Building Classroom Discipline

C. M. Charles
Emeritus, San Diego State University

Collaboration by
Gail W. Senter
California State University San Marcos

PEARSON

Boston   New York   San Francisco
Mexico City   Montreal   Toronto   London   Madrid   Munich   Paris
Hong Kong   Singapore   Tokyo   Cape Town   Sydney

Senior Editor: Arnis E. Burvikovs
Series Editorial Assistant: Erin Reilly
Marketing Manager: Erica DeLuca
Editorial Production Service: Omegatype Typography, Inc.
Composition Buyer: Linda Cox
Manufacturing Buyer: Linda Morris
Electronic Composition: Omegatype Typography, Inc.
Cover Administrator: Kristina Mose-Libon

For related titles and support materials, visit our online catalog at www.ablongman.com.

Between the time website information is gathered and then published, it is not unusual for some sites to have closed. Also, the transcription of URLs can result in typographical errors. The publisher would appreciate notification where these errors occur so that they may be corrected in subsequent editions.

ISBN-13: 978-0-205-51072-6   ISBN-10: 0-205-51072-8

Library of Congress Cataloging-in-Publication Data
Charles, C. M.
    Building classroom discipline / C. M. Charles; collaboration by Gail W. Senter.—9th ed.
       p.   cm.
    Includes bibliographical references and index.
    ISBN 0-205-51072-8
      1. School discipline.   2. Classroom management.   I. Senter, Gail W.   II. Title.

    LB3012.C46 2008
    371.5—dc22   2006052008

Printed in the United States of America

10   9   8   7   6   5   4   3   2   1   RRD-VA   10   09   08   07

Credits: pp. 3–6, The Interstate New Teacher Assessment and Support Consortium (INTASC) standards were developed by the Council of Chief State School Officers and member states. Copies may be downloaded from the Council's website at http://www.ccsso.org. Council of Chief State School Officers. (1992). Model standards for beginning teacher licensing, assessment, and development: A resource for state dialogue. Washington, DC: Author. http://www.ccsso.org/content/pdfs/corestrd.pdf; p. 29, Photo copyright 2004 by Arthur Meyersen; p. 84, Photo by Jason Threlfall.

CONTENTS

Preface   xv

1 Classroom Discipline: The Problem and the Solution   1

- Chapter Preview   1
- Competencies Required for Teaching in Today's Schools   2
  - INTASC Recommendations   2
  - The Praxis Series of Tests   6
  - Danielson and Professional Teaching Competencies   7
- Discipline as a Basic Teacher Competency   7
  - The Meanings of Behavior and Misbehavior   8
  - Types of Misbehavior You Will Encounter   8
  - Clarifying the Terms *Discipline* and *Behavior Management*   9
- Toward Resolving the Discipline Problem   10
  - Suggestions for Working with Students Effectively   10
- Building a Personal System of Discipline   11
  - Five Principles for Building a Personal System of Discipline   11
  - Twenty Questions for Clarifying Your Ideas about Discipline   14
- Getting Started   16
  - Standards of Professionalism   16
  - Legalities Pertaining to Student Safety and Well-Being   17
  - Ethics of Instruction   18
- Key Terms and Concepts Emphasized in This Chapter   19
- Activities   19
- References   19

2 Potential Influences of Cultural and Economic Backgrounds on Student Behavior   20

- Chapter Preview   20
- Value Systems   20

■ Information about Selected Ethnic and Cultural Groups   21

    Middle-Class Caucasian American Students   21

    Hispanic American Students   22

    African American Students   23

    Asian American and Pacific Islander Students   24

    American Indian/Alaska Native Students   26

    Recently Arrived Immigrant Students   28

■ Information about Economically Disadvantaged Students   28

■ General Suggestions for Working with Students from All Ethnic and Economic Groups   30

■ Key Terms and Concepts Emphasized in This Chapter   31

■ Activities   31

■ References   31

3   The Special Challenges of Neurological-Based Behavior   34

■ Chapter Preview   34

■ Introduction to Neurological-Based Behavior (NBB)   35

    Extent of the Problem   36

    A Word about Brain Injuries   37

    Indicators of NBB   38

    Sensory Integration Dysfunction   39

■ Common Pediatric/Adolescent Mental Health Diagnoses   40

    Attention-Deficit Hyperactivity Disorder (ADHD)   40

    Oppositional Defiant Disorder (ODD)   40

    Bipolar Disorder   41

    Learning Disabilities (LD)   42

    Autism Spectrum Disorder (ASD)   44

    Fetal Alcohol Spectrum Disorder (FASD)   45

    Rage   46

■ Medications for Students with Behavioral Issues   49

■ In Summary   50

■ Key Terms and Concepts Emphasized in This Chapter   51

■ Activities   51

■ References   52

4   Twentieth-Century Pioneers in Classroom Discipline   54

- Chapter Preview   54
- The Evolution of Classroom Discipline   54
- Fritz Redl and William Wattenberg: Discipline through Influencing Group Behavior   55
  - Redl and Wattenberg's Principal Teachings   55
  - Review of Redl and Wattenberg's Contributions   56
- B. F. Skinner: Discipline through Shaping Desired Behavior   57
  - Skinner's Principal Teachings   57
  - Review of Skinner's Contributions   58
- Jacob Kounin: Improving Discipline through Lesson Management   58
  - Kounin's Principal Teachings   58
  - Review of Kounin's Contributions   59
- Haim Ginott: Discipline through Congruent Communication   60
  - Ginott's Principal Teachings   60
  - Review of Ginott's Contributions   62
- Rudolf Dreikurs: Discipline through Democratic Teaching   63
  - Dreikurs's Principal Teachings   63
  - Review of Dreikurs's Contributions   64
- Lee and Marlene Canter: Discipline through Assertive Tactics   65
  - The Canters' Principal Teachings   65
  - Review of the Canters' Contributions to Discipline   69
- Key Terms and Concepts Emphasized in This Chapter   70
- Questions and Activities   70
- References   71

5   Three Bridges to Twenty-First-Century Discipline   72

- Chapter Preview   72
- **Part 1   William Glasser: Discipline Guided by Choice Theory**   73
- Glasser on Student Needs, Quality, and Choice Theory   73
  - Meeting Students' Needs   73
  - Choice Theory in the Classroom   74
  - Quality Curriculum   74
  - Quality Teaching   75

More on Lead Teaching   75

Standards of Conduct   76

When Behavior Agreements Are Broken   76

Seven Deadly Habits and Seven Connecting Habits   77

Establishing Quality Classrooms   77

Part 2   **Thomas Gordon: Discipline through Inner Self-Control**   79

■ Gordon on Influence Techniques and Helping Skills   79

I-Messages and You-Messages   80

Gordon's Plan for Discipline   80

Influence Rather Than Control   80

Preventive Skills   80

Discipline and Who Owns the Problem   81

Confrontive Skills   81

Helping Skills   82

No-Lose Conflict Resolution   83

Part 3   **Alfie Kohn: Beyond Discipline**   84

■ Kohn on Classrooms as Communities   84

The Trouble with Discipline for Compliance   85

The Classroom Management We Need   86

The Trouble with Today's Teaching   87

How Instruction Should Be Done   88

■ Key Terms and Concepts Emphasized in This Chapter   89

■ Selected Seven—Summary Suggestions from Glasser, Gordon, and Kohn   90

■ Concept Cases   90

■ Activities   91

■ References   91

6 Discipline through Belonging, Cooperation, and Self-Control   93

■ Chapter Preview   93

Part 1   **Linda Albert: Belonging and Cooperation**   93

■ Albert's Fundamental Hypothesis   93

Albert's Cooperative Discipline   94

Genuine and Mistaken Goals   94

The Three C's of Cooperative Discipline   94

Class Code of Conduct   96

Types of Misbehavior   96

Albert's Plethora of Strategies   97

Avoiding and Defusing Confrontations   97

Dealing with More Severe Confrontations   98

Implementing Consequences   98

Part 2   Barbara Coloroso: Inner Self-Control   99

■ Coloroso's Fundamental Hypothesis   99

Coloroso's Inner Discipline   99

Principles of Good Discipline   100

How Punishment Differs from Discipline   100

Misbehavior and How to Deal with It   101

How Classroom Discipline Leads to Inner Discipline   102

Mistakes, Reality, and Problem Solving   103

Part 3   Jane Nelsen and Lynn Lott: Encouragement and Support   104

■ Nelsen and Lott's Fundamental Hypothesis   104

Nelsen and Lott's Positive Discipline   104

Relationship Barriers and Relationship Builders   105

The Role of Classroom Meetings   106

Building Blocks for Classroom Meetings   106

Standard Format for Class Meetings   108

When Classroom Meetings Fail to Function as Intended   109

■ Key Terms and Concepts Emphasized in This Chapter   109

■ Selected Seven—Summary Suggestions from This Chapter   110

■ Concept Cases   110

■ Activities   111

■ You Are the Teacher   111

■ References   112

7   Discipline through Active Student Involvement   113

■ Chapter Preview   113

■ Fundamental Hypothesis of Jones's Approach   113

■ Overview of the Nature and Practice of Jones's Approach   113

■ Jones on Teaching and Learning   114

Misbehavior and Loss of Teaching–Learning Time   114

How Effective Teachers Teach   115

How Students Misbehave   116

Recouping Lost Time   116

Skill Clusters in Jones's Model   117

Study Group Activity Guide   125

■ Initiating Jones's Approach in the Classroom   126

■ Key Terms and Concepts Emphasized in This Chapter   126

■ Selected Seven—Summary Suggestions from Fred Jones   127

■ Concept Cases   127

■ Activities   128

■ You Are the Teacher   128

■ References   129

8 Discipline through Pragmatic Classroom Management   130

■ Chapter Preview   130

■ Fundamental Hypothesis of the Wongs' Approach   130

■ A Quick Read of the Wongs' Principal Suggestions   130

About School   131

About Teaching   131

About Classrooms and Procedures   132

About Roles and Responsibilities   132

About Discipline   133

About Testing and Evaluation   133

About the First Day of Class   133

About the First Week of Teaching   133

■ The Problem Is Not Discipline   134

■ A Discipline Plan Is Necessary, However   134

■ Why Planning and Organizing Are So Important   135

■ Procedures, and What They Entail   136

How to Decide on Procedures for Your Classroom   136

Classroom Procedures Must Be Taught   136

Examples of Procedures in a Fourth Grade Classroom   137

■ How to Begin a Class Successfully   141

The First Five Minutes Are Critical   144

Mrs. Pantoja's Plan for the First Day   144

The First Ten Days of School   145

Procedures for Cooperative Work Groups   146

For Additional Ideas from the Wongs   146

- A Special Word to Secondary Teachers   147
- Initiating the Wongs' Pragmatic Approach in the Classroom   147
- Key Terms and Concepts Emphasized in This Chapter   148
- Selected Seven—Summary Suggestions from Harry and Rosemary Wong   148
- Concept Cases   148
- Activities   149
- You Are the Teacher   149
- References   150

9 Discipline through Same-Side Win-Win Strategies   151

- Chapter Preview   151
- Fundamental Hypothesis of Win-Win Discipline   151
- Win-Win Discipline   151

The Goal of Win-Win Discipline   152

The Premises of Win-Win Discipline   153

Key Elements in Win-Win Discipline   153

- How Win-Win Discipline Works   155

Before the Class Begins   155

During Instruction and Other Class Interactions   156

More on Types of Disruptive Behavior—ABCD   157

More on Student Positions and Associated Misbehavior   157

Intervention Strategies for Types of Disruption   158

More on Responding in the Moment of Disruption   160

More on Follow-Ups and Long-Term Goals   161

- Promoting Life Skills   162
- Parent and Community Alliances and Schoolwide Programs   163
- Initiating Kagan, Kyle, and Scott's Win-Win Discipline   163
- Summary Review of Kagan, Kyle, and Scott's Advice   164
- Key Terms and Concepts Emphasized in This Chapter   165
- Selected Seven—Summary Suggestions from Kagan, Kyle, and Scott   165
- Concept Cases   166
- Questions and Activities   166
- You Are the Teacher   167
- References   167

10   Discipline through Dignity and Hope for Challenging Youth   168

- Chapter Preview   168
- Fundamental Hypothesis of Discipline with Dignity   168
- The Nature and Practice of Discipline with Dignity   168
- A Four-Phase Plan for Schools and Educators   170
    - Identify the Core Values   170
    - Create Rules and Consequences   170
    - Model the Values   170
    - Use No Interventions That Violate Core Values   171
- Preparing Oneself in Advance   171
- Working with Students Who Are Behaviorally at Risk of Failure   172
- Disciplining Students Who Are Difficult to Control   173
    - Rules and Consequences   174
    - Preventing Escalation   175
- Dealing with Aggression, Hostility, Violence, and Conflict   176
- Dealing with Bullying and Hate Crimes   178
- Helping Students Regain Hope   179
- Motivating Students Who Are Difficult to Manage   180
- Making Changes in Yourself   180
- Putting Curwin and Mendler's Ideas into Practice   182
- Key Terms and Concepts Emphasized in This Chapter   183
- Selected Seven—Summary Suggestions from Curwin and Mendler   183
- Concept Cases   184
- Activities   184
- You Are the Teacher   185
- References   186

11   Discipline through Self-Restitution and Moral Intelligence   187

- Chapter Preview   187
- **Part 1   Diane Gossen: Restitution Self-Discipline   187**
- Fundamental Hypothesis of Self-Restitution   187
- Self-Restitution Theory   188
- The Restitution Triangle and How It Is Used   189
- The Least Coercive Road   190
    - Open Up the Territory—Maximizing Freedom   191

Establish the Social Contract—Building a Sense of Belonging   191

Establish Limits—Clarifying Personal Power   192

Self-Restitution—Making Things Right and Healing Oneself   194

Part 2   Michele Borba: Building Moral Intelligence   195

■ Fundamental Hypothesis of Moral Intelligence   195

■ Moral Intelligence and the Foundations of Character   196

Empathy   196

Conscience   197

Self-Control   198

Respect   198

Kindness   199

Tolerance   199

Fairness   200

■ Reasons for Building Moral Intelligence   200

■ Fostering Moral Intelligence   201

Accentuate a Character Trait or Virtue   201

Tell the Meaning and Value of the Trait   202

Teach What the Trait Looks and Sounds Like   202

Provide Opportunities to Practice the Moral Habits of the Trait   202

Provide Effective Feedback   203

■ Fostering Prosocial Behavior   203

■ The Relation of Moral Intelligence to Classroom Discipline   204

■ Key Terms and Concepts Emphasized in This Chapter   205

■ Selected Eight—Summary Suggestions from Gossen and Borba   205

■ Concept Cases   206

■ Questions and Activities   206

■ You Are the Teacher   207

■ References   207

12 Discipline through Raising Student Responsibility   208

■ Chapter Preview   208

■ Fundamental Hypothesis of Marshall's Raise Responsibility System   208

■ The Nature and Practice of the Raise Responsibility System   208

Theories of How to Manage Others   209

Moving toward Responsible Behavior   209

The Hierarchy of Social Development, Its Value, and How It Is Used   210

Focus on Internal Motivation   213

Twenty-Five Tactics to Stimulate Students to Behave Responsibly   214

How to Intervene When Misbehavior Occurs   218

■ Initiating the Raise Responsibility System in the Classroom   220

■ Summary of the Raise Responsibility System   221

■ Raise Responsibility Self-Analysis   222

■ Key Terms and Concepts Emphasized in This Chapter   223

■ Selected Seven—Summary Suggestions from Marvin Marshall   223

■ Concept Cases   224

■ Questions and Activities   224

■ You Are the Teacher   225

■ References   225

13 Discipline through Careful Teacher Guidance and Instruction   227

■ Chapter Preview   227

■ Fundamental Hypothesis of Real Discipline   227

■ Morrish on Discipline Gone Wrong   228

■ Real Discipline   228

■ Maxims Regarding the Mindset for Real Discipline   229

■ Real Discipline's Three-Phase Approach   230

Phase 1. Training for Compliance   230

Phase 2. Teaching Students How to Behave   233

Phase 3. Managing Student Choice   233

■ Planning the Discipline Program   234

■ Developing Teacher–Student Relationships   237

■ Consequences in Real Discipline   238

■ About Motivation and Rewards   239

■ Don't Promote Self-Indulgence   240

■ When Students Fail to Comply   240

■ Moving to Real Discipline   241

■ Initiating Real Discipline in the Classroom   241

■ Key Terms and Concepts Emphasized in This Chapter   242

■ Selected Seven—Summary Suggestions from Ronald Morrish   242

- Concept Cases   242
- Activities   243
- You Are the Teacher   243
- References   244

14   Discipline through Synergy and Reducing Causes of Misbehavior   245

- Chapter Preview   245
- Fundamental Hypothesis of Synergetic Discipline   245
- The Nature and Practice of Synergetic Discipline   245
  - Synergy and Synergetic Discipline   246
- Establishing Conditions That Elevate Class Spirit and Energy   247
  - Discuss and Take into Account Student Needs   247
  - Emphasize Class Conditions and Activities Students Are Known to Like   248
  - Work to Develop Class Ethics and Trust   248
  - Emphasize and Use Your Personal Charisma   248
  - Improve the Quality of Communication in Your Classroom   249
  - Make Use of Coopetition   249
  - Resolve Class Problems and Conflicts Amicably and Productively   249
- Addressing the Causes of Student Misbehavior   250
  - Causes of Misbehavior That Reside in Individual Students   250
  - Causes of Misbehavior That Reside in Class Peers and Groups   253
  - Causes of Misbehavior That Reside in Instructional Environments   254
  - Causes of Misbehavior That Reside in Teachers and Other School Personnel   255
- Recognizing and Correcting Teacher Misbehavior   258
- Establishing a Discipline Plan with Your Class   258
  - Session 1   258
  - Session 2   259
  - Session 3   259
  - Session 4   259
  - Session 5   260
  - Session 6   260
- Intervening When Students Misbehave   261
  - First Intervention   261
  - Second Intervention   261

Third Intervention   261

Fourth Intervention   262

■ Key Terms and Concepts Emphasized in This Chapter   263

■ Selected Seven—Summary Suggestions from Synergetic Discipline   263

■ Concept Cases   263

■ Questions and Activities   264

■ You Are the Teacher   264

■ References   265

15 Formalizing Your Personal System of Discipline   266

■ Chapter Preview   266

■ Reflecting on a Philosophy of Discipline   266

■ Reflecting on a Theory of Discipline   267

■ Reflecting on the Practice of Discipline   268

The Instruction Aspect of Discipline   268

The Prevention Aspect of Discipline   268

The Support and Intervention Aspects of Discipline   269

Other Considerations in the Practice of Discipline   270

■ The Five Principles and Your Personal System of Discipline   273

■ Thoughts from Students Preparing Themselves to Be Teachers   274

■ Two Sample Discipline Plans from Teachers in Service   275

Sample 1. An Approach That Emphasizes Rules and Consequences   275

Sample 2. An Approach That Emphasizes Prevention and Teacher–Student Cooperation   278

■ Finalizing Your Personal System of Discipline   281

Step 1. Specify How You Will Present and Conduct Yourself   281

Step 2. Specify the Behavioral Goals for Your Students   281

Step 3. Describe the Classroom Conditions You Will Provide   282

Step 4. Specify How You Will Help Students Conduct Themselves Appropriately   282

Step 5. Indicate How You Will Intervene When Misbehavior Occurs   283

Step 6. Think Through and Write Out How You Will Introduce and Explain the System to Your Students   283

■ Your Formula for Success Is in Your Hands   284

■ Key Terms and Concepts Emphasized in This Chapter   284

Glossary   285

Bibliography   294

Index   301

PREFACE

A pleasant classroom environment in which students behave responsibly is essential for high-quality teaching and learning. Teachers, in their efforts to maintain such environments, routinely exert influence on students to help them show initiative, responsibility, and positive interactions with others. This influence is commonly called *discipline*, which consists of a number of different strategies and techniques. In the past, discipline was often demanding and occasionally harsh. Although it helped students behave civilly and stay on task, it produced undesirable side effects such as student fearfulness, loss of motivation, and dislike for school. That kind of discipline is being replaced with discipline that promotes self-control, responsibility, and positive attitudes toward school, teachers, and learning. Techniques for establishing and maintaining that type of discipline are presented in this book.

The Purpose of This Book

Beginning with the first edition of *Building Classroom Discipline* almost three decades ago, the overriding purpose of this book has been to help teachers develop personal systems of discipline tailored to their individual philosophies and personalities as well as to the needs, traits, and social realities of their schools and communities. None of the excellent commercial models of discipline described herein is likely to provide a perfect match for any given teacher's needs. For that reason, teachers are urged to examine the strategies, tactics, and hundreds of ideas presented in the chapters that follow and select from them elements that can be organized into comprehensive approaches to discipline that suit their needs. Guidance for completing that process is presented in Chapter 1 and Chapter 15.

In recent years, many advances have been made in discipline, as outlined in the timeline beginning on page xxi. Whereas earlier discipline was characterized by coercion, reward, and punishment, newer techniques encourage students to behave acceptably because they feel it is the right thing to do and see it as advantageous to themselves and their classmates. This ninth edition of *Building Classroom Discipline* describes a variety of such approaches set forth by leading authorities. These approaches show teachers how to work with students helpfully and respectfully, to ensure learning while preserving student dignity and positive teacher–student relationships.

Nature of This Book and Primary Audiences

Building Classroom Discipline describes laudable models of discipline developed by some of the most astute educational thinkers of the past half century. Six of these models, summarized in Chapter 4, are considered to be historical models. They were all groundbreaking approaches in their day and have powerfully contributed to the best of today's approaches. Chapter 5 presents three transitional models of discipline that reflect the movement from late twentieth century discipline toward new focuses in the early twenty-first century. An additional twelve approaches to discipline, featuring the latest developments in classroom discipline, are examined in greater detail in Chapters 6 through 14. The final chapter in the book helps readers formalize personal systems of discipline that meet their needs and those of their students.

This book, comprehensive enough to serve as a single or primary text, yet compact enough for use with other texts, is designed for use in preservice courses in discipline and classroom management, learning and instruction, methods of teaching, and educational psychology. It is equally appropriate for teachers already in service who are seeking more effective and enjoyable ways of working with students. Instructors in school district training programs and teacher institutes will also find the book useful.

New to This Edition

New and promising approaches to discipline are appearing regularly that help educators work with students in ways that are ever more humane and productive. Accordingly, several new chapters appear in this edition. At the same time, certain older models of discipline have declined in popularity and hence attention to them is minimized, although many of their ideas figure prominently in newer approaches. These changes are made specific in the following overview.

You will notice that the Contents section has been changed for this edition. In previous editions, application chapters were devoted mainly to the work of specific discipline authorities, showing each authority's suggestions concerning the purpose and practice of discipline. In this new edition, **chapters emphasize themes** rather than individual approaches. This change permits joint examination of the work of authorities whose discipline approaches have much in common. The theme approach, reflected in the chapter titles, will help you more easily construct your own personal system of discipline.

Overview of Chapters in the Book

The following is a list of chapters in this edition of *Building Classroom Discipline*. Several new chapters have been added in this edition, others have been reorganized, and some of the older ones have been deleted. Chapter titles have been changed to indicate the theme emphasized in each chapter.

Chapter 1. Classroom Discipline: The Problem and the Solution

As in the previous edition, this chapter reviews the widespread concern about student behavior and school discipline, pointing out problem areas and suggesting remedies for those problems. The nature of misbehavior is discussed, its effects on students and teachers are described, and schools' attempts to deal with behavior problems are reviewed. The chapter describes the INTASC competencies that are desired in teachers and used for teacher licensing in many states, the Praxis Series from Educational Testing Service for assessing teacher competencies, and Charlotte Danielson's observations concerning competencies required for effective classroom teaching. Finally, the chapter reviews the nature of teacher professionalism and provides a framework for developing one's personal system of discipline.

Chapter 2. Potential Influences of Cultural and Economic Backgrounds on Student Behavior

As in the previous edition, this chapter presents information to help teachers better serve students from seven economic and cultural groups: (1) middle-class Caucasian American, (2) Hispanic American, (3) African American, (4) Asian American and Pacific Islander, (5) American Indian/Alaska Native, (6) recently arrived immigrants, and (7) economically disadvantaged.

Chapter 3. The Special Challenges of Neurological-Based Behavior

This new chapter is devoted to working with students who have difficulty controlling their behavior because of neurological dysfunctions that are largely outside their control and are unresponsive to normal management techniques. The chapter identifies those students, explains why they behave as they do, and indicates how teachers can best help them. Diagnoses that receive attention include attention-deficit hyperactivity disorder, learning disabilities, sensory integration dysfunction, bipolar disorder, oppositional defiant disorder, autism spectrum disorder, fetal alcohol spectrum syndrome, and brain injuries.

Chapter 4. Twentieth-Century Pioneers in Classroom Discipline

As in the previous edition, this chapter describes contributions made between 1951 and 1980 by highly influential pioneers in classroom discipline: Fritz Redl and William Wattenberg, B. F. Skinner, Jacob Kounin, Haim Ginott, Rudolf Dreikurs, and Lee and Marlene Canter. Although the approaches of these authorities are not often used as complete behavior management systems today, elements from them contribute strongly to current discipline programs.

Chapter 5. Three Bridges to Twenty-First-Century Discipline

This chapter has been restructured for this edition. Between the latter part of the twentieth century and the early part of the twenty-first century, the general approach to classroom discipline changed significantly. That change is exemplified by the following approaches to behavior management: *Choice Theory*, formulated and popularized by William Glasser, which focused on how to meet students' predominant needs while striving for overall quality in teaching and learning; *Self-Discipline*, formulated and popularized by Thomas

Gordon, which emphasized the crucial role of sensitive communication between teacher and students; and *Classrooms as Communities,* described and popularized by Alfie Kohn, which focused on transforming classrooms into "communities of learners" where cooperation and helpfulness predominated. Those three approaches established trends that now play strongly in almost all systems of discipline.

Chapter 6. Discipline through Belonging, Cooperation, and Self-Control

This newly structured chapter examines the views of authorities who believe good discipline depends on students attaining a sense of belonging, participating in making class decisions, and relating to others with kindness and consideration. Featured are Linda Albert on *Cooperative Discipline,* Barbara Coloroso on *Inner Discipline,* and Jane Nelsen and Lynn Lott on *Positive Discipline* and classroom meetings.

Chapter 7. Discipline through Active Student Involvement

This chapter features the contributions of Fred Jones, author of *Tools for Teaching: Discipline, Instruction, Motivation.* Jones believes discipline problems can be reduced to low levels by keeping students actively involved in lessons. Toward that end he advocates a classroom seating arrangement that enhances teacher mobility, the reduction of chronic help seeking by students, a highly interactive style of teaching, constant monitoring of student performance, incentives for students to complete their assigned work, a program of responsibility training to reduce time wasting, and teacher body language that communicates "meaning business."

Chapter 8. Discipline through Pragmatic Classroom Management

This new chapter details the classroom management suggestions of Harry and Rosemary Wong. The Wongs maintain that discipline problems largely disappear when students are carefully taught to follow procedures for all classroom activities. The chapter presents the Wongs' suggestions for what teachers should do during the first minutes and days of school and how they should train students to follow the various procedures that come into play in the classroom.

Chapter 9. Discipline through Same-Side Win-Win Strategies

This chapter features the work of Spencer Kagan, Patricia Kyle, and Sally Scott. They call their approach *Win-Win Discipline.* It focuses on teaching students to manage themselves responsibly, as teachers and students work together cooperatively from the same side to find a common ground in dealing with problems they encounter. This approach helps students develop self-management, responsibility, and other autonomous life skills. Everyone in the classroom benefits or "wins," hence, the label Win-Win Discipline.

Chapter 10. Discipline through Dignity and Hope for Challenging Youth

This chapter features the ideas of Richard Curwin and Allen Mendler, set forth in their book *Discipline with Dignity* and other publications. Also included is advice from Barbara Coloroso on dealing with bullying at school. Curwin and Mendler believe behavior can be greatly improved when teachers unfailingly maintain student dignity and provide genuine hope for and expectation of success. Although this approach is intended for all students, in recent years the authors have emphasized its effectiveness with "challenging youth"—students considered difficult to manage and thus likely to fail in school.

Chapter 11. Discipline through Self-Restitution and Moral Intelligence

This new chapter presents the contributions of Diane Gossen on *Discipline through Self-Restitution* and Michele Borba on *Building Moral Intelligence*. Self-restitution, which involves regular reflection on personal behavior, helps students learn to profit from mistakes and become better able to conduct themselves in harmony with their needs and inner sense of morality. Moral intelligence, comprised of seven essential virtues that can be taught and developed, affects how students deal with ethical and moral challenges encountered in school and elsewhere. It stresses distinguishing right from wrong, establishing strong ethical convictions, and willingness to act on those convictions in an honorable way.

Chapter 12. Discipline through Raising Student Responsibility

This chapter describes Marvin Marshall's *Raise Responsibility System*. Marshall contends that desirable classroom behavior is best achieved by promoting responsibility—rather than obedience—and by articulating expectations and then empowering students to reach those expectations. The system has three main parts: (1) *Teach* students about four levels of social development and relate the levels to behavior and learning. (2) *Check for understanding* when inappropriate behavior occurs. (3) Provide *guided choices* when disruptions continue. A major tactic used in Marshall's approach is called *elicitation* (also referred to as "authority without punishment"), which brings misbehavior to an end and helps students develop a procedure for behaving appropriately.

Chapter 13. Discipline through Careful Teacher Guidance and Instruction

This new chapter features the work of behavior specialist Ronald Morrish. He calls his approach *Real Discipline*, which he believes can restore proper behavior to today's schools. Morrish explains that Real Discipline is not a new theory, but an organized set of techniques that great teachers and parents have used for generations to teach children to be respectful, responsible, and cooperative. It emphasizes careful teacher guidance to teach students how to behave acceptably, while helping them avoid self-defeating behavior.

Chapter 14. Discipline through Synergy and Reducing Causes of Misbehavior

This chapter presents C. M. Charles's suggestions concerning the judicious classroom use of synergy—a mutually energizing phenomenon that raises motivation and enjoyment for students and teachers. Charles contends that good classroom behavior results when teachers and students cooperate to meet individuals' needs, minimize the causes of misbehavior, and energize the class for greater enjoyment and easier learning. The Synergetic Discipline approach obtains willing cooperation from students within a sense of class community that emphasizes ethical behavior.

Chapter 15. Formalizing Your Personal System of Discipline

As in previous editions, this culminating chapter helps readers organize and finalize personal systems of discipline that address the needs and realities of teacher and students. From the beginning, readers of this book have been encouraged to explore various philosophical, theoretical, and practical views on discipline that lead toward this final activity. Suggestions are presented to help readers

1. Present and conduct themselves in a manner that complies with legal requirements and reflects high standards of professionalism
2. Clarify major types of behavior they want their students to display, now and in the future
3. Stipulate classroom conditions they will provide to help students learn responsibility and self-control and conduct themselves ethically and considerately
4. Indicate how they will relate to students to promote behavior that is considerate and responsible
5. Specify tactics they will use when students behave inappropriately—tactics that lead to better decision making while enhancing positive relations between teacher and students

How Chapters Are Presented

Chapters 1, 2, and 3 contain information readers will find helpful concerning (1) new pushes and expectations in discipline, (2) considerations in working with students from various economic and cultural groups, and (3) the special challenges of working with students with neurological-based behavior (NBB). Chapters 4 and 5 explore the significant contributions to discipline by pioneers in the field and later thinkers who paved the way into the present century. All of these chapters contain end of chapter activities.

Chapters 6 through 14 are organized in a consistent format. Previous users of the book will notice the change in chapter structure from descriptions of single models of discipline to a thematic approach that at times presents information from several different authorities. As always, chapter organization and style of writing aim at maximum clarity, understanding, and applicability. Chapters 6 through 14 are structured as follows:

1. An indication or preview of the main thrust of the chapter, indicating the fundamental hypothesis that underlies each authority's contentions
2. Brief biographical sketches of contributing authorities, including their principal publications
3. A description of each authority's approach to discipline
4. How the approaches are implemented in the classroom
5. Terms and concepts featured in the chapter
6. The Selected Seven—seven selected points that summarize each chapter
7. Application exercises including questions, activities, concept cases, and a "You Are the Teacher" scenario that calls on readers to consider how they would resolve real-life discipline situations
8. References

Note that chapters include a number of terms shown in **bold type.** These terms are highlighted to indicate they are included in the key terms section at the end of the chapter and in the glossary near the end of the book.

Review and Feedback from Authorities

Authorities whose approaches are presented as application models have cooperated with the author by providing detailed feedback to ensure accurate depiction of their concepts, approaches, and terminology. The ongoing cooperative liaison between discipline authorities and the author ensures that the information you read is accurate and up to date.

Timeline of Major Contributions in Discipline

The following shows the chronology of important themes in classroom discipline, together with names of originating authorities and titles of publications in which they set forth their contentions.

 1951 *Group Dynamics*—Fritz Redl (psychiatrist) and William Wattenberg (educational psychologist)

In their book *Mental Health in Teaching*, Redl and Wattenberg explained forces that cause students to behave differently in groups than they do when by themselves. Roles students assume and roles they expect of teachers are indicated. This work was the first systematic theory-based approach to discipline and inaugurated the "modern" period of classroom discipline.

1954 *Reinforcement Theory Applied to Teaching*—B. F. Skinner (behavioral psychologist)

In his article titled "The Science of Learning and the Art of Teaching," Skinner explained how student behavior is, and can be, shaped through the process of reinforcement. Skinner set forth principles of reinforcement for teachers and provided the paradigm for positive reinforcement and behavior modification, both widely used today.

1969 *Behavior as Student Choice*—William Glasser (psychiatrist and educational consultant)

In his book *Schools without Failure,* Glasser made two major contributions of lasting influence to the theory and practice of classroom discipline:

1. *Behavior as choice.* Glasser contended that students choose their behavior, that they are not forced by circumstances to behave in particular ways.

2. *Classroom meetings.* Glasser advocated regularly scheduled meetings in which teachers and students discuss and jointly resolve behavior problems and other matters of concern to the class.

1971 *Congruent Communication*—Haim Ginott (teacher and psychologist)

In his book *Teacher and Child,* Ginott described the use and value of teacher communication that is harmonious with student perceptions and emotions. This work, which urged teachers to address situations rather than the character of offending students, established a style of communication that is now advocated in all programs of classroom discipline.

1971 *Class and Lesson Management*—Jacob Kounin (educational psychologist)

In his book *Discipline and Group Management in Classrooms,* Kounin reported his research into how teachers maintain proper student behavior through classroom organization, lesson management, and attention to individual students. He concluded that management was more effective than punishment or other known sanctions in ensuring acceptable student behavior.

1972 *Primary Need for Belonging*—Rudolf Dreikurs (psychiatrist and family counselor)

In a book titled *Discipline without Tears,* which he coauthored with Pearl Cassel, Dreikurs pinpointed desire to belong as a primary need of students in school. He explained how to help students fill the need for belonging and identified types of misbehavior that occur when students are unable to do so.

1976 *Assertively Taking Charge*—Lee and Marlene Canter (teachers and consultants)

In their book *Assertive Discipline: A Take-Charge Approach for Today's Educator,* the Canters showed how teachers can take charge of student behavior in their classrooms in a firm yet kindly manner, in which teachers' right to teach—and students' right to learn—are maintained without unnecessary disruptions. This approach revolutionized discipline in classrooms and was hugely popular for more than twenty years.

1986 *Control Theory*, later changed to *Choice Theory*—William Glasser (psychiatrist and educational consultant)

In his books *Control Theory in the Classroom* (1986) and *Choice Theory in the Classroom* (1998), Glasser strongly made the points that we cannot control anyone's behavior except our own, and that teachers cannot successfully force students to do anything they don't want to do. What teachers can do is help students envision a quality existence in school and plan the choices that lead to it.

1988 *Discipline with Dignity*—Richard Curwin (teacher educator) and Allen Mendler (school psychologist)

In their book *Discipline with Dignity*, Curwin and Mendler established that a key principle in effective discipline is maintaining student dignity (allowing students to maintain self-respect), which reduces student defensiveness and helps promote positive relations between teacher and student.

1989 *Cooperative Discipline*—Linda Albert (educator and consultant)

In her book *A Teacher's Guide to Cooperative Discipline: How to Manage Your Classroom and Promote Self-Esteem*, Albert urged teachers to work with students in a cooperative manner to manage inappropriate behavior. She provided tactics to help students make *connections* with others, *contribute* to the class, and see themselves as *capable*, all of which contribute to responsible classroom behavior.

1989 *Self-Discipline*—Thomas Gordon (psychologist and consultant)

In his book *Discipline That Works: Promoting Self-Discipline in Children*, Gordon made three significant contributions that have had lasting effects in discipline:

1. *Noncontrolling influence*. Power-based authority doesn't work with students. Teachers should replace it with noncontrolling influence, which Gordon describes.

2. *No-lose conflict resolution*. Conflicts can and should be resolved in a manner that allows both parties to receive much of what they want. This tactic has been incorporated into many approaches to discipline and today is more often called *Win-Win Conflict Resolution*.

3. *Facilitators of communication*. Roadblocks to communication with students, such as lecturing and giving advice, should be replaced with facilitators of communication, such as attentive listening and I-messages that do not make students defensive.

1992 *Maintaining Hope*—Richard Curwin (teacher educator and consultant)

In his book *Rediscovering Hope: Our Greatest Teaching Strategy*, Curwin established that a sense of hope is necessary if difficult-to-manage students are to be brought back into the mainstream of acceptable behavior. He presented tactics for helping students feel that school is worthwhile, two of which are building competencies in matters students consider important and teachers' showing they care about each student as a person.

1993   *Positive Discipline in the Classroom*—Jane Nelsen and Lynn Lott (educators and consultants)

In their book *Positive Discipline in the Classroom: How to Effectively Use Class Meetings and Other Positive Discipline Strategies,* Nelsen and Lott contend that almost all students can learn to behave with dignity, self-control, and concern for others if they are helped to see themselves as capable, significant, and able to control certain aspects of their lives in school. Nelsen and Lott present a number of tactics for use toward that end.

1994   *Inner Discipline*—Barbara Coloroso (educator and consultant)

In her book *Kids Are Worth It!: Giving Your Child the Gift of Inner Discipline,* Coloroso provides tactics for helping students develop self-control. Her plan urges teachers to establish classrooms that provide a climate of trust and responsibility, and in which students are given power to make decisions about many of the problems they encounter and are required to manage the outcomes of their decisions.

1998   *Discipline through Pragmatic Classroom Management*—Harry Wong and Rosemary Wong (teachers and consultants)

In their book *The First Days of School: How to Be an Effective Teacher,* the Wongs firmly state that the main problem in teaching is not poor discipline, but poor classroom management. They urge teachers to use all the time necessary to teach students how to follow routines and complete work assignments. They add that the most effective teachers spend most of the first two weeks teaching students those crucial matters.

2000   *Synergetic Discipline*—C. M. Charles (teacher educator)

In his book *The Synergetic Classroom: Joyful Teaching and Gentle Discipline,* Charles describes how teachers can energize their classes, when desirable, through conditions and activities that interest and motivate students—as seen in athletic competitions, artistic productions, and displays of student work. Factors that tend to promote synergy include teacher charisma, topics and activities of high interest, competition, cooperative work with give and take, and recognition of accomplishment. During periods of synergy, little misbehavior occurs and students hold a positive attitude toward school.

2000   *Discipline through Active Student Involvement*—Fred Jones (psychologist and educational consultant)

In his book *Tools for Teaching: Discipline, Instruction, Motivation,* Jones contends that students seldom misbehave if they are continually kept active during instruction. He shows teachers how to engage productively with students by using effective body language, interacting frequently with individual class members, and using Say See Do teaching.

2000 *Realistic Discipline*—Ronald Morrish (behavior specialist and consultant)

In his book *With All Due Respect,* Morrish describes three things he says teachers can realistically do to establish good discipline in the class: (1) train students through clear expectations and insistence on compliance to accept adult authority and automatically follow teacher directions; (2) teach students the skills, attitudes, and knowledge needed for cooperation, proper behavior, and responsibility; and (3) increasingly offer students opportunities to make choices that take into account the needs and rights of other students and school personnel. When they do something wrong, they are asked to correct their behavior by redoing it properly.

2001 *Building Moral Intelligence*—Michele Borba (educator and consultant)

In her book *Building Moral Intelligence: The Seven Essential Virtues That Teach Kids to Do the Right Thing,* Borba describes moral intelligence as comprising (1) the ability to distinguish right from wrong, (2) the establishment and maintenance of strong ethical convictions, and (3) the willingness to act on those convictions in an honorable way. Borba's program provides suggestions to strengthen students in these three areas, thus promoting better behavior in school.

2001 *Classrooms as Communities of Learners*—Alfie Kohn (educator and consultant)

In his book *Beyond Discipline: From Compliance to Community*, Kohn made the case for organizing classes to function as communities of learners. Kohn has soundly criticized teaching and discipline approaches that *do things to* students rather than involving them as partners in the process, where they can work cooperatively, support each other, and participate fully in resolving class problems.

2001 *Raising Responsibility*—Marvin Marshall (educator and consultant)

In his book *Discipline without Stress, Punishments, or Rewards: How Teachers and Parents Promote Responsibility and Learning,* Marshall describes the Raise Responsibility System, in which students are taught, without coercion, to (1) understand four levels of social development and relate the levels to behavior and learning, (2) identify the level of their personal behavior at any given time, and (3) select better courses of action, when necessary, from self-perceptions or from *guided choices* the teacher provides if disruptions continue.

2001 *Hidden Rules of Poverty*—Ruby Payne (educator and consultant)

In her book *A Framework for Understanding Poverty,* Payne explains that each economic class has its own set of hidden rules that help it survive, rules that are seldom understood by people from other economic classes. Payne's depiction of the hidden rules of poverty greatly helps teachers understand the behavior of students from poverty and work with those students more effectively.

2002   *Same-Side Win-Win Strategy*—Spencer Kagan (psychologist and educator), Patricia Kyle (teacher educator), and Sally Scott (school administrator)

Kagan introduced this approach in 2002 in a website article titled "What Is Win-Win Discipline?" In the Kagan, Kyle, and Scott book, *Win-Win Discipline*, that followed in 2004, the authors explain how students and teachers can work together on the same side to help students develop long-term, self-managed responsibility. The approach emphasizes "three pillars," called *same-side, collaborative solutions*, and *learned responsibility*.

2004   *Self-Restitution Theory*—Diane Gossen (educator and consultant)

In her book *It's All About We*, Gossen explains Self-Restitution as an activity in which students who have behaved inappropriately are encouraged, in a needs-satisfying environment, to reflect on their behavior, identify the need that prompted it, and create a new way of behaving as the responsible person they want to be. This is the first system to place emphasis on misbehaving students learning how to make things right within themselves and improve from the experience.

Supplements

An **Instructor's Manual/Test Bank**, which provides sample syllabi and chapter summaries, is available online to adopters by contacting your local representative.

Videos of many of the authorities noted in this text, as well as numerous other resources, are available at MyLabSchool.

MyLabSchool

mylabschool is a collection of online tools for your success in this course, on your licensure exams, and in your teaching career. Visit www.mylabschool.com to access the following:

- Video footage of real-life classrooms, with opportunities for you to reflect on the videos and offer your own thoughts and suggestions for applying theory to practice
- An extensive archive of text and multimedia cases that provide valuable perspectives on real classrooms and real teaching challenges
- Allyn & Bacon's Lesson and Portfolio Builder application, which includes an integrated state standards correlation tool
- Research paper assistance using Research Navigator™, which provides access to three exclusive databases of credible and reliable source material: EBSCO's ContentSelect Academic Journal Database, The *New York Times* Search-by-Subject Archive, and "Best of the Web" Link Library
- Career Center with resources for Praxis exams and licensure preparation, professional portfolio development, and job search and interview techniques

Acknowledgments

The author gratefully acknowledges the valuable contributions made by the following teachers and administrators: Roy Allen, Constance Bauer, Linda Blacklock, Tom Bolz, Michael Brus, Gail Charles, Ruth Charles, Diana Cordero, Keith Correll, Barbara Gallegos, Nancy Girvin, Kris Halverson, Leslie Hays, Charlotte Hibsch, Elaine Maltz, Colleen Meagher, Nancy Natale, Linda Pohlenz, David Sisk, Deborah Sund, Mike Straus, and Virginia Villalpando.

The author would like to thank the following reviewers for this edition for their comments: Karen Bosch, Virginia Wesleyan College; Heather Carter, Arizona State University; Robert Gates, Bloomsburg University; John Kesner, Georgia State University; Lisa Kirtman, California State University at Fullerton; Denise Salsbury, Ball State University; Beverly Schumer, University of Michigan, Flint; Caroline Sullivan, The University of Texas at Austin; Patrick G. Thomas, Armstrong Atlantic State University; Margaret Torrie, Iowa State University; Eileen Van Wie, New Mexico State University, Las Cruces; Edward Vockell, Purdue University; Louis Warren, East Carolina University; and David Yellin, Oklahoma State University.

The author would also like to acknowledge other critical reviewers: Linda Albert, Cooperative Discipline; Dale Allee, Southwest Missouri State University; Michele Borba, Moral Intelligence; James D. Burney, University of North Alabama; Lee and Marlene Canter, Assertive Discipline; Barbara Coloroso, Kids Are Worth It!; Paula Cook, University of Manitoba; Richard Curwin, Discipline with Dignity; Philip DiMattia, Boston College; Karen M. Dutt, Indiana State University; Carolyn Eichenberger, St. Louis University; James D. Ellsworth, Northern Arizona University; Sara S. Garcia, Santa Clara University; William Glasser, Choice Theory in the Classroom; Thomas Gordon (deceased), Effectiveness Training International; Diane Gossen, Self-Restitution Theory; Marci Green, University of South Florida at Ft. Myers; C. Bobbi Hansen, University of San Diego; Fredric and JoLynne Jones, Tools of Teaching; David I. Joyner, Old Dominion University; Deborah Keasler, Southwestern Oklahoma State University; Spencer Kagan and Associates, Win-Win Discipline; Alfie Kohn, Beyond Discipline: From Compliance to Community; Thomas J. Lasley, The University of Dayton; Lawrence Lyman, Emporia State University; Bernice Magnus-Brown, University of Maine; Marvin Marshall, Raise Responsibility System; Vick McGinley, West Chester University; Janey L. Montgomery, University of Northern Iowa; Ronald Morrish, Real Discipline; Janice L. Nath, University of Houston; Jane Nelsen and Associates, Positive Discipline in the Classroom; Merrill M. Oaks, Washington State University; Jack Vaughan Powell, University of Georgia; Elizabeth Primer, Cleveland State University; Mary C. Shake, University of Kentucky; Alma A. Shearin, University of Central Arkansas; Terry R. Shepherd, Southern Illinois University at Carbondale; JoAnne Smatlan, Seattle Pacific University; Kay Stickle, Ball State University; Marguerite Terrill, Central Michigan University; Sylvia Tinling, University of California, Riverside; Bill Weldon, Arizona State University; Kathlegen Whittier, State University of New York at Plattsburgh; and Harry and Rosemary Wong, The First Days of School.

Finally, the author would like to thank the editorial staff: Arnis E. Burvikovs, Senior Editor, Allyn and Bacon; Erin Reilly, Editorial Assistant, Allyn and Bacon; and Shannon Foreman and the team at Omegatype Typography, Inc.

About the Author

C. M. Charles was a public school teacher from 1953 to 1959, then moved into higher education and held professorships at the University of New Mexico, Teachers College Columbia University, Pepperdine University, Universidade Federal do Marahao (Brazil), and San Diego State University, where he is now professor emeritus. At San Diego State, Charles directed innovative programs in teacher education and five times received outstanding professor and distinguished teaching awards. He also served on several occasions as advisor in teacher education and curriculum to the governments of Peru and Brazil. Charles has authored or coauthored more than 25 books, many of which have attracted wide audiences in the United States and abroad, with translations into several foreign languages. Those dealing most directly with school discipline are *Teacher's Petit Piaget* (1972); *The Synergetic Classroom: Joyful Teaching and Gentle Discipline* (2000); *Essential Elements of Effective Discipline* (2002); *Classroom Management for Middle-Grades Teachers* (2004); *Elementary Classroom Management* (fifth edition, 2008); *Building Classroom Discipline* (ninth edition, 2008), and *Today's Best Classroom Management Strategies: Paths to Positive Discipline* (2008).

Gail W. Senter earned her doctorate in Curriculum and Instruction from the University of Southern California. After teaching in public schools, she moved her professional focus to university-level teacher-training programs in Southern California. In that capacity, she has held faculty positions at the San Diego campus of Chapman University, California State University San Bernardino, and California State University San Marcos, working with preservice and veteran teachers at both the elementary and secondary levels. She assisted C. M. Charles on his book *Introduction to Educational Research*, collaborated with Charles on multiple editions of *Building Classroom Discipline* (ninth edition, 2008), and is principal author of *Elementary Classroom Management* (fifth edition, 2008).

CHAPTER 1

Classroom Discipline
The Problem and the Solution

CHAPTER PREVIEW

This chapter reviews the unsettling realities of student misbehavior, often referred to as "poor discipline," and presents a plan for helping teachers resolve most of the problems associated with it. The plan clarifies the place of discipline skills among the central competencies that teachers require today, and it directs attention to five clusters of skills for maintaining positive work climates in the classroom. It is strongly suggested that readers begin at this point to develop personal systems of discipline that meet the needs of their students while remaining consonant with their individual personalities and views on teaching. Information and guidelines for developing personal systems are presented in this chapter.

Comparing Classrooms 314 and 315

The scene is an inner-city school. Classroom 314 is quiet as students listen attentively to the teacher's questions about a recent lesson. Suddenly, eager hands begin to wave and bodies twist out of their seats amidst shouts of Aooh me! I know! Aooh-oh! Quiet returns when one student is chosen to answer. As soon as she has responded, others begin to yell out refutations or additions and compete again for teacher recognition. When the questions end and seat work begins, some students gaze out the window while others offer to help classmates who are unsure of how to proceed.

But across the hall in room 315, chaos reigns. The room is noisy with the shouting, laughter, and movement of many children. Though most students are seated, many are walking or running aimlessly around the classroom. Some stop at others' desks, provoke them briefly, and move on. Several students who are lining up textbooks as "race courses" for toy cars laugh when the teacher demands their attention. As the teacher struggles to ask a question over the noise, few if any students volunteer to answer. When one student does respond correctly, others yell out, "You think you're so smart." (adapted from Schwartz, 1981, p. 99)

By most teachers' standards, the discipline in Room 314 is acceptable, whereas that in Room 315 is not. But what is the difference? In both rooms students are making noise and behaving in ways not usually condoned. Yet the teacher in Room 314 is probably well satisfied with the lesson, whereas the teacher in Room 315 is not. Why? The answer involves the extent to which the teachers feel their classroom situations are productive. The students in 314 are showing initiative, but are still responsive to the teacher. Their personal interactions are positive and reasonably respectful. The teacher feels progress is being made and is happy to see students displaying reasonable manners while actively involved in the lesson.

In contrast, the students in 315 are barely in touch with the lesson. They are accomplishing little that is worthwhile. They are doing more or less what they want, disregarding what the teacher says. Their behavior is haphazard and their interactions are frequently disrespectful of the teacher and each other. The teacher is rightfully concerned about the behavior in this class, for it is keeping students from learning and is encouraging habits that are self-defeating for students. An impartial judge would consider the lesson a failure.

If you were the teacher in Room 315, what would you hope to see? Think about this a moment. How would you want students to respond to your lessons? How would you want them to relate to you? To each other? What would, or could, you do to make things as you'd like them to be? Could you develop a detailed plan for how you would work with the class so it would be productive and rewarding? Suppose you made such a plan and found that students disregarded what you asked them to do. Then what? Questions such as these are difficult to answer, and in truth are more difficult to answer in a real classroom than when discussing hypothetical situations. If the answers were easy, we'd have no teachers feeling unfulfilled or ready to leave teaching because they could no longer tolerate dealing with students who seem disrespectful and unmotivated.

Competencies Required for Teaching in Today's Schools

Through the years, many individuals, groups, and agencies have listed sets of competencies they believed beginning and experienced teachers should possess. Today, much attention is being paid to competencies suggested by the Interstate New Teacher Assessment and Support Consortium (INTASC). We will examine these suggestions and see how they relate to classroom discipline. The INTASC recommendations are embodied in the Praxis Series of tests produced by Educational Testing Service. Those tests will be discussed briefly, as will further suggestions from Charlotte Danielson, who helped develop the Praxis III tests of teacher competence.

INTASC Recommendations

In 1987 the Interstate New Teacher Assessment and Support Consortium (**INTASC**) was established for the purpose of identifying what beginning teachers needed to know and be able to do in order to meet their responsibilities in a professional manner. The Consortium articulated ten outcomes that should be held up as goals in teacher education; they are presented here in abridged form. These ten principles are widely emphasized in programs of teacher education and are often used to evaluate beginning and experienced teachers. You will probably come in contact with them again during your professional development. For a more detailed presentation of INTASC, consult the following Internet site: www.ccsso.org/intasc. Here are the ten principles. Please note that several of them, especially items 5 and 6, directly affect classroom discipline.

Principle 1. *The teacher understands the central concepts, tools of inquiry, and structures of the discipline(s) he or she teaches and can create learning experiences that make these aspects of subject matter meaningful for students.* Examples of evidence of such understanding are noted when the teacher

- Uses multiple representations and explanations of disciplinary concepts that capture key ideas and link them to students' prior understandings
- Represents and uses differing viewpoints, theories, "ways of knowing," and methods of inquiry in his or her teaching of subject matter concepts
- Engages students in generating knowledge and testing hypotheses according to the methods of inquiry and standards of evidence used in the discipline
- Develops and uses curricula that encourage students to see, question, and interpret ideas from diverse perspectives

Principle 2. *The teacher understands how children learn and develop, and can provide learning opportunities that support their intellectual, social and personal development.* Examples of evidence of such understanding are seen when the teacher

- Assesses individual and group performance to design instruction that meets learners' current needs and that leads to the next level of development
- Stimulates student reflection on prior knowledge and linking new ideas to already familiar ideas, making connections to students' experiences, providing opportunities for active engagement, manipulation, and testing of ideas and materials, and encouraging students to assume responsibility for shaping their learning tasks
- Accesses students' thinking and experiences as a basis for instructional activities by, for example, encouraging discussion, listening and responding to group interaction, and eliciting samples of student thinking orally and in writing

Principle 3. *The teacher understands how students differ in their approaches to learning and creates instructional opportunities that are adapted to diverse learners.* Evidence of this understanding is seen when the teacher

- Identifies and designs instruction appropriate to students' stages of development, learning styles, strengths, and needs
- Uses teaching approaches that are sensitive to the multiple experiences of learners and that address different learning and performance modes

- Makes appropriate provisions (in terms of time and circumstances for work, tasks assigned, and communication and response modes) for individual students who have particular learning differences or needs
- Seeks to understand students' families, cultures, and communities, and uses this information as a basis for connecting instruction to students' experiences (e.g., drawing explicit connections between subject matter and community matters, making assignments that can be related to students' experiences and cultures)
- Creates a learning community in which individual differences are respected

Principle 4. *The teacher understands and uses a variety of instructional strategies to encourage students' development of critical thinking, problem solving, and performance skills.* Evidence of this understanding is seen when the teacher

- Carefully evaluates how to achieve learning goals, choosing alternative teaching strategies and materials to achieve different instructional purposes and to meet student needs (e.g., developmental stages, prior knowledge, learning styles, and interests)
- Uses multiple teaching and learning strategies to engage students in active learning opportunities that promote the development of critical thinking, problem solving, and performance capabilities and that help students assume responsibility for identifying and using learning resources
- Constantly monitors and adjusts strategies in response to learner feedback
- Develops a variety of clear, accurate presentations and representations of concepts, using alternative explanations to assist students' understanding and presenting diverse perspectives to encourage critical thinking

Principle 5. *The teacher uses an understanding of individual and group motivation and behavior to create a learning environment that encourages positive social interaction, active engagement in learning, and self-motivation.* Evidence supporting this understanding emerges as the teacher

- Creates a smoothly functioning learning community in which students assume responsibility for themselves and one another, participate in decision making, work collaboratively and independently, and engage in purposeful learning activities
- Engages students in individual and cooperative learning activities that help them develop the motivation to achieve, by, for example, relating lessons to students' personal interests, allowing students to have choices in their learning, and leading students to ask questions and pursue problems that are meaningful to them
- Organizes, allocates, and manages the resources of time, space, activities, and attention to provide active and equitable engagement of students in productive tasks
- Helps the group concerning interactions, academic discussions, and individual and group responsibility that create a positive classroom climate of openness, mutual respect, support, and inquiry

Principle 6. *The teacher uses knowledge of effective verbal, nonverbal, and media communication techniques to foster active inquiry, collaboration, and supportive interaction in the classroom.* Examples of evidence that support these communication qualities are seen when the teacher

- Models effective communication strategies in conveying ideas and information and in asking questions (e.g., monitoring the effects of messages; restating ideas and drawing connections; using visual, aural, and kinesthetic cues; and being sensitive to nonverbal cues given and received)
- Supports and expands learner expression in speaking, writing, and other media
- Asks questions and stimulates discussion in different ways for particular purposes, for example, probing for learner understanding, helping students articulate their ideas and thinking processes, promoting risk taking and problem solving, facilitating factual recall, encouraging convergent and divergent thinking, stimulating curiosity, and helping students to question
- Communicates in ways that demonstrate a sensitivity to cultural and gender differences (e.g., appropriate use of eye contact, interpretation of body language and verbal statements, and acknowledgment of and responsiveness to different modes of communication and participation)

Principle 7. *The teacher plans instruction based upon knowledge of subject matter, students, the community, and curriculum goals.* Evidence of this capability is seen when the teacher

- Plans for learning opportunities that recognize and address variation in learning styles and performance modes
- Creates short-range and long-term plans that are linked to student needs and performance, and adapts the plans to ensure and capitalize on student progress and motivation

Principle 8. *The teacher understands and uses formal and informal assessment strategies to evaluate and ensure the continuous intellectual, social, and physical development of the learner.* Evidence of this understanding is seen when the teacher

- Uses a variety of formal and informal assessment techniques (e.g., observation, portfolios of student work, teacher-made tests, performance tasks, projects, student self-assessments, peer assessment, and standardized tests)
- Solicits and uses information about students' experiences, learning behavior, needs, and progress from parents, other colleagues, and the students themselves
- Uses assessment strategies to involve learners in self-assessment activities, to help them become aware of their strengths and needs, and to encourage them to set personal goals for learning
- Evaluates the effect of class activities on both individuals and the class as a whole, collecting information through observation of classroom interactions, questioning, and analysis of student work

- Monitors his or her own teaching strategies and behavior in relation to student success, modifying plans and instructional approaches accordingly
- Maintains useful records of student work and performance and can communicate student progress knowledgeably and responsibly, based on appropriate indicators, to students, parents, and other colleagues

Principle 9. *The teacher is a reflective practitioner who continually evaluates the effects of his or her choices and actions on others (students, parents, and other professionals in the learning community) and who actively seeks out opportunities to grow professionally.* Evidence of reflective practice is seen when the teacher

- Uses classroom observation, information about students, and research as sources for evaluating the outcomes of teaching and learning and as a basis for experimenting with, reflecting on, and revising practice
- Seeks out professional literature, colleagues, and other resources to support his or her own development as a learner and a teacher

Principle 10. *The teacher fosters relationships with school colleagues, parents, and agencies in the larger community to support students' learning and well-being.* Evidence that supports the existence of such relationships is seen when the teacher

- Participates in collegial activities designed to make the entire school a productive learning environment
- Makes links with the learners' other environments on behalf of students, by consulting with parents, counselors, teachers of other classes and activities within the schools, and professionals in other community agencies
- Identifies and uses community resources to foster student learning
- Establishes respectful and productive relationships with parents and guardians from diverse home and community situations, and seeks to develop cooperative partnerships in support of student learning and well-being
- Talks with and listens to the student, is sensitive and responsive to clues of distress, investigates situations, and seeks outside help as needed and appropriate to remedy problems

The Praxis Series of Tests

In 1987, Educational Testing Service (ETS) constructed tests that schools could use to assess the professional capabilities of their teachers and that teacher licensing agencies could use in granting certification to new teachers. Called the **Praxis** Series (*praxis* is a word that refers to reflection on and application of accepted ways of doing things—in other words, what one should do in practice), many states now use these tests in teacher licensing. There are three phases of Praxis tests. Praxis I assesses teachers' skills in reading, writing, and mathematics. Praxis II assesses competencies needed for teaching, as empha-sized in programs of teacher education. Praxis III assesses the competence levels of teach-ers as they work in the classroom. Several states and individual writers have worked to align the INTASC principles with the Praxis criteria. To see one such example from the Utah State Department of Education, consult the following website: www.ed.utah.edu/ TandL/ NCATE/correlationINTASC-PRAXIS.pdf.

Danielson and Professional Teaching Competencies

Charlotte Danielson (1996) was involved in the development of Praxis III. In the course of that work, it became evident to her that teachers have, or make, little opportunity to dis-cuss teaching with each other. Yet, teachers trained to serve as assessors in Praxis III re-ported that interactions among professionals provide many insights into teaching. Danielson, therefore, devised a framework for discussions that teachers can use to enrich their professional lives. The framework lists four components of professional teaching: (1) planning and preparation, (2) the classroom environment, (3) communicating clearly and accurately, and (4) reflecting on teaching. Danielson also devised forms that help clarify the relationship between the INTASC principles and teacher performance. To learn more about Danielson's efforts, consult the following website: www.stevens.clarion.edu/ ncate/intasc.htm.

Discipline as a Basic Teacher Competency

Student misbehavior is one of the most troubling realities in education today. In many classes it interferes with teaching, stifles learning, produces great stress, leads to poor class morale, and causes more teachers to fail than does any other factor. This needn't be the case, however. Misbehavior can be rather easily brought to manageable proportions by employing three strategies simultaneously. The first strategy is to *prevent* the occurrence of as much misbehavior as possible. This is done by identifying factors that lead to misbe-havior and then eliminating or reducing those factors. The second is to *introduce classroom conditions* that lead to student enjoyment, sense of purpose, self-direction, and sense of re-sponsibility. The third is to deal with misbehavior that does occur in a *positive manner* rather than a negative one. This is done by encouraging students, relating with them per-sonally, teaching them how to behave acceptably, and helping them understand how to conduct themselves responsibly while seeing the personal value of doing so.

These three strategies are routinely employed by a great many very successful teach-ers, working in all types of schools with all types of students. They find teaching joyful and rewarding. They are proud to see their students interacting positively and behaving con-siderately. They feel close to many of their students and maintain trusting relationships with them. Of course, at times they experience problems and stress, as will always happen in teaching. But they have learned that by working together with students in a spirit of good will, they can keep behavior problems to a minimum. Unfortunately, many teachers have not yet learned how to employ these discipline strategies. As a result, their days are burdened with turmoil that wears them down. Their students are adversely affected, too, with little prospect of enjoying or adequately profiting from their school experience.

Let's begin to eradicate fears you might have about student misbehavior. In the following pages, you will see how to work happily and productively with your students, helping them become solid, productive citizens able to control themselves and get along with each other. The results will bring you great satisfaction and, perhaps, the greatest prize in teaching—the esteem of your students.

The Meanings of Behavior and Misbehavior

Misbehavior is best understood as a condition of overall behavior. **Behavior** refers to everything people do, good or bad, right or wrong, helpful or useless, productive or wasteful. Desirable school behavior is that in which students show self-control, responsibility, and consideration and respect for others. It usually involves cooperation and helpfulness. You can see that this definition of good behavior is somewhat different from the traditional definition, which implies obedience, acquiescence, being quiet, following directions, and doing as expected.

Misbehavior is behavior that is *inappropriate* for the setting or situation in which it occurs. Some people find fault with the term *misbehavior*, feeling it is overly subjective and negative in connotation. They prefer terms such as *inappropriate* or *disruptive*. However, those terms are equally subjective. *Misbehavior* is used in this book because it is a familiar term that is widely used and understood. If you look back to what students were doing in Room 315, you will see that some of their actions merely showed careless disregard for expectations whereas others seemed to be intentional transgressions. Through the history of education, misbehavior has been a catchall term for behavior teachers didn't like. To gain a better, more useful perspective on misbehavior, let's agree on the following: Classroom misbehavior is any behavior that, through *intent or thoughtlessness*

1. Interferes with teaching or learning
2. Threatens or intimidates others
3. Oversteps society's standards of moral, ethical, or legal behavior

Types of Misbehavior You Will Encounter

You can expect to encounter thirteen **types of student misbehavior.** Take note of them here. As you progress through this book, you will learn how to deal positively with all of them.

1. *Inattention.* Daydreaming, doodling, looking out the window, thinking about things irrelevant to the lesson
2. *Apathy.* Having a general disinclination to participate, sulking, not caring, being afraid of failure, not wanting to try or do well
3. *Needless talk.* Chatting during instructional time about things unrelated to the lesson

4. *Moving about the room.* Getting up and moving about without permission, congregating in parts of the room
5. *Annoying others.* Provoking, teasing, picking at, calling names
6. *Disruption.* Shouting out during instruction, talking and laughing inappropriately, causing "accidents"
7. *Lying.* Falsifying to avoid accepting responsibility or admitting wrongdoing, or to get others in trouble
8. *Stealing.* Taking things that belong to others
9. *Cheating.* Making false representations or wrongly taking advantage of others for personal benefit
10. *Sexual harassment.* Making others uncomfortable through touching, sex related language, or sexual innuendo
11. *Aggression and fighting.* Showing hostility toward others, threatening them, shoving, pinching, wrestling, hitting, bullying
12. *Malicious mischief.* Doing intentional damage to school property or the belongings of others
13. *Defiance of authority.* Talking back to the teacher, hostilely refusing to do as the teacher requests

It is natural for teachers to feel that students are to blame when they exhibit these misbehaviors. At this point, let's suspend judgment about blame. As we move ahead, we will see that many different factors can lead to student misbehavior. Instead of blaming students or teachers, we will give attention to factors that often foster misbehavior and will learn how to limit those factors.

Clarifying the Terms *Discipline* and *Behavior Management*

Overall, the tactics teachers use to manage student behavior are referred to as discipline or behavior management. These terms are used interchangeably. **Discipline** is the more familiar and has two meanings in relation to behavior. The first refers to a condition of misbehavior, for example, "The discipline in that room is pretty bad." The second refers to what teachers do to try to get students to behave acceptably, for example, "Mr. Smythe's discipline system is one of the best I've seen." Both meanings are used in this book, with the context indicating which is intended.

Because the term *discipline* has traditionally suggested teacher control, coercion, and forceful tactics, educators today often use the term **behavior management** to indicate preventing, suppressing, and redirecting misbehavior. That term, however, is rarely used in this book because emphasis should be placed on working with students as individuals, rather than on thinking of their behavior as something that can be managed apart from them. Further, please understand that when the word *discipline* is used as a verb in this book, it does not refer to harsh, abusive tactics but rather to positive actions that lead to improved student behavior and good relations between teacher and students.

Educators once considered teaching and discipline to be separate endeavors. They believed teaching was concerned with imparting knowledge, whereas discipline was concerned with making students conduct themselves in an acceptable manner. As recently as thirty years ago, teachers expected students to misbehave and were ready to impose harsh measures when they did. Today we have a different conception of discipline. We now see it as an integral part of teaching, not an effort that stands apart. Furthermore, we know that instruction affects behavior, and behavior affects instruction. That is why discipline is now considered a strand of teaching, along with instruction, communication, classroom structure and management, and relations with parents.

Toward Resolving the Discipline Problem

There is a relatively simple solution to the discipline problem: It is for teachers to develop teaching approaches that meet the needs of their students while remaining consistent with teacher personality and social realities of the community. The remainder of this book provides a great deal of advice on how that can be done.

Suggestions for Working with Students Effectively

Maintain focus on your major task in teaching. Your major task is to help your students become more capable and successful, both in school and in later years. Inform them of this task and indicate what you will do to help them. Then back up your words with actions. Help students develop self-direction and responsibility. Help them become progressively better at making good decisions, treating others well, and accepting responsibility for their actions. They do not learn these things by reading about them or listening to lectures. They learn them through experience, a process in which they try to make good choices, accept mistakes as inevitable, and reflect on mistakes and use them as opportunities to learn. Through this process, students gradually develop responsible self-control.

Know what causes misbehavior and how to deal with those causes. Understand the known causes of student misbehavior, where they reside, and how they are manifested. Take steps to soften or remove those causes.

Understand your students' needs and how to meet them. Know what motivates students. Know what they like and find attractive, as well as what they dislike and try to avoid. Know their typical behaviors and how age, economic level, ethnicity, and social factors contribute to those behaviors. Know how students typically react to teachers and school situations. Align your program to meet student needs. Emphasize topics important to students. Keep them involved. Use activities they enjoy. Keep learning lively and upbeat. Allow groups to work cooperatively. Eliminate drudgery, boredom, frustration, and overload.

Don't try to coerce students. Effective teaching and behavior management depend on enticement rather than coercion. When you use force, students resist. When you speak derogatorily, they lose respect for you. It is true that when you have very highly motivated learners (or very fearful ones) you can deal with them demandingly and abrasively and get some of the results you want. But most students today are not highly motivated to please you, some are not afraid of you, and a few are quite willing to defy you in front of others.

Treat all students as your social equals. Although you must maintain a mature, adult viewpoint, talk with students as your social equals. Confer dignity on all students. Communicate clearly and effectively. Never embarrass students, put them down, speak sarcastically, or make fun of them. Don't make demands or threats. Don't argue with them. Don't spend a lot of time telling them what to do or what they should have done.

Teach and relate to students in a charismatic way. Keep yourself interesting and your outlook positive. Share some of your talents, experiences, and interests. Show personal attention to all your students.

Involve students meaningfully in making decisions. These include decisions about the class, instructional activities, behavioral expectations, and how interventions should occur in the event of misbehavior. Take students seriously. Communicate with them respectfully. Encourage them to look for ways to treat each other well and help each other be successful. Encourage them to assume individual responsibility.

Establish a positive set of tactics for responding to misbehavior. Involve students, depending on their age and maturity, in determining this process and adapting to the decisions that result. The tactics should stop the misbehavior, keep students on track, and preserve good relations.

Involve parents and guardians. To a reasonable degree, keep parents and guardians informed about your class and what it is doing for their children. Show that you want and need their support and will do all you can to help their children succeed in school.

Building a Personal System of Discipline

The major thrust of this book is to encourage and help you develop a **personal system of classroom discipline**—one that meets the needs of your students and is also compatible with your personality. You may wonder why you are advised to develop a personal system, since many outstanding programs of discipline are readily available to you. Those programs, as described in this book, contain marvelous concepts and strategies. Any of them can produce most of the results you hope for in working productively with students. However, none of the discipline programs alone is likely to address all of your particular needs and contingencies. Students differ from place to place and from class to class. Their behavior is strongly affected by the realities of their social situations. Additionally, you have your own distinct personality, philosophy, and preferred ways of teaching. You will find it easy, and reassuring, to design a discipline system that is consonant with the needs and preferences of your students while compatible with your own personality and needs.

Five Principles for Building a Personal System of Discipline

In keeping with the INTASC, Praxis, and Danielson contributions, **five principles for a personal system of discipline** are set forth here to help you prepare for working with students in ways that bring satisfaction to all. It is suggested that you make a practice of reflecting on these principles and taking notes related to them as you read the chapters in this book. By doing so, you will progressively compile a variety of ideas for developing a well-rounded personal system of discipline. The development of your personal discipline system will be finalized in Chapter 15.

Principle 1. *Present, conduct yourself, and interact with students and others in a professional manner.* Make sure you know and put into practice

- Standards of professionalism
- Ethical considerations
- Legal requirements

Principle 2. *Clarify how you want your students to behave, now and in the future.* Identify attitudes and behaviors, such as

- Showing positive attitude
- Behaving considerately toward others
- Taking initiative
- Showing self-direction
- Making a strong effort to learn
- Assuming personal responsibility for behavior

Principle 3. *Establish and maintain classroom conditions that help students enjoy and profit from their educational experience.* You may wish to give attention to

- Good environment for learning
- Compatibility with students' natures, needs, interests, and preferences
- Sense of community
- Positive attention
- Good communication
- Consideration for others
- Special needs
- Trust
- Interesting activities
- Student knowledge of expectations
- Continual helpfulness
- Preservation of dignity
- Minimizing causes of misbehavior
- Teacher charisma
- Student involvement in planning the program

Principle 4. *Do all you can to help students learn to conduct themselves responsibly.*

- Identify and reduce the known causes of misbehavior.
- Build a sense of community in your classroom that emphasizes collaboration, joint decision making, responsibility, and consideration for others.

- Communicate clearly and effectively with students. Keep them fully informed.
- Speak with students in ways that build dignity and invite cooperation.
- Work in a collaborative way with students and allow them to help make class decisions.
- Reach a set of agreements about how the class is to function and how you and the students will conduct yourselves.
- Build group spirit and otherwise energize the class.
- Bring parents into meaningful partnership with your class and program.
- Use activities that increase student self-direction and responsibility.
- Resolve class problems effectively and fairly while maintaining good personal relationships.

Principle 5. *Intervene supportively and productively when common disruptions, neurological-based behavior, or serious infractions occur in the classroom.*

- Understand the nature of helpful interventions and devise approaches that are suited to you and your students.
- Develop a repertoire of helpful things to say and do when students misbehave.
- Identify tactics and words you want to avoid using.
- Establish a clear procedure for dealing with misbehavior. Involve students in developing the procedure. Follow that procedure consistently.
- Help students accept responsibility for their behavior and commit to better behavior in the future.

These five principles work together to help you develop an organized approach to discipline that is suited to the needs and social realities of the students with whom you work, as well as to your personality and preferences. This personal system will enable you to effectively work with all students, no matter what their age or background. It will also build a sense of togetherness in the classroom, with a high likelihood of the following:

- *An effective environment for learning.* Learning generally occurs best in environments that are reasonably well ordered, free from threat, free from disruptions, and encouraging of exploration and interaction.
- *A heightened sense of purpose for students.* Each of us, knowingly or unknowingly, tries to identify what is important to us, how our lives are made better by those things, how we can best pursue them, and how we can avoid damaging others or the environment in their pursuit. Good discipline helps students develop a clearer sense of purpose concerning what they wish to experience, what they want to learn, and how they want their lives to progress.
- *Increased learning.* As class behavior improves, students become more likely to focus on instructional activities and put forth their best effort. When threat and fear of failure are removed, students become more likely to willingly engage in activities.

■ *A joyful, satisfying experience in school.* Far too many students don't enjoy school because they find it to be boring. Many say the only thing they like about school is the opportunity to be with friends. This picture changes significantly when you make your classes enjoyable and satisfying.

■ *Positive personal relations.* Our personal sense of accomplishment and satisfaction is dependent in large measure on how we are treated by others. And, of course, the treatment we receive from others depends in large part on how we treat them. Most of us want to be respected, accepted as worthwhile, and treated with consideration. We want to enjoy friendships and work with others harmoniously. We are more likely to experience those benefits when we accord the same things to others. When we have disagreements, we would like to resolve them equitably, while maintaining positive feelings. We cannot expect to do so if we don't treat others respectfully. In order to work effectively with others, we must remember and apply the Golden Rule.

■ *Student self-control.* One of our major goals in teaching is to help students develop inner discipline, the ability to control and direct themselves in various situations. When this is accomplished, students gain a sense of purpose and direction and avoid incidents that lead to damaging confrontations or undesirable acts.

■ *Student responsibility.* Our society emphasizes individual freedom concerning expression, activity, and relationships. However, those freedoms are linked to responsibility, where the rights of others are taken into account and not transgressed. Responsibility entails showing consideration, behaving ethically, and accepting the legitimate consequences of one's behavior, whether positive or negative. Effective discipline heightens student initiative and choice, but is always anchored in responsibility.

Twenty Questions for Clarifying Your Ideas about Discipline

Please take a few minutes to reflect on the following twenty questions concerning students and their behavior. The purpose of this activity is to open and orient your thinking still further. Discuss these questions with colleagues, if at all possible. As you proceed through this book, you will be able to answer all these questions in a professional manner.

1. *How should students behave at school?* How, generally and specifically, do you want your students to conduct themselves at school and in your class? Clarify your reasons for wanting them to behave in the manner you envision.

2. *What are appropriate behavior and misbehavior?* What is meant by the terms *appropriate behavior* and *misbehavior* as used in education? What are two examples of each? Do teachers ever misbehave when working with students? If so, in what ways?

3. *What is bad about misbehavior?* In what ways does misbehavior interfere with teaching and learning? How seriously does it affect effort, progress, and morale? Is there a positive side to misbehavior?

4. *Why do students misbehave when they know they shouldn't?* Why don't students always behave as teachers would like them to? Identify some factors that seem to lead to misbehavior. Do teachers have any control over those factors?

5. *What should we know about student needs?* What do we know about the nature and needs of students that can help us work with them more effectively? What about students with special needs related to disabilities, economic realities, or racial, ethnic, cultural, or linguistic diversity?

6. *What do we mean by "positive" discipline?* Is there a "negative" discipline? If so, how do the two differ, and what is each good for?

7. *What can teachers do to help students behave properly?* How would you explain the teacher's role in helping today's students behave more appropriately? List five things teachers could do toward this end.

8. *Does teaching method affect behavior?* In what ways can method(s) of teaching affect student behavior? Is it possible to teach in ways that encourage students to want to conduct themselves appropriately?

9. *Does the physical environment affect behavior?* Can you identify some of the ways in which the physical learning environment affects student behavior? What can you do to enhance the quality of the physical environment in which you and your students work?

10. *Does the psychosocial environment affect behavior?* In what ways can the psychosocial learning environment (including emotions, feelings, and attitudes) affect student behavior? What can you and your students do to enhance the quality of the psychosocial environment?

11. *What role does communication play in discipline?* How, specifically, can you speak with and otherwise communicate with students to influence them in a positive manner?

12. *How can you help students work together productively?* What, specifically, can you do to help all members of your class work together effectively, enjoy success, and interact with each other in a positive manner?

13. *What role can parents or guardians play in discipline?* What do you see as advantages of establishing and maintaining good relationships with students' parents or guardians? How can those people be helpful to you and your students?

14. *How can teachers establish good relations with parents?* What can you do to enhance your relationship with students' parents? How can you best communicate with them? How can you enlist their support?

15. *In what ways do trust, ethics, and teacher charisma affect student behavior?* To what do these terms refer? What effects can they produce? Who is responsible for ensuring that they become part of the class environment and procedures?

16. *What should you do when students misbehave?* When students misbehave, how can you intervene positively to stop the misbehavior, keep students on track, and maintain positive feelings and relationships? What are specific things you feel comfortable saying and doing?

17. *How can you best deal with problems in your classroom?* What is the difference between a problem and misbehavior? When general problems involving students and their behavior arise in your classes, how can you best deal with them?

18. *How can you best deal with conflict?* What is meant by conflict? How does it differ from misbehavior and problems? When conflicts occur among students or between you and students, how can you positively deal with them?

19. *How do you make your class energetic and lively when you want it that way?* What steps can you take to energize your class so students enjoy learning in a helpful, active, cooperative manner?

20. *Why is a structured approach to discipline desirable?* Why is it important for you to rely on a well-organized strategy for maintaining positive behavior in your classroom? Why is it important that you organize the strategy to suit your specific needs?

Getting Started

To begin your personal system of discipline, please attend once more to the five principles for building a personal system of discipline. At this point, we will consider Principle 1, present, conduct yourself, and interact with students and others in a professional manner. This principle concerns professional, ethical, and legal considerations for teachers. Later in this book we will consider the other four principles. Please note that *the author is not qualified to provide legal advice.* The legal considerations in the following section are believed to be correct, but the interpretations presented here cannot be considered the final word. Please, therefore, obtain a description of legal responsibilities of your local school district's teachers and consider that information authoritative.

Standards of Professionalism

The National Education Association (1975) has set forth professional and ethical provisions for educators. All teachers are expected to abide by them. This code stipulates, among other things, that the educator

- Shall not misrepresent his or her professional qualifications in any way
- Shall not knowingly make false or malicious statements about a colleague
- Shall not accept any gratuity, gift, or favor that might impair or appear to influence professional decisions or action
- Shall not suppress or distort subject matter relevant to the students' progress
- Shall not intentionally expose students to embarrassment or disparagement
- Shall not disclose information about students obtained in the course of professional service, unless disclosure serves a compelling professional purpose or is required by law

In addition to the NEA stipulations, professionalism requires that you

- Dress professionally, as an adult in a professional situation
- Use appropriate language for the educational setting, with correct speech patterns and complete avoidance of obscenities
- Treat others with respect and courtesy

Legalities Pertaining to Student Safety and Well-Being

It is important that you familiarize yourself with certain legal concerns involved in teaching. Schools operate under the doctrine of *in loco parentis,* which means "in place of parents." This doctrine involves student care and safety; it means you should watch over students as if you were their parent (actually, even more closely than that). It gives you and other school officials authority over students in school matters involving academics and discipline and permits you to take actions that a reasonable parent would take under similar circumstances.

Due Diligence

Teachers and other school personnel have a duty to oversee—to exercise reasonable care to protect students from harm (see Goorian and Brown, 2002). Many teachers are not aware they are required to keep a diligent eye on all students under their supervision. They may feel that their mere presence satisfies their duty. In general, diligence means taking reasonable care or giving reasonable attention to a matter. In school settings this principle is applied in relation to established policies and is judged in terms of what a reasonable and prudent professional would do in a similar circumstance.

Negligence and Breach of Duty

If a student is injured mentally or physically while at school, and the teacher on duty did not exercise due diligence, the teacher and school may be sued for negligence (Drye, 2000). The following guidelines will help you make sure you are in a defensible position should questions arise about negligence and breach of duty:

- Perform your assigned duties as directed, even those that seem boring and unnecessary.
- Oversee your students. Be vigilant in monitoring their behavior. Do not leave students unattended in your classroom, shop, or instructional area.
- Provide thorough instructions and teach safety procedures before undertaking activities that involve risk to students.
- Be vigilant for signs that students might harm themselves. Pay attention to what they do, say, and write. Observe them for changes in behavior.
- Be aware of signs of abuse. You are required by law to report if you suspect one of your students is being abused. Follow your school guidelines to familiarize yourself with signs of abuse. If concerns arise, report them to the school counselor or administrator, who will then follow up.

Concerns Related to Physical Contact with Students

Don't allow yourself to be alone in the classroom with a student, unless you are in plain sight of others. If you are male, refrain from touching students, other than on the hands or arms or with pats to the head or shoulder. If students frustrate or anger you, never grab any part of their body; it is difficult to justify physical contact motivated by anger. Also make sure you never throw pencils, pens, erasers, books, desks, or chairs, no matter how strongly you are provoked.

Ethics of Instruction

Ethics refer to right and wrong, proper and improper. There are certain ethics of the profession by which all teachers are expected to abide. They affect your approach to teaching and your overall strategy for working with students. They also influence many factors associated with interacting with students, presenting lessons, and managing behavior. It is strongly recommended that you emphasize the following ethical qualities in your overall teaching style.

1. *Give your genuine best effort to the profession.* Your obligation is to do the best you can to help each and every student profit from the educational experience and experience satisfaction in doing so. This applies to all students under your direction, without favoritism. It also applies to how you work and relate with parents and colleagues.

2. *Do your best to teach effectively.* Teach in a manner deemed most conducive to success for all learners. This implies careful selection of subject matter, provision of worthwhile topics and activities for learning, relating with students effectively, and insisting on considerate, humane treatment by and for everyone in the class.

3. *Always do what you can to help students.* Helpfulness is an indispensable ingredient of effective teaching. You will see it emphasized and reemphasized in the most popular models of classroom discipline. As Haim Ginott (1971) said, always ask yourself what you can do, at a given moment, that will be most helpful to your students.

4. *Treat students civilly, respectfully, and fairly.* Treat all students as your social equals. Give each of them some personal attention every day. Learn their names quickly and remember important things about them. Give them credit for work well done and for exemplary behavior. Smile and interact with them in a friendly manner, but don't single out any as your favorites. Spread your attention around evenly. Be friendly, but don't try to be pals with students.

5. *Emphasize same-side cooperation with students.* Involve students in planning and decision making. Try to establish the understanding that you and they must work together to attain class goals in a satisfying manner. Show you are considerate of their desires and feelings. Always treat them as you would like to be treated in similar circumstances. Do not attack their dignity or disparage them in any way.

6. *Communicate effectively.* Make sure students know what is expected of them. Take time to listen to their concerns. Consider using class meetings to discuss important matters with the class. When you listen to students, try to see their perspectives. When you speak to them, be helpful and encouraging, but take care that you don't give too much advice or begin preaching or moralizing. Don't grill students about their behavior or otherwise put them on the defensive. Instead, politely ask them to help you understand why they have

done or said a certain thing. When they explain, listen to them attentively. When you reply with a suggestion, indicate it is something for them to consider or is simply your opinion.

7. *Maintain a charismatic demeanor.* Charisma is a quality of attractiveness that draws attention and makes others want to be in your presence and interact with you. You acquire charisma by making yourself personally interesting to students. Be upbeat and pleasant, with a touch of wit (don't try to overdo it). Share some of your interests, experiences, and talents. Let students know a bit about your family life and what you like to do outside of school. Use humor, but without being silly. Never weave sarcasm into what you say. Show personal interest, be helpful, and treat students considerately.

KEY TERMS AND CONCEPTS EMPHASIZED IN THIS CHAPTER

INTASC	types of misbehavior (13)	five principles for a personal system
Praxis	discipline	of discipline
behavior	behavior management	
misbehavior	personal system of discipline	

ACTIVITIES

1. In pairs or small groups, discuss the twenty questions for clarifying your ideas about discipline (pp. 14–16). See if you can arrive at group consensus concerning answers to the questions.

2. Think through the advice from INTASC, the Praxis Series, and Charlotte Danielson. Incorporate these ideas into your personal system of discipline. Also consider suggestions related to professional, ethical, and legal aspects of teaching.

3. Refer to the five principles for building a personal system of discipline. In a notebook or journal, copy the outline headings, leaving a few blank pages following each of the five principles. Then review this chapter and enter in your notebook information you feel applies to each of the principles. By repeating this activity at the end of each chapter, you will accumulate a wealth of ideas and techniques to use in organizing your own personal system of discipline.

REFERENCES

Danielson, C. 1996. *Enhancing professional practice: A framework for teaching.* Washington, DC: Association for Supervision and Curriculum Development.

Drye, J. 2000. *Tort liability 101: When are teachers liable?* Atlanta, GA: Educator Resources. www.educator-resources .com.

Ginott, H. 1971. *Teacher and child.* New York: Macmillan.

Goorian, B., and Brown, K. 2002. Trends and Issues: School Law. ERIC Clearinghouse on Educational Management. http://eric.uoregon.edu/trends_issues/law/index.html.

Interstate New Teacher Assessment and Support Consortium. 2003. www.ccsso.org/intasc.

National Education Association. 1975. Code of Ethics of the Education Profession. www.nea.org/aboutnea/code.html.

Schwartz, F. 1981. Supporting or subverting learning: Peer group patterns in four tracked schools. *Anthropology and Education Quarterly, 12*(2), 99–120.

CHAPTER 2

Potential Influences of Cultural and Economic Backgrounds on Student Behavior

Geneva Gay (2005) reminds us that teaching and learning do not take place in culture-free settings, but in rich social contexts, to which teachers and students bring a vast array of personal ideas, beliefs, and behaviors. Teachers and students typically feel the customs and beliefs they have grown up with are proper and natural, whereas those of other groups are quaint or incorrect. Where differences exist among values and customs of people who live and work together, it is a challenge to make sure that everyone enjoys equal opportunity and feels valued within the group. This challenge is one that teachers must deal with successfully if all students are to flourish under their guidance.

In the United States, schools are said to reflect the values, traditions, and customs of Caucasian American society, although in 2004 approximately 43 percent of the public school students were members of non-Caucasian racial and ethnic groups. In larger urban schools, the number was considerably higher (National Center for Educational Statistics, 2006). In addition, significant numbers of students from all cultural groups live in poverty—the overall percentage is estimated to range from 10 percent (National Center for Educational Statistics) to 25 percent (Payne, 2001). This chapter presents information to help teachers better serve students from all segments of society.

Value Systems

A **value system** is a composite of what certain individuals or groups believe to be important in various life matters. Value systems are reflected in personal habits, interactions, work ethics, aspirations, spiritual beliefs, and myriad other activities. In times past, teachers and students in most societies held similar values, but with time and rapid changes in demographics, the difference in life views between teachers and many of their students has widened.

Information about Selected Ethnic and Cultural Groups

The following sections present information selected from the literature about a few of the largest cultural subgroups within U.S. society. This information can help teachers work more effectively with students whose life views differ from their own. The groups are listed in order of size within the overall population.

Middle-Class Caucasian American Students

Most teachers, school administrators, and other educators in the United States reflect the beliefs and behaviors characteristic of white middle-class society. This value system stems from the Judeo-Christian ethic, influenced by a capitalistic outlook and democratic, individualistic traditions of work ethic, future orientation, enterprise, and self-sufficiency. The following are a few examples of white middle-class values held by a large proportion of students and teachers in schools, regardless of their ethnic or racial origins. (Please remember that values vary from person to person within any societal group.)

- *Time orientation.* Promptness is valued; orientation is toward the future.
- *Planning ahead.* Plans are laid ahead of time, often for years in advance.
- *Work.* Hard work brings financial rewards, but is also good in its own right. It is not good to be "lazy" in either the classroom or the workplace.
- *Relations with others.* A sense of equality prevails; others are to be treated with consideration and respect.
- *Personal achievement and competition.* Individuals are urged to aspire to personal achievement in all matters. It is good to compete as individuals and rise above the norm.
- *Child-to-adult relations.* Adults are shown respect, but are not seen as infallible.
- *Adult-to-child relations.* Children require guidance, but are not to be treated subserviently.
- *Opportunity.* Potential to advance in life is available to everyone; one has only to seize the opportunity and follow through.
- *Verbal learning.* Much learning, especially in school, occurs verbally, through listening, reading, and discussing.
- *Success.* Success is seen as obtaining a good job, holding responsible positions, providing a good home, and acquiring a degree of wealth.
- *Personal behavior.* Individuals are all ultimately responsible for their own behavior. Most people behave ethically; laws and regulations serve as guidelines.

Human behavior and values across all groups of people are far more similar than they are different. Nevertheless, certain cultural differences have strong bearing on learning in school. In contrast to the white middle-class values, some groups frown on individual achievement and recognition. Some place great emphasis on traditions. Some see little purpose in working at school activities that do not seem useful or are not inherently interesting. Students in some groups adopt a subservient manner when interacting with teachers and are made uncomfortable by eye contact. Many do not want to voice opinions that disagree with what the teacher believes. Many do not look for educational opportunities to "advance" themselves, and many consider class rules and school regulations merely restrictions imposed by teachers in power. A failure to approach such differences sensitively can lead to malaise between teachers and students, promote misunderstandings, and put strain on relationships, thus making teaching and learning more difficult than necessary.

Hispanic American Students

Hispanic refers to a person who is of Mexican, Puerto Rican, Cuban, Central or South American, or other Spanish cultures or origins, regardless of race. Hispanic American students, often called Latinos, are members of various ethnic groups whose native or ancestral language is Spanish. These students now comprise just over 17 percent of public school enrollment, up from 6 percent in 1972 and expected to reach 25 percent by the year 2025 (Latinos in School: Some Facts and Findings, 2001). Large numbers of these students have blended into the dominant society, speak English perfectly, and assume leadership roles in the broader society. However, as a group, Hispanic American students are the second most likely, after American Indian and Alaska Native (AI/AN) students, to drop out of school. Their high school completion rate in 1999 was 63 percent, as compared with 81 percent for African Americans and 90 percent for Anglo Americans. They are less likely than African American and Caucasian students to have had early childhood education, including preschool or Head Start (Strategies for Teaching Minorities, 2004). Although there are strong common characteristics across the larger Hispanic American population, the group as a whole is composed of distinct subcultures that vary significantly in customs, values, and educational orientation (Griggs and Dunn, 1996). One characteristic common to all subgroups is family commitment, which involves loyalty, a strong support system, a belief that a child's behavior reflects on the honor of the family, a hierarchical order among siblings, and a duty to care for family members. The dignity of each individual and respect for authority figures are also strongly valued throughout Hispanic American culture.

Teachers should ensure that Hispanic cultural concerns are addressed in the curriculum. They should emphasize hands-on cooperative activities, while ensuring that students' intellectual and emotional well-being is protected. Wendy Schwartz (2000) and Anne Lockwood and Walter Secada (2000) have presented several additional suggestions for improving the quality of classroom experiences for Hispanic American youth. To make the classroom safe and inviting, they advise the following:

- Personalize instruction and give students the opportunity to assume positions of leadership and responsibility.
- Provide help in reducing student anger and building trust as a means of countering attitudes produced by negative experiences with schools and adults.

- Treat Hispanic students' language and culture as desirable resources.
- Convey high expectations, provide options, and furnish resources needed for an effective education.
- Emphasize the prevention of problems and respond to early warning signs that a student is beginning to disengage from school.
- Respect and show interest in students' language, culture, and ethnicity.
- If possible, identify for each Hispanic student an adult in the school who is committed to nurturing a sense of self-worth and supporting the student's efforts to succeed. Such mentors can help students withstand the peer, economic, and societal pressures that lead to dropping out.
- Bring attention to the lives and contributions of outstanding people of Hispanic origin, and engage family members and the community in the education of their children.

As for the learning environment, a somewhat more formal design has been identified as helpful to Hispanic American elementary and middle school students (Dunn, Griggs, and Price, 1993). Hispanic Americans seem to like a higher degree of structure than do Anglo American students (Yong and Ewing, 1992). Hispanic American students enjoy and profit from cooperative learning with peers, kinesthetic instructional resources, a high degree of structure, and a variety of activities.

African American Students

African American, not of hispanic origin, refers to a person having origins in any of the black racial groups of Africa. African American students comprise approximately 17 percent of the public school population. The Education Trust reported in 2003 that 61 percent of African American fourth graders were lagging behind the established standards for reading proficiency and mathematics. Earlier, Ashcher (1991) cited evidence that low-achieving students from all groups seldom catch up with their peers, but instead fall farther behind over time.

The following observations and suggestions for working with African American students are adapted from a website presentation titled "Strategies for Teaching Science to African American Students" (2005). This resource, which also makes many suggestions concerning avoiding bias, suggests that many African American students profit from visual, kinesthetic, and tactile learning, more than from verbal explanations from the teacher. They tend to respond well to cooperative learning. Their preferred discussion style is simultaneous talk instead of alternating talk. They tend to use colorful language in verbal communication. Many African American students are physically active and do not adjust well to sedentary learning environments. They are sensitive to and responsive to what others feel and think, and they consider how their actions may affect others. They enjoy close proximity to other students and respond well to praise, smiles, and pats on the back. The Education Trust (2003) reports that African American students also respond well to clear public standards for what students should learn at benchmark grade levels, challenging curricula with standards, and extra instruction for students who need it.

Jackie Irvine and James Fraser (1998) suggest the following for teachers of African American students:

- Think of yourself as a surrogate parent for your students.
- Use a teaching style filled with rhythmic language and rapid intonation with many instances of repetition, call and response, high emotional involvement, creative analogies, figurative language, gestures and body movements, symbolism, aphorisms (short sayings), and lively and often spontaneous discussions.
- Use students' everyday cultural and historical experiences as links to new knowledge, and strive to develop good personal relationships with your students.

Johnnie McKinley (2003) reported a study involving twenty-nine teachers in a large urban district that showed African American students responded well to culturally relevant curriculum and materials, cooperative group instruction, structured lessons, heavy use of questions, and student recitation. Other authorities (Diller, 1999; Foster, 1999; Ladson-Billings, 2000; McCollough, 2000; Bempechat, 2001; Schwartz, 2002; North Central Regional Educational Laboratory, 2005) advise teachers to spend classroom and non-classroom time developing personal relationships with students, frequently teasing and joking with them, and showing solidarity with them and their concerns.

Asian American and Pacific Islander Students

Asian American refers to a person having origins in any of the original peoples of East Asia, Southeast Asia, and the Indian subcontinent. This area includes China, India, Indonesia, Japan, Korea, Vietnam, Thailand, Cambodia, and other smaller nations. *Pacific Islander* refers to a person having origins in any of the original peoples of Hawaii; the U.S. Pacific Territories of Guam, American Samoa, and the Northern Marinas; the U.S. Trust Territory of Palau; the islands of Micronesia and Melanesia; and the Philippines. Jianhua Feng (1994) points out that the term *Asian American* covers a variety of national, cultural, and religious groups, more than twenty-nine of which differ in language, religion, and customs. These various groups are commonly categorized into four subgroups: East Asian, Southeast Asian, South Asian, and Pacific Islanders. Although these distinct groups often get lumped together as "Asian," they differ considerably from each other.

Asian Americans are generally viewed as successful, conforming, and high achieving. Their school behavior is much in keeping with those perceptions, and they rarely present behavior problems for teachers. Asian American students tend to be strongly group and family oriented, which may interfere with newly arrived students' adaptation to the independence, competition, and individualism emphasized in Western education.

Students from many East and Southeast Asian cultures are imbued with Confucian ideals, which value learning, respect for elders, responsibility for relatives, deferred gratification, and self-discipline (Feng, 1994). They tend to view failure as representing a lack of will. They tend to be conforming and willing to place family welfare ahead of individual wishes. They are usually self-effacing, willing to wait patiently, and seem to learn best in well-structured, quiet environments (Baruth and Manning, 1992). They tend to dislike having attention drawn to them as individuals. Most listen carefully, think before they speak, use soft voices, and are modest in personal dress and grooming.

In conversations and other verbal communication, Asians seldom speak their minds as plainly as do Westerners. They often display verbal hesitancy and ambiguity to avoid giving offense, and they do not make spontaneous or critical remarks (Kim, 1985). Their body language is noticeably different from that of Westerners, too, characterized by head nodding and lack of eye contact (Matsuda, 1989). The Japanese and Vietnamese are noted for being unwilling to use the word *no* even when they disagree (Coker, 1988; Wierzbicka, 1991). Seldom are Asian students, their family members, or their teachers aware of the cultural differences that affect communication. This leads to one side or the other being misunderstood or ignored.

A sense of time unfamiliar to most teachers in Western schools can also cause difficulties. Many Asian cultures operate on what is called "polychronic time" as distinct from the "monochronic time" familiar to Western people (Storti, 1999). Polychronic time allows different social interactions to occur at the same time, whereas monochronic time is linear—you do one thing at a time, in a fixed sequence. This difference in time orientation sometimes causes misunderstandings because Asians may not be prompt or ready to get down to business as quickly as Westerners would like. (Note, however, that the traditional sense of monochronic time among Western people seems to be changing somewhat among today's middle-class youth, evident in their use of technology for multitasking.)

Teachers of Asian American students should also understand that when their students show delay or hesitation, it may be because they are unsure of an answer, unfamiliar with the discourse style, or simply disengaged and lost. When they fail to stick with the topic, it may be due to insufficient knowledge, unfamiliarity with how to gain the floor, or fear and avoidance of interactions. They often make what teachers consider inappropriate nonverbal expressions, such as avoiding eye contact with adults (a sign of respect), frowning (a sign of concentration rather than displeasure), or giggling (a sign of embarrassment or lack of understanding rather than a response to something humorous). When they make short responses, it is sometimes because their English proficiency does not permit replies in long, cohesive utterances, or they may be too shy to respond. They may use an overly soft voice, which is typical for children in some Asian cultures. If they show unwillingness to take risks, it is probably from fear of being embarrassed or ridiculed. When they are reluctant to participate, it might be because volunteering information is considered overly bold. When they receive praise, they may be embarrassed because their native culture values humility and self-criticism. They may divert their eyes downward and offer no greeting when the teacher approaches, but this can be because of respect or fear rather than impoliteness or unfriendliness.

Li-Rong Cheng (1998) adds that Asian students who have had school experience in their native countries are accustomed to learning through (1) listening, observing, reading, and imitating; (2) responding to teachers' questions based on lectures and textbooks;

and (3) taking tests that require only the recall of factual information. They may be left feeling ambivalent and confused by class work that involves group efforts, discussions, and creative activities.

Matsuda (1989), Baruth and Manning (1992), Trueba and Cheng (1993), Huang (1993), Feng (1994), and Cheng (1996, 1998) make a number of suggestions to help teachers work more effectively with Asian students, including:

- Carefully observe and understand students' sense of communication and time, and adjust your interactions accordingly.
- Learn at least a few words of the students' native languages. Ask students to teach them to you.
- Help students understand that, while at school, they may offer their opinions and challenge the views of others.
- Explain to family members that parental involvement in their child's education is a tradition in the Western world.
- Be patient during verbal exchanges. Consider periods of silence opportunities for reflection on what has been said. Be attentive to nonverbal cues.
- When you can do so, meet with students individually and communicate with them orally, rather than in writing.
- Encourage students to join student clubs to increase their exposure to language, socialization, and different types of discourse.
- Facilitate students' transition into mainstream culture through activities and discussions of culturally unique experiences and celebrations, such as birthday parties and Thanksgiving.
- Role-play, practice colloquialisms, and act out skits that involve typical verbal exchanges.
- Read to students to increase their vocabulary, and expose them to various narrative styles used in letters, stories, articles, biographies, and poetry.

American Indian/Alaska Native Students

American Indian/Alaska Native refers to a person having origins in any of the native or indigenous peoples of North America, and who maintains cultural identification through affiliation or community recognition. Susan Faircloth and John Tippeconnic reported in 2000 that there were approximately 500,000 American Indian/Alaska Native students attending K–12 schools in the United States, just over 1 percent of the total school population. These students come from more than 500 tribal groups that have their own government and social systems and speak an estimated 200 different languages. Many of the tribes are matrilineal, with females in positions of authority and owning property.

Overall, the students from these various tribal groups have been experiencing below-average success in school and have the highest dropout rate of all racial/ethnic groups in the United States (National Center for Education Statistics, 2001a). The reasons for American Indian/Alaska Native students' relative lack of success in school are not known, although possible causes include poverty, a curriculum that is unconnected to students' lives, and the feeling that success in school suggests selling out older traditions in favor of "white man's ways" (St. Germaine, 1995).

It has been suggested that American Indian/Alaska Native students may have learning styles that differ somewhat from those of students in the dominant culture (Cornett, 1983; Swisher, 1991). Many American Indian/Alaska Native students have strong capabilities for learning visually, perceptively, and spatially, and tend to use mental images in thought processes rather than word associations. They may learn better by seeing the entire overview of what is to be learned, rather than by learning bits of information that slowly build to the full picture. They show an affinity for manipulatives and hands-on activities and seem to learn better in cooperative groups than individually. They show an ability to learn from experience without constant supervision and feedback. They best demonstrate their learning in contexts similar to those from which they have learned.

Caucasian American teachers usually consider American Indian/Alaska Native students to be quiet and not very talkative in the classroom. Although these students may be hesitant to participate in large and small group recitations, they have been described as more talkative than other students when working in student-led group projects (Philips, 1983). Philips explains that American Indian/Alaska Native students seem to acquire competence best through a process of observation, careful listening, supervised participation, and individualized self-correction or testing.

A number of other sources offer information about working with American Indian/Alaska Native students (see Cox and Ramirez, 1981; Cornett, 1983; Cajete, 1986; Swisher, 1991; Butterfield, 1994; and Portland Oregon Schools, 2003). These studies indicate that American Indian/Alaska Native students become uncomfortable when asked, in school, to behave in ways not valued in the communities where they live. They are more cooperative and less competitive, individually, than Caucasian American students, emphasizing group, rather than individual, achievement. Very able students often hide their academic competence to avoid appearing superior. Many do not like to make direct eye contact; when students divert their eyes, teachers should not interpret it as disobedience or disrespect. Before singling students out to talk about their culture or community, make sure that doing so will not cause embarrassment. Many of their parents have had negative experiences in school and are hesitant to become involved in their child's educational process. They will respond and participate, however, when approached sensitively, sincerely, and respectfully.

Cornel Pewewardy and Patricia Hammer (2003) urge teachers of American Indian/Alaska Native students to

- Acquire better awareness and understanding of American Indian/Alaska Native culture and learning styles.
- Analyze their own attitudes and beliefs.
- Develop caring, trusting, inclusive classrooms.
- Model respect for American Indian/Alaska Native knowledge and ways of knowing.
- Provide a curriculum that promotes critical thinking and social justice.

- Provide much helpful feedback, which should be immediate and as private as possible.
- Include art and other creative activities in lessons.
- Enrich class experiences by asking American Indian/Alaska Native speakers or performers to become involved in the class.
- Allow students to relate learning activities to their personal experiences.
- Hold and express high expectations of American Indian/Alaska Native students.
- Evaluate progress in terms of goal attainment, behavior, and involvement.
- Work to develop positive rapport with family members. Invite them to school and to your class.

Recently Arrived Immigrant Students

Recently arrived immigrant students have needs not only for academic learning, but also (and sometimes more importantly) for socialization and language development. Suggestions for working with these students have been put forth by several writers (see Lucas, Henze, and Donato, 1990; Walsh, 1991; the National Coalition of Advocates for Students, 1994; Benard, 1997; Qualities of Effective Programs for Immigrant Adolescents with Limited Schooling, 1998; Krovetz, 1999; and Chavkin and Gonzalez, 2000). Here is a summary of their advice.

- Use a repertoire of instructional approaches that upholds high expectations of students, while affirming the acceptance of differences among students.
- Learn as much as possible about students' families and request support from family members. Hold high expectations of students and frequently recognize their achievement.
- Become familiar with English as a Second Language (ESL) and sheltered English instruction.
- Learn a bit of the students' native language.
- Give much personal attention to each student.
- Use a flexible approach that involves peer tutoring, mentoring by sympathetic adults, home–school liaisons, and links with community agencies.
- Work to increase student self-esteem, motivation, and willingness to accept responsibility. Emphasize prosocial skills and academic success.
- Develop personal relationships with students to increase motivation.

Information about Economically Disadvantaged Students

The term **economic disadvantage** is used synonymously with "living in poverty," a condition that increasingly affects students in school. Students in poverty are defined as students who are members of households that must spend more than one-third of their disposable income for food adequate to meet the family's nutritional needs. Karen Pellegrino (2005) writes about the exceedingly high educational price that students of poverty must pay. She lists poverty as a leading factor that puts students at risk of failure in school. She notes that students in poverty often have single parents who are very young. The parents tend to be poorly educated and place relatively little importance on education. They often live in dangerous neighborhoods. Some are homeless. Their rate of mobility is high, and many do not stay in the same community or neighborhood long enough for the children to become established in school.

Ruby Payne (2001; Claitor, 2003) has made many important contributions by describing the impact of poverty on education. She noted that in 1996 approximately one out of four individuals under the age of 18 in the United States was living in poverty. Payne says poor children are much more likely than other children to suffer developmental delay and damage, to drop out of high school, and to give birth during the teen years. She explains that each economic class has its own set of hidden rules that help it survive. The hidden rules for schools, teachers, and the majority of students reflect the values of white middle-class society, which were summarized previously. The hidden rules for students from "generational poverty" (long-term poverty) are different than the rules in the mainstream. Payne urges teachers to learn the hidden rules because they provide keys to understanding and communicating with students.

Payne (2001) illustrates her conclusions by comparing the hidden values of three different groups—those in generational poverty, those in middle-class society, and those in a society of wealth. For people from the middle class, the major driving forces are work and achievement, with high value placed on material possessions. For people of wealth, the driving forces are social, financial, and political connections, with high value placed on legacies and pedigrees. For people in poverty, the driving life forces are survival, personal relationships, and entertainment.

Students in poverty usually value relationships over achievement. One's mother is the most important person in one's life, and insults against her will not be tolerated. Relatives and close friends are also defended, no matter what they have done. The world is defined in local terms. Too much education can be disquieting because the educated person might leave the community. Conflict is resolved by fighting, and respect is accorded to those who can defend themselves. School discipline is about penance and forgiveness, not about behavior change. Students often save face by laughing when they are disciplined. One's sense of personal value is tied up with the ability to entertain others. Money is to be used, to be spent, not to be managed and saved. Destiny and fate govern most matters, with individuals feeling they have relatively little control over their lives.

Students in poverty often use a casual, informal style of speech that contrasts with the more formal style of speech used in school. Teachers should point out the difference, help students use the appropriate language for various situations, and help them understand that a formal style is helpful in school and the workplace. Clothing is very important and is seen as an expression of personality. Noise level among people of poverty is high, with frequent displays of emotion. At home, the television is almost always turned on and the sound mixes with participatory conversation in which two or more people are talking at the same time, in contrast to classrooms where everything is quieter and speakers take turns.

As with other groups, a first step in working with students who are economically disadvantaged is to learn about their values, customs, and lifestyles. Payne, in an interview with Diana Claitor (2003), explains that in addition to understanding their students, teachers must work to build personal relationships with them. More specific suggestions from Ruby Payne and Shirley Heath have been presented by Linda F. Hargan (2003), such as the following:

■ Teach and model explicitly how students should organize, prioritize, and set timelines for completion of tasks.
■ Help students "procedural self-talk," in which they verbalize how to break tasks down into steps and write down their conclusions.
■ Teach students how to speak and write in a formal manner.
■ Give students examples and model acceptable behavior. Have them practice that behavior in school.

Donna Beegle (Oregon School Boards Association, 2004) further urges teachers to act as mentors for their students. At times, teachers are the only people children from poverty know that live outside poverty. She says that if we treat students as competent, they will begin to behave competently.

General Suggestions for Working with Students from all Ethnic and Economic Groups

In the preceding sections, you have seen many suggestions for helping teachers understand and work more effectively with their students. Although descriptions and suggestions given are considered typical of students from particular groups, teachers should not allow themselves to stereotype students. The following suggestions apply to teaching students from all cultural and economic groups:

■ Learn as much as you can about the value systems of your students, including what they consider important, how they relate to each other and to adults, and how they relate to teachers and school in general.
■ Become knowledgeable about the "hidden rules" that regulate group and personal behavior.
■ Show acceptance of your students, their families, and their lifestyles.
■ Show solidarity with students and eagerness to help them learn and find success.
■ Emphasize the knowledge, skills, and values needed for school success and for a healthy personal and cultural identity.
■ Link curriculum content to students' out-of-school experiences.
■ Attempt to mentor students, an especially effective tactic for motivation and good personal relations between student and teacher.
■ Create a more hospitable environment by communicating the expectation that all students can succeed and all will be helped to do so.

■ Develop codes of class behavior that are culturally sensitive while emphasizing responsibility and respect.

■ Keep family members informed about their child's performance and behavior and ask them to work with you for the child's benefit.

KEY TERMS AND CONCEPTS EMPHASIZED IN THIS CHAPTER

value system   economic disadvantage

ACTIVITIES

1. Add notes you find helpful from this chapter to augment your journal for building a personal system of discipline.

2. Working with one or more peers, select one of the groups described in the chapter and decide what you would do to make their school experience more enjoyable and rewarding.

REFERENCES

Ascher, C. 1991. School programs for African American males. ERIC Digests. ED334340. www.ericdigests.org.

Baruth, L., and Manning, M. 1992. *Multicultural education of children and adolescents.* Boston: Allyn & Bacon.

Bempechat, J. 2001. Fostering high achievement in African American children: Home, school, and public policy influences. http://eric-web.tc.columbia.edu/monographs/ti16_index.html.

Benard, B. 1997. Drawing forth resilience in all our youth. *Reclaiming Children and Youth, 6*(1), 29–32.

Butterfield, R. 1994. Blueprints for Indian education: Improving mainstream schooling. ERIC Digests. ED372898. www.ericdigests.org.

Cajete, G. 1986. Science: A Native American perspective (A Culturally Based Science Education Curriculum). Ph.D. dissertation, International College/William Lyon University, San Diego, CA.

Chavkin, N., and Gonzalez, J. 2000. Mexican immigrant youth and resiliency: Research and promising programs. ERIC Digests. ED447990. www.ericdigests.org.

Cheng, L. 1996. Enhancing communication: Toward optimal language learning for limited English proficient students. *Language, Speech and Hearing Services in Schools, 28*(2), 347–354.

Cheng, L. 1998. Enhancing the communication skills of newly-arrived Asian American students. ERIC Digests. www.ericdigests.org/1999-1/asian.html.

Claitor, D. 2003. Breaking through: Interview of Ruby Payne. www.hopemag.com/issues/2003/septOct/breaking Through.pdf.

Coker, D. 1988. Asian students in the classroom. *Education and Society, 1*(3), 19–20.

Cornett, C. 1983. What you should know about teaching and learning styles (Fastback No. 191). Bloomington, IN: Phi Delta Kappa Foundation.

Cox, B., and Ramirez, M. 1981. Cognitive styles: Implications for multiethnic education. In J. Banks (Ed.), *Education in the 80s: Multiethnic education* (pp. 61–71). Washington, DC: National Education Association.

Diller, D. 1999. Opening the dialogue: Using culture as a tool in teaching young African American children. *Reading Teacher, 52*(8), 820–858.

Dunn, R., Griggs, S., and Price, G. 1993. Learning styles of Mexican-American and Anglo-American elementary-school students. *Journal of Multicultural Counseling and Development 21*(4), 237–247.

Faircloth, S., and Tippeconnic, J. 2000. Issues in the education of American Indian and Alaska Native students with disabilities. ERIC Digests. EDO-RC-00-3. www.ericdigests.org.

Feng, J. 1994. Asian-American children: What teachers should know. ERIC Digests. EDO-PS-94-4. www.ericdigests.org.

Foster, M. 1999. Teaching and learning in the contexts of African American English and culture. *Education and Urban Society, 31*(2), 177ff.

Gay, G. 2005. A synthesis of scholarship in multicultural education. North Central Regional Educational Laboratory. www.ncrel.org/sdrs/areas/issues/educatrs/leadrshp/le0gay.htm.

Griggs, S., and Dunn, R. 1996. Hispanic-American students and learning style. http://ceep.crc. uiuc.edu/eecearchive/digests/1996/griggs96.html.

Hargan, L. 2003. Teaching students of poverty, NCL brief. www.ctlonline.org/ESEA/newsletter.html.

Huang, G. 1993. Beyond culture: Communicating with Asian American children and families. ERIC Digests. ED366673. www.ericdigests.org.

Irvine, J., and Fraser, J. 1998. Warm demanders. Education Week on the WEB. www.edweek.org/ew/1998/35 irvine.h17.

Kim, B. 1985. (Ed.). *Literacy and languages. The second yearbook of literacy and languages in Asia, International Reading Associations special interest group.* International Conference on Literacy and Languages (Seoul, South Korea, August 12–14, 1985).

Krovetz, M. 1999. *Fostering resiliency: Expecting all students to use their minds and hearts well.* Thousand Oaks, CA: Corwin Press.

Ladson-Billings, G. 2000. Fighting for our lives: Preparing teachers to teach African American students. *Journal of Teacher Education 51*(3), 206–214.

Latinos in school: Some facts and findings. 2001. ERIC Digests. www.ericdigests.org.

Lockwood, A., and Secada, W. 2000. Transforming education for Hispanic youth: Exemplary practices, programs, and schools. U.S. Department of Education. www.ncela. gwu.edu/pubs/resource/hispanicyouth/ch6.htm.

Lucas, T., Henze, R., and Donato, R. 1990. Promoting the success of Latino language minority students. An exploratory study of six high schools. *Harvard Educational Review, 60*, 315–340.

Matsuda, M. 1989. Working with Asian family members: Some communication strategies. *Topics in Language Disorders, 9*(3), 45–53.

McCollough, S. 2000. Teaching African American students. *Clearing House 74*(1), 5–6.

McKinley, J. 2003. Leveling the playing field and raising African American students' achievement in twenty-nine urban classrooms. New Horizons for Learning. www.newhorizons.org.

National Center for Education Statistics. 2006. Minority enrollment in public schools 2004. http://nces.ed.gov/programs/coe/charts/chart05.asp.

National Coalition of Advocates for Students. 1994. Delivering on the promise: Positive practices for immigrant students. Boston: Author.

North Central Regional Educational Laboratory. 2005. Culturally responsive African-American teachers. info@ncrel.org.

Oregon School Boards Association 2004. Breaking barriers: Poverty—The elephant in the room. www.osba.org/hotopics/gap/poverty.htm.

Payne, R. 2001. *A framework for understanding poverty.* Highlands, TX: Aha! Process.

Pellegrino, K. 2005. The effects of poverty on teaching and learning. www.teach-nology.com/tutorials/teaching/poverty.

Pewewardy, C., and Hammer, P. 2003. Culturally responsive teaching for American Indian students. ERIC Digests. ED482325. www.ericdigests.org.

Philips, S. 1983. *The invisible culture.* New York: Longman.

Portland Public Schools. 2003. Supporting American Indian/Alaska Native students in school. Title IX Indian Education Project Staff and Parent Board. http://comped.salkeiz.k12.or.us/indian-ed/ai-an.htm.

Qualities of effective programs for immigrant adolescents with limited schooling. 1998. ERIC Digests. ED423667. www.ericdigests.org.

Rowe, D. (Ed.). 2003. Reducing adolescent risk: Toward an integrated approach. Newbury Park, CA: Sage Press. www.sagepub.com/book.aspx?pid=9315.

Schwartz, W. 2000. New trends in language education for Hispanic students. ERIC Digests. ED442913. www.ericdigests.org.

Schwartz, W. 2002. School practices for equitable discipline of African American students. ERIC Digests. ED455343. www.ericdigests.org.

St. Germaine, R. 1995. Drop-out rates among American Indian and Alaska Native Students: Beyond cultural discontinuity. ERIC Digests. Eric document reproduction service no ED 388 492.

Strategies for teaching science to African American students. 2005. www.as.wvu.edu/~equity/african.html.

Strategies for teaching minorities. 2004. www.as.wvu.edu/~equity/general.html.

Swisher, K. 1991. American Indian/Alaskan Native learning styles: Research and practice. ERIC Digest. ED335175. www.ericdigests.org.

The Education Trust. 2003. African American Achievement. Washington, DC. www.edtrust.org.

Trueba, H., and Cheng, L. 1993. *Myth or reality: Adaptive strategies of Asian Americans in California.* Bristol, PA: Falmer Press.

Walsh, C. 1991. Literacy and school success: Considerations for programming and instruction. In C. Walsh and H. Prashker (Eds.), *Literacy development for bilingual students.* Boston: New England Multifunctional Resource Center for Language and Culture Education.

Wierzbicka, A. 1991. Japanese key words and core cultural values. *Language in Society, 20*(3), 333–385.

Yong, F., and Ewing, N. 1992. A comparative study of the learning-style preferences among gifted African-American, Mexican-American and American born Chinese middle-grade students. *Roeper Review, 14*(3), 120–123.

CHAPTER 3

The Special Challenges of Neurological-Based Behavior

Authoritative Input
■ Paula Cook / Teacher specialist in neurological-based behavior

Most students can control their behavior when they wish to do so. A few cannot, however, or have great difficulty in doing so. This chapter explains who those students are, why they behave as they do, and how teachers can best help them. The undesirable behavior they often display, which is largely outside their control, is referred to as neurological-based behavior (NBB). Such behavior, unresponsive to normal behavior management techniques, often leaves teachers feeling powerless. More and more, however, we are learning how to provide helpful support for those students, whose diagnoses include attention-deficit hyperactivity disorder, learning disabilities, sensory integration dysfunction, bipolar disorder, oppositional defiant disorder, autism spectrum disorder, fetal alcohol spectrum disorder, and brain injuries. Please remember that students affected by these disorders are real people struggling to do the best they can in life. They are referred to herein using **people first language,** as exemplified by expressions such as "students with dyslexia" rather than "dyslexic students." This chapter includes six scenarios depicting student behavior. The scenarios are true accounts with the names of people involved changed to maintain anonymity.

Scenario 1
Tyler began the morning by refusing to participate in opening activities. He chose instead to make beeping sounds. After the opening activities, the class was to read quietly on their own for ten minutes, but Tyler decided to sing loudly. When asked to stop, he began to hoot. He was belligerent and noisy for some time. He poked Jackie with a pencil, chewed the eraser off his pencil and swallowed it, and insisted on writing on his math sheet with a tiny piece of pencil lead moistened with spittle. He

refused to comply with academic instructions until almost time for recess. During recess, Tyler pushed, poked, hit, and tried to choke other students. He laughed when they protested. He engaged in violent play fantasies and was extremely argumentative with the teachers on duty, swearing at them and insisting they could not make him do anything he didn't want to do. Finally, Tyler had to be physically lead back to the classroom. He screamed that his rights were being violated and that he would sue the school and kill the teachers. Tyler worked the rest of the morning alone in the resource room with the resource teacher. In the afternoon, Tyler was well behaved, compliant, and willing to participate and learn.

Application: After you have read this chapter, you will be asked in the activities to return to this scenario and, with a fellow teacher or classmate, discuss the situation and reflect on how one might deal with it effectively.

Introduction to Neurological-Based Behavior (NBB)

Virtually all students behave inappropriately at times, regardless of age, gender, ethnicity, or socioeconomic background. In Chapter 1, you saw the kinds of misbehavior you can expect in school, brought on by familiar conditions such as fatigue, perceived threat, general boisterousness, disregard for authority, or ignorance of expectations. Later in this book you will learn how to manage those factors and their associated behaviors easily.

However, not all misbehavior originates from those familiar causes. In some cases, students misbehave erratically or inconsistently for no apparent reason, and their behavior does not respond reliably to normal discipline tactics. This puzzling condition seems to result from difficulties students experience in processing information, due to compromised cerebral functioning from chemical imbalances, congenital brain differences, brain injuries, or brain diseases. The resulting diagnoses are considered to be "mental health issues" (American Academy of Child and Adolescent Psychiatry, 2004a). Students with those diagnoses usually show high degrees of inattention, hyperactivity, impulsivity, emotionality, anxiety, inconsistent emotional responses,

About Paula Cook

Paula Cook teaches in a highly specialized program for students with behavioral, emotional, and psychiatric disorders, with mild to moderate cognitive impairment. Her responsibilities include curriculum modifications and adaptations, individualized educational planning, advocacy, behavior management, and social skills and life skills education. She also teaches at Red River Community College and the University of Manitoba. She has made numerous presentations at regional, national, and international conferences and was a 2003 recipient of the Council for Exceptional Children's Outstanding Educator of the Year award.

unpredictable intense mood swings, withdrawal, and episodes of rage (Kranowitz, 1998; Greene, 2001; Papolos and Papolos, 2002; Hall and Hall, 2003; Cook, 2004a). However, because **neurological differences** and mental health issues can be difficult to diagnose, they are sometimes not identified until several years after individuals experience the onset of symptoms (Papolos and Papolos, 2002). Because of that lag, many students with neurological differences have not been formally diagnosed, even though teachers know something is producing behavior that is erratic and unpredictable.

We must understand that when ordinary classroom discipline procedures do not help students with neurological issues remain productively at work, it is not because the students are "bad" or "too far gone" or come from "horrible families." Rather, they behave as they do because of the way their brains work. They cannot always control their behavior in ways that serve them best, or as we would like them to. In this chapter, we refer to behavior of that type as **neurological-based behavior (NBB).** Two of the major characteristics of such behavior are inconsistency and unpredictability (Kranowitz, 1998).

Extent of the Problem

Few educators realize how prevalent mental health issues are among students. Some of the categories of mental health diagnoses prominent in the literature include the following:

- **Attention-deficit hyperactivity disorder (ADHD).** Accompanied by restlessness and short attention span
- **Affective disorders.** Affect mood or feeling, such as **bipolar disorder,** in which individuals cycle between mania and depression
- **Anxiety disorders.** Involve fear and extreme uneasiness
- **Posttraumatic stress disorder.** Adversely affects students who have witnessed or heard about traumatic events
- **Conduct disorder.** Involves regularly breaching society's moral constraints
- **Oppositional defiant disorder.** Involves opposing and defying teachers and others
- **Autism spectrum disorder.** Involves failure to develop normal speech patterns or personal relationships
- **Fetal alcohol spectrum disorder.** Includes poor impulse control, poor judgment, lack of common sense, and learning difficulties

Most of these disorders are treated with medications, some of which may adversely affect students' attention, concentration, and stamina (National Institute of Mental Health, 2005). Also consider the following:

- Childhood mental health conditions are now so common that some psychiatrists are calling them a "plague" (DeAngelis, 2004).
- You can expect, on average, about one in five of your students to have one or more mental health conditions that affect behavior in school (DeAngelis, 2004).

- As many as one in ten students may suffer from a serious emotional disturbance (National Institute of Mental Health, 2005).
- Only 20 percent of children with mental health disorders get the kind of treatment they need (DeAngelis, 2004).
- Attention-deficit hyperactivity disorder (ADHD) is the most commonly diagnosed mental health disorder in children, affecting 3 to 5 percent of school-age children (National Institute of Mental Health, 2005).
- Suicide is the third leading cause of death for 15- to 24-year-olds and the sixth leading cause of death for 5- to 14-year-olds (American Academy of Child and Adolescent Psychiatry, 2004c).
- 22 percent of youths in juvenile justice facilities have a serious emotional disturbance, and most have a diagnosable mental disorder (Jans, Stoddard, and Kraus, 2004).
- Diagnosis of a single individual often reveals a constellation of mental health symptoms existent simultaneously (Feldman, 2004). Two or more diagnoses that exist simultaneously are called "comorbid diagnoses."
- Mental health disorders are biological in nature. They cannot be overcome through willpower and are not related to a person's character or intelligence.
- Serious mental illnesses can now be treated effectively, bringing a 70 to 90 percent reduction in symptoms. Treatment usually includes a combination of pharmacological and psychosocial support (National Institute of Mental Health, 2005).

Although ADHD is the mental health condition found most often in students and those conditions listed here are among the most common, there are numerous others as well. You may encounter students with generalized anxiety disorder (GAD), explosive behavior disorder, paranoia, obsessive compulsive disorder (OCD), substance dependence, phobias, eating disorders, and Tourette's syndrome. Treatment for these disorders varies. If you wish to learn more about any of them, you can find them discussed at length on the Internet. As noted, these disorders are usually treated with medication, which oftentimes affects students' attention, memory, abstract thinking, and organizational skills (Davidson, 1993).

A Word about Brain Injuries

Physical injuries to the brain often affect its ability to function normally. The incidence of brain injuries has increased dramatically in recent years (Brain Injury Society, 2006). They are categorized as traumatic or nontraumatic. **Traumatic brain injuries** result from blows to the head incurred during events such as accidents, sporting events, or assaults. **Nontraumatic brain injuries** result from disrupted blood flow to the brain (as in strokes), or from tumors, infections, drug overdoses, and certain medical conditions (Acorn and Offer, 1998). The effects of severe injuries are readily apparent, but mild injuries may go unrecognized even though they have a significant effect on student behavior.

Indicators of NBB

Three indicators can alert you to the possibility that a given student has NBB—behavior difficulties, language difficulties, and academic difficulties. Behavior difficulties are frequently the first indication that something unusual is occurring in the student, especially if the behavior is atypical, inconsistent, perhaps compulsive, and immune to normal behavior management. Such behavior may stem from a neurological event that is promoting student confusion, uncertainty, fear, or frustration. Language difficulties include problems in understanding, processing, and expressing information verbally. Classroom interactions operate on the assumption that language is understood more or less the same by all students and teachers, but this is not so for students with NBB, who often do not interpret, understand, process, respond to, or use language properly (Cook, Kellie, Jones, and Goossen, 2000; Greene, 2001; Hall and Hall, 2003; Cook, 2004a). Language difficulties can be further exaggerated by environmental stimulation, fatigue, medication, hunger, or stress. To give yourself a feeling of what students with language difficulties may experience, try reading the following:

```
   is      the        research, assumes        of  treatment                . Because  of colla
active    are             dependent      indep dent      measured       and    res hers
         depen                                            ables.                subjects
 research,"  dent       vari        "         in    abs    title.   T he        isinclusive
            seventh    and                          track
     pertinent    . The of    is sta ted   coll   borative      and  is
    investigating      concept      a     and    attitudes          teaching
```

If you notice students who seem to have difficulty understanding or who are not complying with expectations or requests, try using fewer words and increase the wait time for compliance. Make your directions clear, concrete, and consistent. Physically show directions, if necessary, in addition to telling. Ask the student to repeat the directions and show you what they are supposed to do.

Academic difficulties vary among students with NBB. Some of those difficulties are easily recognized, and teachers know how deal with them. Not all, however, are easily remedied. Memory is often compromised in students who have NBB, causing highly variable gaps in learning. Difficulties with fine and gross motor skills, comprehension, and language and mathematic skills add to the problem. Comprehensive assessments by school psychologists often reveal student difficulties that require special attention, making affected students eligible for special services.

If you have a student with NBB who has been approved for special services, take note of what the special teachers do. You can adapt and use some of their strategies in your normal teaching. This will benefit students with NBB and often other students as well. One example of such adaptation would be the provision of differentiated instruction, using Howard Gardner's theory of multiple intelligences (1999) to teach concepts in as many different ways as possible. This provides support for students by helping with comprehension, while pinpointing specific student strengths and weaknesses.

Sensory Integration Dysfunction

Sensory integration dysfunction (SID), also called **sensory processing disorder,** seems to be a core factor in NBB. Sensory integration refers to the process we use to take in information from our senses, organize the information, interpret it, and respond to it. This process occurs automatically and keeps us informed, ready to act, and better able to protect ourselves. At times, however, and for some people, flaws occur in the process so an individual does not receive information properly and does not interpret it correctly, resulting in poor learning and inappropriate behavior. This flawed process is known as sensory integration dysfunction (see Kranowitz, 1998; Cook, 2004b; and Kranowitz, Szkut, Balzer-Martin, Haber, and Sava, 2003). SID seems to be a major cause of hyperactivity, inattention, fidgety movements, inability to calm down, impulsivity, lack of self-control, disorganization, language difficulties, and learning difficulties (Kranowitz, 1998; Cook, 2004b). Yet, most teachers know little about it.

Some students' sensory processing systems seem to become easily overwhelmed by excess visual and auditory stimulation. You can help those students by keeping the classroom neat and tidy, removing sources of loud or unpredictable noise, enlarging printed questions or directions, and standing in front of a solid white overhead screen when giving instructions and directing lessons, all of which reduce distractions from extraneous sources. You can also give directions more slowly and distinctly, check to ensure students have understood correctly, and maintain a sense of calm in the classroom.

Scenario 2

Jimmy entered kindergarten in September. By January, his behavior was worse than when he began school. Every day he had a series of tantrums, usually beginning when he arrived at school. He sometimes complied with directions, but more often, especially during changes of activity, he would scream, cry, kick, flail his arms, fall to the floor, or run out of the classroom. During these episodes, he kicked or hit staff members and has assaulted students who were in his way. Jimmy's home life is unremarkable. He has an older sibling, both parents, and lives in a quiet neighborhood. His family environment is loving and stable. His parents are very concerned about his behavior. Jimmy does not have any diagnosed neurological conditions. His mother did not drink or use illicit substances during her pregnancy. The pregnancy and his birth were deemed "typical."

Commentary: This child, with no diagnosis other than his behavior to suggest neurological dysfunction, was having a terrible experience in school. His teacher ultimately changed the classroom environment to cut down sensory stimulation. Jimmy's behavior then improved considerably.

Common Pediatric/Adolescent Mental Health Diagnoses

As we have seen, a wide range of disorders is included under the mental health/psychiatric diagnostic umbrella. Unfortunately, people with mental health issues are often portrayed unfairly in society, and the media tend to perpetuate stereotypes that have a negative impact on students with mental health difficulties. The following sections present information about a few mental health diagnoses that are common in today's classrooms—attention-deficit hyperactivity disorder, oppositional defiant behavior, bipolar disorder, learning disabilities, autism spectrum disorder, and fetal alcohol spectrum disorder.

Attention-Deficit Hyperactivity Disorder (ADHD)

Attention-deficit hyperactivity disorder is characterized by short attention span, weak impulse control, and hyperactivity—all of which inhibit learning and can lead to misbehavior. ADHD can begin in infancy and extend into adulthood, with negative effects on the individual's life at home, in school, and in the community. It is estimated that ADHD affects 3 to 5 percent of the school-age population. The cause of ADHD is not known, but research suggests a hereditary component. Males are more likely than females to have the condition. Among students with ADHD, males typically have attention-deficit disorder (ADD) with hyperactivity, while females typically have ADD without hyperactivity (Amen, 2001). ADHD is very often comorbid with other diagnoses.

Oppositional Defiant Disorder (ODD)

Teachers know that from time to time some of their students will talk back, argue, and disregard directives. Teachers don't enjoy such behavior, but they realize it is a normal occurrence in human development. However, occasionally a student will behave in a manner that is so uncooperative and hostile that it damages the student's social, family, and academic life. That sort of behavior is typical in a diagnosis called oppositional defiant disorder (ODD). The American Academy of Child and Adolescent Psychiatry (2004b) lists the following as symptoms of ODD:

- Frequent temper tantrums
- Excessive arguing with adults
- Active defiance and refusal to comply with adult requests and rules
- Belligerent and sarcastic remarks, made when directly praised
- Deliberate attempts to annoy or upset people
- Blaming others for one's own mistakes or misbehavior
- Being touchy or easily annoyed by others
- Speaking hatefully when upset
- Seeking revenge

The AACAP (2004b) reports that 5 to 15 percent of all school-age children have ODD. Its cause is not known. If you have a student who displays the characteristics of ODD, you might consider using positive reinforcement when the student shows flexibility or cooperation. Indirect or earshot praise sometimes works well, such as when the student "overhears" two adults talking positively about him or her (intentionally to be overheard). It is also helpful to reduce the number of words you use when speaking to a student with ODD (Hall and Hall, 2003). A suggested procedure is to say and show what you mean once and with no further explanation. Students will ask for more information if they need it, and then you can provide what they need. Also consider taking a personal time-out if you feel your responses are about to make the conflict worse. This allows you to calm down, and it also presents a good model for the student.

Bipolar Disorder

Bipolar is an affective disorder characterized by severe mood swings that occur in cycles of mania and depression, or highs and lows. Individuals with bipolar disorder can change abruptly from irritable, angry, and easily annoyed, to silly, goofy, giddy, and disruptive, after which they return again to low energy periods of boredom, depression, and social withdrawal (University of Sheffield, 2005). The abrupt swings of mood and energy, which in some cases occur several times a day, are often accompanied by poor frustration tolerance, outbursts of temper, and ODD. Students with bipolar disorder are also frequently diagnosed with SID (Papolos and Papolos, 2002).

The cause of bipolar disorder is not known. The disorder was once thought to be rare in children, but recent research shows it can begin very early in life and is much more common than previously believed. The condition in children is sometimes misdiagnosed as one or more of the following: ADHD, depression, ODD, obsessive compulsive disorder, or separation anxiety disorder. The misdiagnosis can lead to treatment with stimulants or antidepressants—medications that can make the bipolar disorder worse. Proper drugs can stabilize mood swings, and cognitive therapy and counseling can often help. Indicators of bipolar disorder in school students include the following:

- Hysterical laughing and infectious happiness for no evident reason
- Belligerence and argumentation, followed by self-recrimination
- Jumping from topic to topic in rapid succession when speaking
- Blatant disregard of rules because they think they do not pertain to them
- Arrogant belief that they are exceptionally intelligent
- Belief they can do superhuman deeds without getting seriously hurt

The bipolar condition interferes with the quality of sleep; hence, students who are affected often wake up tired. At school, they may show irritability and nebulous thinking during morning hours, but become able to function better in the afternoon (Papolos and Papolos, 2002).

Learning Disabilities (LD)

Learning disabilities (LD) are neurobiological disorders that interfere with learning in specific subjects or topics and are categorized by the academic areas in which difficulties are identified. They affect students of average to above average intelligence, making it difficult for them to receive and process information. Some of the common learning disabilities include: *dyslexia,* difficulty in processing language; *dyscalculia,* difficulty with basic mathematics; *dysgraphia,* difficulty with handwriting and spelling; and *dyspraxia,* difficulty with fine motor skills (National Council for Learning Disabilities, 2005).

Because LD is so often confused with other diagnoses, it is useful to note that learning disabilities are *not* the same as attention disorders such as ADHD, although the two may occur together. Nor are learning disabilities the same as mental retardation, autism, hearing or visual impairment, physical disabilities, or emotional disorders. Learning disabilities are *not* caused by lack of educational opportunities, frequent changes of schools, poor school attendance, or lack of instruction in basic skills.

Learning disabilities *are* difficulties in learning certain topics, especially in reading, writing, and mathematics. They appear to be inherited, and they affect girls as frequently as boys. Students never outgrow their particular LD, but with support and intervention can be successful in learning and life.

Indicators of LD

At various stages, individuals with normal or above normal intelligence may reveal characteristics that point to learning disabilities. Indicators of LD that you might notice include the following (adapted from material from the National Council for Learning Disabilities, 2005):

- Inability to discriminate between/among letters, numerals, or sounds
- Difficulty sounding out words; reluctance to read aloud; avoidance of reading or writing tasks
- Poor grasp of abstract concepts; poor memory; difficulty telling time
- Confusion between right and left
- Difficulty being disciplined; distractible, restless, impulsive; trouble following directions
- Saying one thing but meaning another; responding inappropriately in certain situations
- Slow work pace; short attention span; difficulty listening and remembering
- Eye–hand coordination problems; poor organizational skills

Specialized psychological and academic testing is needed to confirm diagnoses of LD. The law requires that the diagnosis be made by a multidisciplinary group, which includes teacher, student, other school staff, family members, and diagnostic professionals, such as psychologists, reading clinicians, and speech and language therapists. Based on their assessment and on the availability of resources, special services may be provided to the student at school.

About Dyslexia

Dyslexia is the most widespread and commonly recognized of all learning disabilities, affecting about 30 million American children and adults (Dolphin Education, 2006). It is characterized by difficulties in word recognition, spelling, word decoding, and occasionally with the phonological (sound) component of language. From a young age, students with dyslexia show deficits in coordination, attention, and reading, which often damage their self-concept and sense of competence. The other cognitive faculties in people with dyslexia are believed to function properly.

The cause and effects of dyslexia are of much interest to doctors and research scientists. Harold Levinson (2000), a psychiatrist and neurologist, concluded in the late 1960s that dyslexia is due to a signal-scrambling disturbance involving the inner ear and the cerebellum. Levinson reports that the inner ear–cerebellum interaction can also promote attention deficits, fears, phobias, and panic. Levinson's examinations of thousands of students with reading disabilities showed that whereas none of the students showed evidence of a thinking, brain, or linguistic impairment, over 95 percent had clear-cut balance/coordination/rhythmic difficulties diagnostic of an inner ear–cerebellum dysfunction. Levinson hypothesized that the inner ear acts as a "fine-tuner" to the brain. The degree of dyslexia is dependent on (1) the number of inner-ear circuits that are not working properly, (2) the degree of signal scrambling, and (3) the ability of normal cerebral processors to descramble or otherwise compensate for scrambled signals. Levinson points out that many people with dyslexia are very high achievers, including Albert Einstein, Thomas Edison, and Winston Churchill. Sally Shaywitz and Bennett Shaywitz (2003) also helped establish the neurological basis for the disorder.

Scenario 3

The class had just finished a discussion of a chapter in the book they were reading. Justin actively participated in the discussion, making correct and well thought-out responses. Mr. Gatta, the teacher, then instructed the class to complete a chapter summary sheet at their desks. Justin needed to be told a second time to get started. He put his feet up on his desk top and began to belch loudly. The students laughed. Mr. Gatta asked Justin to stop belching and take his feet off his desk, whereupon Justin put his feet down and wrapped his legs around the legs of his desk. He then leaned back and made himself fall backwards, pulling his desk on top of him. When Mr. Gatta came to help disentangle Justin from the furniture, Justin grabbed the desk, wrapped his legs tighter around it, squealed loudly, and laughed uncontrollably.

Commentary: Justin shows great reluctance to write down answers, even though he can say them correctly. His behavior may be linked to a learning disability, and there may also be other intricate neural issues involved. What do you think Mr. Gatta might do to help Justin behave more normally and enjoy greater success in school?

Autism Spectrum Disorder (ASD)

Autism spectrum disorder (ASD) includes various diagnoses of abnormal development in verbal and nonverbal communication, along with impaired social development and restricted, repetitive, and stereotyped behaviors and interests (Faraone, 2003). It also includes pervasive developmental disorder (delays in the development of socialization and communication skills) and Asperger syndrome. Asperger syndrome is a pattern of behavior among students of normal intelligence and language development who also exhibit autistic-like behaviors and marked deficiencies in social and communication skills. About 1.5 million American children and adults are thought to have some form of autism. It occurs in every ethnic and socioeconomic group and affects four times as many males as females. Students with ASD may show extreme hyperactivity or extreme passivity in relating to people around them. In its milder form, autism resembles a learning disability. Indicators of ASD include:

- Self-stimulation, spinning, rocking, and hand flapping
- Obsessive compulsive behaviors, such as lining objects up evenly
- Repetitive odd play for extended periods of time
- Insistence on routine and sameness
- Difficulty dealing with interruption of routine schedule and change
- Monotone voice and difficulty carrying on social conversations
- Inflexibility of thought and language (For example, one student with autism refused to wear his winter jacket during subzero weather in early December because he had learned winter did not officially begin until December 21st.)

Manifestations of autism vary enormously in severity. Sensory integration dysfunction is also common in students with ASD, and sensory overload can lead to behavior problems in school. Modifying the physical environment can do much to improve behavior and academic achievement of students with ASD.

Some people with autism never develop language and need around-the-clock care; others become fully functioning, independent members of society, as exemplified by Temple Grandin (2005), perhaps the world's most accomplished and well-known adult with autism. Dr. Grandin has appeared on major television programs such as the *Today* show, *Larry King Live, 48 Hours,* and *20/20,* and has been featured in publications such as *Time, People, Forbes, U.S. News and World Report,* and the *New York Times.* (See www.templegrandin.org.)

Scenario 4

Tay is extremely noisy. Even during quiet work time, she taps, hums, or makes other noises. When the teacher asks her to stop, she denies doing anything. She talks very loudly. When classmates ask her to be quiet, she ignores them. Tay wears three pairs of socks all the time and adjusts the cuffs on each pair a number of times a day. She cannot settle down and focus until her socks are just right. She will not change shoes for gym class. When the gym teacher tried to make her do so, Tay swore at her and then ran out of the gym and away from school, crying hysterically. When dashing across the street, Tay ran into the side of a parked car, then fell to the road and sobbed until a teacher came to get her.

Commentary from Tay's Teacher: Tay is diagnosed with ASD with extreme SID. Outside noise bothers her greatly, so she makes her own noise to drown it out. It is speculated that she wears the three pairs of socks to put extra pressure on her feet, which would be an indicator of SID, as is her continual cuff adjustment. Things that have been done to help her benefit more from school include:

- Providing ear covers to block outside noise
- Using a portable radio/CD player with headphones to drown other noise
- Giving her gum or mints to help keep her mouth quiet
- Overlooking her sock rituals, which are not a major issue
- Compromising by allowing Tay to decide whether she will change shoes for gym class or move to an alternate activity arranged for her, which includes teaching of social skills in her individualized education program

Fetal Alcohol Spectrum Disorder (FASD)

Fetal alcohol spectrum disorder is a group of neurobehavioral and developmental abnormalities that includes fetal alcohol syndrome (FAS), alcohol related neurodevelopmental disorder (ARND), and partial fetal alcohol syndrome (pFAS). The spectrum affects about 1 percent of the population in the United States (Clark, Lutke, Minnes, and Ouellette-Kuntz, 2004). The disorder results from the fetus being exposed to alcohol from the mother's blood. Ingestion of even small amounts of alcohol by the mother, as little as one ounce per week, has been linked to ADHD and delinquent and aggressive behavior in the child. The Centers for Disease Control and Prevention contend that no level of alcohol consumption during pregnancy is considered to be safe (CDC, 2004). It is now accepted that women who drink during pregnancy, even in the earliest stages, are at risk of having a child with fetal alcohol spectrum disorder.

The symptoms and characteristics of FASD appear in a variety of combinations, with the overall condition ranging in severity from mild to extreme. Individuals with FASD can exhibit any combination of the behaviors in any degree of severity (American Academy of Pediatrics, 2004). Two people with the same diagnosis can behave differently from each other and can have different levels of skills.

Alcohol is the most toxic and damaging substance to which unborn children are normally exposed, and it is the leading cause of mental retardation in the Western world (Institute of Medicine, 1996). Even so, most individuals with FAS and other diagnoses on the FASD continuum have normal intelligence (Streissguth, Barr, Kogan, and Bookstein, 1997). At the same time, many have compromised adaptive and social skills, including poor impulse control, poor judgment, tendency to miss social cues, lack of common sense, learning difficulties, and difficulty with the tasks of daily living. ADHD is usually comorbid with FASD, and behavior difficulties are a main issue for students with FASD (Kellerman, 2003).

Scenario 5
Ten-year-old Sam never sits still in class. He is always talking and always calling out answers in class even though they are usually wrong. Yesterday he pushed a classmate when they were coming in from recess. The teacher spoke to him, reminded him of the rules, and told him he could not go out for recess that afternoon. This morning, Sam was reminded to keep his hands to himself or he would lose recess again. Sam repeated word for word what he was told: "I will keep my hands to myself, and if I don't, I won't be able to go out for recess this afternoon." Fifteen minutes later Sam pushed Jonathan. When the teacher spoke to him, Sam claimed he didn't do anything and it wasn't his fault.

Commentary: Sam has been diagnosed with FASD and ADHD. His repeating back the words and consequences indicates language processing difficulties common to FASD. Like other students with the condition, he reacts automatically to situations without always remembering what he did. Calling out and inability to sit still indicate ADHD.

Rage

Rage is not a type of neurological disorder, but rather an extreme kind of behavior sometimes exhibited by students with NBB. It is manifested as an explosion of temper that occurs suddenly with no real warning and may turn violent (Packer, 2005). The process is traumatic for everyone and should be understood as a neurological event that leads to behavior over which the student has little control. Rage differs from tantrum, which is goal directed, with the purpose of getting something or getting somebody to do something. Rage is not goal oriented, but rather a release of built up tension or frustration. (Tantrums sometimes evolve into rage.) Once a rage episode has begun, there is little one can do to stop it. It may only last for a few minutes, or may continue for hours. Although it usually has to run its course, it can be softened and controlled somewhat by teachers and other adults.

The **rage cycle** proceeds through five phases, identified as pre-rage, triggering, escalation, rage, and post-rage. These phases, their characteristics, and how you can help in each of them are described in the paragraphs that follow (adapted from Greene, 2001; Echternach and Cook, 2004; Cook, 2005; Hill, 2005; and Packer, 2005).

Phase 1:

This is the time preceding the rage just before something triggers the rage event and sets it in motion.

Phase 2:

Triggers are precipitating events that provoke episodes of rage, apparently by stimulating neurochemical changes in the brain that greatly heighten the fight/flight/freeze reactions (self-protective responses). Triggering conditions seem to be associated frequently with work transitions, sensory overload, being told no, fatigue, frustration, confusion, hunger, central nervous system executive dysfunction, anxiety, and mood swings. For children with ADHD, triggers tend to be related to sensory or emotional overstimulation. For children with bipolar disorder, triggers are often related to having limits set on their behavior (Papolos and Papolos, 2002). In the triggering phase students may appear angry, confused, frustrated, dazed, tense, or flushed, and they may swear and use other rude language.

> *What you can do to help at this phase*
> - Recognize that a rage episode may be forthcoming and you may not be able to prevent it.
> - Understand that this is a neurological event. The student's flight/fight/freeze responses are strongly activated.
> - Understand that the rage is not intentional or personal toward you.
> - Stay calm. Use a quiet tone of voice. Do not become adversarial.
> - Use short, direct phrases and nonemotional language.
> - Do not question, scold, or become verbose.
> - Use nonthreatening body language. Stand on an angle off center to the student, at least a long stride away. Make sure the student can see your hands.
> - Use empathetic verbal support ("It sounds like you're upset." "That would upset me too.").
> - Deflect control elsewhere ("The clock says it's time to clean up." "The big rule book in the office says . . . ").
> - Calmly, quietly, and succinctly use logical persuasion to provide the student an alternative behavior.

Phase 3:

Following the triggering, the rage may escalate mildly or rapidly. In *mild escalations,* the student may begin to get angry, call names, swear, exhibit startled verbal or physical responses, talk rapidly, increase the volume and cadence of speech, and show tension in arms, hands, and body. *Rapid escalations* are characterized by violent temper, hostility, aggressive comments ("Leave me alone." "I'm going to kill you."), profanity, flushed face, and clammy body. The student may show fists and throw objects or furniture.

> *What you can do to help during this phase*
> - Stay calm.
> - Ensure the safety of others by clearing them from the room or supporting them to ignore the escalation.
> - If the student threatens you, walk away.
> - Calmly direct the student to a safe place (e.g., Quiet Room or designated area) to allow the energy to dissipate.
> - When speaking to the student, use short, direct phrases and nonemotional language.
> - Use body language that is nonthreatening and nonconfrontational.
> - Use supportive empathy to acknowledge the student's feelings.

- Calmly, quietly, and succinctly use logical persuasion to provide the student an alternative.
- Praise the student as soon as he or she begins to respond to your direction.
- Do not address the student's inappropriate language, threats, or other behavior at this time. The student cannot process the information and may only become further inflamed.

Phase 4:

During the rage, or meltdown phase, the student is caught up in the rage.

What you can do to help during this phase
- Allow the student space to go through the physical manifestations.
- Do not restrain the student unless there is an immediate threat to physical safety.
- Do not bully, question, make sarcastic comments, yell, scream, or try to talk the student out of the rage.
- Do not try to make the student understand instructions.
- While the student is going through the cycle of reactions, support others in the room and help ensure that their interpretations of the rage event are correct.

Phase 5:

After a rage event, in the post-rage or post-meltdown phase, the student may or may not remember the behavior or the triggering causes. This is a low point for the student because he or she has expended a great amount of energy and is left confused and often embarrassed. The student will now be tired, passive, headachy, and sometimes remorseful and apologetic. The student may be in need of sleep, or may be ready to continue the day.

How you can help at this phase
- Reassure the student that he or she is all right now.
- Do not talk about consequences or punishments; they are not appropriate.
- When the student is ready, help him or her put language to the event.
- Help him or her plan what to do the next time a rage occurs—such as finding a sensory-friendly refuge (a safe place or room in which to rage), using words to get what he or she needs, and timing him- or herself out (that is, remaining in a safe place until able to calm down).
- After the rage event and when the student is calm, take care of yourself. Relax, drink water, and remind yourself that it was not personal and that you did the best you could. Meanwhile, document your observations, hold debriefing conversations with a colleague, and listen to reflections made by anyone involved. Take note of any evident triggers, sensory influences, or other environmental characteristics that may

be implicated in the rage. It is perfectly acceptable for you *not* to talk during the rage, but just "be there" with the student, without crowding.

Scenario 6

Calley is noncompliant, argumentative, and loud. He often tries to slap, bite, and scratch teachers and classmates. He makes personal threats and has defaced desks and walls. He often prints f‑‑‑ on papers, desks, and walls. His profanity distances him from others in the class. At the same time, he is vulnerable because his aggressive profanity sometimes brings reprisals from other students.

Calley is also a danger to himself. When angry, he chews on things such as pencils, paper, erasers, math manipulatives, and his clothing. He usually spits the material out, but sometimes swallows it. One of his disturbing traits is tying himself up when distressed. Once, he tied his wrists together with his shoe laces while in the Quiet Room. The next time he was sent to the Quiet Room, he had to remove his shoes, but Calley used his socks to tie his wrists together. A few days after that, he tore up his T‑shirt, knotted it into a rope, and again tied himself up. Then he began to scream for the teacher, "Help me, I'm choking! Untie me you stupid c‑‑‑! I'm dying, you wh‑‑‑‑! Are going to let me die, you bi‑‑‑ ?!!"

Commentary from Calley's teacher: Teaching Calley was a real experience. Something set him off about three days each week. But he really taught me a lot during the two years I worked with him. He was assessed several times and was diagnosed with ADHD, SID, language processing disorder, and severe academic delay. The poor boy was terribly frustrated, and as you can imagine, his behavior very much got in the way of his academic progress.

Medications for Students with Behavioral Issues

The National Institute of Mental Health (2006) reports that most childhood mental health problems are treatable with medication. However, because medication is controversial, the decision whether to use it is ultimately made by the parents. If they allow medication at school, established policies stipulate where the medication must be stored, who is responsible for administering it, and what teachers and other educators are allowed to say about the medication. Teachers should inform themselves about medication policies at their school and what their attendant responsibilities are.

Monitoring the effects of medication is usually a shared responsibility among parents, school, and the medical practitioner, with school personnel asked to watch for any unusual behavior or symptoms during the school day. If teachers are asked to give reports of how the child behaved, they are to state them in this manner: "During the math lesson, Jason got up five times without permission. On one occasion he berated another student." Teachers should not make emotionally charged commentary, such as, "Jason was badly out of control and seriously disrupted the class with his antics." In other words, teachers should make sure they avoid vocabulary that reflects their own emotional reactions to the student's behavior.

In Summary

Mel Levine (2003) says that from the moment students get out of bed in the morning until they are back in bed at night, they have one mission that overrides all others—the avoidance of humiliation at all costs. He also says that we need to demystify NBB for affected students and peers. He says to explain plainly to the class and others that some people function (are "wired up," if you prefer) in such a way that they lose control at times, more often than others do. Students need to be reassured that teachers can help them avoid getting into trouble and will partner with them out of care and concern. Linda Rammler (Ask the Expert, 2005) adds that as difficult as it may be at times, we need to think of NBB students separately from their behavior. We should always model the calm, soothing behavior we want them to display, while making sure they feel loved and respected as human beings.

When working with students with NBB it important to be as proactive as possible in ensuring student success. Strategies for this purpose include:

■ Establish a positive and nurturing rapport with the students. Warmly greet them when they arrive at class. Show interest and talk about pop culture or something they are interested in.

■ Modify the classroom to make it sensory friendly. Sit in the student's seat and look at the room from the student's perspective. See if there are things that might be distracting or annoying. It is far more productive to change the classroom than try to change the student.

■ Provide a calm, structured, and nurturing classroom environment. Structure provides a framework for the development of responsible behavior.

■ Add structure to time periods that are ordinarily unstructured, such as recess and free time. Students with NBB often have difficulty with unstructured time.

■ Use and teach humor, which is effective with all students.

■ Be careful of eye contact. It can stimulate upper cortex activity, which is good for academic thinking, but it can at times trigger episodes of misbehavior—eye contact combined with a stern tone of voice is often interpreted as a challenge or threat.

■ Be careful how you react to situations. If you raise your voice, students with NBB will often raise their voices in return.

■ When giving students a choice, provide two alternatives you can live with and let the students select the one they prefer.

A positive teacher attitude can greatly improve the quality of service provided to students with NBB and their families. Students experiencing difficulties in neurological processing are human beings first and foremost, who badly need our help. They are not predestined to fail. They have many qualities and strengths that can be nurtured and built on as they develop life competencies. One of our most valuable strategies is to use a "strengths" perspective, rooted in the here and now, that is solution orientated and devoted to practical outcomes. All small improvements by students with NBB should be celebrated as important steps to a better quality life, now and in the future. This closing anecdote is reflective of some of the foregoing points. The principal brought a top-level administrator from the school district to visit the class for students with special needs. The class had been working on a science unit about the human body, and several students were very impressed that exercise can make your muscles bigger. During the visit, 12-year-old Kelly, diagnosed with ASD, looked at the administrator and said, "Wow, if I was you I wouldn't breathe very hard." When the Superintendent asked why, Kelly replied, "You won't want that nose to get any bigger." According to reports, the teacher privately celebrated Kelly's learning.

KEY TERMS AND CONCEPTS EMPHASIZED IN THIS CHAPTER

people first language
neurological differences
neurological-based behavior (NBB)
attention-deficit hyperactivity
    disorder
affective disorders
bipolar disorder

anxiety disorders
posttraumatic stress disorder
conduct disorder
oppositional defiant disorder
autism spectrum disorder
fetal alcohol spectrum disorder
traumatic brain injuries

nontraumatic brain injuries
sensory integration dysfunction (SID)
    or sensory processing disorder
learning disabilities (LD)
dyslexia
rage
rage cycle

ACTIVITIES

1. In your journal devoted to the principles for building a personal system of discipline, make entries from this chapter that you might wish to incorporate into the system of discipline you will create.

2. In cooperation with one or more classmates or fellow teachers, go back to Scenario 1 at the beginning of the chapter. Discuss how you might help Tyler move past his inappropriate behavior. The commentary from Tay's teacher in Scenario 4 might help you organize your thoughts. Share your conclusions with peers and ask for their comments.

3. Individually or in collaboration with others, select Scenario 4, 5, or 6. With a partner discuss what you might do to minimize the disruptive behavior of the student involved and otherwise improve the overall situation.

4. Select one of the NBB diagnoses described in the chapter and see how much information you can find about it on the Internet. Report back to your peers or classmates.

REFERENCES

Acorn, S., and Offer P. (Eds.). 1998. *Living with brain injury: A guide for families and caregivers.* Toronto: University of Toronto Press.

Amen, D. 2001. *Healing ADD: The breakthrough program that allows you to see and heal the six types of attention deficit disorder.* New York: G. P. Putnam's Sons.

American Academy of Child and Adolescent Psychiatry. 2004a. Child psychiatry facts for families: Recommendations, help and guidance from the AACAP. http://pediatrics.about.com/library/bl_psych_policy_statements. htm.

American Academy of Child and Adolescent Psychiatry. 2004b. Children with oppositional defiant disorder. www.aacap.org/publications/factsfam/72.htm.

American Academy of Child and Adolescent Psychiatry. 2004c. Teen suicide. www.aacap.org/publications/factsfam/suicide.htm.

American Academy of Pediatrics. 2004. Fetal alcohol syndrome. www.aap.org/advocacy/chm98fet.htm.

Ask the Expert. 2005. Interview with Linda H. Rammler. www.explosivekids.org/pdf/rammler.pdf.

Brain Injury Society. 2006. 1998 Newsletter: Fall Issue. www.bisociety.org.

Centers for Disease Control and Prevention (CDC). 2004. Alcohol consumption among women who are pregnant or who might become pregnant—United States, 2002. www.acbr.com/fas.

Clark, E., Lutke, J., Minnes, P., and Ouellette-Kuntz, H. 2004. Secondary disabilities among adults with fetal alcohol spectrum disorder in British Columbia. *Journal of FAS International* (2), 1–12.

Cook, P. 2004a. Behaviour, learning and teaching: Applied studies in FAS/FAE (Distance Education Curricula). Winnipeg, MB: Red River College.

Cook, P. 2004b. Sensory integration dysfunction: A layperson's guide. Booklet available from Paula Cook. pcook59@shaw.ca.

Cook, P. 2005. Rage: A layperson's guide to what to do when someone begins to rage. Booklet available from Paula Cook. pcook59@shaw.ca.

Cook, P., Kellie, R., Jones, K., and Goossen, L. 2000. Tough kids and substance abuse. Winnipeg, MB: Addictions Foundation of Manitoba.

Davidson, H. 1993. Just ask! A handbook for instructors of students being treated for mental disorders. Calgary, AB: Detselig Enterprises.

DeAngelis, T. 2004. Children's mental health problems seen as "epidemic." *APA Monitor on Psychology,* 35(11), 38.

Dolphin Education. 2006. Dyslexia research: 4. The incidence of dyslexia. www.dolphinuk.co.uk/education/case_studies/dyslexia_research.htm.

Echternach, C., and Cook, P. 2004. The rage cycle. Paper available from Paula Cook. pcook59@shaw.ca.

Faraone, S. 2003. *Straight talk about your child's mental health.* New York: The Guilford Press.

Feldman, E. 2004. Impact of mental illness on learning. Keynote Address at the 9th Midwest Conference on Child and Adolescent Mental Health. Grand Forks, ND.

Gardner, H. 1999. *Intelligence reframed: Multiple intelligences for the 21st century.* New York: Basic Books.

Grandin, T. 2005. www.templegrandin.org.

Greene, R. 2001. *The explosive child.* New York: Harper Collins.

Hall, P., and Hall, N. 2003. *Educating oppositional and defiant children.* Alexandria, VA: Association for Supervision and Curriculum Development.

Hill, P. 2005. Pharmacological treatment of rage. www.focusproject.org.uk/SITE/UPLOAD/DOCUMENT/Hill.

Institute of Medicine. 1996. Fetal alcohol syndrome: Diagnosis, epidemiology, prevention, and treatment. www.come-over.to/FAS/IOMsummary.htm.

Jans, L., Stoddard, S., and Kraus, L. 2004. Chartbook on mental health and disability in the United States. An InfoUse report. Washington, DC: U.S. Department of Education, National Institute on Disability and Rehabilitation Research.

Kellerman, T. 2003. The FAS community resource center. www.come-over.to/FASCRC.

Kranowitz, C. 1998. *The out-of-sync child.* New York: Skylight Press.

Kranowitz, C., Szkut, S., Balzer-Martin, L., Haber, E., and Sava, D. 2003. Answers to questions teachers ask about sensory integration. Las Vegas, NV: Sensory Resources.

Levine, M. 2003. *A mind at a time.* New York: Simon and Schuster Adult Publishing Group.

Levinson, H. 2000. *The discovery of cerebellar-vestibular syndromes and therapies: A solution to the riddle—Dyslexia* (2nd ed.). Lake Success, NY: Stonebridge Publishing.

National Council for Learning Disabilities. 2005. The ABCs of learning disabilities. www.ncld.org.

National Institute of Mental Health. 2005. Health information quick links. www.nimh.nih.gov.

National Institute of Mental Health. 2006. Medications. www.nimh.nih.gov/publicat/medicate.cfm#ptdep1.

Packer, L. 2005. Overview of rage attacks. www.tourettesyndrome.net/rage_overview.htm.

Papolos, D., and Papolos, J. 2002. *The bipolar child.* New York: Broadway Books.

Shaywitz, S., and Shaywitz, B. 2003. Drs. Sally and Bennett Shaywitz on brain research and reading. www.schwablearning.org/Articles.asp?r=35.

Streissguth, A., Barr, H., Kogan, J., and Bookstein, F. 1997. Primary and secondary disabilities in fetal alcohol syndrome. In Streissguth, A., and Kanter, J. (Eds.), *The challenge of fetal alcohol syndrome: Overcoming secondary disabilities* (pp. 23–39). Seattle: University of Washington Press.

University of Sheffield. 2005. Teaching students with mental health conditions. www.shef.ac.uk/disability/teaching/mental/10_examples.html.

CHAPTER 4

Twentieth-Century Pioneers in Classroom Discipline

CHAPTER PREVIEW

This chapter describes contributions made between 1951 and 1998 by six influential pioneers in classroom discipline. Although their approaches are rarely used as complete systems of discipline today, elements from their programs are strongly evident in current discipline programs. Prior to 1951, teachers used an authoritative approach to discipline. Discipline was not considered to be a part of real teaching, but an onerous and necessary duty to keep classes from falling into chaos. In 1951, this picture began to change, and it is still changing today. Now, discipline is seen as an integral part of teaching and a valuable way to help students develop important life skills, such as responsibility, civility, and perseverance. The groundwork for that major change was laid by authorities featured in this chapter.

The Evolution of Classroom Discipline

Prior to the middle of the twentieth century, classroom discipline was forceful and demanding, often harsh and punitive. Teachers were persons of good intent doing the best they could to help students learn, but in those days, everyone expected teachers to make students toe the mark. When students got out of line, they were to be reprimanded and, if necessary, punished. Teachers possessed authoritative power and used it, believing their efforts were helpful to learning, rather than harmful.

The years following World War II brought many societal changes toward greater equality and democracy, and those changes slowly affected classroom discipline. Today's discipline uses tactics that entice, persuade, and assist students, rather than intimidate and attempt to force them into compliance. The first comprehensive discipline system to gain acceptance appeared in 1951. Created by Fritz Redl and William Wattenberg, it combined the theory of human dynamics with humane treatment. That work opened educators' minds to new possibilities and set a pattern for changes to come.

You may notice that the early discipline approaches reported in this chapter were set forth by professors in psychology and psychiatry, whose ideas reflected work they were doing in their academic pursuits. For example, B. F. Skinner worked in experimental psychology, Rudolf Dreikurs in psychiatry and clinical psychology, Fritz Redl in psychiatry and developmental psychology, and William Wattenberg in educational psychology. It was not until the mid-1970s that education practitioners began to set forth approaches that more closely reflected the concerns of teachers and students in schools.

This chapter examines the contributions of those early pioneers who led the way toward modern discipline. We begin with Redl and Wattenberg's conclusions concerning group behavior and proceed to the pivotal discoveries by B. F. Skinner on behavior shaping, Jacob Kounin on lesson management, Haim Ginott on communication in discipline, Rudolf Dreikurs on discipline through democratic teaching, and Lee and Marlene Canter on assertively taking charge in the classroom.

Fritz Redl and William Wattenberg: Discipline through Influencing Group Behavior

Fritz Redl and William Wattenberg (1951), specialists in human behavior and educational psychology, presented the first theory-based approach to humane classroom discipline. Their work, which inaugurated the modern era in classroom discipline, was designed specifically to help teachers understand and deal considerately with group misbehavior and the effects it had on individual students.

Redl and Wattenberg's Principal Teachings

Redl and Wattenberg based many of their conclusions on evidence that people in groups behave differently than individuals. They explained that students in classrooms *are likely* to do things they would not do if alone, and *unlikely* to do certain things they would do if by themselves or in small groups. Their work helped teachers understand how groups affect personal behavior.

Redl and Wattenberg called the forces they detected in groups group dynamics. They defined **group dynamics** as forces that are generated by and within groups and that strongly affect behavior. They claimed that for teachers to deal effectively with group behavior, they must understand group dynamics, how those dynamics develop, and how they affect students in the classroom. Group dynamics account for effects such as group spirit, imitative behavior, desire to excel, scapegoating, hiding places for nonachievers, group norms and expectations, and the adoption of certain roles by members of the group. Redl and Wattenberg said that, in any class, students take on **student roles,** such as leader, follower, clown (those who show-off), instigator (those who provoke misbehavior), and scapegoat (those on whom blame is placed even when not deserved). They urged teachers to be watchful for the emergence of these roles, bring them to the class's attention, be prepared to encourage or discourage them as appropriate, and know how to limit their detrimental effects.

Students are not the only ones whose behavior is affected by classroom conditions. Students have in mind certain **teacher roles** they expect teachers to fill, and they put pressure on teachers to do so. For example, students expect teachers to serve as role model, source of knowledge, referee, judge, and surrogate parent. Teachers need to be aware that students hold these expectations, and they should discuss them openly with students.

Redl and Wattenberg further urged teachers to show a clear desire to be helpful, remain as objective as possible, show tolerance, keep a sense of humor, and help students maintain positive attitudes toward school and the class. All these things, they said, could be fostered by influence techniques that teachers could (and should) use instead of punishment to control student behavior. Positive influence techniques include **supporting student self-control,** offering **situational assistance,** and **appraising reality** (helping students become aware of underlying causes of proper and improper behavior.) One of Redl and Wattenberg's suggestions that did not appear widely in practice until many years later was that teachers should involve students in setting class standards and deciding how transgressions should be handled, an idea featured strongly in most of today's systems of discipline.

Redl and Wattenberg said that **punishment,** if it had to be used at all, should never be physically hurtful, but should consist only of preplanned consequences that are unpleasant to the student, such as sitting by themselves, making up work that has not been done, or not being allowed to participate in certain class activities. Never should it involve angry outbursts from the teacher or attempts to "teach the student a lesson."

Review of Redl and Wattenberg's Contributions

In summary, Redl and Wattenberg made five notable contributions to modern discipline. First, they described how groups behave differently from individuals, thus helping teachers understand classroom behaviors that are otherwise perplexing. Second, they provided the first well-organized, systematic approach to improving student behavior in the classroom, replacing aversive techniques with humane approaches that promote long-term positive relationships. Third, they placed emphasis on understanding the causes of student misbehavior, believing that by attending to causes teachers could eliminate most misbehavior. Fourth, they established the value of involving students in making decisions about discipline, now advocated by virtually all authorities. And fifth, they pointed out the detrimental effects of punishment and showed why it should not be used in class discipline. These five contributions established trends that propelled classroom discipline in new directions.

But despite Redl and Wattenberg's remarkable contributions, their approach was never put widely into practice. Teachers found it difficult to grasp the concept and implications of group dynamics, and they did not understand how to deal with roles expected of students and themselves. They found they could not put the recommended procedures into effect quickly enough, given the harried context of the classroom, and felt they had insufficient expertise to carry them out properly. Thus, although Redl and Wattenberg's work broke new ground in discipline and teachers found it interesting, persuasive, and in many ways helpful, the approach was too cumbersome to be implemented efficiently.

B. F. Skinner: Discipline through Shaping Desired Behavior

Even before Redl and Wattenberg published their suggestions based on group dynamics, Harvard behavioral psychologist Burrhus Frederic Skinner (1904–1990) was discovering how our behavior is influenced by what happens to us immediately after we perform a given act. Skinner earned his doctorate in psychology at Harvard in 1931, and from that time almost until his death in 1990, he published articles and books based on his findings and beliefs about human behavior. Skinner never concerned himself directly with classroom discipline. In the early 1960s, his followers devised and popularized **behavior modification,** the principles of which have been widely used in teaching, child rearing, and human relations.

Skinner's Principal Teachings

Skinner's work, done first with laboratory animals, convinced him that much if not most of our voluntary behavior is shaped by reinforcement we receive immediately after performing an act. For our purposes here, reinforcement can be thought of as reward, though *reward* is a term Skinner never used in his work. Simply put, when we do something and are rewarded for it, we are more likely to repeat that act and even try harder.

The reward, what Skinner called the reinforcing stimulus, must be received soon after the behavior occurs, if it is to have an effect. Reinforcing stimuli common in the classroom include knowledge of results, peer approval, awards and free time, and smiles, nods, and praise from the teacher. In years past, teachers used rewards such as candy, popcorn, and tangible objects, but that practice died out quickly as teachers came to understand that students often worked mainly to get the reward, with unsatisfactory residual learning once the rewards were no longer in place.

The term *behavior modification,* a term that Skinner never used, today refers to the overall procedure of **shaping behavior** intentionally through systematic reinforcement. The way in which reinforcement is provided affects subsequent behavior. **Constant reinforcement,** given every time a student behaves as desired, helps new learning become established. The teacher might praise Jonathan every time he raises his hand, or privately compliment Mary every time she turns in required homework. **Intermittent reinforcement,** given occasionally, is sufficient to maintain desired behavior once it has become established. After students have learned to come into the room and immediately begin work, the teacher will only occasionally need to express appreciation. Behaviors that are not reinforced eventually disappear. If Roberto raises his hand in class but is never called on, he will eventually stop raising his hand. The shaping of desired behavior is done through **successive approximation,** in which behavior comes closer and closer to a preset goal. This process is helpful in building skills incrementally. Skinner stressed that **punishment** should not be used in behavior shaping because its effects were unpredictable.

Review of Skinner's Contributions

Although Skinner did not concern himself with classroom discipline per se, his discoveries concerning the shaping of behavior led directly to behavior modification, which is still used to speed and shape academic and social learning. In the 1960s, many primary grade teachers used behavior modification as their entire discipline system, rewarding students who behaved properly and ignoring those who misbehaved. The procedure was considered very effective in promoting desired behavior. Today, behavior modification is not used so much for discipline as for encouraging and strengthening learning. Even teachers who previously enjoyed its effectiveness are now concerned about its being tantamount to bribing students to behave properly.

Beyond primary grades, teachers found behavior modification unsuitable as an overall discipline approach for several reasons. A major concern was that although it was helpful in teaching students desirable behavior, it was inefficient in teaching them what *not* to do. Teachers grew tired of hoping that by ignoring misbehavior they could get students to behave properly. They found that misbehavior was often sustained by social rewards from peers. Teachers also found that it is simply easier to teach students how to behave desirably and show them how they should *not* behave. They don't have to learn those things through lengthy processes of reinforcement or extinction.

Jacob Kounin: Improving Discipline through Lesson Management

As mentioned earlier, teaching and discipline were once thought of as separate and relatively unrelated aspects of education. Although everyone knew they affected each other, teaching was thought of as helping students learn, whereas discipline was considered the means to make students do their work, pay attention, and behave themselves so learning could occur. We have seen that this view began to change with the contributions of Redl and Wattenberg and was furthered by the teachings of B. F. Skinner. That trend continued with the work of Jacob Kounin (1971), an educational psychologist at Wayne State University, who focused on how classroom management and lesson management affect student behavior in school.

Kounin's Principal Teachings

The central factor in managing behavior, Kounin asserted, was teacher ability to know what was going on in all parts of the classroom at all times and dealing with incipient problems before they turned into misbehavior. Kounin based his conclusions on hundreds of hours of observing effective teachers at work, and he found that teachers whose classes were best behaved displayed this teacher awareness, which he called **withitness.** He found that such teachers were able to monitor and interact with groups of students doing independent work even while the teacher was teaching lessons to smaller groups. He called the act of attending to two or more classroom events simultaneously **overlapping** and considered it one of the most valuable capabilities teachers can possess.

Kounin also focused a great deal on lesson management as a means of keeping students on task and involved. He noted that effective teachers use identifiable tactics for gaining student attention and clarifying expectations. One such tactic is what Kounin called **group alerting,** where teachers gain students' full attention before giving directions or making explanations. They then keep students actively involved in the lesson. Another tactic he found useful was what he called student accountability, maintained by regularly calling on students to respond, demonstrate, or explain. He found that good lesson **momentum** helped keep students alert and involved. He used the term *momentum* to refer to a condition where teachers started lessons with dispatch, kept lessons moving ahead, made transitions among activities efficiently, and brought lessons to a satisfactory close. He also emphasized **smoothness** in lesson presentation, referring to the steady progression of lessons, without abrupt changes.

Kounin went to some lengths to explain how good teachers keep students from getting bored or otherwise frustrated with lessons. He reminded teachers to guard against over-exposure to a given topic, as a means of avoiding **satiation,** his term for students' getting all they can tolerate of a topic. He emphasized that teachers should make instructional activities enjoyable and challenging. Students usually indicate satiation, he said, by misbehavior and disengagement from the lesson.

Review of Kounin's Contributions

Kounin identified a number of teacher strategies that help students remain engaged in lessons, with resultant reduction in misbehavior. The interconnection he identified between ways of teaching and control of behavior led to a new line of thought concerning how teaching influences behavior. Kounin explained that he had expected to find a relationship between what teachers did when students misbehaved and the subsequent misbehavior of those students. But no such findings emerged from his research. This prompted Kounin to write:

> That unexpected fact required unlearning on my part, in the sense of having to replace the original question by other questions. Questions about disciplinary techniques were eliminated and replaced by questions about classroom management in general, [and] *preventing* misbehavior was given higher investigative priority than *handling* misbehavior. (1971, p. 143, italics added)

He went on to describe what teachers should understand about operating their classrooms:

> . . . the business of running a classroom is a complicated technology having to do with developing a nonsatiating learning program; programming for progress, challenge, and variety in learning activities; initiating and maintaining movement in classroom tasks

with smoothness and momentum; coping with more than one event simultaneously; observing and emitting feedback for many different events; directing actions at appropriate targets; maintaining a focus upon a group; and doubtless other techniques not measured in these researches. (1971, pp. 144–145)

Kounin made outstanding contributions concerning the relation of classroom management to student behavior, and he provided a valuable service in drawing attention to the close connection between teaching and discipline. However, teachers never found his approach satisfactory as a total system of discipline. They agree that certain teaching tactics can cut down markedly on the incidence of class misbehavior. But misbehavior occurs even in the best of circumstances, and Kounin provided no help concerning what teachers should do when misbehavior disrupts the class. Kounin stated that he couldn't identify teacher tactics that, when used in response to misbehavior, did anything to improve the behavior. Improve it or not, teachers feel they must be able to put a stop to disruptive or defiant behavior simply in order to continue with their lessons. They found little in Kounin's work that helped in that regard.

Haim Ginott: Discipline through Congruent Communication

In the same year that Kounin published his work on lesson management, there appeared another small book that had even greater influence. That was Haim Ginott's *Teacher and Child* (1971) in which Ginott illuminated the critical role of communication in discipline, especially concerning how teachers talk to and with their students. In many ways, Ginott did more than anyone else to set the personal, caring tone that prevails in today's systems of discipline.

Ginott was a classroom teacher early in his career. Later, he earned his doctorate at Columbia University and went on to hold professorships in psychology at Adelphi University and at New York University Graduate School. He also served as a UNESCO consultant in Israel, was resident psychologist on the *Today* show, and wrote a weekly syndicated column titled "Between Us" that dealt with interpersonal communication.

Ginott's Principal Teachings

Ginott's small book was packed with valuable suggestions for teachers. First, he reminded teachers that learning always takes place in the present tense. By that, he meant that teachers must not prejudge students or hold grudges. He pointed out that learning is always a personal matter to the student. Teachers who have to work with large classes must remember that each student learner is an individual who must be treated as such. The key to working effectively with students is communication, and the style teachers should use is called **congruent communication,** which is communication that is harmonious with students' feelings about situations and themselves. The cardinal principle of congruent communication is that it addresses *situations,* not students' character or personality. Ginott emphasized that **teachers at their best,** using congruent communication, do not preach, moralize, impose guilt, or demand promises. Instead, they **confer dignity** on their students by treating them as social equals capable of making good decisions. On the other hand, **teachers at their worst** label students, belittle them, and denigrate their character. They usually do these things inadvertently.

Effective teachers **invite cooperation** from their students by describing the situation and indicating what needs to be done. They do not dictate to students or boss them around, which are acts that provoke resistance. Effective teachers have a **hidden asset** they call on, which is always to ask themselves, "How can I be most helpful to my students right now?" Most classroom difficulties are avoided when teachers employ that asset.

Ginott said teachers should feel free to express their anger and other feelings, but when doing so should use **I-messages** rather than **you-messages.** Using an I-message, the teacher might say, "I am very upset." Using a you-message, the teacher might say, "You are being very rude." Ginott said it is also wise to use **laconic language** when responding to or redirecting student misbehavior. *Laconic* means short and to the point, which describes the sort of responses Ginott advocated.

Ginott had a great deal to say about praise, and his contentions came as a surprise to most teachers. For example, he insisted that **evaluative praise** is worse than none at all and should never be used. An example of evaluative praise is, "Good boy for raising your hand." Instead of evaluative praise, which evaluates student character, teachers should use **appreciative praise** when responding to effort or improvement. This is praise in which the teacher shows appreciation for what the student has done, without directly evaluating the student's character or talent (e.g., "I can almost smell those pine trees in your drawing").

In personal relations with students, Ginnot asked teachers always to respect students' privacy. Teachers should never pry when students do not wish to discuss personal matters, but should show they are available should students want to talk. With regard to correcting inappropriate behavior, Ginott advised simply teaching students how to behave properly, instead of reprimanding them when they misbehave. Teachers should also assiduously avoid asking **why questions** when discussing behavior. Why questions make students feel guilty and defensive. Examples of why questions are, "Why did you speak to Susan that way?" and "Why didn't you get your homework done?"

Ginott also placed sanctions on sarcasm and punishment. Sarcasm is almost always dangerous and should not be used when discussing situations with students. Punishment should not be used at all in the classroom. It only produces hostility, rancor, and vengefulness, while never making students really want to improve.

As for teachers, they should continually strive for **self-discipline** in their work with students. They must be very careful not to display the behaviors they are trying to eradicate in students, such as raising their voice to end noise, acting rude toward students who are impolite, and berating students who have used inappropriate language.

Finally, according to Ginott, classroom discipline is attained gradually. It is a series of little victories in which the teacher, through self-discipline and helpfulness, promotes humaneness and self-control within students.

Review of Ginott's Contributions

Ginott maintained that the only true discipline is self-discipline, which all teachers should try to promote in students and in themselves. He made a number of especially helpful contributions concerning how teachers can communicate with students to foster positive relations while reducing and correcting misbehavior. He showed the importance of the teacher being self-controlled and, beyond that, the value of congruent communication, which is teacher communication that is harmonious with student feelings and self-perception.

Ginott urged teachers to use **sane messages** when addressing misbehavior, messages that focus calmly on what needs to be corrected without attacking the student's character or personality. He helped clarify his contentions by describing teachers at their best and at their worst, pointing out the positive effects that accrue from treating students considerately and helpfully and the negative effects that result when teachers lose self-control, berate students, or speak to them sarcastically. He cautioned educators that his suggestions would not produce instantaneous results. Guidance through communication had to be used repeatedly over time for its power to take effect. Although misbehavior can be squelched, **genuine discipline,** by which Ginott meant self-discipline, never occurs instantaneously, but rather in a series of small steps that result in genuine changes in student attitude.

Ginott's (1971) overall view on teaching and working with students is summarized in the following excerpt from *Teacher and Child:*

> As a teacher I have come to the frightening conclusion that I am the decisive element in the classroom. It is my personal approach that creates the climate. It is my daily mood that makes the weather. As a teacher I possess tremendous power to make a child's life miserable or joyous. I can be a tool of torture or an instrument of inspiration. I can humiliate or humor, hurt or heal. In all situations it is my response that decides whether a crisis will be escalated or de-escalated, and a child humanized or dehumanized. (p. 13)

It would be difficult to find a teacher who disagrees with Ginott's views on the value of communication and his suggestions concerning how it should be done. Indeed, his ideas are reiterated in virtually all of today's popular systems of discipline. Yet, teachers who have tried to use Ginott's suggestions as their total system of discipline have found something lacking. Teachers want their discipline system to be humane, but they also want it to put a quick stop to behavior that is offensive or disruptive. Ginott did not provide adequate suggestions to meet that need. His suggestions are more helpful in maintaining good relationships with students and providing encouragement than in dealing with students who are disruptive.

Rudolf Dreikurs: Discipline through Democratic Teaching

On the heels of the influential books by Jacob Kounin and Haim Ginott there appeared yet another great contribution to discipline, one by psychiatrist Rudolf Dreikurs that emphasized seeking out and dealing with underlying causes of misbehavior. Dreikurs formulated strategies for helping students acquire self-discipline based on understanding of its social value. Dreikurs taught that self-discipline could best be achieved within the context of a democratic classroom.

Dreikurs (1897–1972) was born in Vienna, Austria. After receiving his medical degree from the University of Austria, he entered into a long association with the renowned Austrian psychiatrist Alfred Adler, with whom he worked in family and child counseling. Dreikurs immigrated to the United States in 1937 and eventually became director of the Alfred Adler Institute in Chicago. He also served as professor of psychiatry at the Chicago Medical School. In keeping with his interest in child and family counseling, he turned his attention to misbehavior and discipline in school classrooms.

Dreikurs's Principal Teachings

Discipline at its best is seen in student **self-control,** based on social interest. Self-controlled students are able to show initiative, make reasonable decisions, and assume responsibility in ways that benefit themselves and others, thus improving the school experience for all concerned. Good discipline occurs best in a **democratic classroom,** one in which teacher and students work together to make decisions about how the class will function. Good discipline cannot occur in autocratic or permissive classrooms. In **autocratic classrooms,** the teacher makes all decisions and imposes them on students, leaving no opportunity for student initiative and responsibility. In **permissive classrooms,** the teacher fails to require that students comply with rules, conduct themselves humanely, or deal with the consequences for their misbehavior.

Almost all students have a primary and compelling desire to feel they are a valued member of the class and that they belong. This sense of belonging is the **genuine goal** of most school behavior. Students sense **belonging** when the teacher and others give them attention and respect, involve them in activities, and do not mistreat them. When students are unable to gain a sense of belonging in the class, they often turn to the **mistaken goals** of **attention-seeking, power seeking, revenge seeking,** and **inadequacy.** When seeking attention, students talk out, show off, interrupt others, and demand teacher attention. When seeking power, they drag their heels, make comments under their breath, and sometimes try to show that the teacher can't make them do anything. When seeking revenge, they try to get back at the teacher and other students by lying, subverting class activities, and maliciously disrupting the class. When displaying inadequacy, they withdraw from class activities and make no effort to learn.

Teachers should learn how to identify mistaken goals and deal with them. When teachers see evidence that students are pursuing mistaken goals, they should point out the fact by identifying the mistaken goal and discussing the faulty logic involved. They should do this in a friendly, nonthreatening manner. Dreikurs suggests calmly asking, "Do you need me to pay more attention to you?" or "Could it be that you want to show that I can't make you do the assignment?"

Rules for governing class behavior should be formulated jointly by teacher and students. **Logical consequences** for compliance or violation should be associated with those rules. Good behavior, shown in following the rules, brings pleasant consequences, such as enjoyment of learning and associating positively with others. Misbehavior brings unpleasant consequences, such as having to complete work at home or being excluded from normal class activities.

Punishment should never be used in the classroom. Punishment is a way for teachers to get back at students and show who's boss. It usually humiliates the student and has additional undesirable effects. It should therefore be replaced with logical consequences that have been agreed to by the class.

Review of Dreikurs's Contributions

Dreikurs contributed several valuable concepts and strategies, many of which are evident in today's most popular systems of discipline. He called self-discipline **true discipline,** and was the first to base his discipline scheme on the premise of **social interest,** that is, on students' seeing that their personal well-being is closely associated with what is good for the group. He was among the first to clarify how democratic teachers and democratic classrooms promote sound discipline. He was the first to pinpoint a prime goal (that of belonging) as an underlying motivator of student behavior, and to identify the mistaken goals of attention, power, revenge, and inadequacy that students turn to when unable to achieve the primary goal of belonging. He urged teachers to involve students jointly in formulating rules of class behavior and link those rules with logical consequences that occur as students comply with, or violate, the class rules.

Dreikurs also provided a number of more specific suggestions concerning how teachers should interact with students. He said teachers should never use punishment and should avoid using praise, which he felt made students dependent on teacher reactions. Instead of praise, Dreikurs would have teachers use **encouragement.** Praise, by its nature, is directed at the character of the student. Encouragement, by its nature, is directed at what the student does or can do. Instead of saying "You can certainly play the piano well," an enlightened teacher would say, "I notice a great deal of improvement," or "I can see you enjoy playing very much." Dreikurs gave considerable attention to how teachers should speak and relate with students. He made the following suggestions (Dreikurs and Cassel, 1972, pp. 51–54):

- Always speak in positive terms; never be negative.
- Encourage students to strive for improvement, not perfection.
- Emphasize student strengths while minimizing weaknesses.
- Help students learn from mistakes, which are valuable parts of the learning process.
- Encourage independence and the assumption of responsibility.

- Show faith in students; offer them help in overcoming obstacles.
- Encourage students to help each other.
- Show pride in students' work; display it and share it with others.
- Be optimistic and enthusiastic—a positive outlook is contagious.
- Use encouraging remarks, such as, "You have improved." "Can I help you?" "What did you learn from that mistake?"

Because Dreikurs contributed so much to discipline, it might seem strange that teachers did not adopt his approach wholeheartedly. Teachers like his ideas, but have found his system a bit daunting, too unwieldy to be implemented easily. They had trouble seeing the interconnections among democracy, prime motive, mistaken goals, social interest, and logical consequences. But most of all, they found it lacking in the ingredient they most wanted, namely, what do you do to put an immediate stop to student disruptions, aggression, and defiance?

Lee and Marlene Canter: Discipline through Assertive Tactics

In 1976, Lee Canter founded Canter & Associates. Their first product was a book titled *Assertive Discipline: A Take-Charge Approach for Today's Educator* (1976). In subsequent years, Canter & Associates provided a large quantity of materials and programs involving Assertive Discipline for educators and parents. They brought *Assertive Discipline* to millions of teachers and administrators worldwide. In 1998, Canter & Associates merged with Sylvan Learning Systems, which in 2003 made the decision to focus exclusively on postsecondary education. The company changed its name to Laureate Education, Incorporated, and no longer produces materials or provides workshops on Assertive Discipline.

The Canters' Principal Teachings

By 1978, Assertive Discipline was the most popular of all discipline systems, and it remained so for almost 20 years. The Canters described Assertive Discipline as an approach to help teachers take charge in the classroom by interacting with students in a calm, insistent, and consistent manner. They continually emphasized that **student rights** included learning in a calm, orderly classroom, and that **teacher rights** included teaching without interruptions. They expected school administrators and students' parents to support the system they advocated.

The Canters maintained that students choose to behave as they do—that nothing makes them do so against their will. Accordingly, their system attempted to establish an environment in which students would choose to behave in an acceptable manner. To make this possible, they attempted to ensure that students' and teachers' needs were met and that behavior was managed assertively but humanely. Further, they advocated the use of clear rules of classroom behavior. When students complied with those rules, the teacher applied positive consequences, such as recognition and praise. When students broke the rules, teachers applied negative consequences in accordance with a carefully structured hierarchy, which would ultimately involve consequences so distasteful that students would choose to comply with class rules. In later years, as more humane measures became popular, the Canters added suggestions for teaching students how to behave properly. They emphasized regularly giving students positive attention, talking helpfully with students who misbehaved, and establishing a sense of mutual trust and respect.

A primary reason for Assertive Discipline's early popularity was the Canters' insistence on the following: Teachers have the right to teach in a professional manner, without disruption. Students have the right to learn in a safe, calm environment, with full support. These rights are best met by take-charge teachers who allow nothing to violate students' best interests. These notions were extremely attractive during a time when students were generally beginning to behave atrociously, and teachers had no method, and no support, to make them do otherwise.

Central to Assertive Discipline was the concept of three contrasting types of teachers. **Hostile teachers** behave in a manner that makes it appear they view students as adversaries. They seem to feel that to maintain order and teach properly, they must keep the upper hand, which they attempt to do by laying down the law, accepting no nonsense, and using commands and stern facial expressions. They sometimes give needlessly strong admonishments, such as, "Sit down, shut up, and listen!" Such messages suggest a dislike for students and make students feel they are being treated unjustly.

Nonassertive teachers take an overly passive approach to students. They fail to help the class formulate reasonable expectations or are inconsistent in dealing with students, allowing certain behaviors one day while strongly disapproving them the next. They often make statements as, "For heaven's sake, please try to behave like ladies and gentlemen" or "How many times do I have to tell you no talking?" They come across as wishy-washy, and after a time, students stop taking them seriously. Yet, when those teachers become overly frustrated, they sometimes come down very hard on students. This inconsistency leaves students confused about expectations and enforcement.

Assertive teachers clearly, confidently, and consistently model and express class expectations. They work to build trust with the class. They teach students how to behave so they can better learn and relate to others, and they implement a discipline plan that encourages student cooperation. Such teachers help students understand which behaviors promote success and which lead to failure. Assertive teachers are not harsh taskmasters. They recognize students' needs for consistent limits on behavior, but at the same time are ever mindful of students' needs for warmth and encouragement. Because they know that students may require direct instruction in how to behave acceptably in the classroom, they might be heard to say, "Our rule is no talking without raising your hand. Please raise your hand and wait for me to call on you."

Each of the response styles produces certain effects on teachers and students. The **hostile response style** takes away most of the pleasure that teachers and students might otherwise enjoy in class. Its harshness curtails the development of trusting relationships and can produce negative student attitudes toward teachers and school. The **nonassertive response style** leads to student feelings of insecurity and frustration. Nonassertive teachers cannot get their needs met in the classroom, which produces high levels of stress for them. These teachers frequently become hostile toward chronically misbehaving students. Students in turn feel manipulated and many feel little respect for their teachers. The **assertive response style** provides several benefits that the other styles do not. Assertive teachers create a classroom atmosphere that allows both teacher and students to meet their needs. They invite student collaboration and help students practice acceptable behavior. Students learn they can count on their teacher to provide clear expectations, consistency, and an atmosphere of warmth and support. All this engenders a feeling of comfort for everyone and allows teaching and learning to flourish.

The operation of Assertive Discipline is understood through its details. The Canters urged teachers to make a written discipline plan that clarifies rules, positive recognition, and corrective actions. **Rules** state exactly how students are to behave. They should indicate observable behaviors, such as, "Keep your hands to yourself" rather than vague ideas, such as, "Show respect to other students." Rules should be limited in number (three to five) and refer only to behavior, not to academic issues.

Positive recognition refers to giving sincere personal attention to students who behave in keeping with class expectations. Positive recognition should be used frequently, as it tends to increase self-esteem, encourage good behavior, and build a positive classroom climate. Common ways of providing recognition include encouragement, expressing appreciation, and positive notes and phone calls to parents.

Corrective actions are applied when students interfere with other students' right to learn. Corrective actions are never harmful physically or psychologically, although they will usually be slightly unpleasant for students. The Canters stress that it is not severity that makes corrective actions effective, but rather consistency in application. When corrective actions must be invoked, students are reminded that, by their behavior, they have chosen the consequence. Teachers usually don't like to invoke corrective actions, but the Canters remind us that we fail our students when we allow them to disrupt or misbehave without showing we care enough to limit their unacceptable behavior.

When misbehavior occurs, it should be dealt with calmly and quickly. The Canters advised making a **discipline hierarchy** that lists corrective actions and the order in which they will be imposed within the day. Each day or secondary class period begins afresh. Each consequence in the hierarchy is a bit more unpleasant than its predecessor. The Canters (1993, p. 85) illustrate the discipline hierarchy with the following examples:

- *First time a student disrupts.* Consequence: "Bobby, our rule is no shouting out. That's a warning."
- *Second or third time the student disrupts.* Consequence: "Bobby, our rule is no shouting out. You have chosen 5 minutes time-out at the back table."
- *Fourth time the student disrupts.* Consequence: "Bobby, you know our rules about shouting out. You have chosen to have your parents called." The teacher informs Bobby's parents. This is done by telephone and is especially effective if Bobby is required to place the call and explain what has happened.

- *Fifth time the student disrupts.* Consequence: "Bobby, our rule is no shouting out. You have chosen to go to the office to talk with the principal about your behavior."
- *Severe clause.* Sometimes behavior is so severe that it is best to invoke the *severe clause,* in which the student is sent to the principal on the first offense. Consequence: "Bobby, fighting is not allowed in this class. You have chosen to go to the principal immediately. We will talk about this later."

To employ the discipline hierarchy effectively, teachers must keep track of offenses that students commit. This can be done by recording on a clipboard students' names and the number of violations. Other options include recording this information in the plan book or, in primary grades, using a system of colored cards that students turn or change after each violation.

The Canters stressed that in order to make a discipline plan work effectively, teachers must teach the plan to their students. It is not enough only to read it aloud or display it on a poster. The Canters provided a number of sample lessons showing how the plan could be taught at different grade levels. The plans followed this sequence:

1. Explain why rules are needed.
2. Teach the specific rules.
3. Check for understanding.
4. Explain how you will reward students who follow rules.
5. Explain why there are corrective actions for breaking the rules.
6. Teach the corrective actions and how they are applied.
7. Check again for understanding.

When the discipline program is first implemented, students are clearly informed of positive recognition and negative corrective actions associated with class rules, and they may participate in role-played situations involving both. They realize that negative corrective actions naturally follow misbehavior. The Canters make these suggestions for invoking negative corrective actions:

- Provide corrective actions calmly in a matter-of-fact manner: "Nathan, speaking like that to others is against our rules. You have chosen to stay after class."
- Be consistent: Provide a consequence every time students choose to disrupt.
- Find the first opportunity after a student receives a consequence to recognize that student's positive behavior: "Nathan, I appreciate how you are working. You are making a good choice."
- Provide an escape mechanism for students who are upset and want to talk about what happened: Allow the student to describe feelings or the situation in a journal or log.

- When a younger student continues to disrupt, move in: Nathan again speaks hurtfully to another student. The teacher moves close to Nathan and quietly and firmly tells him his behavior is inappropriate. She reminds him of the corrective actions he has already received and of the next consequence in the hierarchy.
- When an older student continues to disrupt, move out: Marta once again talks during work time. The teacher asks Marta to step outside the classroom, where she reminds Marta of the inappropriate behavior and possible corrective actions. All the while, the teacher stays calm, shows respect for Marta's feelings, and refrains from arguing.

The Canters concluded that these techniques help almost all students behave in a responsible manner, but they recognize that a few students require additional consideration. Those are the difficult-to-handle students who the Canters (1993, p. 6) describe as "students who are continually disruptive, persistently defiant, demanding of attention or unmotivated. They are the students who defy your authority and cause you stress, frustration and anger." These students are not pleasant to work with, but they are most in need of attention and adult guidance. The Canters suggest making special efforts to (1) reach out to difficult students by trying to establish trust, (2) meet the special needs of difficult students that are not being met in school, and (3) take pains to find ways of communicating more with difficult students.

As time passed, other discipline systems appeared that called for humane cooperation and increased student responsibility in the classroom. Assertive Discipline gave way to the newer approaches to discipline and by the end of the twentieth century, it had largely disappeared from the educational picture, although remnants still form parts of many of the newer discipline systems.

Review of the Canters' Contributions to Discipline

The Canters made several major contributions to classroom discipline. They popularized the concept of rights in the classroom—the rights of students to have teachers help them learn in a calm, safe environment and the rights of teachers to teach without disruption. They explained that students need and want limits that assist their proper conduct and that it is the teacher's responsibility to set and enforce those limits. The Canters were the first to insist that teachers have a right to backing from administrators and cooperation from parents in helping students behave acceptably, and also the first to provide teachers with a workable procedure for correcting misbehavior efficiently through a system of easily administered corrective actions. Over the years, the Canters continually modified their popular approach to ensure that it remained effective as social realities change. Earlier, they focused mainly on teachers' being strong leaders in the classroom, but later moved to greater emphasis on building trusting, helpful relationships with students, providing positive recognition and support, and taking a proactive approach to dealing with problems of behavior.

KEY TERMS AND CONCEPTS EMPHASIZED IN THIS CHAPTER

The following terms and concepts are pivotal in the contentions of pioneers in modern discipline and appear frequently in systems of discipline now in use.

From Redl and Wattenberg's Group Dynamics
group dynamics
student roles
teacher roles
supporting student
  self-control
situational assistance
appraising reality
punishment

From Skinner's Behavior Shaping
behavior modification
shaping behavior
constant reinforcement
intermittent reinforcement
successive approximations
punishment

From Kounin's Lesson and Group Management
withitness
overlapping
group alerting
momentum
smoothness
satiation

From Ginott's Discipline through Communication
congruent communication
teachers at their best
confer dignity
teachers at their worst
invite cooperation
hidden asset
I-messages
you-messages
laconic language
evaluative praise
appreciative praise
why questions
self-discipline
sane messages
genuine discipline

From Dreikurs's Discipline through Democratic Teaching
self-control
democratic classroom
autocratic classroom
permissive classroom
genuine goal of behavior
belonging
mistaken goals
attention-seeking

power seeking
revenge seeking
inadequacy
logical consequences
punishment
true discipline
social interest
encouragement

From the Canters' Assertive Discipline
student rights
teacher rights
hostile teachers
nonassertive teachers
assertive teachers
hostile response style
nonassertive response style
assertive response style
rules
positive recognition
corrective actions
discipline hierarchy

QUESTIONS AND ACTIVITIES

1. Enter into your journal items of information from this chapter that are pertinent to the five guiding principles for building a personal system of discipline.

2. It was noted that except for Assertive Discipline, none of the discipline systems described in this chapter found widespread use *as a total system*. What do you understand to be the reason for this, given the number of excellent suggestions they contain?

3. Of the approaches reviewed in this chapter, which seemed most useful to you? Which seemed least useful? Why?

4. Despite the presence today of many effective systems of discipline, some teachers still try to maintain discipline by out-shouting their students, speaking sarcastically, and treating students disrespectfully. Why do you believe they persist with these tactics? How effective do you think these tactics are with today's students?

REFERENCES

Canter, L., and Canter, M. 1976. *Assertive Discipline: A take-charge approach for today's educator.* Seal Beach, CA: Lee Canter & Associates. The second and third editions of the book, published in 1992 and 2001, are titled *Assertive Discipline: Positive behavior management for today's classroom.*

Canter, L., and Canter, M. 1993. *Succeeding with difficult students: New strategies for reaching your most challenging students.* Santa Monica, CA: Lee Canter & Associates.

Dreikurs, R., and Cassel, P. 1972/1995. *Discipline without tears.* New York: Penguin-NAL.

Ginott, H. 1971. *Teacher and child.* New York: Macmillan.

Ginott, H. 1972. I am angry! I am appalled! I am furious! *Today's Education, 61,* 23–24.

Ginott, H. 1973. Driving children sane. *Today's Education, 62,* 20–25.

Kounin, J. 1971. *Discipline and group management in classrooms.* New York: Holt, Rinehart & Winston. Reissued in 1977.

Redl, F., and Wattenberg, W. 1951. *Mental hygiene in teaching.* New York: Harcourt, Brace & World. Revised and reissued in 1959.

Skinner, B. 1953. *Science and human behavior.* New York: Macmillan.

Skinner, B. 1954. The science of learning and the art of teaching. *Harvard Educational Review, 24,* 86–97.

Skinner, B. 1971. *Beyond freedom and dignity.* New York: Knopf.

CHAPTER 5

Three Bridges to Twenty-First-Century Discipline

Authoritative Input
- William Glasser / Choice Theory
- Thomas Gordon / Self-Discipline
- Alfie Kohn / Beyond Discipline

CHAPTER PREVIEW

In Chapter 4 we saw how discipline changed during the last half of the twentieth century. It went from teacher authoritarianism to a more benign and humane relationship between teachers and students. Further significant changes were occurring as the twentieth century merged into the twenty-first. Those changes reflected the strong influence of three persons of note—William Glasser, Thomas Gordon, and Alfie Kohn—who provided bridges between older approaches to discipline and newer concepts that brought students into ever closer cooperation with teachers, where both play roles in working together for the benefit of the class as a whole. The primary concepts contributed by those authorities were *Choice Theory,* formulated and popularized by William Glasser, *Tactics of Communication,* emphasized by Thomas Gordon, and *Classrooms as Communities,* formalized and popularized by Alfie Kohn. Glasser's Choice Theory moved toward meeting students' predominant needs while striving for overall quality in teaching and learning. Gordon's communication tactics focused on influencing students rather than making demands on them. And Kohn's Classrooms as Communities helped teachers establish in their classes "communities of learners" where cooperation and helpfulness predominate. Those three approaches established trends so well-received that they now play strongly in almost all systems of discipline. Here, we explore the nature of those approaches and the practices they advocate.

Part 1. William Glasser
DISCIPLINE GUIDED BY CHOICE THEORY

Glasser on Student Needs, Quality, and Choice Theory

Glasser says that most classroom misbehavior occurs when students are bored or frustrated by class expectations, conditions that occur when students' basic needs are not being met in school. Glasser identified five prime **student needs** that the school must meet if students are to flourish—needs he called survival, belonging, power, fun, and freedom. Curriculum and instruction must be aimed at meeting those needs, Glasser insisted, and teaching should be done in a leading manner, using noncoercive techniques, rather than a bossing manner. Throughout the process, teachers should give prime emphasis to quality in teaching, learning, and curriculum.

Meeting Students' Needs

Glasser says education that does not give major attention to meeting students' **basic needs** is bound to fail. Meeting **basic student needs** is not difficult. Need for survival is met by keeping the school environment safe and free from personal threat. Need for

About William Glasser

William Glasser, a psychiatrist and educational consultant, has for many years written and spoken extensively on issues related to education and discipline. He achieved early acclaim for his 1965 book, *Reality Therapy: A New Approach to Psychiatry,* which shifted the focus in treating personal problems in people's lives from earlier events to present realities. Not long after the appearance of that book, Glasser applied his ideas to schooling. His work with juvenile offenders convinced him that teachers could help students make better personal choices that would result in better behavior in the classroom. He explained those views in *Schools without Failure* (1969), extolled as one of the twentieth century's most influential books in education. In 1986, Glasser added yet another facet to school discipline with his contention that for students to learn properly in school, they must "believe that if they do some work, they will be able to satisfy their needs enough so that it makes sense to keep working" (1986, p. 15). Since that time, Glasser has focused on meeting students' basic needs as the primary means of ensuring class participation and desirable behavior. He first called his new approach "Control Theory," but now calls it "Choice Theory." His ideas on teaching and discipline are presented in his books *Choice Theory in the Classroom* (1998a), *The Quality School: Managing Students without Coercion* (1998b), *The Quality School Teacher* (1998c), and *Every Student Can Succeed* (2001), which Glasser says will be his last book in education. The Glasser website is www.wglasser.com.

belonging is met by involving students in class matters and seeing they receive attention and recognition from teachers and others. Need for power is met by giving students responsible tasks to carry out in the class and allowing them to participate in making decisions about curriculum, activities, and class procedures. Need for fun is met by allowing students to work and talk with others, engage in interesting activities, and share their accomplishments. And the need for freedom is met by allowing students to make choices concerning what they will study and how they will demonstrate their accomplishments.

Choice Theory in the Classroom

When students like the topics being studied, and thus want to learn more about them, they almost always do well and rarely misbehave seriously. Glasser says educators have traditionally assumed, erroneously, that "external control" (what we do to students or for them) is teachers' most reliable means of motivating students to learn. That assumption is incorrect, he maintains, for two reasons: First, students will do what is most satisfying to them at any given time, if they can. Second, the key to genuine motivation in school lies in **Choice Theory,** which acknowledges that we cannot control anyone's behavior except our own, and cannot successfully make a student do anything. What we can do instead is help students envision a quality existence in school and plan the choices that lead to it. From that vision come student involvement and responsible behavior.

Quality Curriculum

Glasser claims that the present-day school curriculum contains two major flaws in design. The first flaw lies in too much emphasis on memorizing facts that are irrelevant to students' lives. The second major flaw lies in judging the quality of education on the basis of how many fragments of information students can retain long enough to be measured on tests. He says the best way to improve schools is to convert them into places where students learn useful information and learn it well. To make that possible, a **quality curriculum** is needed that consists of topics students find enjoyable and useful. The rest of the typical curriculum should be discarded as "nonsense" (Glasser, 1992).

The quality of the curriculum becomes evident when teachers introduce new topics for learning. Done properly, teachers should hold discussions with students and, if the students are old enough, ask them to identify what they would like to explore in depth. Adequate time should then be spent on instruction that helps students learn the identified topics well. **Quality learning,** which leads to **quality education,** is made evident in depth of understanding, together with a good grasp of its usefulness. Learning a smaller number of topics very well is always preferable to covering many topics superficially. To evaluate the quality of learning, educators should ask students to explain why the material they have learned is valuable and how and where it can be used. As part of the process, students should be asked regularly to assess the quality of their own efforts.

Quality Teaching

Quality teaching is as important in education as a quality curriculum. Glasser (1993, p. 22 ff) says teachers can furnish high-quality instruction by providing the following:

- *A warm, supportive classroom climate.* Help students know and like you. Use natural occasions to tell students who you are, what you stand for, what you will and will not ask them to do, and what you will and will not do for them. Show you are always willing to help.
- *"Lead teaching" rather than "boss teaching."* Use methods that encourage students and draw them out. Don't try to force information into them.
- *School work that is useful.* Useful work centers on knowledge and skills that are useful in students' lives. At times you may have to point out the value of new learning, but that value must become quickly apparent to students or they will not make a sustained effort to learn. Students should not be required to memorize information beyond what is essential for the skill being learned. Criteria for judging the suitability of new material include (1993, p. 48):
  1. The information is directly related to an important skill.
  2. The information is something that students express a desire to learn.
  3. The information is something the teacher believes especially useful.
  4. The information is required for college entrance exams.
- *Encouragement for students to do the best they can.* The process of doing quality work develops slowly and must be nurtured. Glasser (1998b) advises teachers to do the following: Discuss quality work enough so that students understand what you mean. Begin with an assignment that is clearly important enough to do well. Ask students to do their best work on the assignment. Do not grade their work because grades suggest to students that the work is finished.
- *Opportunity for students to evaluate work they have done and improve it.* Quality usually accrues by means of modifications to the work through continued effort. When students feel they have completed a piece of work, ask them to make value judgments about it, in which they explain why the work shows high quality and how they think it might be improved further. As students strive to improve their work still further, quality results occur naturally. In this process, teachers can progressively help students learn to use **SIR,** a process of self-evaluation, improvement, and repetition, until quality is achieved.

More on Lead Teaching

Glasser says that teachers must move away from "boss teaching" and replace it with "lead teaching." **Boss teachers,** as Glasser describes them, set the tasks and standards for student learning. They talk rather than demonstrate and rarely ask for student input. They grade the work without involving students in the evaluation. They use coercion to try to make students comply with expectations.

Lead teachers work differently. They understand that genuine motivation to learn resides within students, in the form of needs and interests. They spend most of their time organizing interesting activities and providing assistance. They discuss the curriculum with the class in such a way that many topics of interest are identified, then they encourage students to identify topics they would like to explore in depth. They discuss with students the kind of schoolwork that might ensue, emphasizing quality. They explore resources that might be needed for **quality schoolwork** and the amount of time such work might require. When necessary, they demonstrate how the work can be done, using samples of work that reflect quality. They make it clear they will do all they can to provide students good tools and a workplace that is noncoercive and nonadversarial.

Standards of Conduct

Within this approach to quality, Glasser urges teachers to work together with students to establish class standards of conduct. He advises beginning with a discussion of the importance of quality work and assuring students that everything possible will be done to help them learn and enjoy themselves. That discussion leads naturally to asking students about class behavior that will help them get their work done in a satisfactory manner. Glasser says that if teachers can get students to see the importance of courtesy, no other rules may be necessary.

Teachers should also involve students in determining what should happen when behavior agreements are broken. Students usually suggest punishment, even though they know punishment does not actually make them want to behave better. If asked further, they will conclude that behavior problems are best solved by looking for ways to remedy whatever is causing the rule to be broken. Glasser urges teachers to ask, "What could I do to help?" Once agreements and consequences are established, they should be put in writing and all students should sign the resultant document, attesting that they understand the agreements and that, if they break them, they will, with the teacher's help, do their best to remedy the underlying problem.

When Behavior Agreements Are Broken

When rules the class has agreed on are violated, the teacher must intervene, but in a nonpunitive manner that stops the misbehavior and gets the student's mind back on class work. Suppose that Jonathan has come into the room obviously upset. As the lesson begins, he turns heatedly and throws something at Michael. Glasser suggests the following as an appropriate teacher response:

> **Teacher:** It looks like you have a problem, Jonathan. How can I help you solve it? (Jonathan frowns, still obviously upset.)

> **Teacher:** If you will calm down, I will discuss it with you in a little while. I think we can work something out.

If Jonathan doesn't calm down, you should make it clear you cannot help him until he does so. Indicate this without emotion in your voice. Glasser (1990) says to allow him 20 seconds, and if he isn't calm by then, simply acknowledge that there is no way to solve the problem at that time. Give Jonathan time-out from the lesson, but don't threaten or warn him.

> **Teacher:** Jonathan, I want to help you work this out. I am not interested in punishing you. Whatever the problem is, let's solve it. But for now you must go sit at the table. When you are calm, come back to your seat.

Later, at an opportune time, discuss the situation with Jonathan:

> **Teacher:** What were you doing when the problem started? Was it against the rules? Can we work things out so it won't happen again? What could you and I do to keep it from happening?

If the problem involves hostilities between Jonathan and Michael, the discussion should involve both boys and proceed along these lines:

> **Teacher:** What were you doing, Jonathan? What were you doing, Michael? How can the three of us work things out so this won't happen anymore?

Don't assign blame to either Jonathan or Michael or spend time trying to determine whose fault it was. Remind the boys you are only looking for a solution so the problem won't occur again. If you treat Jonathan and Michael courteously, if you show you don't want to punish or throw your weight around, and if you talk to them as a problem solver, their classroom behavior and class work will improve.

Seven Deadly Habits and Seven Connecting Habits

Teachers can be seen, at various times, to use **seven deadly habits** in trying to control student behavior. Those habits are called "deadly" because they damage caring relationships with students. The habits are criticizing, blaming, complaining, nagging, threatening, punishing, and rewarding. To maintain good relationships with your students and gain their willing cooperation, you must put those deadly habits aside and replace them with tactics that increase a sense of connection with students. Glasser identifies seven **connecting habits** that serve teachers well—caring, listening, supporting, contributing, encouraging, trusting, and befriending. Glasser believes all students who come to school can do competent work, provided teachers connect with them strongly.

Establishing Quality Classrooms

To enjoy the benefits of a quality classroom, here is what you need to do.

- *Habits.* Assiduously avoid the seven deadly habits when working with students. Replace them with connecting habits.
- *Your message.* "We are in this class together. I want to help you become competent or go beyond. My job is to teach you and help you learn, not to find out what you don't know and punish you for not knowing it. If you have a question, ask me. If you need more time, I'll give it to you. If you have an idea how to do what we are trying to do better, tell me. I'll listen" (Glasser, 2001, p. 113).

- *Friendships.* Instead of telling students what they must do and not do, endeavor to befriend all of them. Say, "I think an important part of my job is to do all I can to make sure you have a good time learning. You have to come to school and no one's going to pay you for doing schoolwork. So the least I can do is make this class fun for both you and me. I think we can learn a lot and still have a very good time" (Glasser, 2001, p. 54). From that time forward, use the seven connecting habits.

- *Class rules.* Rely on one fundamental rule of behavior—the Golden Rule. You may think of it simply as "courtesy." Discuss the concept with students. A few other rules may occasionally be necessary, but the Golden Rule is fundamental to all others.

- *Intervening.* Do away with traditional discipline (applying external control) and replace it with talking and listening to students whenever you sense impending trouble. Listen carefully. Inject humor into the situation if you can, without making light of students' concerns or giving the impression you consider their concerns frivolous.

- *Knowledge.* Assure students you will not ask them to learn anything that is not useful to them, and when there is doubt, you will explain clearly the benefits of the new learning. There will be no memorizing just for the sake of remembering.

- *Competency.* Tell students you have a way of teaching in which everyone can do competent work and everyone will make good grades (meaning a grade of B or better). Explain that you will ask students to work at any given assignment until they have brought it to a competent level. Nobody will fail or receive a low grade. They can use any resources available to help them, including textbooks, parents, and other students. The primary objective is to do competent work.

- *Quality.* Often encourage students to work for still higher quality. This means working at assignments until they have been brought up to the A level.

- *Tests.* Use tests as much as you want. Teach students using your best techniques, then give them a test. Explain that tests are for learning only. Since memorization is not emphasized, use short essay or multiple choice tests. Promise students no one will fail or receive a bad grade. When they have completed the test, have them go back over it and correct any incorrect or incomplete answers. Ask them to explain why the correction is better. Give them the time and help needed to get everything right.

- *Understanding and using.* Always have students use the information and skills being taught. Ask them to share and discuss new learnings with parents and guardians.

- *For older students.* Explain that you will teach and test for educational competence. This will involve using new knowledge when speaking, listening, reading, writing, and problem solving. This is done to improve and strengthen knowledge.

- *Competence.* Students who complete their work competently are given the option of helping other students or working to achieve still higher quality.

Part 2. Thomas Gordon
DISCIPLINE THROUGH INNER SELF-CONTROL

Gordon on Influence Techniques and Helping Skills

Gordon believed classroom discipline is best accomplished by helping students acquire an inner sense of **self-control.** He insisted that teachers can no longer rely on the traditional intervention techniques of power-based authority, reward and punishment, and win–lose conflict resolution. About reward and punishment, Gordon (1989) wrote:

> Using rewards to try to control children's behavior is so common that its effectiveness is rarely questioned. . . . the fact that rewards are used so often and unsuccessfully by so many teachers and parents proves they don't work very well. . . . (pp. 37–38)

Gordon urged teachers to replace reward and punishment with **noncontrolling methods,** such as modifying the environment to reduce student misbehavior; sending I-messages that do not set off coping mechanisms in response to power; practicing the no-lose method of conflict resolution; acknowledging feelings and perceptions; actively listening to students; and avoiding roadblocks to communication, such as giving orders, warning, preaching, advising, lecturing, criticizing, name-calling, analyzing, praising, reassuring, questioning, and withdrawing.

The development of student self-control is possible in the classroom, but only if teachers give up their "controlling" power over students. As Gordon (1989) put it:

> You acquire more influence with young people when you give up using your power to control them . . . [and] the more you use power to control people, the less real influence you'll have over their lives. (p. 7)

About Thomas Gordon

Clinical psychologist Thomas Gordon (1918–2002) was founder and, until his death, head of Gordon Training International, one of the largest human relations training organizations in the world. He was a pioneer in the teaching of human relations skills and conflict resolution to parents, teachers, youth, and managers of organizations. Well over two million people have taken advantage of his training programs worldwide. Gordon authored a number of books, including *Parent Effectiveness Training* (1970), *Teacher Effectiveness Training* (1974), *Leader Effectiveness Training* (1977), and *Discipline That Works: Promoting Self-Discipline in Children* (1989). In 1999 Gordon received the American Psychological Foundation's Gold Medal Award for Enduring Contributions to Psychology in the Public Interest. Gordon Training International can be contacted at www.gordontraining.com.

However, permissiveness in dealing with students is just as bad as authoritarianism. The desired middle ground is reached when teachers help students make positive decisions, become more self-reliant, and take control of their own behavior.

I-Messages and You-Messages

Gordon strongly believed that teacher effectiveness is greatly enhanced when teachers use I-messages rather than you-messages for expressing their needs and feelings to students. **I-messages** state how teachers personally think or feel about situations and behavior. The following is an example of an I-message: "I am having trouble concentrating because there is so much noise in the room."

You-messages, on the other hand, are statements of blame leveled at students' behavior. They activate students' coping mechanisms (flee, fight, submit), with counterproductive results. This is an example of a you-message: "You girls are making too much noise. You need to quiet down."

Gordon's Plan for Discipline

Gordon's plan for classroom discipline involves six major elements: (1) influence rather than control, (2) preventive skills, (3) determining **who owns the problem**, (4) confrontive skills, (5) helping skills, and (6) no-lose conflict resolution. These elements, their functions, and their implementation are explained in the following paragraphs.

Influence Rather than Control

The more you try to control students, the less you are able to exert **positive influence** on them. Control activates students' **coping mechanisms,** which are: *fighting* (combating the person with whom they have the conflict), *taking flight* (trying to escape the situation), and *submitting* (giving in to the other person). Coping mechanisms cut off communication and willingness to cooperate. Teachers should use noncontrolling methods to influence student behavior. Presently we will see how this is done.

Preventive Skills

Teachers can do three things to prevent most discipline problems: Use preventive I-messages, set rules collaboratively with students, and use participative management. **Preventive I-messages** influence students' future actions. Unenlightened teachers might say, "You didn't show the level of responsibility I hoped for yesterday. You are going to have to do better than that today." This message is ineffective because it carries blame. A more effective message would be: "We are now ready to work in our new groups. I need to feel sure that I have helped everyone remember to do their part responsibly." **Collaborative rule setting** means students and teachers collaborate in deciding how they will conduct themselves in the classroom and in formulating a set of rules for class behavior. **Participatory classroom management** refers to teachers sharing power with students in making decisions about class matters such as rules, room arrangement, seating, preferred activities, and the like. This style of management motivates students, gives them greater confidence and self-esteem, and encourages them to take risks and behave responsibly.

Discipline and Who Owns the Problem

Gordon (1976) explained that **misbehavior** is behavior that "produces *undesirable consequences for the adult*" (p. 107, italics added). In the classroom, it is the teacher who usually experiences and is made uncomfortable by the "badness" in student behavior. Because the effect is experienced mainly by the teacher, the teacher is said to own the problem. At other times, students may own the problem. For example, when Kyla feels the other girls in the class have slighted her, she becomes upset and morose, but when only Kyla is affected, she owns the problem, not the teacher or other students. This differentiation is important in Gordon's plan because discipline techniques (confrontive skills and helping skills) are applied in accordance with who owns the problem.

Confrontive Skills

When the *teacher owns the problem* (is upset by student behavior), he or she employs confrontive discipline skills, from among the following:

1. *Modifying the physical environment (rather than the student).* Teachers can often eliminate or minimize behavior problems by enriching the environment or minimizing its distractions. They might play quiet background music during certain activities, enrich the room with learning centers and colorful posters, and display student murals about the topic being studied. If these effects are too distracting for some students, teachers can provide an area without displays or have study carrels for students who sometimes need a more subdued atmosphere.

2. *Sending I-messages regularly.* When teachers are upset, they should express their feelings through I-messages instead of through scolding. Complete I-messages communicate three things that do not activate students' coping mechanisms: (1) the behavior that is presenting a problem for the teacher, (2) what the teacher is feeling about the behavior, and (3) why the behavior is causing a problem. For example, Mrs. Watson might say, "When class rules are broken, as they are now, I feel upset because that keeps us from getting our work done, and because it shows a lack of consideration for others." Or, "When I have to wait too long for quiet and readiness, I have to rush through the directions, and then I have to spend more time repeating myself because the directions are not clear. Do you have any suggestions that might help me with this problem?" As we have seen, I-messages contrast with you-messages that carry heavy judgments and put-downs, evident in statement such as, "You've been very careless with this work" or "You shouldn't tattle like that" or "Can't you follow a simple direction?"

3. *Shifting gears.* Sometimes teachers' I-messages provoke defensive responses from students. When this happens, it is important that the teacher listen sensitively to the

resistance and change from a sending/assertive posture to a posture of listening/understanding, a change that causes students to react more positively. Gordon calls this change shifting gears. When Mr. Johnson sends a confrontive I-message to Marcos about his irregular attendance, such as "I am very bothered, Marcos, when any of my students miss class," Marcos heatedly responds, "School is not the only thing. I have responsibilities at home. I can't help missing class sometimes." Shifting gears, Mr. Johnson replies, "It sounds like you have some difficult things to deal with outside of school. Is there anything I can do to help?"

Helping Skills

When *the student owns the problem,* teachers are advised to use two main helping skills: listening and avoiding communication roadblocks. Listening skills enable teachers to acknowledge students' concerns without trying to solve them. Gordon described four kinds of listening skills—*passive listening, acknowledgment responses, door openers,* and *active listening.* **Passive listening** consists of little more than attentive silence, but is often enough to encourage students to talk about what is bothering them. The teacher shows attention through posture, proximity, eye contact, and alertness. Mr. Aragon demonstrates this skill when he sits down beside Julian as the boy begins to speak of difficulties at home. *Acknowledgment responses* can be verbal ("uh-huh," "I see") or nonverbal (nods, smiles and frowns, and other body movements). They demonstrate the teacher's interest and attention. **Door openers** invite students to discuss their problems. When the student needs encouragement, the teacher may say, "Would you like to talk about it?" or "It sounds like you have something to say about that." These comments are nonjudgmental and open ended, and because they are nonthreatening, they invite the student to talk. Sensing that Eduardo is distressed about the math assignment, Mr. Sutton says, "I think there might be something bothering you about this assignment, Eduardo. Would you like to talk about it?" **Active listening** is a process of mirroring back what students are saying. It confirms that the teacher is attentive and understands the student's message. No judgment or evaluation is made. The teacher might say, "You've been late to class this week because you've been working the closing shift at the restaurant, and that makes you so tired you sleep through your alarm."

Avoiding communication roadblocks is a major requirement in communicating effectively with students. Gordon went to some lengths to help teachers recognize and avoid the following **communication roadblocks**: giving orders, warning, preaching, advising, lecturing, criticizing, name calling, analyzing, praising, reassuring, questioning, and withdrawing. At Del's middle school, for example, all students are required to take physical education. Del, who is very self-conscious about his weight, detests physical education and has been offering various excuses for not participating.

When *giving orders,* a teacher says to Del, "You might as well stop complaining about things you can't control. Go ahead and get ready now." A more effective response might be, "Do you see any way I might be able to make this easier for you?"

When *warning,* the teacher threatens Del, "That's enough. Change into your PE clothes now, or I'll have you running laps." A more effective response might be, "I can see this matter is bothering you a great deal. Would you like to discuss it after school?"

When *preaching,* the teacher reminds Del of "shoulds" and "oughts": "You should try to get yourself in shape." "You ought to know that exercise is important." A more effective response might be "Some people like to exercise, and others don't, but everyone needs it. How do you think we might help you get the exercise you need?"

When *advising,* the teacher offers Del suggestions or gives solutions: "If you feel you can't keep up with the others, try setting your own personal goal and work to meet it." A more effective response might be "Sometimes even good athletes don't like PE classes. Have you heard any of them discuss their feelings?"

When *lecturing,* the teacher presents logical facts to counter Del's resistance: "I can assure you that if you develop a habit for exercise now, you will be pleased and will carry it with you for the rest of your life." A more effective response might be "Sometimes it is certainly tempting to stop exercising and just sit out the class. If you do, what effect do you think it might have on your health?"

When *criticizing,* the teacher points out Del's faults and inadequacies: "I can't believe you just said that. That's nothing but excuse making." A more effective response might be "I think I'm beginning to understand what you are saying. Could you tell me a bit more about that?"

When *name calling,* the teacher labels or makes fun of Del: "I might expect third graders to argue about dressing out for PE, but aren't you a bit large for third grade?" A more effective response might be "Frankly, I haven't fully understood why you are reluctant. Can you help me understand a bit better?"

When *analyzing,* the teacher diagnoses or interprets Del's behavior: "What you are really saying is that you are afraid others will laugh about your weight." A more effective response might be "Go ahead with that thought. Can you explain it further?"

When *praising,* the teacher uses positive statements and praise to encourage Del: "You have above-average coordination. You'll handle yourself well out there." A more effective response might be "I understand your concern. What might I do to make physical education more pleasant for you?"

When *reassuring,* the teacher tries to make Del feel better by offering sympathy and support: "I know how you feel. Remember, there are a lot of boys just like you. You will forget your concerns after a while." A more effective response might be "Have you known other students with concerns like yours? How did they deal with them?"

When *questioning,* the teacher probes and questions Del for more facts: "What exactly are you afraid of? What do you think is going to happen?" A more effective response might be, "We often anticipate the worst, don't we? Have you had other experiences like this that troubled you?"

When *withdrawing,* the teacher changes the subject in order to avoid Del's concerns: "Whose team do you want to be on?" A more effective response might be "Do you think this matter might be bothering others, too? Do you think I should talk to the class about it, or should we keep it between us?"

No-Lose Conflict Resolution

One of Gordon's greatest contributions to discipline is his concept of the **no-lose method of conflict resolution,** which is now often called win-win conflict resolution. This procedure has been adopted by most other authorities in discipline. Its power lies in helping disputants reach agreements that satisfy both parties. When Samuel and Joaquin get in an angry scuffle, the teacher takes them aside and asks sincerely, "I wonder what we might do so you boys won't feel like fighting any more?" The discussion is aimed at finding a solution that prevents either boy from feeling he has been unjustly treated or has "lost" the dispute. No power is applied by the teacher; hence, egos are preserved and relations remain undamaged.

This no-lose approach contrasts with the more common procedure in which one side emerges as winner and the other as loser, sometimes with undesirable effects for both. For example, if Samuel and Joaquin scuffle and Samuel is ordered to apologize to Joaquin, the conflict may seem to have been resolved. It is not resolved properly, however, because Samuel feels wronged and humiliated and therefore declines to cooperate for a time with Joaquin or the teacher.

Part 3. Alfie Kohn
BEYOND DISCIPLINE

Kohn on Classrooms as Communities

Kohn's main emphasis has been on developing caring, supportive classrooms in which students are able to pursue topics of interest in depth. For this to happen, students must be able to participate fully in class matters, including solving problems that affect all class members. Kohn has roundly criticized teaching and discipline that do things *to* students rather than *involving* students as partners in the process. Particularly scathing have been his attacks on discipline that involves reward and punishment. He says that not only does nothing of value come from such discipline, the process is actually counterproductive for two reasons: First, it produces side effects such as mistrust, avoidance, and working for rewards only. Second, it causes students to mistrust their own judgment and hinders their becoming caring and self-reliant.

Kohn's solution is to transform school and classrooms into **learning communities.** By *community* Kohn (2001) means

> . . . a place in which students feel cared about and are encouraged to care about each other. They experience a sense of being valued and respected; the children matter to one another

About Alfie Kohn

Alfie Kohn, a former teacher, is now a full-time writer and lecturer. He has several influential books to his credit, including *Punished by Rewards: The Trouble with Gold Stars, Incentive Plans, A's, Praise, and Other Bribes* (1993) and *Beyond Discipline: From Compliance to Community* (2001). He has appeared on well over 200 radio and television programs, including *Oprah* and the *Today* show, and speaks at major conferences across the nation. His website is www.alfiekohn.org.

and to the teacher. They have come to think in the plural: they feel connected to each other; they are part of an "us." And, as a result of all this, they feel safe in their classes, not only physically but emotionally. (pp. 101–102)

Kohn suggests some strategies to help teachers and schools move toward a greater sense of community. Among them are the following:

■ *Building relationships between teachers and students.* Students behave more respectfully when important adults in their lives behave respectfully toward *them.* They are more likely to care about others if they know *they* are cared about. If their emotional needs are met, they show a tendency to help meet other people's needs rather than remaining preoccupied with themselves.

■ *Enhancing connections among students.* Connections among students are established and enhanced through activities that involve interdependence. Familiar activities for enhancing connections include cooperative learning, getting-to-know-you activities, such as interviewing fellow students and introducing them to the class, and finding a partner to check opinions with on whatever is being discussed at the moment. Kohn also suggests using activities that promote **perspective taking,** in which students try to see situations from another person's point of view.

■ *Classroom meetings.* Kohn says the overall best activity for involving the entire group is a class meeting (Chapter 6 explains how class meetings are structured and used). Kohn suggests holding class meetings at the beginning of the year to discuss questions such as, "What makes school awful sometimes? Try to remember an experience during a previous year when you hated school, when you felt bad about yourself, or about everyone else, and you couldn't wait for it to be over. What exactly was going on when you were feeling that way? How was the class set up?" Kohn says not enough teachers encourage this practice, particularly in elementary schools where an aggressively sunny outlook prevails.

■ *Undertaking classwide and schoolwide activities.* To develop a sense of community, students need many opportunities for the whole class to collaborate on group endeavors. This might involve producing a class mural, producing a class newsletter or magazine, staging a performance, or doing some community service activity as a class.

■ *Using academic instruction.* The quest for community is not separate from academic learning. Class meetings can be devoted to talking about how the next unit in history might be approached, or what the students thought was best and worst about the math test. Academic study pursued in cooperative groups enables students to make connections while learning from each other. Units of study in language arts and literature can be organized to promote reflection on helpfulness, fairness, and compassion.

The Trouble with Discipline for Compliance

Kohn is scornful about most approaches to discipline, but has nevertheless made significant contributions to discourse on the topic. As we have seen, he would have teachers convert their classrooms into communities where students support each other and the teacher. He believes discipline becomes irrelevant if school is organized in accordance with **constructivist theory,** which holds that students cannot receive knowledge directly from teachers but must construct it from experience. Such instruction involves students so deeply in topics they consider important that there is little need for discipline of any sort.

Kohn is deeply troubled by the notion that schooling is usually structured to force, or at least entice, **compliant behavior** from students. Kohn often begins workshops by asking teachers, "What are your long-terms goals for the students you work with? What would you like them to be—to be like—long after they've left you?" (2001, p. 60). Teachers say they want their students to be caring, happy, responsible, curious, and creative, a conclusion that, according to Kohn (2001)

> . . . is unsettling because it exposes a yawning chasm between what we want and what we are doing, between how we would like students to turn out and how our classrooms and schools actually work. We want children to continue reading and thinking after school has ended, yet we focus their attention on grades, which have been shown to reduce interest in learning. We want them to be critical thinkers, yet we feed them predigested facts and discrete skills—partly because of pressure from various constituencies to pump up standardized test scores. We act as though our goal is short-term retention of right answers rather than genuine understanding. (p. 61)

Kohn points out that even when students are rewarded into compliance, they usually feel no commitment to what they are doing, no genuine understanding of the act or why they are doing it, and no sense that they are becoming people who *want* to act this way in the future. In addition, classroom rules are self-defeating because they cause students to look for ways of subverting the rules and cast teachers as police who feel obliged to take action when students break the rules. Kohn (2001) concludes that the entire process of behavior management works against what we hope to achieve:

> The more we "manage" students' behavior and try to make them do what we say, the more difficult it is for them to become morally sophisticated people who think for themselves and care about others. (p. 62)

Kohn says that if compliance is *not* what teachers are looking for in the long run, then we are faced with a basic conflict between our ultimate goals for learners and the methods we are using to achieve those goals. One or the other, Kohn asserts, has to give.

The Classroom Management We Need

If we give up reward and punishment as means of ensuring desired behavior, then what are we left with? Most people ask, "Aren't there times when we simply need students to do what we tell them?" Kohn suggests that teachers think carefully about how often "students need to do what the teacher tells them." He notes that the number of such occasions varies widely from one teacher to another, which suggests that the need for student compliance is seated in the teacher's personality. He says teachers ought to examine their preferences and bring them to a conscious level. If one teacher needs more student compliance than another, however, is that teacher entitled to use a coercive discipline program to meet his or her particular needs?

When reflecting on this point, many teachers are inclined to ask whether the abandonment of compliance suggests that anything goes, and that students don't have to comply with expectations of participation and learning. Can they be allowed, for example, to ignore assignments, shout obscenities, and create havoc?

Kohn does not answer this question directly, contending that it misses the point. He says the question isn't whether it's all right for students to act in those ways, but rather, if they are likely to do so if their teacher does not demand control and compliance, but instead emphasizes a curriculum that appeals to students. Teachers do not have to choose between chaos on the one hand and being a strong boss on the other. There is a third, better option, which is to work with students in creating a democratic community where students comply with teacher expectations when it is truly necessary for them to do so, as when personal abuse, safety, or legal matters are concerned.

Most teachers feel it is necessary to place structure and limits on student behavior if the class is to function efficiently. Kohn presents criteria for assessing the defensibility of structure and limits.

- *Purpose.* A restriction is legitimate to the extent its objective is to protect students from harm, as opposed to imposing order for its own sake.
- *Restrictiveness.* The less restrictive a structure or limit, the better. It is more difficult to justify a demand for silence than for quiet voices.
- *Flexibility.* Although some structure is helpful, one must always be ready to modify the structure in accordance with student needs.
- *Developmental appropriateness.* Kohn uses the example that although we need to make sure that young children are dressed for winter weather, it is better to let older students decide on such matters for themselves.
- *Presentation style.* The way in which restrictions are presented makes a big difference in how students accept them. If they are suggested respectfully, students are more accepting than if the restrictions sound like orders.
- *Student involvement.* Most importantly, it is student input that makes structure acceptable. When concerns arise, the teacher can ask students, "What do you think we can do to solve this problem?"

The Trouble with Today's Teaching

Kohn thinks traditional instruction is falling well short of the mark it could be reaching. By *traditional instruction,* he means the type in which the teacher selects the curriculum; does the planning; delivers the lessons through lecture, demonstration, guided discussion, reading assignments, worksheets and homework; and tests students to evaluate their progress. That kind of instruction emphasizes helping students reach certain specific objectives—information and skills that students can demonstrate behaviorally. But it gives little attention to exploring ideas, seeking new solutions, looking for meaning or connections, or attempting to gain deeper understanding of the phenomena involved. Students remain relatively passive during traditional instruction. They listen, read assignments, answer questions when called on, and complete worksheets. There is little give and take. Instruction and learning are deemed successful to the extent that students show on tests they have reached most of the stated objectives.

Kohn (1999, p. 28) says such instruction counterproductively puts emphasis on *how well* students are doing rather than *on what* they are doing. Instruction concerned with *how well* tends to focus on outcomes that are shallow, relatively insignificant, and of little interest or relevance to learners. Students come to think of correct answers and good grades as the major goals of learning. They rarely experience the satisfaction of exploring in depth a topic of interest and exchanging their views and insights with others. Kohn says an impressive and growing body of research shows that the traditional approach undermines student interest in learning, makes failure seem overwhelming, does not encourage students to challenge themselves, reduces the quality of learning (that is, it has little depth or relevance), and causes students to think of how smart they are instead of how hard they are trying.

He goes on to say that students taught in this way develop a poor attitude toward learning. They think of learning as getting the work done rather than something they could be excited about exploring. Once they have done the "stuff," they quickly forget much of it as they move on to learn more new stuff. They strive to get the right answer, and when they do not, or if they don't make top scores on the test, they experience a sense of failure that is out of place in genuine learning, in which making mistakes is the rule rather than the exception. They never have reason to challenge themselves intellectually. The overall result is that although students seem to be learning well, they are actually doing poorly because they are not thinking widely and exploring ideas thoughtfully.

How Instruction Should Be Done

Kohn argues for instruction that is notably different from traditional teaching. He says, first, that students should be taken seriously, meaning that teachers must honor them as individuals and seek to determine what they need and enjoy. Enlightened teachers recognize that students must construct knowledge and skills out of the experiences provided in school. These teachers look for students' interests, continually try to imagine how things look from the child's point of view, and try to figure out what lies behind the child's questions and mistakes. Such teachers know that knowledge cannot be absorbed from the teacher, so they lead students to explore topics, grapple with them, and make sense of them. They provide challenges and emphasize that making mistakes is an important part of learning.

How do teachers help students move into deeper levels of thinking? Kohn says the best way is by asking them for examples or asking the question, "How do we know that?" This helps students maintain a critical mind, a healthy skepticism, a need for evidence, a willingness to hear different points of view, and a desire to see how things are connected. It encourages them to appraise the importance of what they are learning and to explore how it can be useful in their lives.

Kohn argues for a curriculum that allows students to be purposefully active most of the time, rather than passive. He says the way to bring that about is to "... start *not* with facts to be learned or disciplines to be mastered, but with questions to be answered" (1999, p. 145). He says these questions should not lead students to correct answers, but make students pause, wonder, and reflect. Kohn gives examples of what he means in questions such as, "How could you improve the human hand?" and "Why were America's founding fathers so afraid of democracy?" (1999, p. 146).

Kohn urges educators to remember three key facts about teaching: (1) Students learn most avidly and have their best ideas when they get to choose which questions they want to explore; (2) all of us tend to be happiest and most effective when we have some say about what we are doing; and (3) when students have no choice and control over learning, their achievement drops. Given these facts and the difference they make in learning, Kohn finds it astonishing that present-day instruction ignores them.

It is unnerving to most teachers, at least at first, to try to organize instruction in accordance with Kohn's suggestions. Kohn, however, says it is breathtaking to be involved in learning in which students have a say in the curriculum and can decide what they will do, when, where, with whom, and toward what end. Kohn points out that this approach must be adjusted to the maturity levels of students, but he maintains it is a rule of thumb that "the more students' questions and decisions drive the lesson, the more likely [it is] that real learning will occur" (1999, p. 151). The best teachers, he insists, are those who ask themselves, "Is this a decision I must make on my own, or can I involve students in it?"

KEY TERMS AND CONCEPTS EMPHASIZED IN THIS CHAPTER

Glasser's Choice Theory
student needs
basic needs
basic student needs
Choice Theory
quality curriculum
quality learning
quality education
quality teaching
SIR
boss teachers
lead teachers
quality schoolwork
seven deadly habits
connecting habits

Gordon's Student Self-Control
self-control
noncontrolling methods
I-messages
you-messages
who owns the problem
positive influence
coping mechanisms
preventive I-messages
collaborative rule setting
participatory classroom
    management
misbehavior
passive listening
door openers

active listening
communication roadblocks
no-lose method of conflict
    resolution

Kohn's Beyond Discipline
learning communities
perspective taking
constructivist theory
compliant behavior

SELECTED SEVEN—SUMMARY SUGGESTIONS FROM GLASSER, GORDON, AND KOHN

1. You can largely remove misbehavior as a problem if you take students seriously, develop a sense of community, provide an engaging curriculum based on student interests, draw students into meaningful decision making, and think in terms of "we" rather than "I."

2. Encourage your students to pursue in-depth information about socially approved topics they consider useful or relevant in their lives.

3. Instead of coercing, scolding, and punishing your students to get them to learn and behave properly, befriend them, provide encouragement and stimulation, and show unending willingness to help.

4. Ask students what kinds of class behaviors will help them acquire quality learning. Ask them to reach agreements about such behavior in the class. Ask them what should happen when anyone breaks a behavior agreement. Ensure the suggestions are positive, not negative.

5. When class concerns arise, ask students, "What do you think we can do to solve this problem?" Involve them, and keep communication open and easy.

6. You cannot transfer your knowledge to students. The best you can do is lead students to explore topics and try to make sense of them. Provide challenges and emphasize that making mistakes is an important part of learning.

7. The best education emphasizes quality in all aspects of teaching, learning, and schooling.

CONCEPT CASES

Case 1: Kristina Will Not Work

Kristina, a student in Mr. Jake's class, is quite docile. She socializes little with other students and never disrupts lessons. However, despite Mr. Jake's best efforts, Kristina will not do her work. She rarely completes an assignment. She is simply there, putting forth no effort at all. *How would William Glasser help Kristina?*

Glasser would first suggest that Mr. Jake think carefully about the classroom and the program to try to determine whether they contain obstacles that prevent Kristina from meeting her needs for survival, belonging, power, fun, and freedom. He would then have Mr. Jake discuss the matter with Kristina, not blaming her but noting the problem of nonproductivity and asking what the problem is and what he might be able to do to help. In that discussion, Mr. Jake might ask Kristina questions such as the following:

1. You have a problem with this work, don't you? Only you can decide whether to do it. Is there anything I can do to help you?

2. Is there anything I could do to make the work more interesting for you?

3. Is there anything in this class that you especially enjoy doing? Do you think that, for a while, you might like to do only those things?

4. Is there anything we have discussed in class that you would like to learn very, very well? How could I help you do that?

5. What could I do differently that would help you want to learn?

Glasser would want Mr. Jake to talk with Kristina every day about nonschool matters such as trips, pets, and movies. He would do this casually, showing he is interested in her and willing to be her friend. Glasser would remind Mr. Jake that there is no magic formula for success with all students. Mr. Jake can only encourage and support Kristina. Scolding and coercion are likely to make matters worse, but as Mr. Jake befriends Kristina she is likely to begin to do more work and of better quality.

Case 2: Sara Cannot Stop Talking

Sara is a pleasant girl who participates in class activities and does most, though not all, of her assigned work. She cannot seem to refrain from talking to classmates, however. Her teacher, Mr. Gonzales, has to speak to her repeatedly during lessons, to the point that he often becomes exasperated and loses his temper. *What suggestions would Thomas Gordon and Alfie Kohn give Mr. Gonzales for dealing with Sara?*

Case 3: Joshua Clowns and Intimidates

Joshua, larger and louder than his classmates, always wants to be the center of attention, which he accomplishes through a combination of clowning and intimidation. He makes wise remarks, talks back (smilingly) to the teacher, utters a variety of sound-effect noises such as automobile crashes and gunshots, and makes limitless sarcastic comments and put-downs of his classmates. Other students will not stand up to him,

apparently fearing his size and verbal aggression. His teacher, Miss Pearl, has come to her wit's end. *Would Joshua's behavior be likely to improve if Thomas Gordon's techniques were used in Miss Pearl's classroom? Explain.*

Case 4: Tom Is Hostile and Defiant

Tom has appeared to be in his usual foul mood ever since arriving in class. On his way to sharpen his pencil, he bumps into Frank, who complains. Tom tells him loudly to shut up. Miss Baines, the teacher, says, "Tom, go back to your seat." Tom wheels around, swears loudly, and says heatedly, "I'll go when I'm damned good and ready!" *How would William Glasser have Miss Baines deal with Tom?*

ACTIVITIES

1. Make notes in your journal concerning ideas from Glasser, Gordon, and Kohn that relate to the five principles for developing a personal system of discipline.

2. Summarize the contentions of Glasser, Gordon, and Kohn in fifteen words or less for each. Share your results with the class.

3. Select a grade level and/or subject you enjoy teaching. Outline what you would consider and do, along the lines of Glasser's suggestions, concerning:

   a. Organizing the classroom, class, curriculum, and activities to better meet your students' needs for belonging, fun, power, and freedom

   b. Your continual efforts to help students improve the quality of their work

4. Do a comparative analysis of Gordon's system with that of Kohn, as concerns:

   a. Effectiveness in suppressing inappropriate behavior
   b. Effectiveness in improving long-term behavior
   c. Ease of implementation
   d. Degree to which each model accurately depicts realities of student attitude and behavior

REFERENCES

Glasser, W. 1969. *Schools without failure.* New York: Harper & Row.

Glasser, W. 1986. *Control theory in the classroom.* New York: HarperCollins.

Glasser, W. 1990. *The quality school.* New York: Perennial Library.

Glasser, W. 1992. The quality school curriculum. *Phi Delta Kappan, 73*(9), 690–694.

Glasser, W. 1993. *The quality school teacher.* New York: HarperPerennial.

Glasser, W. 1998a. *Choice theory in the classroom.* New York: HarperCollins.

Glasser, W. 1998b. *The quality school: Managing students without coercion.* New York: HarperCollins.

Glasser, W. 1998c. *The quality school teacher.* New York: HarperCollins.

Glasser, W. 2001. *Every student can succeed.* Chatsworth, CA: William Glasser Incorporated.

Gordon, T. 1970. *Parent Effectiveness Training: A tested new way to raise responsible children.* New York: New American Library.

Gordon, T. 1974, 1987. *T.E.T.: Teacher Effectiveness Training.* New York: David McKay.

Gordon, T. 1976. *P.E.T. in action.* New York: Bantam.

Gordon, T. 1977. *Leader Effectiveness Training, L.E.T.* New York: Wyden Books.

Gordon, T. 1989. *Discipline that works: Promoting self-discipline in children.* New York: Random House.

Kohn, A. 1993. *Punished by rewards: The trouble with gold stars, incentive plans, A's, praise, and other bribes.* Boston: Houghton Mifflin.

Kohn, A. 1999. *The schools our children deserve: Moving beyond traditional classrooms and "tougher standards."* Boston: Houghton Mifflin.

Kohn, A. 2001. *Beyond discipline: From compliance to community.* Upper Saddle River, NJ: Merrill/Prentice Hall. 1996 edition published Alexandria, VA: Association for Supervision and Curriculum Development.

CHAPTER 6

Discipline through Belonging, Cooperation, and Self-Control

Authoritative Input
- Linda Albert / Cooperative Discipline
- Barbara Coloroso / Inner Discipline
- Jane Nelsen and Lynn Lott / Positive Discipline

CHAPTER PREVIEW

This chapter presents the views of selected authorities who believe good discipline depends on students' attaining a sense of belonging, participating in making class decisions, and relating to others with kindness and consideration. As students acquire these attitudes and capabilities, they experience an inner sense of discipline that is manifested in self-control and responsible behavior.

Part 1. Linda Albert
BELONGING AND COOPERATION

Albert's Fundamental Hypothesis

Discipline occurs best when teachers and students work together in a genuinely cooperative manner to (1) establish a classroom that is safe, orderly, and inviting; (2) provide students a sense of connectedness and belonging; and (3) turn all behavior mistakes into opportunities for learning.

About Linda Albert

Linda Albert, author and disseminator of *Cooperative Discipline,* is a counselor, syndicated columnist, university professor, and former classroom teacher who consults nationally and internationally with educators and parents. She has written a number of books, including *Cooperative Discipline* (1996) and *A Teacher's Guide to Cooperative Discipline* (2003), from which the information in this chapter was drawn.

Albert's Cooperative Discipline

Albert has found that teachers everywhere are troubled by student misbehavior, which is reducing student learning, affecting the quality of teaching, and ruining job satisfaction for teachers. She believes this picture can be reversed through classroom discipline that permits teachers to work with students in a genuinely cooperative manner. She emphasizes teachers' and students' making class decisions together, while keeping students' parents informed and involved. She has devised tactics to help students make *connections* with others, *contribute* to the class, and see themselves as *capable*. She calls connections, contributions, and capabilities the Three C's. Albert, strongly influenced by the earlier work of Rudolf Dreikurs, maintains that students urgently want to feel they "belong" in the class. When they do not obtain the desired sense of belonging, they tend to behave inappropriately by pursuing "mistaken goals" they erroneously believe will provide a sense of belonging.

Genuine and Mistaken Goals

For students to meet their need for belonging in the class, they must come to see themselves as important, worthwhile, and valued as class members. When unable to gain a sense of **belonging** (their **genuine goal**), students frequently misbehave by pursuing **mistaken goals** in an attempt to gain acceptance. These mistaken goals are typically **attention** (look at me), **power** (you can't make me), **revenge** (I'll get even), and withdrawal (I won't participate).

The Three C's of Cooperative Discipline

Fundamental to Albert's Cooperative Discipline are the **Three C's,** which help students see themselves as capable, connected with others, and contributing members of the class.

For the first C, capable, Albert stresses students' sense of "I can," meaning the belief they are capable of accomplishing work given them in school. Albert says teachers can increase student sense of capability by doing four things:

1. *Counter fear of mistakes.* Countering students' fear of making mistakes, which keeps some students from trying, is done by helping students understand what mistakes are, that everyone makes mistakes, that mistakes are a part of learning, and that no progress ever occurs without mistakes being involved.
2. *Build confidence.* Building students' confidence that success is possible is done by helping students see that learning is a process of improvement, not an end product. They should see, too, that people can be successful in a number of ways that do not involve written work. Teachers should look for activities that maximize the likelihood of success.
3. *Make progress tangible.* Progress can be made tangible by having students compile albums and portfolios that display their accomplishments at school. Albert also suggests talking with students about "yesterday, today, and tomorrow." For example, the teacher might say: "Remember when you couldn't spell these words? Look how easy

they are now. You are learning fast. By the end of the year you will be able to . . ." or, "Remember three weeks ago when you couldn't even read these Spanish verbs? Now you can use all of them in present tense. By next month, you'll be able to use them in past tense as well."

4. *Recognize achievement.* Recognizing achievement can be done by having students acknowledge each other's accomplishments in class, at awards assemblies, at exhibits, and at presentations for parents and community.

For the second C, connected, Albert advocates emphasizing the the **Five A's of connecting:** acceptance, attention, appreciation, affirmation, and affection.

Acceptance means communicating that it is all right for each student to be as he or she is, regardless of culture, abilities, disabilities, and personal style.

Attention means making oneself available to others, by sharing time and energy with them.

Appreciation involves positive acknowledgment of others' accomplishments, through compliments given orally, in writing, or behaviorally through how we treat others. In these cases, it is important to focus on the deed, not the doer.

Affirmation refers to showing you recognize and appreciate acts of courage, cheerfulness, dedication, enthusiasm, friendliness, helpfulness, kindness, loyalty, originality, persistence, sensitivity, and thoughtfulness. Teachers can find something positive to say about all students, even those whose behavior is often undesirable: "I have noticed your thoughtfulness" or "Your kindness is always evident."

Affection shows closeness and caring. It is quite different from reward, which comes when students behave in a desired way. Affection is freely given, with nothing required in return.

For the third C, contributing, students need to see that they can make school better for everyone when they contribute to it and to each other. Some of Albert's suggestions for doing so are as follows:

1. *Encourage student input in class matters.* Ask their opinions and preferences about class requirements, routines, and how the class might be improved. Sincerely indicate you appreciate their contributions.
2. *Encourage student contributions to the school.* Albert suggests creating a **Three C Committee** to think of ways to help all students feel more capable, connected, and contributing. Students can play an active role in performing class duties, beautifying classrooms, and keeping the grounds neat, which help build a sense of pride in the school.
3. *Encourage student contributions to the community.* This can be done through such things such as performing random acts of kindness and helpfulness, volunteering in libraries and sporting activities, and contributing to community drives.
4. *Encourage students to work to protect the environment.* One of Albert's suggestions is for the class to adopt a street or area of the community and keep it litter free.
5. *Encourage students to help other students.* Albert's suggestions include peer tutoring, peer counseling, and establishing a **circle of friends** who make sure that everyone has a partner to talk with, to sit with during lunch, and to walk with between classes.

Class Code of Conduct

From the first contact with students, teachers should involve students cooperatively in developing a **class code of conduct.** This code stipulates behavior expected of everyone in the class. As part of the process, teachers and students jointly decide on **consequences** to be invoked when students transgress the class code. When students participate in developing consequences to be applied when misbehavior occurs, they become much more likely to consider those consequences reasonable and abide by them. Even so, conflict will sometimes occur between teacher and students. When that happens, the teacher should remain calm and relaxed, listen to the students, and attempt to address their concerns. They should adopt a businesslike attitude and use a calm, firm tone of voice. Always, teachers should remember that **encouragement** is their most powerful teaching tool.

Types of Misbehavior

Albert identifies four types of classroom misbehavior, associated with the mistaken goals that students pursue in a vain attempt to gain a sense of belonging. They are attention seeking, power seeking, revenge seeking, and avoidance of failure.

Attention-Seeking Behavior

When students do not receive the positive attention they desire, they frequently seek it, actively and passively. Active attention seeking involves **attention-getting mechanisms (AGMs),** such as pencil tapping, showing off, calling out, and asking irrelevant questions. Passive attention seeking is evident when students dawdle, lag behind, and are slow to comply—tactics they use to get attention from the teacher.

Albert says there is a silver lining to attention seeking: It shows that the offending student desires a positive relationship with the teacher but does not know how to connect. For such students, Albert would provide abundant recognition when they behave properly. If attention seeking becomes excessive, teachers can use the numerous intervention techniques Albert provides. Two examples are standing near the student or saying, "I find it difficult to keep my train of thought when talking is occurring."

Power-Seeking Behavior

When attention seeking doesn't work, students sometimes resort to power-seeking behavior. Through words and actions they try to show that they cannot be controlled by the teacher. They may mutter replies, disregard instructions, comply insolently, or directly challenge the teacher. Active power-seeking may take the form of temper tantrums, back talk, disrespect, and defiance. Passive power seeking may take the form of quiet noncompliance with teacher requests.

When students engage in power seeking behavior, teachers often feel angry and frustrated. They worry they will lose face or lose control of the class. Albert says that power seeking also has its silver lining, in that many students who behave in this manner show good verbal skills and leadership ability, as well as assertiveness and independent thinking. Keeping the silver lining in mind, teachers can give students options from which to choose (e.g., You may do this work alone or with a partner), delegate responsibilities, and grant them legitimate power when appropriate. Once teachers find themselves engaged in a power struggle with a student, they should look for what Albert calls a graceful exit, described in the section on dealing with more severe confrontations.

Revenge-Seeking Behavior

When students suffer real or imagined hurts in the class, a few may set out to retaliate against teachers and classmates. This often happens when teachers deal forcefully with students, and sometimes when students are angry at parents or others. Revenge seeking usually takes the form of verbal attacks, such as, "You really stink as a teacher!" At times it may involve destruction of materials or room environment or physical attacks on teachers or other students. Strategies effective with power-seeking behavior are also effective when students seek revenge. (These matters are addressed in sections titled "Avoiding and Defusing Confrontations" and "Dealing with Severe Confrontations.")

Avoidance-of-Failure Behavior

Many students dread failure. A few, especially when assignments are difficult, withdraw and quit trying, preferring to appear lazy rather than stupid. Albert tells teachers to counter withdrawal by altering assignments and providing plentiful encouragement. Specific suggestions include (1) using concrete learning materials that students can see, feel, and manipulate; (2) teaching students to accomplish one step at a time so they enjoy small successes; and (3) teaching to the various intelligences that allows students to use special talents they might have in different areas (see Gardner, 1983). Special individual help can be provided by the teacher, adult volunteers, and peer tutors. Withdrawn students should constantly be encouraged to try. The teacher must show belief in them and help remove their negative beliefs about their ability to succeed.

Albert's Plethora of Strategies

Albert suggests many strategies teachers can employ at "the moment of misbehavior," so they are never at a loss for what to do when a student misbehaves. Because space within this chapter does not permit presentation of the numerous strategies she presents, readers are directed to the appendixes of her book, *Cooperative Discipline* (1996), especially Appendix C which provides a summary chart of the numerous interventions she advocates.

Avoiding and Defusing Confrontations

Direct confrontations between teacher and students sometimes occur. Although they worry teachers a great deal, they can be handled effectively. It is well to think through and practice how you will conduct yourself when students challenge you through power or revenge behaviors. Albert suggests the following:

1. *Focus on the behavior, not the student.* Describe aloud the behavior that is occurring without evaluating it. Use objective terms, while avoiding subjective words such as *bad, wrong,* or *stupid.* Deal with the moment, talking only about what is happening now, not what happened yesterday or last week. Be firm but friendly. Indicate that the behavior must stop, but at the same time show continuing concern for the student's well-being.
2. *Take charge of your negative emotions.* Even when you feel angry, frustrated, or hurt, you can still respond calmly, objectively, and noncombatively. Doing so reduces student antagonism and helps everyone calm down.
3. *Discuss the misbehavior with the student later.* Wait an hour or until the next day when both of you have cooled down.
4. *Allow the student to save face.* Students know you have the ultimate power in confrontations, so eventually they comply with your expectations. However, to save face with their peers and make it seem they are not backing down completely, they often mutter, take their time complying, or repeat the misbehavior one more time before stopping. It is best to overlook those face-saving behaviors rather than confront the student anew.

Dealing with More Severe Confrontations

Suppose that a very upset student is having a real tantrum, yelling and throwing things. What do you do then? Albert offers a number of suggestions that she calls **graceful exits,** which allow teachers to distance themselves from the situation. These exits are made calmly, with poise, and without sarcasm. First, acknowledge the student's power, but also state your expectation: "I can't make you write this essay, but it does need to be turned in by Friday. Let me know your plan for completing the assignment." Then, move away from the student and table the matter. You might say, "Let's talk about it later" or "I am not willing to talk with you about this right now." If the defiance persists, call the student's bluff and deliver a closing statement: "Let me get this straight. I asked you to complete your assignment and you are refusing. Is this correct?" Stand with a pencil and clipboard and write down what the student says. You may wish to say, "You've mistaken me for someone who wants to fight. I don't." If you see that the student will not calm down, have the student take time-out in the classroom or a designated room.

Implementing Consequences

If a student seriously or repeatedly violates the classroom code of conduct, you should invoke consequences in keeping with previous agreements. Think of consequences as tools for helping students learn to make better behavior choices. Talk with your class about four categories of consequences: (1) loss or delay of privileges, such as a favorite activity; (2) loss of freedom of interaction, such as talking with other students; (3) restitution, such as return, repair, or replacement of objects, doing school service, or helping students that have been offended; and (4) relearning appropriate behavior, such as practicing correct behavior for given situations.

Albert says to remember the **Four R's of consequences**—related, reasonable, respectful, and reliably enforced. *Related* means the consequence calls on students to do something related directly to their misbehavior. If Courtney continues to talk disruptively, her consequence is to sit in the back of the room where she can't talk to others. *Reasonable* means the consequence is proportional to the misbehavior. We use consequences to teach students, not to punish them. If Juan fails to turn in an assignment, the consequence should be to redo the assignment. *Respectful* means the consequence is invoked in a friendly but firm manner, with no blaming, shaming, or preaching. *Reliably enforced* means teachers invoke consequences and follow through in a consistent manner.

Resolution of more serious misbehavior or repeated violations should be done in a private conference with the student. The purpose of the conference is never to cast blame, but rather to work out ways for helping the student behave responsibly. Albert presents a **Six-D conflict resolution plan** to help resolve matters under dispute.

1. Define the problem objectively, without blaming or using emotional words.
2. Declare the need; that is, tell what makes the situation a problem.
3. Describe the feelings experienced by both sides.
4. Discuss possible solutions. Consider pros and cons of each.
5. Decide on a plan. Choose the solution with the most support from both sides. Be specific about when it will begin.
6. Determine the plan's effectiveness. A follow-up meeting is arranged after the plan has been in use for a time in order to evaluate its effectiveness.

Part 2. Barbara Coloroso
INNER SELF-CONTROL

Coloroso's Fundamental Hypothesis

Discipline occurs best when teachers help students acquire an inner sense of self-control, which is developed through earning trust, assuming responsibility, and acquiring the power to make decisions.

Coloroso's Inner Discipline

Coloroso's approach to discipline emphasizes helping students develop self-control. Her plan urges teachers to establish classrooms that provide a climate of trust and responsibility, in which students are given power to make decisions about their problems and are required to manage the outcomes of those decisions. She says classrooms are ideal places to learn the process of responsible decision making, but teachers and students must work

About Barbara Coloroso

Barbara Coloroso has been a Franciscan nun, parent, teacher, workshop leader, author, and affiliate instructor at the University of Northern Colorado. She has expressed her ideas on discipline and child rearing in a number of books, articles, and conference presentations. In recent years, she has emphasized working with students with special needs and talents, with troubled students, and with matters related to bullying (presented in her book *The Bully, the Bullied, and the Bystander: How Parents and Teachers Can Break the Cycle of Violence* (2003). Her ideas included in this chapter come mostly from her book, *Kids Are Worth It: Giving Your Child the Gift of Inner Discipline* (2002). The Kids Are Worth It! series includes videos, audiotapes, and workbooks to help teachers develop a discipline system that creates trust, respect, and success in school. See Coloroso's website: www.kidsareworthit.com.

closely together in the process. Teachers must truly believe students are worth every effort made on their behalf. This requires unconditional commitment to developing needed behavior skills. Teachers must treat students as they, themselves, wish to be treated. When students encounter difficulties, teachers should help by asking how they plan to solve the problems, thus requiring that students take responsibility for resolving problems they encounter.

Principles of Good Discipline

Discipline should be thought of as a means of teaching students to take positive charge of their lives. Students have the right to be in school, but they also have the responsibility to respect the rights of those around them. Good discipline shows students what they have done wrong, has them assume ownership of the problem that has resulted, and teaches them ways to solve the problem. All of this is done while keeping student dignity intact. The result is **inner discipline** that helps students manage problems they encounter. They learn to think for themselves and believe they are capable solving most of the problems they encounter.

How Punishment Differs from Discipline

Coloroso describes **punishment** as treatment that is psychologically hurtful to students and likely to provoke anger, resentment, and additional conflict. Students typically respond to punishment with the Three F's—fear, fighting back, or fleeing. Threatened with punishment, they become afraid to make a mistake. Coloroso advises against using punishment because it removes good opportunities for developing integrity, wisdom, compassion, and mercy—all of which contribute to inner discipline.

In contrast to punishment, proper discipline does four things that lead students toward positive behavior: (1) shows students what they have done wrong; (2) gives them ownership of the problems involved; (3) provides them strategies for solving the problems; and (4) leaves their dignity intact. Discipline, unlike punishment, helps students learn how to handle problems they will encounter throughout life. The following case illustrates these points:

> Alexis is a starting player on the high school basketball team, but because she received a detention from her chemistry teacher for being tardy several times, Coach Stein informs her she will have to sit out the next game. Even though this is school policy, Alexis thinks the chemistry teacher holds a grudge against her. Alexis is upset that Coach Stein doesn't back her up. While angry, Alexis writes some unacceptable comments on the locker room wall. When Coach Stein finds the damage, she knows other girls have seen it, and she feels hurt, disappointed, and angry. Her first reaction is to call Alexis in and suspend her for another game, but after considering the situation further she realizes punishment of that sort would be unproductive and might not help Alexis make better choices in the future. Coach Stein decides to encourage Alexis to accept ownership of the problem and deal constructively with the turmoil she has created. Coach Stein realizes she must show compassion, kindness, gentleness, and patience. This will make it easier for Alexis to repair the damage she did to the locker room, make a plan to ensure it won't happen again, and mend fences with her coach, teammates, and the chemistry teacher. Coach Stein makes plans to meet with Alexis to help her acknowledge what she has done wrong, assume ownership of the problem, and identify options for dealing with the problem. Coach Stein knows all this must be done in a way that preserves Alexis's sense of personal dignity.

Misbehavior and How to Deal with It

Coloroso describes behavior as falling into three categories—mistakes, mischief, and mayhem—which are addressed in different ways. Mistakes are simple errors that provide opportunity for learning better choices. Mischief, although not necessarily serious, is intentional misbehavior. It provides an opportunity to help students find ways to fix what they did wrong and learn how to avoid doing it again. Mayhem, which is willfully serious misbehavior, calls for application of the **Three R's of reconciliatory justice**—restitution, resolution, and reconciliation.

Restitution means doing what is necessary to repair damage that occurred. **Resolution** means identifying and correcting whatever caused the misbehavior so it won't happen again. **Reconciliation** entails healing relationships with people who were hurt by the misbehavior. In all cases, students are allowed to experience natural discomfort associated with their misbehavior. They are not bribed, rewarded, or punished. Bribes make them dependent on others for approval. Rewards cause students to behave in certain ways only to please the teacher. Punishment only makes students think about how to avoid getting caught the next time they misbehave.

The best way to help students who misbehave is to allow them to make decisions and grow from the results, whatever the results may be. The main caution is to make sure that student decisions do not lead to situations that are physically dangerous, morally threatening, or unhealthy. Otherwise, encourage students to face situations that require decisions and, without making judgments, let them proceed through the process. When they are in situations that call for decisions, ask them to make the decision (you may need to provide guidance without expressing judgments) and let them experience the results. This process may seem inefficient, but it produces rapid growth in ability to solve problems. Mistakes and poor choices become the students' responsibility. If they experience discomfort, they have the power to behave more responsibly in the future.

Coloroso believes that teachers should never rescue students by solving thorny problems for them. Doing so sends the message that students don't have power in their lives and another person must take care of them. When students make mistakes, as they will, teachers should not lecture them with comments such as, "If you had studied more, you wouldn't have failed the test." Students already know this. What they now need is opportunity to correct the situation they have created. It is best for the teacher to say, "You have a problem. What is your plan for dealing with it?"

When students take on **ownership of the problem** and situation they have created, they know it is up to them to make matters better. Teachers are there to offer advice and support, but not provide solutions. Rather than telling a student, "You can't go to the library during choice time until you finish your math assignment" (punishment), a teacher should say, "You can go to the library during choice time when you finish your math assignment" (discipline). This simple response difference helps students take responsibility for their actions.

How Classroom Discipline Leads to Inner Discipline

As you have seen, Coloroso believes the ultimate purpose of discipline is to enable students to make intelligent decisions, accept the consequences of their decisions, and use the consequences to help them make better decisions in the future. Coloroso advises teachers to prepare for their role in this process by asking themselves two questions and answering them honestly: "What is my goal in teaching?" and "What is my teaching philosophy?" The first has to do with what teachers hope to achieve with learners, and the second with how they think they can best accomplish the task. Because teachers act in accordance with their beliefs, it is important for them to clarify those beliefs: "Do I want to empower students to take care of themselves, or do I want to make them wait for teachers and other adults to tell them what to do and think?" Teachers who feel they must control students turn to bribes, rewards, threats, and punishment to restrict and coerce behavior. Those who want to empower students to make decisions and resolve their own problems give students opportunities to think, act, and take responsibility.

When given this opportunity, students will not always make the best choices. For that reason they must be provided a safe, nurturing environment in which to learn to deal with consequences. Teachers should allow and respect student decisions, even those clearly in error, and let students experience the consequences. Even when consequences are unpleasant, students learn from them and at the same time learn that they have control over their lives through the decisions they make. When teachers understand this process, they realize it is counterproductive to nag, warn, and constantly remind students of what they ought to be doing.

Mistakes, Reality, and Problem Solving

Students learn problem solving better and more quickly when they know it is all right to make mistakes. They should begin by distinguishing between reality and problem, with *reality* being an accurate appraisal of what has occurred and *problem* being the discomfort caused by the reality. In learning to solve problems, we first accept the realities, then we solve the problems that come from them. As students make the distinction between reality and problem they begin to see that there is no problem too great to be solved. But when faced with a problem, students need a way of dealing with it, which they should formalize into a plan similar to the following:

1. *Identify the reality and define the problem.* Josh asks Melissa to return the book he checked out from the library and then lent to Melissa. Melissa can't find the book, but remembers she left it on the kitchen table near the books her mother was donating to the library. The *reality* is, she cannot find the book. The associated *problem* is discomfort for Melissa, and later for Josh, as well, because Josh has a report due on the book. From Melissa's perspective, how is the problem to be resolved?

2. *List possible solutions for dealing with the problem.* Melissa's first thought is to say she left the book on Josh's desk or avoid Josh as long as possible. After she thinks about it, she identifies three more options: see if she can find the book at the library, buy a new book for Josh, or borrow Randy's copy of the book for Josh to use.

3. *Evaluate the options.* Melissa considers the options. She rejects lying because she is unwilling to think of herself in those terms. She does not want to avoid Josh, either, because they usually do homework together and avoidance would only prolong the problem. She doesn't want to purchase a replacement book for Randy—she borrowed the book in the first place because she didn't have money for a new one.

Melissa's teacher has taught her to ask herself four questions about each of the options she has identified: Is it unkind? Is it hurtful? Is it unfair? Is it dishonest? Melissa recognizes that the options she first considered would be dishonest, unfair, and maybe hurtful to Josh. She is in the process of learning that negative actions lead to further trouble. That leaves her two options: check with the library, and if they can't find it, buy a replacement book.

4. *Select the option that seems most promising.* The best options seem to be to check with the library or, if necessary, purchase a new book.

5. *Make a plan and carry it out.* Melissa decides go to the library, tell them what happened, and see if the book can be found. If it is located, she will ask for its return. If it can't be found, she will purchase a new copy. Admitting to and owning a problem, making a plan, and following through are difficult things to do, for adults as well as children. Excuses are not acceptable. If the plan does not work, then a new option must be tried. Melissa may have to borrow money from her parents to replace the book. That will mean taking on extra chores to repay them, but she must accept that responsibility.

6. *In retrospect, reevaluate the problem and the solution.* This step is very important in learning and involves three questions:

What caused the problem in the first place?
How can a similar problem be avoided in the future?
Was the problem solution satisfactory?

As she ponders these questions, Melissa's self-esteem remains intact and her ability to solve problems has grown stronger.

Part 3. Jane Nelsen and Lynn Lott
ENCOURAGEMENT AND SUPPORT

Nelsen and Lott's Fundamental Hypothesis

Discipline occurs best when teachers provide classrooms that are accepting, encouraging, respectful, and supportive. Such classrooms enable students to behave with dignity, self-control, and concern for others.

Nelsen and Lott's Positive Discipline

Jane Nelsen and Lynn Lott contend that almost all students can learn to behave with dignity, self-control, and concern for others. The key to fostering this development is providing structure that allows students to see themselves as capable, significant, and able to control their own lives.

About Jane Nelsen and Lynn Lott

Jane Nelsen and Lynn Lott are educators who share their views on discipline through lectures, workshops, printed material, and video material. Their goal is to help adults and children learn to respect themselves and others, behave responsibly, and contribute to the betterment of the groups of which they are members. Their book *Positive Discipline in the Classroom* (1993, 2000, 2006) explains how to establish classroom climates that foster responsibility, mutual respect, and cooperation. They believe such climates do away with most discipline problems because they teach students the value of respect and helpfulness. Nelsen and Lott have authored a number of books and teaching materials that can be viewed on the Positive Discipline website, www.positivediscipline.com, and the Empowering People website, www.empoweringpeople.com. Their former coauthor H. Stephen Glenn died in 2002.

Relationship Barriers and Relationship Builders

Nelsen and Lott identify five pairs of contrasting teacher behaviors they call barriers and builders. **Barriers to relationships** prevent good relationships because they are disrespectful and discouraging, whereas **builders of relationships** foster good relationships because they are respectful and encouraging. Here are some examples of barriers versus builders (the barrier is shown first, followed by the builder).

1. *Assuming versus Checking.* Too often teachers *assume*, without checking with students, that they know what students think and feel, can and cannot do, and how they should or should not respond. Teachers then deal with students on the basis of those assumptions. Rather than assuming they know what students think and feel, it is better that teachers *check* with them.

2. *Rescuing/Explaining versus Exploring.* Teachers think they are being helpful when they make lengthy explanations, rescue students from difficulties, or do a portion of students' work for them. Students progress better, however, when allowed to perceive situations for themselves and proceed on the basis of those perceptions. Elementary teachers explain and rescue, for example, when they say, "It's cold outside, so don't forget your jackets." They help explore when they say, "Take a look outside. What do you need to remember in order to take care of yourself?"

3. *Directing versus Inviting/Encouraging.* Teachers do not realize they are being disrespectful when they tell students, "Pick that up" or "Put that away" or "Straighten up your desk before the bell rings." But such commands build dependency while suppressing initiative and cooperation. In contrast, teachers should *invite* and *encourage* students to become self-directed. They might say, "The bell will ring soon. I would appreciate anything you might do to help get the room straightened up for the next class."

4. *Expecting versus Celebrating.* Teachers should hold high expectations of students and believe in their potential. Students become easily discouraged if they are judged negatively when they fall short of expectations, as when teachers say, "I really thought you could do that" or "I thought you were more responsible than that." Students respond far better when teachers look for improvements and call attention to them.

5. *Adult-isms versus Respecting.* Nelsen and Lott use the term adult-ism for teacher statements that suggest what students *ought to do*, such as: "How come you never . . . ?" or "Why can't you ever . . . ?" or "I can't believe you would do such a thing!" These adult-isms produce guilt rather than provide encouragement. Instead of handing an unacceptable paper back and saying, "You knew what I wanted on this project!" a teacher could say, "What is your understanding of the requirements for this project?" In 1993, Nelsen, Lott, and Glenn flatly stated:

> We guarantee 100% improvement in student–teacher relationships when teachers simply learn to recognize barrier behaviors and stop demonstrating them. Where else can you get such a generous return for ceasing a behavior? And when the builders are added, the payoff is even greater. (p. 18)

The Role of Classroom Meetings

Nelsen and Lott believe **classroom meetings** are uniquely suited to implementing the tactics they suggest for building positive discipline. Those meetings promote social skills such as listening, taking turns, hearing different points of view, negotiating, communicating, helping one another, and taking responsibility for one's behavior. Academic skills are strengthened in the process, as well, because students must practice language skills, attentiveness, critical thinking, decision making, and problem solving.

In addition, class meetings help students see that teachers and other adults need support as much as students do. When teachers involve themselves as partners with students in class meetings, a climate of mutual respect begins to grow. Teachers and students listen to one another, take each other seriously, and work together to solve problems for the benefit of all. Antagonisms often seen in many classrooms tend to fade away.

Building Blocks for Classroom Meetings

Nelsen and Lott suggest **eight building blocks** for effective class meetings, each focusing on a particular skill. It takes about two hours to introduce the eight building blocks. After that, about four additional class meetings are required to give adequate attention to what they entail.

Before putting classroom meetings in place, introduce the concept and get students to buy into the activity. Explain that you would like to begin holding class meetings in which students can express concerns and use their power and skills to help make decisions. Elementary students seldom hesitate to try class meetings, but middle school and high school students may need some persuading. A way to begin with them is to initiate a discussion about power, how problems are usually handled in school, and how power involves teachers' telling students what to do.

Next, ask students, "Who has an example they would like to share about what happens when someone tries to control you? What do you feel? What do you do? What do you learn?" Students usually say that they feel angry or scared and manipulated, and feel like withdrawing or rebelling. Ask them also, "Do you, yourself, ever try to control or manipulate others, including teachers? If so, how do you do so?"

Continue by asking students if they would like to be more involved in making decisions that affect their lives at school. Would they be willing to do the work to come up with solutions they like? Point out that some students actually *prefer* having adults boss them around, so they can rebel or so they don't have to take responsibility themselves. Make it clear that you don't intend to waste time teaching and learning a respectful method if they prefer continuing with the usual way, in which the teacher is in control and students' only options are to comply, rebel, and/or spend time in detention. Once students indicate support, decide together when the classroom meetings will be held. Preferences vary from weekly half-hour meetings to three shorter meetings per week. A meeting every day is advisable for the first week, as students learn the process.

Building Block 1. Form a Circle

A circular seating arrangement works best because it allows face-to-face contact. Ask students for suggestions about how to form the circle. Write their ideas on the board and make a decision based on their suggestions.

Building Block 2. Practice Giving Compliments and Showing Appreciation

Begin class meetings on a positive note, which can be done by saying complimentary things to each other. Many students have difficulty giving and receiving compliments. Practice helps. Ask them to recall when someone said something that made them feel good about themselves. Let them share their examples with the group. Then ask them to think about something they would like to thank others for, such as thanking a classmate for lending a pencil or eating lunch together. See if they can put their feelings into words.

Receiving compliments is often as difficult as giving them. The best response to a compliment is often a simple thank-you. Giving and receiving compliments seems especially embarrassing to some middle school students. When that is the case, use the term *show appreciation* instead of *compliment*.

Building Block 3. Create an Agenda

All class meetings should begin with a specific agenda. When students and teachers experience concerns, they can jot them down in a special notebook. This can be done at a designated time and place, such as when students leave the room. The class meetings will address only the concerns that appear in the notebook.

Building Block 4. Develop Communication Skills

A number of activities help develop communication skills, such as taking turns speaking (begin by going around the circle and letting each person speak), listening attentively to what others say, learning to use **I-statements** (saying "I think," "I feel," and so forth), seeking solutions to problems rather than placing blame on others, showing respect for others by never humiliating or speaking judgmentally about them, learning to seek and find mutually acceptable solutions to problems, and framing conclusions in the form of "we decided," showing it was a group effort and conclusion.

Building Block 5. Learn about Separate Realities

In this building block, help students understand that not everyone is the same or thinks the same way. Nelsen and Lott describe an activity that poses problem situations faced by turtles, lions, eagles, and chameleons. For example, the animals might need to cover a distance quickly, contend with weather, or hide from enemies. Students discuss how each of the animals might feel or deal with the problem. This can lead to helping students see that different people feel and behave differently in various situations.

Building Block 6. Recognize the Reasons
People Do What They Do

Ask students if they have ever wondered why different students behave as they do. Acknowledge their thoughts and then ask if they have ever heard of the primary goal of belonging and the four mistaken goals of misbehavior. Proceed by using examples to illustrate the goal of belonging and the mistaken goals of undue attention, power, revenge, and giving up. (Note: Nelsen and Lott use Rudolf Dreikurs's explanation of why students behave as they do. As you will see later, there are alternative explanations concerning student motivation and causes of misbehavior.)

Building Block 7. Practice Role-Playing
and Brainstorming

By the third class meeting, students are usually ready to begin considering problems and solutions. Here are some suggestions for exploring problems tactfully: (1) Discuss the key elements of the problem situation. (2) Have students act out roles involved in the problem. (3) Brainstorm a number of possible solutions to the difficulty or problem and allow students to select a solution they believe will be best.

Building Block 8. Focus on Nonpunitive Solutions

Ask students the following and write their answers on the board: "What do you feel like when someone bosses you? What do you want to do when someone calls you names or puts you down? When others do these things to you, does it help you behave better?" Then ask them how their behavior is affected when someone is kind to them, helps them, or provides stimulation and encouragement. With their answers written on the board, ask students to compare them. Use the comparison to draw attention to the value of encouragement versus punishment.

Tell the students that you intend never to punish or belittle them in any way, and that when they do something wrong you will try to help them behave more appropriately. Explain that the help you provide will always be *related* to what they have done wrong, *respectful* of them as persons, and *reasonable*. These are what Nelsen and Lott call the **Three R's of solutions.**

Standard Format for Class Meetings

Consistent with the building blocks, Nelsen and Lott suggest the following format for class meetings. The teacher normally initiates the meeting and makes sure everyone abides by the rules and has an equal right to speak:

1. *Express compliments and appreciation.* Each session begins in this way as a means of setting a positive tone.
2. *Follow up on earlier solutions applied to problems.* Any suggested solution is to be tried only for a week, so it is important to determine if the solution has been working. If it hasn't, the class may wish to put the issue back on the agenda for future problem solving.

3. *Go through agenda items.* When an agenda item is read, ask the person (student or teacher) who raised the issue if he or she still wants help with it. If so, ask that person what a satisfactory solution could be. If he or she can't think of any, go around the circle giving every student an opportunity to offer a suggestion. Ask the person with the issue to select the most helpful solution from the suggestions offered.

4. *Make future plans for class activities.* End the class meeting by discussing an enjoyable activity for the entire class at a future date. For example, the class might decide to set aside some time on Friday to discuss an upcoming event, view a videotape, or complete homework assignments with a friend.

When Classroom Meetings Fail to Function as Intended

When new procedures are implemented, it often takes awhile for them to function smoothly. If students do not respond to class meetings with the expected enthusiasm, don't be discouraged. Trust in the procedure; it will eventually come together. The goal is for long-term quality, not short-term convenience. When putting class meetings into practice, be willing to give up *control over* students in favor of gaining *cooperation with* students. Instead of pontificating, ask for thoughts and opinions; doing so will improve cooperation, collaboration, and problem resolution.

Aside from that, if classroom meetings are not working as intended, it is probably due to one or more of the following:

- Not forming a circle
- Not having the meetings regularly (three to five times per week for elementary; less often for secondary)
- Censoring what students say
- Not helping students learn nonpunitive problem-solving skills
- Talking down to students instead of showing faith in their abilities
- Not going around the circle giving every student a chance to speak or pass

KEY TERMS AND CONCEPTS EMPHASIZED IN THIS CHAPTER

Linda Albert	Five A's of connecting	graceful exits
belonging	Three C Committee	Four R's of consequences
genuine goal	circle of friends	Six-D conflict resolution plan
mistaken goal	class code of conduct	
attention	consequences	**Barbara Coloroso**
power	encouragement	inner discipline
revenge	attention-getting	punishment
Three C's	mechanisms (AGMs)	Three R's of reconciliatory justice

restitution
resolution
reconciliation
ownership of the problem

Jane Nelsen and Lynn Lott
barriers to relationships
builders of relationships
classroom meetings

eight building blocks
I-statements
Three R's of solutions

SELECTED SEVEN—SUMMARY SUGGESTIONS FROM THIS CHAPTER

1. Promote a sense of belonging in your classroom by helping students feel important, worthwhile, and valued. Help them feel capable, show them how to connect with others, and help them contribute to the class.

2. To relate better with students, remove the normal barriers to relationships and replace them with builders of relationships. Help students see themselves as capable and in control of their own lives.

3. Work cooperatively with your students to determine how students (and teacher) are to conduct themselves in class. When you must deal with misbehavior, (1) describe the behavior that is occurring, but without evaluating it, (2) deal only with what is happening now (not what happened in the past), and (3) be firm, but friendly. Always make sure you speak reasonably and respectfully and treat students as you would like to be treated.

4. Use a discipline approach that does four things: (1) shows students what they have done wrong, (2) gives them ownership of the problems created, (3) provides them ways to solve the resultant problems, and (4) leaves their dignity intact.

5. Strive for win-win solutions to problems and disputes. When discussing class problems, always focus on solutions rather than consequences.

6. Show you truly care about your students by learning about them as individuals, encouraging them to see mistakes as opportunities to learn and grow, and having faith in their ability to make meaningful contributions.

7. Hold regular classroom meetings, in accordance with the eight building blocks of effective classroom meetings. Give up some of your power in these meetings and allow students to make decisions that work for the class.

CONCEPT CASES

Case 1: Kristina Will Not Work

Kristina, a student in Mr. Jake's class, is quite docile. She socializes little with other students and never disrupts lessons. However, despite Mr. Jake's best efforts, Kristina will not do her work. She rarely completes an assignment. She is simply there, putting forth no effort at all. *How would Linda Albert deal with Kristina?*

Albert would advise Mr. Jake to do the following: Work hard at the Three C's with Kristina. Give her work she can do easily so she begins to feel more capable, then gradually increase the difficulty, teaching one new step at a time. Help her connect through a buddy system with another student and through participation in small group work. Give her opportunities to contribute by

sharing information with the class about hobbies, siblings, and the like. Perhaps she has a skill she could teach to another student. Encourage her at every opportunity. Talk with her; ask her if there is something that is preventing her from completing her work. Show that you will help her however you can.

Case 2: Sara Cannot Stop Talking

Sara is a pleasant girl who participates in class activities and does most, though not all, of her assigned work. She cannot seem to refrain from talking to classmates, however. Her teacher, Mr. Gonzales, has to speak to her repeatedly during lessons, to the point that he often becomes exasperated and loses his temper. *What sugges-*

tions would Barbara Coloroso give Mr. Gonzales for dealing with Sara?

Case 3: Joshua Clowns and Intimidates

Joshua, larger and louder than his classmates, always wants to be the center of attention, which he accomplishes through a combination of clowning and intimidation. He makes wise remarks, talks back (smilingly) to the teacher, utters a variety of sound-effect noises such as automobile crashes and gunshots, and makes limitless sarcastic comments and put-downs of his classmates. Other students will not stand up to him, apparently fearing his size and verbal aggression. His teacher, Miss Pearl, has come to her wit's end. *Would Joshua's behavior be likely to improve if Nelsen and Lott's techniques were used in Miss Pearl's classroom? Explain.*

Case 4: Tom Is Hostile and Defiant

Tom has appeared to be in his usual foul mood ever since arriving in class. On his way to sharpen his pencil, he bumps into Frank, who complains. Tom tells him loudly to shut up. Miss Baines, the teacher, says, "Tom, go back to your seat." Tom wheels around, swears loudly, and says heatedly, "I'll go when I'm damned good and ready!" *How would Albert, Coloroso, or Nelsen and Lott have Miss Baines deal with Tom?*

ACTIVITIES

1. In your journal, make entries from the chapter that you feel contribute importantly to the five principles of building a personal system of discipline.

2. Compare the suggestions made by Albert, Coloroso, and Nelsen and Lott. Which group of suggestion do you find most helpful? Explain.

3. See if you can summarize in twenty-five words or less the central message of this chapter.

YOU ARE THE TEACHER

Middle School Library

You are a media specialist in charge of the middle school library. You see your job as serving as resource person to students who are seeking information and you are always eager to give help to those who request it. About half the students in your school are Caucasian. The remainder are African American, Hispanic, and Asian American. For each period of the day you have a different number and type of students under your direction. Usually, small groups have been sent to the library to do cooperative research. Some unexpected students always appear. Usually, they have been excused from physical education for medical reasons but hate to be sent to the library, or they bear special passes from their teachers for a variety of purposes.

Typical Occurrences

You have succeeded in getting students settled and working when Tara appears at your side, needing a book to read as makeup work for missing class. You ask Tara what kinds of books interest her. She resignedly shrugs her shoulders. You take her to a shelf of newly published books. "I read this one last night," you tell her. "I think you might like it. It's a good story and fast reading." Tara only glances at it. "That looks stupid," she says. "Don't you have any good books?" She glances down the shelf. "These are all stupid!" Another student, Jaime, is tugging at your elbow, with a note from his history teacher, who wants the source of a particular quotation. You ask Tara to look at the books for a moment while you take Jaime to the reference books. As you pass by a table of students supposedly doing research, you see that the group is watching Walter and Teo have a friendly pencil fight by hitting pencils together until one of them breaks. You address your comments to Walter, who appears to be the more willing participant. Walter answers hotly, "Teo started it! It wasn't me!" "Well," you say, "if you boys can't behave yourself, just go back to your class." The other students smile, and Walter feels he is being treated unjustly. He sits down and pouts. Meanwhile, Tara has gone to the large globe and is twirling it. You start to speak to her but realize that Jaime is still waiting at your side with the request from his teacher. Somehow, before the period ends, Tara leaves with a book she doesn't want and Jaime takes a citation back to his teacher. The research groups have been too noisy. You know they have done little work and wonder if you should speak to their teacher about their manners and courtesy. After the period is over, you notice that profane remarks have been written on the table where Walter was sitting.

Conceptualizing a Strategy

If you followed the suggestions provided in this chapter, what would you conclude or do with regard to the following?

1. Preventing the problem(s) from occurring in the first place
2. Involving other or all students in addressing the situation
3. Maintaining student dignity and good personal relations
4. Applying follow-up procedures that would prevent the recurrence of the misbehavior
5. Using the situation to help the students develop a sense of greater responsibility and self-control

REFERENCES

Albert, L. 1996. *Cooperative discipline.* Circle Pines, MN: American Guidance Service.

Albert, L. 2003. *A teacher's guide to cooperative discipline.* Circle Pines, MN: American Guidance Service.

Coloroso, B. 1990. *Discipline: Creating a positive school climate.* [Booklet, video, audio.] Littleton, CO: Kids are worth it!

Coloroso, B. 2002. *Kids are worth it: Giving your child the gift of inner discipline.* New York: Quill.

Coloroso, B. 2003. *The bully, the bullied, and the bystander: How parents and teachers can break the cycle of violence.* New York: HarperCollins.

Gardner, H. 1983. *Frames of mind: The theory of multiple intelligences.* New York: Harper and Row.

Nelsen, J. 1996. *Positive discipline.* New York: Ballantine.

Nelsen, J., Lott, L., and Glenn, H. 1993, 2000. *Positive discipline in the classroom.* Rocklin, CA: Prima. 2006 edition by Nelsen, J., and Lott, L.

CHAPTER 7

Discipline through Active Student Involvement

Authoritative Input
■ Fred Jones / Tools for Teaching: Discipline, Instruction, Motivation

CHAPTER PREVIEW

The approach to teaching and discipline that Jones advocates establishes a classroom environment and class routines that encourage good behavior. Within that approach, Jones spells out several teaching tools that promote student attention and participation, such as interactive teaching, providing help efficiently, and using incentive systems to foster responsibility.

Fundamental Hypothesis of Jones's Approach

Most discipline problems can be prevented by maintaining active student involvement in lessons. This can be done by providing for (1) an effective seating arrangement to facilitate teacher mobility, (2) the reduction of chronic help seeking by students, (3) a highly interactive style of teaching, (4) constant monitoring and adjusting of student performance, (5) incentives for correct work completion, and (6) a program of responsibility training to reduce time wasting. Discipline problems that do occur can be remediated by effective limit setting, which combines commitment and consistency with the body language of "meaning business" so the use of negative sanctions becomes rare.

Overview of the Nature and Practice of Jones's Approach

Jones explains how teachers can relate to students in ways that promote consideration, responsibility, and nondisruptive behavior. First, teachers must do what they can to prevent behavior problems before they occur. Good classroom organization, effective

113

About Fred Jones

Fred Jones is the developer and disseminator of Tools for Teaching (an approach to work-ing with students that was formerly known as Positive Classroom Management). A clinical psychologist, Jones has developed training procedures for improving teacher effectiveness in motivating, managing, and instructing students. His procedures were first developed from extensive field observations of effective teachers, observations he conducted while on the faculties of the UCLA Medical Center and the University of Rochester School of Medicine and Dentistry. An independent consultant since 1978, Jones now devotes full efforts to his training programs.

Jones's management system is described in his books, *Positive Classroom Discipline* (1987a), *Positive Classroom Instruction* (1987b), and *Fred Jones's Tools for Teaching* (2007). Jones also makes available a video course of study called *The Video Toolbox* (2002). A free Study Group Activity Guide, which divides his book into twelve study sessions, complete with focus questions and practice exercises, is available on the Fred Jones website, www.fredjones.com.

body language, and efficiently provided help combine to reduce misbehavior. Interactive teaching, which Jones calls "Say, See, Do teaching," is very effective in holding student attention. Jones also places great emphasis on effective body language and group incentives to manage incipient misbehavior. He says we must teach students responsibility by never doing for them what they can do for themselves. Jones has found that through specific training episodes, almost all teachers can acquire the techniques that were formerly used by only the most effective.

Jones on Teaching and Learning

Misbehavior and Loss of Teaching–Learning Time

In the 1970s, Jones and his associates spent thousands of hours observing and recording what transpires in hundreds of elementary and secondary classrooms. Jones's main interest was to pinpoint methods of teaching and classroom management that keep students working positively and productively. He also wanted to identify what expert teachers do to provide help when students need it and how they deal with misbehavior when it occurs.

Jones's observations led him to several notable conclusions. Principal among them is that discipline problems are usually quite different from the way they are depicted in the media and perceived by the public. Even though many of the classrooms he studied were located in inner-city schools and alternative schools for students with behavior problems, Jones found relatively little hostile student defiance—the behavior that teachers fear and many people believe predominates in schools. Instead, he found what he called **massive time wasting,** in which students talked when they shouldn't, goofed off, daydreamed, and moved about the room without permission. Jones found that in well-managed classrooms, one of those behaviors occurred about every 2 minutes, on average. In loud, unruly classes, they occurred on an average of about 2.5 per minute. In attempting to deal with the more disruptive misbehaviors, teachers lost an average of almost 50 percent of the time available for teaching and learning (Jones, 1987a).

Jones also discovered a critical time during lessons in which misbehavior is most likely to occur. He found that most lessons proceed fairly well until students are asked to work on their own. At that point, Jones (1987b) says, "The chickens come home to roost." Students seem to pay attention and give the impression they are learning perfectly, but when directed to continue work on their own, hands go up, talking begins, students rummage around or stare out the window, and some get out of their seats. At those times, most teachers do not have the skills to control the behavior and resort to admonishing and nagging. That, says Jones, is "another day in the life of a typical classroom" (1987b, p. 14) where the teacher ends up reteaching the lesson to a group of helpless hand-raisers during time that should be devoted to independent work.

Jones reports that teachers everywhere relate to that scenario and acknowledge having experienced the frustration and sense of defeat that comes with it. When discussing the phenomenon, many teachers say they expected they would quickly learn to maintain order in their classrooms, but were only partially successful in doing so and usually found themselves resorting to punitive measures.

Jones established that, at that time, teachers had not received training in behavior management and, further, that many, if not most, were unable to develop needed skills while working on the job. Jones decided to observe and document the methods used by teachers who were notably successful with discipline. He distilled those observations and used them as the basis for his teachings about classroom discipline.

How Effective Teachers Teach

From his studies of outstanding teachers, often referred to as "naturals," Jones was able to identify what they do to make teaching and discipline seem effortless. He found their success came from a set of core competencies that helped students learn the curriculum and, at the same time, taught students how to manage themselves. The combination of learning and self-management greatly reduced the incidence of misbehavior, as well as teacher workload and stress. Presently, we will examine the skill clusters that Jones features in his program.

Today, Jones strongly emphasizes the value of good classroom organization and management and stresses the importance of teaching students to behave responsibly. He was the first theorist—and still the major one—to systematically explain the power that teachers can exert through **nonverbal communication,** such as their body posture and carriage, facial expressions, gestures, eye contact, and physical proximity. He was also the first to provide a workable solution for what he calls helpless handraising by students who get stuck during seat work. He developed an instructional approach he calls **Say, See, Do teaching,** which calls for frequent student response during lessons, thus ensuring attention and active participation.

These tactics, which we will examine more closely in pages that follow, are used not only to prevent misbehavior, but to make teaching more effective and student learning more predictable. The techniques support students' own self-control and lead naturally to proper behavior and positive attitudes.

How Students Misbehave

Jones's research revealed that in normal classes, approximately 95 percent of all student misbehavior consists of talking to neighbors, daydreaming, making noise, being out of one's seat, and otherwise generally goofing off. Those behaviors, in isolation, are not overly disruptive, but Jones's studies showed that, on the average, they cause teachers to lose about 50 percent of their total time for instruction. Jones describes it as adding up to massive time wasting, gross inefficiency, and high frustration for teachers.

Recouping Lost Time

Teachers can avoid losing time for teaching and learning by taking the steps Jones advocates—establishing a classroom structure that discourages misbehavior; using effective body language; using Say, See, Do teaching; using incentive systems; and providing help efficiently to students during independent work. Efficient arrangement of the classroom also increases the likelihood of successful teaching and learning. This includes seating arrangements that permit teachers to **work the crowd** (move about easily and interact with individuals) as they supervise student work and provide help. Equally important is the teacher's use of **body language,** which Jones calls one of the most effective discipline skills available to teachers. Body language includes eye contact, physical proximity, body carriage, facial expressions, and gestures. Jones says that teachers set limits on student behavior not so much through rules as through subtle interpersonal skills, which show students that the teacher means business.

As for instructional methodology, Jones is very enthusiastic about his Say, See, Do teaching, which calls for frequent student response to teacher input. This method keeps students actively alert and involved in the lesson. But that is not the only teaching technique that motivates students. Jones says students will work hard and behave well if provided with certain incentives for doing so. The incentives he advocates are teachers' promises that students will be allowed to engage in favorite activities, if they first behave responsibly. These activities, selected by the group from an approved list, are earned by all members of the class for the enjoyment of everyone. In order to be effective, an incentive must be attractive to all and available to all.

Incentives are but one of the tools for teaching that help students to do their work without the teacher hovering over them. Another tool is a strategy for reducing students' reliance on teacher presence for doing their work. Jones devised a method of efficiently providing help to students who call for teacher assistance during independent work (the Helpless Handraisers). This tactic asks teachers, in Jones's words, to "be positive, be brief, and be gone." We will see more about this tactic presently.

Skill Clusters in Jones's Model

Jones believes the purpose of discipline is to help students profitably and enjoyably engage in learning. Discipline tactics should be positive and as unobtrusive as possible. He set forth six clusters of teacher skills that contribute to this kind of discipline. They are (1) classroom structure to discourage misbehavior, (2) limit setting through class agreements, (3) limit setting through body language, (4) Say, See, Do teaching to maximize student attention and involvement, (5) responsibility training through incentive systems, and (6) efficiently providing help to individual students. Here we explore these skill clusters further.

Skill Cluster 1. Classroom Structure to Discourage Misbehavior

Jones emphasizes that the best way to control misbehavior is to prevent its occurrence, and that the best preventive technique is a **classroom structure** that gives specific attention to room arrangement, class rules, classroom chores, and routines for beginning the class.

Room Arrangement.   An effective way to prevent students' goofing off is to minimize the physical distance between teacher and students. This tactic calls on teachers to work the crowd, moving about, maintaining physical proximity to students, interacting with students, and using occasional pauses, looks, or slow turns when necessary. These efforts keep most students actively attentive and involved, with no inclination to misbehave. For teachers to move easily among students during seat work and cooperative learning, the classroom seating must provide generous walkways. Jones suggests the **interior loop** as ideal, where desks or tables are set with two wide aisles from front to back and enough distance between side-to-side rows for teachers to walk comfortably among the students.

Classroom Rules.   Classroom rules should be both general and specific. **General rules,** few in number, define the teacher's broad guidelines, standards, and expectations for work and behavior. They should be posted and reviewed periodically. **Specific rules** describe procedures and routines, detailing specifically what students are to do and how they are to do it. Specific rules must be taught and rehearsed until they are learned like any academic skill. Jones advocates spending the first two weeks making sure students clearly understand the specific rules.

Classroom Chores.   Jones believes in assigning as many classroom chores to students as possible. This helps them buy in to the class program and helps develop a sense of responsibility.

Opening Routines.   Class sessions in most schools begin in a fragmented way, with announcements, taking attendance, handling tardies, and the like. This fragmentation wastes time and fosters misbehavior. Jones says that, on average, about 5 to 8 minutes are wasted in most classrooms immediately after the bell rings. To remedy that situation, teachers should begin lessons promptly. Jones suggests beginning the class with **bell work,** which does not require active instruction from the teacher. Bell work, which students are to begin by themselves upon entering the room, engages and focuses students on one or more of the day's lessons. Examples of bell work are review questions, warm-up problems, brain teasers, silent reading, and journal writing.

Skill Cluster 2. Limit Setting through Class Agreements

To help class members conduct themselves responsibly, it is suggested that during the first class session you discuss with students the concept of setting limits on behavior. The discussion should deeply involve students in exploring types of desirable and undesirable behavior. Such discussions lead to statements of acceptable behavior for the classroom, which are then formalized as class rules. You should explain to students that when they violate rules, you will help them correct their misbehavior by using your body language to remind them what they should be doing. Examples of body language include eye contact, stares, and physical proximity, which you should demonstrate.

To make limit setting work effectively, incentives and social rewards for proper behavior are provided. Desirable incentives are discussed (see Skills Cluster 5), and procedures for managing incentives are described. Students are reminded that the incentives they select are to have instructional value. Social rewards include acknowledgment and approval from teachers and classmates.

You will also need to discuss with students the backup systems you will use when students misbehave seriously and refuse to comply with rules or your requests. Jones's system attempts to move teachers away from reliance on admonition and threat; yet, Jones acknowledges that at times the teacher may be unable to get misbehaving students to comply with the rules. At those times, teachers may tell the student, "If you are not going to do your work, sit there quietly and don't bother others." For more serious situations of defiance or aggression, teachers must have a plan by which they isolate the student or call for help as needed.

Skill Cluster 3. Limit Setting through Body Language

Jones maintains that good discipline depends in large measure on teachers making effective use of body language. Jones says this is best done when teachers use their bodies correctly but say nothing and take no other action. He reminds teachers that they cannot discipline with their mouths. He says if that were possible, nagging would have fixed every kid a million years ago. When you open your mouth, he says, you run the risk of slitting your own throat. The specific aspects of body language Jones emphasizes are discussed here.

Proper Breathing. Teachers do well to remain calm in all situations. Calm conveys strength. It is attained in part through proper breathing. The way teachers breathe when under pressure signals how they feel and what they are likely to do next. Skilled teachers breathe slowly and deliberately before responding to situations. Jones noted that some teachers take two deep breaths before turning to a misbehaving student. He believes doing so enables them to maintain self-control.

Eye Contact.   Miss Remy is demonstrating and explaining the process of multiplying fractions. She sees that Jacob has stopped paying attention. She pauses in her explanation. The sudden quiet causes Jacob to look at Miss Remy. He finds she is looking directly at his eyes. He straightens up and waits attentively. Few physical acts are more effective than eye contact for conveying the impression of being in control. Jones says that turning and pointing the eyes and the feet toward talking students shows teacher commitment to discipline.

Physical Proximity.   Miss Remy has completed her demonstration of the multiplication of fractions. She has directed students to complete some exercises on their own. After a time she sees from the back of the room that Jacob has stopped working and has begun talking to Jerry. She moves toward him, and Jacob unexpectedly finds her shadow at his side. He immediately gets back to work, without Miss Remy having to say anything. Jones observes that teachers who use physical proximity rarely need to say anything to the offending students to get them to behave.

Body Carriage.   Jones also finds that posture and **body carriage** are quite effective in communicating authority. Students read body language and are able to tell whether the teacher is feeling in charge, tired, disinterested, or intimidated. Good posture and confident carriage suggest strong leadership, whereas a drooping posture and lethargic movements suggest resignation or fearfulness. Effective teachers, even when tired or troubled, tend to hold themselves erect and move assertively.

Facial Expressions.   As with body carriage, teachers' facial expressions communicate much to students. They can show enthusiasm, seriousness, enjoyment, and appreciation, all of which encourage good behavior; or they can reveal boredom, annoyance, and resignation, which may encourage misbehavior. Expressions such as winks and smiles are especially effective because they convey a sense of humor and personal connection, traits that students appreciate in teachers.

Skill Cluster 4. Using Say, See, Do Teaching

Jones says that many teachers beyond primary grades spend major portions of their class periods presenting information to students while the students remain relatively passive. It is not until the end of such lessons that students are asked to do something with the information they have received. Jones (2001) graphically depicts this old-fashioned approach as follows:

(Teacher) input, input, input, input, input—(Student) output

This instructional approach contains some built-in factors that contribute to student misbehavior, including:

- The large amount of teacher input produces cognitive overload in students, which makes them disengage from the lesson.

- The students sit passively for too long. The urge to do something builds up.
- The teacher does not adequately work the crowd, that is, interact with individual students, particularly in the back of the classroom.

Teachers who are more effective, Jones says, put students to work from the beginning. They present information and then quickly have students do something with it. This approach is doing oriented, with activities occurring often at short intervals, and is depicted as follows:

(Teacher) input—(Student) output—(Teacher) input—(Student) output—
(Teacher) input—(Student) output

This Say, See, Do teaching, along with the use of **visual instruction plans (VIPs),** greatly reduces the amount of wasted time because students are kept busy while the teacher circulates and interacts with them. The VIP consists of a series of picture prompts that represent the process of the activity or thinking and guide students through the process.

Skill Cluster 5. Responsibility Training through Incentive Systems

Jones observes that teachers tend to sort themselves into three different management styles: (1) Some teach well and reward well; (2) some nag, threaten, and punish; and (3) some lower their standards and accept whatever they can get from students. These management styles are closely related to success in the classroom. Compare Mr. Sharpe with Mr. Naeve. Mr. Sharpe tells his class that if all of them complete their work in 25 minutes or less, they can have the last 10 minutes of class time to talk quietly with a friend. Mr. Naeve tells his class he will allow them to begin the period by discussing their work with a friend, provided they promise to work very hard afterward. Which teacher is likely to get the best work from his students? This question has to do with incentives and how they affect responsibility.

An **incentive** is something outside of the individual that prompts the individual to act. In classrooms, it is something that is held in abeyance and is promised as a result for students behaving as desired. It might a preferred activity or an unspecified surprise. Its effectiveness is judged by how well students behave properly in order to obtain the reward. Jones gives prominence to incentives in his discipline program. He found that some of the most effective teachers use incentives systematically, although most teachers use them ineffectively or not at all.

What are characteristics of effective incentives, and how should they be used? Responsibility training gains most of its strength, Jones says, from the "bonus" portion of the incentive. Bonuses encourage students to save time they would normally waste so they can get it back in the form of preferred activity time. It gives class members a shared vested interest in cooperating to save time rather than wasting time throughout the period or day. Jones suggests that to make the best use of incentives, teachers should carefully consider (1) Grandma's rule, (2) student responsibility, (3) genuine incentives, (4) preferred activities, (5) educational value, (6) group concern, (7) ease of implementation, (8) omission training, and (9) backup systems. Let us see what is involved in each.

Grandma's Rule.   **Grandma's rule** states: "First eat your vegetables, and then you can have your dessert." Applied to the classroom, this rule requires that students first do what they are supposed to do, and then for a while after that they can do an activity they enjoy doing. Just as children (and most adults) want their dessert first, promising to eat their vegetables afterward, students ask to have their incentive first, pledging on their honor to work feverishly afterward. As we all know, even the best intentions are hard to remember once the reason for doing the work is gone. Thus, teachers who wish to use incentive systems effectively must delay the rewards until students have done the required work acceptably. If they don't eat their broccoli, they don't get their ice cream.

Student Responsibility.   Jones believes that incentives can help everyone take responsibility for their actions. For example, one way students can show responsibility is through carrying their load in group activities. However, when doing so is merely a "teacher expectation," some students will find other things to do or look for the easy way out. Jones suggests that when students show responsibility by doing what teachers ask them to do, it is because teachers have used encouragement and incentives, rather than trying to force responsible behavior through nagging, threatening, or punishing.

Genuine Incentives.   There is a wide difference between what many teachers think might be good incentives (e.g., "Let's all work in such a way that we will later be proud of what we do") and what students consider to be **genuine incentives** (e.g., "If you complete your work on time, you can have 5 minutes of preferred activity time"). By the way, preferred activity time is different than free time. Jones cautions against allowing students to earn free time to do whatever they wish. He says students won't work for long to earn free time, but they will for *activity* time they enjoy.

Another caution about incentives is that certain ones, although effective for some members of the class, are not effective for all. For example, a teacher might say, "The first person to complete a perfect paper will receive two bonus points." This may motivate a few of the most able students, but all the others know they have little chance to win so they don't feel any reason to try. Or the teacher may say, "If you really work hard, you can be the best class I have ever had." This sounds good to the teacher but means little to the students and is not sufficient to keep them diligently at work.

Jones believes that activities students enjoy are the best overall incentives. Students respond well to the anticipation of activities such as art activities, viewing a video, doing class skits, and the like. Almost all students enjoy such activities, and they are available to all students, not just a few. On the other side of the picture, tangible objects, awards, and certificates should not be used as incentives. They tend to be costly or difficult to dispense and usually have little educational value.

Preferred Activity Time.   **Preferred activity time (PAT)** is time allotted for activities such as learning games and enrichment activities. "Preferred activity" is activity that students especially enjoy, such as using vocabulary words to play hangman, doing a class art project, or reading a favorite book. Jones advises that when selecting and introducing PAT, teachers must make sure that students want the activity, that they earn the activity by showing responsibility, and that the teacher can live with the PAT.

PAT may be earned in a number of different ways. Mr. Jorgensen gives his fourth graders 3 minutes to put away their language arts materials and prepare for math. Any time left over from the 3 minutes goes to PAT later in the week. In Mrs. Nguyen's English class, if everyone is seated and ready when the bell rings, the class earns two additional minutes of PAT. However, if the class or some of its members continues to be noisy, the class loses the amount of PAT they wasted. Some PAT may be used the day it is earned, whereas other PAT may be accumulated for a future activity, such as a field trip. In some instances, PAT may be earned as individual bonuses. When Mickey continues to be unprepared and consequently loses PAT for the class, Mr. Duncan decides to work with him individually. In that way, Mickey's irresponsibility does not penalize the entire class, but as he improves, he might earn PAT for the entire class, which enhances his status with peers.

Educational Value.   To the extent feasible, every class period should be devoted to activities that have educational value. Work that keeps students occupied but teaches them trivialities can seldom be justified. This principle applies to incentive systems. Although few educators would be loath never to allow a moment of innocent frivolity, the opposite extreme of daily or weekly parties as incentives is difficult to condone. What then should one use as PAT?

There are many activities with educational value that students enjoy greatly, both individually and in groups. Students are not left to do just anything, nor do they proceed without guidance. The freedom lies in being able to choose from a variety of approved activities. Activities can be chosen by vote, and all students engage in the same activity during the time allotted. Elementary school students often select physical education, art, music, drama, construction activities, or being read to by the teacher. Secondary students often choose to watch a video, hold class discussions on special topics, watch performances by class members, or work together on projects such as producing a class magazine. JoLynne Talbott Jones posts on the Jones website (www.fredjones.com) suggestions from teachers for a large number of educationally sound activities that students of various grade levels enjoy greatly and that therefore serve as good preferred activities.

Group Concern.   Jones emphasizes the importance of making sure every student has a stake in earning the incentive for the entire class. This **group concern** motivates all students to keep on task, behave well, and complete assigned work. Here is how it is done: The teacher agrees to set aside a period of time in which students might be allowed to engage in a preferred activity. In keeping with Grandma's rule, this PAT period must come after a significant amount of effort has been devoted to the normal curriculum. The PAT can be held at the end of the school day for self-contained classes—perhaps 15 to 20 minutes. For departmentalized classes, the time can be set aside at the end of the week—perhaps 30 minutes on Friday. The students can decide on the activity for their dessert time, and to earn it they have to work and behave as expected.

The teacher manages the system by keeping track of the time that students earn. Of course, it is possible that a single student, by misbehaving, can prevent the class from earning full PAT. Teachers often think it unfair to penalize the entire class for the sins of a few. In practice this is rarely a problem, because the class quickly understands that this is a group effort, not an individual one. The group is rewarded together and punished together regardless of who might transgress. A strength of this approach is that it brings peer pressure to bear against misbehavior. Ordinarily a misbehaving student obtains reinforcement from the group in the form of attention or laughter. With proper PAT, the opposite is true. The class is likely to discourage individual misbehavior because it takes away something the class members want. Nevertheless, some students do occasionally misbehave to the detriment of other responsible students. When this occurs, the teacher may decide to work with the offending student individually.

Ease of Implementation.   Incentive systems will not work unless they are easy to implement. Jones (2001) suggests the following:

1. Establish and explain the system.
2. Allow the class to vote from time to time on the approved activities they wish to enjoy during incentive time.
3. Keep track of the bonus time students have earned for PAT.
4. Be prepared when necessary to conduct the class in low-preference activities for the amount of time that students have lost from the time allotted to their preferred activity.

Omission Training.   Generally speaking, incentives and PAT bonuses are earned by the entire class. Teachers cannot possibly monitor incentives for all students individually. As noted, however, occasional misbehavior by a given student may spoil PAT for the rest of the class. To help those few students, Jones suggests **omission training,** a plan that allows a student to earn PAT for the entire class by ceasing to misbehave in a particular way.

Kevin, a student in Ms. VanEtten's class, is one such student. He simply does not seem to care about PAT, and, consequently, is late, loud, and unprepared, thus causing other class members to lose the PAT they have tried to earn. Ms. VanEtten privately explains to Kevin that he doesn't have to participate with the class in earning PAT, but she does want him to be successful with his own work and behavior. She explains that she will use a timer, and when Kevin behaves in accordance with class rules, he will earn time for himself, and also PAT for the class. When he misbehaves, he loses time for himself but not for the class.

Backup Systems.   As a last option for students like Kevin, Jones suggests **backup systems,** which are hierarchical arrangements of sanctions intended to stop unacceptable student behavior. Jones identifies three levels of backup.

1. *Small backup responses.* Said privately or semiprivately to the student: "I expect you to stop talking so we can get on with our work." With such low-keyed messages the student knows the teacher means business. Whispering privately is a constructive way to protect students' dignity.

2. *Medium backup responses.* Delivered publicly in the classroom: "Emily, please go to the thinking chair for 3 minutes and consider how you are acting and why it causes me to send you there" or "Brian, you are late again. You must have detention with me to-morrow after school." Other medium backup responses include warnings, reprimands, loss of privilege, and parent conferences. Because these responses are made publicly, they carry the risk that students may try to get even with teachers if they feel humiliated in front of their peers.

3. *Large backup responses.* Deal with chronically repeated disruptions or other intolera-ble behavior. They require involvement of at least two professionals, usually the teacher and an administrator. They include trips to the office, in- or out-of-school suspension, special class, and special school.

Skill Cluster 6. Providing Efficient Help to Individual Students

One of the most interesting, important, and useful findings in Jones's research has to do with the way teachers help students who are stuck during seat work. Suppose a lesson in verb tenses is in progress. The teacher introduces the topic, explains the concept on the board, asks two or three questions to determine whether the students are understanding, and then assigns exercises for students to complete at their desks. Very soon Arnell raises his hand, signaling that he needs help. If only three or four students raise hands during this time, the teacher has no problem. But if twenty students fill the air with waving arms, most of them sit for several minutes waiting for the teacher. This waiting time is pure waste and an invitation to misbehave.

Jones asked teachers how much time they thought they spent on the average when providing help to individuals who raised their hands for help. The teachers felt they spent from 1 to 2 minutes with each student, but when Jones's researchers timed the episodes, they found that teachers actually spent around 4 minutes with each student. This amount of time made it impossible for the teacher to attend to more than a few students during the work period. Even if the amount of time was only 1 minute per contact, several minutes would pass while some students sat and did nothing.

Jones noted an additional phenomenon that compounded the problem. He called it **helpless handraising,** wherein some students routinely raised their hands for teacher help even when they did not need it. It was rewarding to those students to have the teacher unfailingly come to their side and give them personal attention. Over time, a dependency syndrome developed in those students; they would not work unless the teacher gave them attention.

Jones concluded that independent seat work is typically beset with four problems: (1) insufficient time for teachers to answer all requests for help, (2) wasted student time, (3) high potential for misbehavior, and (4) perpetuation of dependency. Jones deter-mined that all four problems can be solved through teaching teachers how to give help efficiently, which is accomplished as follows:

First, organize the classroom seating so students are within easy reach of the teacher. The interior loop seating arrangement previously described is suggested because it gives the teacher free, easy movement in the room.

Second, use visual instruction plans and graphic reminders, such as models or charts, to provide clear examples and instructions for students to follow, such as the steps in algorithms, proper form for business letters, or things to be done in the lesson. The reminders are posted and can be consulted by students instead of calling on teachers for help.

Third, reduce to a minimum the time spent in giving students individual help. Consider the inefficient procedure teachers often use, for example, a questioning tutorial like the following:

"What's the problem?"
"All right, what did we say was the first thing to do?" *[Waits; repeats question.]*
"No, that was the second. You are forgetting the first step. What was it? Think again." *[Waits until student finally makes a guess.]*
"No, let me help you with another example. Suppose . . ."

In this manner the teacher often reteaches the concept or process to each student who requests help. Four minutes can be spent unexpectedly in each interaction. Jones trains teachers to give help in a very different way, and he insists that each help episode be done in 20 seconds or less, with an optimal goal of about 10 seconds. To reach this level of efficiency, the teacher should do the following when arriving beside the student:

1. (Optional for initial contact.) Quickly find anything that the student has done correctly and mention it favorably: "Your work is very neat" or "Good job up to here."
2. Give a straightforward prompt that will get the student going: "Follow step two on the chart" or "Regroup here." Jones says to teach students to ask themselves, "What do I do next?" instead of tutoring them through the whole task.
3. Leave immediately. Jones puts it like this: "Be positive, be brief, and be gone."

Help provided in this way solves the time and attention problems that teachers face during instructional work time. Every student who truly needs help can receive proper attention. When students do not sit idly while waiting for the teacher, they are far less likely to misbehave. Helpless handraising disappears. Rapid circulation by the teacher permits better monitoring of work being done by students who do not raise their hands. When errors are noted in those students' work, the teacher should provide help just as for students who have raised their hands.

Study Group Activity Guide

Jones makes available a free Study Group Activity Guide for educators that can be downloaded from his website. *The Video Toolbox* aligns with the Study Guide and book and is designed for use by small groups of teachers or student teachers who meet regularly to discuss and put into practice the skills Jones advocates. He stresses the value of working with colleagues in this manner. The Study Group Activity Guide and *The Video Toolbox* structure learning activities that can be used indefinitely as you perfect your management skills. He recommends that the study groups consist of three to eight teachers who meet on a weekly basis. The structure for meetings includes focus questions, study group questions, and performance checklists. The twelve meeting topics are as follows:

1. Working the Crowd and Room Arrangement
2. Praise, Prompt, and Leave
3. Visual Instructional Plans
4. Say, See, Do Teaching
5. Rules, Routines, and Standards
6. Understanding Brat Behavior
7. Calm Is Strength
8. The Body Language of Meaning Business
9. Eliminating Backtalk
10. Responsibility Training
11. Omission Training and Preferred Activity Time
12. Dealing with Typical Classroom Crises

Initiating Jones's Approach in the Classroom

Jones (1987a, p. 321) suggests that his approach to discipline be put in place as a five-tiered system that includes: (1) classroom structure, (2) limit setting, (3) Say, See, Do teaching, (4) incentives, and (5) backup systems. Because they are interrelated, all five tiers are planned out in advance and introduced simultaneously. Teachers can assess their own classroom behavior in light of Jones's suggestions and isolate certain discipline tactics they would like to incorporate into their teaching. They can practice what Jones suggests and apply their new skills in the classroom. Although Jones suggests his five tiers be implemented together, teachers have ample opportunity later for practicing, perfecting, and adding new skills incrementally.

KEY TERMS AND CONCEPTS EMPHASIZED IN THIS CHAPTER

massive time wasting
nonverbal communication
Say, See, Do teaching
work the crowd
body language
classroom structure
interior loop
general rules

specific rules
bell work
body carriage
visual instruction plan
    (VIP)
incentives
Grandma's rule
genuine incentives

preferred activity time
    (PAT)
group concern
omission training
backup systems
helpless handraising

SELECTED SEVEN–SUMMARY SUGGESTIONS FROM FRED JONES

1. Do what you can to save instructional time that is too frequently wasted because of student misbehavior and other factors. A number of simple management techniques will conserve this time.

2. Structure your classroom and program to encourage attention, active involvement, and responsibility. Use an effective seating arrangement, establish clear routines, and assign individual chores to students.

3. Use body language and personal skills more than verbal messages to limit misbehavior and help students stay on track.

4. Emphasize Say, See, Do teaching as a means of increasing student alertness, involvement, and learning.

5. Use class incentives as a means of increasing student involvement and responsibility.

6. Learn how to give individual help to students in 20 seconds or less. Doing so eliminates student dependence on your presence and enables you to provide help as needed to all students quickly.

7. Actively work the crowd, interacting frequently with individual students during instruction.

CONCEPT CASES

Case 1: Kristina Will Not Work

Kristina, a student in Mr. Jake's class, is quite docile. She socializes little with other students and never disrupts the class. However, Mr. Jake cannot get Kristina to do any work. She rarely completes an assignment. She is simply there, putting forth almost no effort at all. *How would Jones deal with Kristina?*

Jones would probably suggest that Mr. Jake take the following steps to improve Kristina's behavior:

1. Make frequent eye contact with her. Even when she looks down, Mr. Jake should make sure to look directly at her. She will be aware of it, and that may be enough to encourage her to begin work.

2. Move close to Kristina. Stand beside her while presenting the lesson.

3. Give Kristina frequent help during seat work. Check on her progress several times during the lesson. Give specific suggestions and then quickly move on.

4. Increase the amount of Say, See, Do teaching with Kristina so she has less information to deal with and is called on to respond frequently.

5. Set up a personal incentive system with Kristina, such as doing a certain amount of work to earn an activity she especially enjoys.

6. Set up a system in which Kristina can earn rewards for the entire class. This brings her peer attention and support.

Case 2: Sara Cannot Stop Talking

Sara is a pleasant girl who participates in class activities and does most, though not all, of her assigned work. She cannot seem to refrain from talking to classmates, however. Her teacher, Mr. Gonzales, has to speak to her repeatedly during lessons, to the point that he often becomes exasperated and loses his temper. *What suggestions would Jones give Mr. Gonzales for dealing with Sara?*

Case 3: Joshua Clowns and Intimidates

Joshua, larger and louder than his classmates, always wants to be the center of attention, which he accomplishes through a combination of clowning and intimidation. He makes wise remarks, talks back (smilingly) to the teacher, utters a variety of sound-effect noises such as automobile crashes and gunshots, and makes limitless sarcastic comments and put-downs of his classmates. Other students will not stand up to him, apparently fearing his size and verbal aggression. His teacher, Miss Pearl, has come to her wit's end. *What specifically do you find in Jones's suggestions that would help Miss Pearl with Joshua?*

Case 4: Tom Is Hostile and Defiant

Tom has appeared to be in his usual foul mood ever since arriving in class. On his way to sharpen his pencil, he bumps into Frank, who complains. Tom tells him loudly to shut up. Miss Baines, the teacher, says, "Tom, go back to your seat." Tom wheels around, swears loudly, and says heatedly, "I'll go when I'm damned good and ready!" *How effective do you believe Jones's suggestions would be in dealing with Tom?*

ACTIVITIES

1. Makes notes in your journal concerning elements from Jones's model that contribute to the five principles of building a personal system of discipline.

2. For each of the following scenarios, first identify the problem that underlies the undesired behavior, then describe how Jones would have the teacher deal with it.

   a. Mr. Anton tries to help all of his students during independent work time but finds himself unable to get around to all who have their hands raised.

   b. Ms. Sevier wants to show trust for her class. She accepts their promise to work hard if she will allow them first to listen to a few favorite recordings. After listening, the students talk so much that they fail to get their work done.

   c. Mr. Gregory wears himself out every day dealing ceaselessly with three class clowns who disrupt his lessons. The other students always laugh at the clowns' antics.

   d. Mrs. Swanson, who takes pride in her lectures, is becoming frustrated because students begin to gaze out the window and whisper before she has completed what she wants to tell them.

YOU ARE THE TEACHER

Student Teacher

You are a student teacher in an inner-city magnet school that emphasizes academics. Half of your students are African American. The other half, of various ethnic groups, have been bused in to take advantage of the instructional program and rich resources. All are academically talented and none has what would be called a bad attitude toward school. Mrs. Warde, the regular teacher of the class, does not seem to rely on any particular scheme of discipline, at least not any which is obvious to you. She simply tells the students what to do and they comply. For the first few lessons you have taught, Mrs. Warde has remained in the room, serving as your aide. The students worked well, and you felt pleased and successful.

When Mrs. Warde Leaves the Room

Mrs. Warde tells you that she will leave the room during the math lesson so you can begin getting the feel of directing the class on your own. Mrs. Warde warns you that the class might test you with a bit of naughtiness, though nothing serious is likely to occur. "Just be in charge," Mrs. Warde counsels. The math lesson begins well, without incident. The lesson has to do with beginning algebra concepts, which you approach through a discovery mode. You tell the class, "I want you to work independently on this. Think your way through the following equations and decide if they are true for all numbers."

$$a + 0 = a$$

$$a + b = b + a$$

$$a (b + c) = ab + c$$

$$a + 1 = 1$$

$$a \times 0 = a$$

The students begin work, but within 2 minutes hands are shooting up. You go to help Alicia, who is stuck on the third equation. "What's the matter?" you whisper.

Alicia: I don't understand what this means.
Teacher: It was like what I showed you on the board. The same.
Alicia: Those were numbers. I don't understand it with these letters.
Teacher: They are the same as the numbers. They take the place of the numbers. I showed you how they were interchangeable, remember? Go ahead, let me see. Tell me what you are doing, step-by-step.

You do not realize it, but you spend almost five minutes with Alicia. Meanwhile, a few of the students have finished and are waiting, but most are holding tired arms limply in the air. You rush to the next student and repeat your questioning procedure. Meanwhile, Matt and Alonzo have dropped their hands and are looking at each other's papers. They begin to talk and laugh. Others follow, and soon all work has stopped and the classroom has become quite noisy. You repeatedly say, "Shhh, shhh!" but with little effect. At last you go to the front of the room, demand attention, and tell the class how disappointed you are in their rude behavior.

Conceptualizing a Strategy

If you followed the suggestions of Fred Jones, what would you conclude or do with regard to the following?

1. Preventing the problem from occurring in the first place.

2. Putting a clear end to the misbehavior.

3. Involving other or all students in addressing the situation.

4. Maintaining student dignity and good personal relations.

5. Using follow-up procedures that would prevent the recurrence of the misbehavior.

6. Using the situation to help the students develop a sense of greater responsibility and self-control.

REFERENCES

Jones, F. 1987a. *Positive classroom discipline.* New York: McGraw-Hill.

Jones, F. 1987b. *Positive classroom instruction.* New York: McGraw-Hill.

Jones, F. 2007. *Fred Jones's tools for teaching.* Santa Cruz, CA: Fredric H. Jones & Associates.

Jones, J. 2002. *The Video Toolbox.* Santa Cruz, CA: Fredric H. Jones & Associates.

CHAPTER 8

Discipline through Pragmatic Classroom Management

Authoritative Input
■ Harry Wong and Rosemary Wong / The First Days of School

The Wongs strive to help all teachers become more effective in their work. They place major emphasis on classroom management, focusing especially on structure and procedures that enable students to work diligently, behave responsibly, and reach high levels of achievement. The Wongs' approach is eminently **pragmatic,** built from practical ideas gleaned from myriad sources, with no attempt to make their suggestions fit any particular theory. They write in an informal manner and use many aphorisms that stick in the mind, such as

- The main problem in teaching is not poor discipline, but poor classroom management.
- Procedures provide the foundation that leads to high student achievement.
- Effective teachers spend most of the first two weeks teaching students to follow classroom procedures.
- The more capable the teacher, the more successful the student.

Fundamental Hypothesis of the Wongs' Approach

Discipline problems largely disappear when students are carefully taught to follow procedures for all classroom activities.

A Quick Read of the Wongs' Principal Suggestions

The following extracted statements provide an overview of the Wongs' principal contentions (from Glavac, 2005; Starr, 1999; and Wong and Wong, 2000a, 2000b, 2004a, 2004b, 2005). As the chapter progresses, some of these statements will be explored in greater detail.

About Harry and Rosemary Wong

For many years, Harry Wong, now an educational speaker and consultant, taught middle school and high school classes in science. He received numerous teaching awards, including Outstanding Secondary Teacher Award, the Science Teacher Achievement Recognition Award, the Outstanding Biology Teacher Award, and the Valley Forge Teacher's Medal. In 2006, he was named one of Education's Superstars by Instructor Magazine. Rosemary Wong taught grades K–8 and served as media coordinator and student activity director. She was chosen as one of California's first mentor teachers and has been awarded the Silicon Valley Distinguished Woman of the Year Award. She works with her husband and is CEO of their publishing company. At the time of this writing, their book, *The First Days of School,* (2004b) had sold over 2.7 million copies, making it the best-selling education book of all time. They have also produced a video series titled *The Effective Teacher,* which won the Gold Award in the International Film and Video Festival and the Telly Award as the best educational staff development video. In this chapter, Harry and Rosemary Wong, in partnership, are referred to as "the Wongs." Because Harry is scheduled for speaking for years in advance, they now write a monthly column so more people can access their ideas. The columns are posted on www.teachers.net. The Wongs' website is www.effectiveteaching.com.

About School

- School is where students go to learn how to be productive citizens and reach their potential as human beings.
- School should be challenging, exciting, engrossing, and thought provoking, but it must have structure to ensure student success.
- You cannot give students self-esteem, but you can make sure they find success in school.

About Teaching

- Teaching is a craft—a highly skilled craft that can be learned.
- By far the most important factor in school learning is the ability of the teacher. The more capable the teacher, the more successful the student.
- Good teachers enhance the life and spirit of students they teach.
- Stop asking, "What am I supposed to do?" Start asking, "What must I know that will help me accomplish what I need to do?"
- What you do on the first day of school determines your success for the rest of the year.
- Start class immediately. Do not take roll until later.
- Learning is most effective when it takes place in a supportive community of learners.
- The more that students work together responsibly, the more they learn.
- Shorter assignments produce higher student achievement.
- Intersperse questions throughout a lesson. Ask a question after you have spoken a few sentences rather than many. By doing so, you significantly increase student learning and retention.
- Students usually learn more from an activity-question approach to teaching than from a textbook-lecture approach.

- Teachers go through four stages of professional development—fantasy, survival, mastery, and impact. Good management will move you quickly from fantasy to mastery.
- You can have your achievements or you can have your excuses.
- Those who teach well never cease to learn.

About Classrooms and Procedures

- The single most important factor governing student learning is not discipline; it is how a teacher manages a classroom.
- Your classroom need not be chaos; it can be a smoothly functioning learning environment.
- A well-managed classroom is task oriented and predictable.
- *Ineffective teachers* begin the first day of school attempting to teach a subject. They then spend the rest of the school year running after their students.
- *Effective teachers* spend most of the first two weeks of the school year teaching students to follow classroom procedures. Then students learn better and conduct themselves better.
- What is done on the first day of school or the beginning of a class—even the first few minutes—can make or break a teacher.
- The very first day, the very first minute, the very first second of school, teachers should begin to establish a structure of procedures and routines for the class.

About Roles and Responsibilities

Help students understand both your responsibilities and their responsibilities in the classroom. The following, appropriate for secondary classes, appears on the cover of *The First Days of School* (2004b):

My Responsibilities as Your Teacher
1. To treat you with respect and care as an individual.
2. To provide you an orderly classroom environment.
3. To provide the necessary discipline.
4. To provide the appropriate motivation.
5. To teach you the required content.

Your Responsibilities as My Students
1. To treat me with respect and care as an individual.
2. To attend classes regularly.
3. To be cooperative and not disruptive.
4. To study and do your work well.
5. To learn and master the required content.

About Discipline

- Classroom rules indicate the behavior you expect from students. In order to provide a safe and effective learning environment, establish and enforce appropriate rules.
- Rules of behavior set limits, just as do rules in games. They create a work-oriented atmosphere in the classroom.
- Behavior associated with rules must be taught through discussion, demonstration, and practice.
- Consequences should be attached to rules—positive consequences for compliance and negative consequences (but not punishment) for noncompliance.
- Explain your discipline plan (expectations, rules, and consequences) to students the first day of school.

About Testing and Evaluation

- If a student cannot demonstrate learning or achievement, it is the teacher's fault, not the student's.
- Use criterion-referenced tests to evaluate student performance.
- The more frequent the tests, the higher the achievement.
- Grade on what is learned, not on the curve—a procedure that has done great harm to education.

About the First Day of Class

- Have your classroom ready for instruction, and make it inviting.
- Organize your classroom in accordance with a script that you follow.
- Stand at the door and greet students as they enter.
- Give each student a seating assignment and a seating chart.
- Position yourself in the room near the students: Problems are proportional to distance between you and them.
- In a consistent location, post an assignment for students to begin when they enter the room.
- Display your diploma and credentials with pride. Dress in a professional manner that models success and shows you expect achievement.

About the First Week of Teaching

- The three most important things you must teach the first week of school are discipline, procedures, and routines.
- Explain your discipline plan to students and put it in effect immediately.
- State your procedures and rehearse them until they become routines.

The Problem Is Not Discipline

The Wongs insist that the main cause of poor behavior in the classroom is not bad discipline, but rather errors teachers make in classroom management. Unless you establish and teach clear class procedures, student behavior will never be as you want it. The Wongs support their contentions with many illustrative cases, such as the following (Wong and Wong, 2000a):

> Bob Marlowe, a typical teacher, continually frets about his lessons and his students' behavior. His main question is always, "What am I going to teach tomorrow?" He considers teaching to consist of three main parts: (1) covering material, (2) doing activities, and (3) disciplining students when they do not comply with expectations. Bob experiences daily frustrations in teaching, yet he continues to repeat the same cycle day after day—cover and discipline, cover and discipline. Bob's difficulties occur because he does not know how to motivate students, get their attention, distribute and retrieve materials, collect and deal with papers and homework, maintain a current grade-record book, explain what students should do if they finish early, and a huge number of other management matters that require ongoing attention.

A Discipline Plan Is Necessary, However

The Wongs say that although classroom misbehavior occurs primarily because of poor classroom management, all teachers still need a discipline plan that contains rules and consequences. As noted, they say (2004b, p. 141) that the three most important things you should teach students during the first days of school are discipline, procedures, and routines. They believe that most teachers are too eager to begin teaching lessons, and when misbehavior occurs, those teachers apply punitive measures to stop it. The Wongs insist if you don't have a discipline plan that begins the first day of school, you are setting yourself up for failure. Effective teachers present their rules clearly and provide reasonable explanations for why they are needed.

The Wongs are not particular about the kind of discipline plan you use. They say that instead of adopting someone else's discipline plan, you should develop one that is suited to your requirements and your students' needs. Any discipline plan should include rules of behavior, procedures for teaching those rules, and consequences that are applied when students comply with rules or break rules.

As for rules, the Wongs (2004b, p. 143) suggest that you carefully think through the kind of behavior you expect from students, write your expectations as rules, post them in the class, and go over them with students on the first day. They point out that you will have firm confidence in your ability to manage the class if you and your students understand clearly what is expected.

The Wongs suggest you limit the number of rules to a maximum of five, stated in a positive manner when possible (although in some cases it is more effective to state them in a negative manner, such as "No fighting."). Here are five universal rules that the Wongs provide for your consideration (2004b, p. 146):

1. Follow directions the first time they are given.
2. Raise your hand and wait for permission to speak.
3. Stay in your seat unless you have permission to do otherwise.
4. Keep hands, feet, and objects to yourself.
5. No cursing or teasing.

Introduce the rules on the first day of class and post them in a prominent place. The Wongs suggest introducing them as follows, using your own language and explanations:

> The rules for our class are to help you learn in a classroom that is safe and effective. They help make sure that nothing will interfere with your success in this class.
>
> We will be working together closely. We need to keep this classroom a place where you will never have fear of being ridiculed or threatened. Because I care about all of you and want you to succeed, I will not allow you to do anything that will interfere with someone else who is trying to learn.
>
> In the same way, my job is to teach you and help you be successful, so I will not allow you to do anything that will interfere with my teaching and our group success and enjoyment.
>
> So I can teach and all of us can learn in the best possible conditions, I have a set of rules that help make this classroom safe, orderly, and productive. I'd like to explain these rules to you so you understand clearly what they mean and how I will enforce them.

Why Planning and Organizing Are So Important

The case of Bob Marlowe, presented earlier, illustrates what the Wongs call the progression from fantasy to reality. In the initial fantasy phase, beginning teachers expect students automatically to rally to them and begin learning and enjoying themselves. But when Bob first met his new class of students, he quickly moved into the 'reality phase' of teaching, which was the opposite of what he expected. Everything seemed to go wrong. The lessons did not succeed and students behaved badly. The Wongs use Bob Marlowe's case to emphasize that there is nothing more important to teaching success than good planning and organization.

Organization, they point out, is about keeping a schedule, knowing where things are, and making your time and space work for you. It eliminates chaos, lets you get things done, and allows you some time to enjoy life. And where do teachers like Bob find good management ideas? The Wongs say you can find those ideas in abundance in the best practices of outstanding teachers. They advise Bob to "beg, borrow, and steal" those good ideas from any sources available. (The Wongs, in their book and website, provide the suggestions Bob needs for a smoothly functioning classroom.)

Procedures, and What They Entail

The Wongs believe most students will conduct themselves acceptably if they are taught the procedures that lead to learning and responsible behavior. As the procedures are taught and used, they become **routines** that students follow habitually. The Wongs say student achievement is directly related to how well teachers establish good, workable classroom procedures, beginning the very first day. Students accept and appreciate uniform procedures that provide security while minimizing confusion. If those procedures are not in place, students are likely to behave undesirably and develop poor work habits that are difficult to correct.

How to Decide on Procedures for Your Classroom

To establish good **procedures,** do two things: (1) Decide what routines are needed for the activities you will provide, and (2) make lists of the procedural steps students must follow to participate in and benefit from the activities. If you do these two things, you will end up with a very large number of procedures. Remember that every time you want students to do something, they need a procedure to follow. The Wongs give specific attention to the following matters and many more:

- How to enter and exit the classroom
- How dismissal occurs at the end of the period or day
- How to begin and finish work
- How to come to attention
- What to do on returning after being absent
- What to do when arriving tardy
- How the class is to get quiet when necessary
- How the period or day is to begin
- How to ask for help from the teacher or others
- How to indicate when you don't understand or need help
- How to move about the classroom
- How papers, materials, and supplies are to be distributed and collected
- How everyone is to listen to and respond to questions
- How to work cooperatively with others
- How groups are changed
- How directions are given for each assignment and how students can find the directions
- How to walk in the corridors
- How students are to keep personal notebooks

Classroom Procedures Must Be Taught

Good procedures allow a great variety of activities to occur, often several at the same time, with little confusion. But you have to teach students the procedures, not just talk about them. The Wongs suggest a three-step method for teaching procedures:

1. *Explain.* Teacher states, explains, and demonstrates the procedure.
2. *Rehearse.* Students rehearse and practice the procedure under teacher supervision.
3. *Reinforce.* Teacher reteaches, rehearses, practices, and reinforces the classroom procedure until it becomes a habit.

Examples of Procedures in a Fourth Grade Classroom

The following procedures, which the Wongs credit to teacher Nathan Gibbs, show how one teacher has structured his fourth-grade class for success. You may teach kindergarten or high school physical education and do not feel these procedures apply to you. The Wongs remind us repeatedly that although this scheme is what works for one particular teacher, it reflects realities that exist in all classrooms. (These procedures may be tedious to read, but please consider them carefully—they touch on many things that are important in all classrooms.)

Nathan makes his classroom a place where students feel genuinely cared for. He provides personal attention within a warm, relaxed, refined learning environment. On the first day of school he gives his students a written list of all the classroom procedures, with a cover page that says, "Follow these procedures to reward yourself with complete success."

Nathan spends the first two weeks of class teaching the procedures, and he expects students to follow them to the letter. The number of procedures may seem overwhelming, but Nathan says his students appreciate them. Here is what Nathan emphasizes (adapted from Wong and Wong, 2004a): "You will be safe in this class. I will do my best for you, and I want you to do your best for yourself. Be ready to learn and do the best you can."

Morning Entry Procedures
1. Empty your backpack, place it neatly outside, and bring in homework and needed supplies.
2. Enter the classroom in a quiet and orderly manner.
3. Greet your teacher as you enter, and say "hi" to all your classmates.
4. Turn in homework or keep it at your desk if it is to be graded in class.
5. Begin your seatwork.

Desk Procedures
1. Only your notebook, assignment book, textbooks, reading book, and supply box belong in your desk.
2. Toys, food, and loose paper do NOT belong in your desk.
3. Keep hands, feet, paper, books, and pencils off your neighbors' desks.
4. Push in your chair EVERY TIME you get up.
5. CLEAN your desk and the area around it before you leave.

Line-Up Procedure, Leaving Classroom
1. When dismissed, stand in two equal lines and wait quietly.
2. The first excused line goes out of the room, and then the second line follows.
3. No talking while you are still in the hallway.

Lunch Procedures

1. When excused for lunch, get your lunch if you brought it.
2. Lunch Leaders stand in front with lunch buckets.
3. Follow the line-up procedures.
4. When dismissed by the teacher, WALK to cafeteria.
5. If you have brought your lunch, go and sit at the correct table.
6. Say "hello" to any adult in the cafeteria.
7. If you are buying lunch, get your card from the slot and wait quietly in line.
8. Eat nicely and neatly.
9. Talk with a low voice.
10. Clean up your mess and encourage others to do so.
11. Raise your hand when you would like to be dismissed.
12. Put all leftover food and trash in the trash cans.
13. Place your lunch box in the bucket when you leave.
14. Walk to the play area.

Lunch Leaders

1. Line up first in line.
2. Bring lunch bucket to multipurpose room and back from multipurpose room.
3. Clean out lunch bucket when needed.
4. Remind classmates at the end of day to retrieve their lunch boxes from buckets.
5. Make sure our class is the cleanest of all in the multipurpose room.

Bus Pick-Up Procedure

1. Walk quickly to bus area.
2. Quietly wait behind the line for the bus.
3. Show respect for the teacher on duty.
4. Show respect for the bus driver.
5. On the bus, stay in your seat and talk quietly.
6. Follow the bus rules or lose your bus pass.
7. Be a good role model and a helper for the younger students on early-out Wednesday.

Car Pick-Up Procedure

1. Walk to car pick-up area near the primary wing.
2. Don't walk onto the blacktop where cars park or drive.
3. Show respect for the teacher on duty.
4. Quietly wait for your ride.
5. If your ride is more than 10 minutes late, go to the office to sit quietly and wait.
6. When your ride arrives, the driver must get out of the car and sign you out in the Late Log.

7. Be a good role model and a helper for the younger students on early-out Wednesday.

Bicycle Rider Procedures
1. Walk your bike on campus before and after school.
2. Lock your bike to the bike rack.
3. Leave other bikes alone.
4. Wear your helmet while riding your bike.
5. Obey all traffic laws.
6. Come straight to school and go straight home.

Walker Procedures
1. Walk straight to school.
2. Walk straight home.
3. Obey all traffic laws.

Going to Other Parts of School
1. Line up quietly when asked.
2. WALK on the right side of the walkway SINGLE FILE.
3. Enter the other classroom or library silently and with good manners.
4. Greet the teacher as you enter.
5. Remember you are representing yourselves and our class.

Basic Assembly Procedures
1. Line up inside or outside our classroom first.
2. Follow the student council representatives to the correct area.
3. Pay attention and sit where you are instructed to.
4. QUIETLY sit on chairs or benches or with legs crossed on the floor.
5. Remember your Lifeskills and guidelines while waiting, watching, and after the assembly.
6. Show respect for the presentation.
7. Be patient if you have a question for the presenter.
8. Return to the classroom in a quiet, orderly manner.

End of the Day Procedure
1. Copy the homework assignment into your notebook.
2. Clean around your desk.
3. Pack your assignment notebook and what you need for homework.
4. Wait for the teacher to call your number to get your backpack.
5. Leave ONLY when dismissed by the teacher.

6. On leaving, say "goodbye" to classmates and the teacher.
7. Make sure you get to the bus on time.
8. Remember to tell your family about your day at school.

Restroom Procedures

1. Only one person at a time may go.
2. Quietly hold up three fingers; shake your fingers if it is an emergency.
3. Wash your hands afterwards.
4. Come right back and enter the classroom QUIETLY.

Drinking Fountain Procedures

1. Drink water at recess, lunch, or when your work is FINISHED.
2. Do NOT line up at the drinking fountain outside or inside the classroom AFTER the recess bell has rung.
3. Maximum of three people at sink area at any time.
4. Wipe the sink after you drink.

Computer Procedures

1. Wash your hands before you use the computer.
2. No more than two people at a computer.
3. Refer your questions to the technology assistant.
4. Clean up the area around you before you leave.
5. Log out of all programs you have been using.
6. Shut off the computer at the end of the day if you are the last to use it.

Goals, Yellow Cards, and Red Cards

1. When you receive a goal, put it in your "safe place."
2. At the end of the week have ALL goals totaled for recording.
3. If you receive your first yellow card of the week, put it in your slot; with your first yellow card, put your entry into the LOGBOOK and see the Peer Counselor.
4. Check in with the recess aide and sit out for that day.
5. If you receive your second yellow card, put your entry in the LOGBOOK; report to Mr. Gibbs to receive counseling.
6. With your second yellow card, for the remainder of the week, sit out at recess after checking with the duty aide.
7. If you ever receive the nasty red card, see Mr. Gibbs when instruction is finished. Choose between the call home and the DISCIPLINE ESSAY.
8. With a red card, sit out at recess for two full weeks.

Peer Council

1. Ensure you are talking to all YELLOW CARD RECIPIENTS.
2. Check LOGBOOK to see that they signed it.

3. Report any problems to the teacher.

4. Settle as many disputes as possible at recess.

When You Have a Substitute Teacher

1. Respect and follow the substitute's directions and rules, even if they are not exactly the same as ours.

2. Remember that the substitute is taking my place and is an equal of mine.

3. Be as helpful as possible. The substitute has a copy of all our class procedures.

4. ASSIST THE SUBSTITUTE IN FINDING SUPPLIES.

Group Work

1. Greet all group members.

2. To be successful, be prepared with the necessary tools and resources.

3. Collaboration is the key to being a successful learning club.

4. All members participate, share, learn from, and help one another.

5. Use the same procedures for speaking as you do during class.

6. No one group member is to do all the work.

7. Practice active listening.

8. Cooperate.

9. Do your personal best.

Nathan Gibbs's lists of procedures include a number of other matters, such as procedures for jobs, technology assistant, messengers, pet and garden caretakers, work organization, cleanup, homework, turning in completed work, correcting assignments, filling out the student planner, and missing a school day. If you are interested in Mr. Gibbs's lists for those matters, you can find them on the Internet at http://teachers.net/wong/MAR04.

How to Begin a Class Successfully

The Wongs place great emphasis on what teachers should do to begin the term or year (see Wong and Wong, 2002). New teachers, the Wongs say (with a note of irony), have bags brimming with lesson plans, boxes of activities, the state performance appraisal instrument, five interpretations of educational foundations, nine theories of child development, conflicting advice from a plethora of educational specialists, and a collection of buzzwords and current educational fads. But new teachers have little idea about what to do during the first days and weeks of school. To help new teachers overcome this problem, the Wongs present a First Day of School Action Plan, which they credit to teacher Sarah Jondahl, who developed a plan of step-by-step procedures associated with the following: preparing the classroom before students arrive, academic expectations, time frames, lesson plans and activities for first days of school, steps in establishing working relations with students and parents, class schedules, maintaining a good learning environment, and documentation and evaluation of student progress. To illustrate,

Sarah lists the following matters that require her attention for preparing the classroom before the first day of school:

- "Be Prepared" sheet
- Preparation checklist
- Getting organized
- Cooperative classroom dry-erase board
- Student contract for classroom materials
- "Our Class Fits Like a Puzzle" bulletin board
- Classroom door decoration
- "Brag About Me Board" bulletin board
- "All About Me" bulletin board
- Room arrangement

In the section on establishing relationships with students and parents, she included matters such as

- Letter to students
- Open house activities
- Substitute teacher handbook
- New student folder
- Parent letter
- Homework policy
- Homework tip list
- Transportation checklist
- "Any Beautiful Collectible" wish list
- Rules, consequences, rewards
- Volunteer sheet
- "Welcoming Phone Call" planning sheet
- "Welcoming Phone Call (to parents of potential problem students)" planning sheet
- "Positive Phone Call" form
- Parent conferences outline

And for maintaining a good learning climate, she detailed what she would do concerning

- Reasons for the behavior management plan
- Rules, consequences, rewards
- Procedures in behavior management
- First morning greeting and seating arrangement
- Housekeeping ideas
- "Duty Wheel" for student jobs

- Intervention plan packet
- Sociogram
- Form used to create a sociogram
- Notes of encouragement
- Student postcard
- "Special News about a Very Special Student" certificate
- "Super Job—Way To Go—Great Day" letter form

The Wongs emphasize that teachers should set high expectations on the first day, plan the entire day right down to the minute, and make sure to give attention to an opening assignment for students, establishing routines, and learning students' names. They stress that during the first week, the most important thing is to provide the security of consistency (Wong and Wong, 2004b). If the furniture is movable, on the first day, align all the desks on facing the teacher and keep them that way until you have a good reason to change. Provide a well-organized, uncluttered, attractive classroom. Have the room ready and inviting when students arrive on the first day. On a bulletin board or elsewhere, post schedules, rules, procedures, and a preview of what is to come. Also post information about yourself, including a picture, and a sign that welcomes students to the class. Wear neat clothing—first perceptions affect how students relate to you. Stand when you speak and use short, clear sentences or phrases. Use a firm but soft voice. When emphasizing, do not point your finger, because it presents an accusatory image.

Your major mission during the first few days is to establish student routines and classroom procedures. If you have very young students, put their names on their coat hooks, desks, and cubbyholes and tell them to use their particular coat hook, desk, or cubbyhole every day. Set up a seating plan beforehand, because this helps you to get to know your students quickly. Address your students by name as soon as possible.

On the first day, go to school early and take time to double-check everything. Have your first bellwork assignment ready (a short assignment that students begin working on when they first arrive in the room). Make it interesting but fairly easy so students will have an initial sense of accomplishment. Students who fail early tend to create problems in the classroom. Before class begins, tell yourself:

1. I will establish classroom management procedures from the beginning.
2. I will convey that this class will be business-like, with a firm, competent, and warm teacher.
3. First I will establish work habits in my students and I will worry about content later.

As the students arrive, position yourself outside the door to greet them. This establishes authority and shows that you consider them important. If young children are to line up before entering, insist on a straight line. If you pick up your class from another area, don't say: "Follow me" or "Come on." Rather, introduce yourself and then teach the procedure you want students to follow as they walk to your room.

The First Five Minutes Are Critical

The Wongs repeat that you should have an assignment for the students to begin working as soon as they walk into the room (Wong and Wong, 2000a). This eliminates 90 percent of discipline problems that would otherwise arise. There should be no student free time in the routines at first. It is better to have too much planned for the class period than too little. The first few minutes are crucial to setting the tone in your class. Students must know what they are expected to do. When they come in, remind them of the materials they need that day, and remind them to have their pencils sharpened and paper ready. When the bell rings, turn on the overhead projector to display a warm-up activity, perhaps important information or a brief review of something learned the previous year or term. As students work, take roll while you walk around and observe them. For the next activity, students might be asked to write a reaction to a quote or newspaper article, copy a timeline, brainstorm emotions felt in response to a piece of music, or (later) take a quiz on the previous night's reading assignment.

Mrs. Pantoja's Plan for the First Day

The Wongs suggest you carefully plan your first day of class or school in detail. They describe how art teacher Melissa Pantoja attends to this task (see Wong and Wong, 2000c). They liken Mrs. Pantoja to a football coach who scripts the first twenty-five plays of a game. They say a teacher should not "wing it" in a classroom any more than a coach would wing it on a football field or a pilot would wing it on a flight from Baltimore to Kansas City. The effective teacher goes in with a plan and modifies that plan if conditions change. Here is Mrs. Pantoja's plan for the first day.

Greet each student at the door
- Hand each child a classroom rules sheet (goes in notebook).
- Direct each child toward his or her assigned seat (alphabetical).
- Tell child to read and follow the instructions that are written on the board.

Welcome students to class and introduce myself
- My name
- My family (husband, kids)
- Education
- Where I'm from and where I live
- Why I wanted to teach

Arriving and leaving class
- Teach procedure for arriving in class.
- Teach procedure for dismissal from class.

Explain rules and daily procedures
- Refer to the rules that are posted at front.
- Explain discipline plan and refer to poster.
- Go over procedures and refer to poster.
- Talk about "We Missed You" chart.

Number assignments
- Each person will have a number that represents them.
- The number will be on all of their art papers and on their art folder.
- This will help all of us keep our papers straight.

Respecting the classroom and the art supplies
- Refer to classroom rules and procedures.
- Teach students to be responsible for the art supplies and room; teach procedures.

Teacher's things and students' things
- Some things are only for me.
- Other things are for you to use as you need them.

Art centers
- Everyone will get a chance to go to all the centers.
- Boards at art centers have names (numbers) that tell us who does what that day.

Portfolios
- Each child will be taking a portfolio home.
- Papers will be filed in a container until end of semester.

Notebooks
- For individual students to record their grades and keep track of them
- To store vocabulary words for future use
- To write a weekly journal entry about what they liked most about the week's lesson

The First Ten Days of School

The Wongs (2005) further provide detailed suggestions for procedures during the first 10 days of school. They present a guide they credit to Jane Slovenske, a National Board

Certified Teacher. Ms. Slovenske's class uses a *self-manager plan* in which students are taught to manage their own behavior in a responsible manner. Behavior standards are established through class discussions about responsible behavior, treatment of others, and working promptly to the best of one's ability. Once a list of behaviors is agreed on, the students are presented with a *self-manager application* to use as a self-evaluation of their behaviors and standards.

When students are able to manage all of the items on the application, they fill in the form and take it home for parental review. When parents are in agreement with their child's self-evaluation, it is to be signed and returned to school. Ms. Slovenske then determines whether she agrees with the student's self-evaluation and discusses any differences of opinion. Most students, with input from their parents, are honest about self-evaluating their performance. Space here does not permit inclusion of Ms. Slovenske's plan in detail, but you might wish to examine it on the Internet at http://teachers.net/wong/JAN05.

Procedures for Cooperative Work Groups

Generally speaking, most students do better in school when allowed to work in cooperative learning groups. The Wongs suggest that you call your groups **support groups,** with each member of the group known as a **support buddy.** Children need lots of support. Instead of isolating them with seat work, surround them with support buddies and teach them how to support each other. It is important that each student in the group have a specific job to do. Group procedures must be taught clearly. *Ineffective* teachers divide students into groups and then simply expect the students to work together. *Effective* teachers teach the students procedures and social skills needed for functioning in a group. Before you begin your first group activity, teach students how to do the following:

1. Be responsible for your own work and behavior.
2. Ask a support buddy for help if you have a question.
3. Help any support buddy who asks for help.
4. Ask for help from the teacher only when support buddies cannot supply it.

For further detailed information on how to work with groups, consult Chapter 24 in *The First Days of School* (Wong and Wong, 2004).

For Additional Ideas from the Wongs

As you can see, the Wongs provide an abundance of practical ideas and suggestions, most of which can be accessed in *The First Days of School* and the Wong gazette articles posted on the teachers.net website. There, they delve into important matters not included in this chapter, such as how to be a professional teacher, how to teach for mastery learning, how to get the class's attention, how to motivate students, how to help students with their assignments, and how to grow as a teacher.

A Special Word to Secondary Teachers

Secondary teachers sometimes comment that the Wong's suggestions appear to be too elementary for use in high school, but the Wongs emphasize that their approach works very well at the high school level. In their website articles, they present testimonials from secondary teachers, many of whom assert that the Wongs' suggestions saved their careers.

For example, Chelonnda Seroyer (see http://teachers.net/wong/FEB05), a first year teacher, used the Wongs' ideas as the basis for managing her class and had a very successful year. She was also senior class sponsor, homecoming parade assistant, and a member of the support team for the school's efforts related to the No Child Left Behind Act. For her efforts she received the Bob Jones High School "First Year Patriot Award," which is given to a first year teacher in recognition for outstanding accomplishments and achievements in academics, athletics, or cocurricular pursuits.

Jeff Smith (see http://teachers.net/wong/APR04) teaches welding at a Career Tech Center in Pryor, Oklahoma. He was almost fired during his first year because of poor classroom management, but he happened to hear one of the Wongs' tapes and wrote to say, "You saved my job, and someday I want to help other beginning teachers just like you helped me." Jeff now holds the state record for the most career tech students certified under the industry standard welding certification. His former students have the highest pay average for high school graduates in the state. He reports that he always knew his subject matter, but had no clue about classroom management until he encountered the Wongs' ideas.

Ed Lucero (see http://teachers.net/wong/MAR05) teaches high school business, marketing, and finance in Albuquerque, New Mexico. He writes, "Last year was my eleventh year of teaching. I was miserable! Students weren't paying attention. I constantly repeated myself. Students would ignore my instructions and at times talk back. Some students would attempt to call me 'bro' instead of Mr. Lucero." Ed decided if things did not improve, he would leave teaching and go back into public accounting. His wife suggested he read the Wongs' *The First Days of School: How to Become an Effective Teacher.* He spent the summer studying their suggestions, and when the next school year began, he was able to implement them and enjoy the pleasures of teaching.

Initiating the Wongs' Pragmatic Approach in the Classroom

This chapter has explained how the Wongs would implement their ideas in the classroom. Their suggestions have mostly touched on what you should do on the first few days of school. If you are past the beginning days of your class and are dissatisfied with the operation of the class, you might consider trying the Wongs' procedural approach. If you do so, it is suggested that you hold a class discussion in which you inform students of your concerns. Tell them you would like to make some changes that will improve everyone's opportunities to enjoy success and pleasure in the class. Explain what you have decided. It will take a few days to reorient the class to functioning in the new way, but it may well resolve the ongoing concerns you are experiencing.

KEY TERMS AND CONCEPTS EMPHASIZED IN THIS CHAPTER

pragmatic   procedures   support buddy
routines   support groups

SELECTED SEVEN—SUMMARY SUGGESTIONS FROM HARRY AND ROSEMARY WONG

1. Before the first day of school, carefully prepare your classroom and class procedures for maximizing student success.

2. Beginning on the first day of school, take pains to help students clearly understand your responsibilities, their responsibilities, the discipline plan, and how the class is to function.

3. To maximize learning and responsible behavior, carefully teach students the procedures involved in all the tasks you expect of them.

4. Script (write out) exactly what you want to do and say for the first few days of class or school.

5. Plan more than seems necessary and leave no free time or dead spots.

6. Use support groups for cooperative learning and teach support buddies how to assist each other.

7. Through the term or year, continue to practice class procedures to ensure they become habituated routines that students are able to follow automatically.

CONCEPT CASES

Case 1: Kristina Will Not Work

Kristina, a student in Mr. Jake's class, is quite docile. She socializes little with other students and never disrupts lessons. However, despite Mr. Jake's best efforts, Kristina will not do her work. She rarely completes an assignment. She is simply there, putting forth no effort at all. *How would Harry and Rosemary Wong suggest Mr. Jake deal with Kristina?*

The Wongs would advise Mr. Jake to carefully teach Kristina the procedures associated with completing assignments and other work activities. He should ask her to show him that she understands the procedures. He might consider having Kristina work with a support buddy with whom she feels comfortable. He would supply positive consequences for all improvements Kristina shows. If Kristina does not improve, Mr. Jake should talk further with her privately, and in a positive, supportive tone reit-

erate that he cares about her, wants her to succeed, will let nothing interfere with her progress if he can help it, and will help correct anything that might be standing in the way of her completing her work. If Kristina still doesn't improve, Mr. Jake should seek help from school personnel who are trained to assess Kristina and help provide conditions that improve her likelihood of success.

Case 2: Sara Cannot Stop Talking

Sara is a pleasant girl who participates in class activities and does most, though not all, of her assigned work. She cannot seem to refrain from talking to classmates, however. Her teacher, Mr. Gonzales, has to speak to her repeatedly during lessons, to the point that he often becomes exasperated and loses his temper. *What suggestions would Harry and Rosemary Wong give Mr. Gonzales for dealing with Sara?*

Case 3: Joshua Clowns and Intimidates

Joshua, larger and louder than his classmates, always wants to be the center of attention, which he accomplishes through a combination of clowning and intimidation. He makes wise remarks, talks back (smilingly) to the teacher, utters a variety of sound-effect noises such as automobile crashes and gunshots, and makes limitless sarcastic comments and put-downs of his classmates. Other students will not stand up to him, apparently fearing his size and verbal aggression. His teacher, Miss Pearl, has come to her wit's end. *Do the Wongs provide suggestions that might improve Joshua's behavior? Explain.*

Case 4: Tom Is Hostile and Defiant

Tom has appeared to be in his usual foul mood ever since arriving in class. On his way to sharpen his pencil, he bumps into Frank, who complains. Tom tells him loudly to shut up. Miss Baines, the teacher, says, "Tom, go back to your seat." Tom wheels around, swears loudly, and says heatedly, "I'll go when I'm damned good and ready!" *What suggestions might the Wongs have for helping improve Tom's behavior?*

ACTIVITIES

1. In your journal, list concepts and procedures from this chapter that you would like to incorporate into your personal system of discipline.

2. Working alone or with peers, compile a comprehensive list of procedures you would want to teach students in a grade or subject of your choice.

3. Working alone or with peers, select five of the procedures you have identified and specify what you would teach your students and how you would do so. Share your efforts with the class.

YOU ARE THE TEACHER

Middle School Library

You are a media specialist in charge of the middle school library. You see your job as serving as resource person to students who are seeking information and you are always eager to give help to those who request it. Each period of the day brings different students to your center. Usually, small groups have been sent to the library to do cooperative research. Always some unexpected students appear who have been excused from physical education for medical reasons but don't like coming to your center, or else they bear special passes from their teachers for a variety of reasons.

Typical Occurrences

You have succeeded in getting students settled and working when Tara appears at your side, needing a book to read as makeup work for missing class. You ask Tara what kinds of books interest her. She resignedly shrugs her shoulders. You take her to a shelf of newly published books. "I read this one last night," you tell her. "I think you might like it. It's a good story and fast reading." Tara only glances at it. "That looks stupid," she says. "Don't you have any good books?" She glances down the shelf. "These are all stupid!" Another student, Jaime, is tugging at your elbow, with a note from his history teacher, who wants the source of a particular quotation. You ask Tara to look at the books for a moment while you take Jaime to the reference books. As you pass by a table of students supposedly doing research, you see that the group is watching Walter and Teo have a friendly pencil fight, hitting pencils together until one of them breaks. You address your comments to Walter, who appears to be the more willing participant. Walter answers hotly, "Teo started it! It wasn't me!" "Well," you say, "if you boys can't behave yourself, just go back to your class." The other student smiles and Walter feels he is being treated unjustly. He sits down and pouts. Meanwhile, Tara has gone to the large globe and is twirling it. You start to speak to her but realize that Jaime is still waiting at your side with the request for his teacher. Somehow, before the period ends, Tara leaves with a book she doesn't want and Jaime takes a citation back to his teacher. The research groups have been too noisy. You know they have done little work and wonder if you should speak to their teacher about their manners and courtesy. After the period is over, you notice that profane remarks have been written on the table where Walter was sitting. *What suggestions might the Wongs make that would improve things for you in the Media Center?*

REFERENCES

Glavac, M., 2005. Summary of Major Concepts Covered by Harry K. Wong. The Busy Educator's Newsletter. www.glavac.com.

Starr, L. 1999. Speaking of Classroom Management—An Interview with Harry K. Wong. Education World. www.education-world.com/a_curr/curr161.shtml.

Wong, H., and Wong, R. 2000a. The First Five Minutes Are Critical. Gazette Article. Teachers.net. http://teachers.net/gazette/NOV00/wong.html.

Wong, H., and Wong, R. 2000b. The Problem Is Not Discipline. Gazette Article. Teachers.net. http:// teachers.net/gazette/SEP00/wong.html.

Wong, H., and Wong, R. 2000c. Your First Day. Gazette Article. Teachers.net. http://teachers.net/gazette/JUN00/covera.html.

Wong, H., and Wong, R. 2002. How to Start School Successfully. Gazette Article. Teachers.net. http://teachers.net/gazette/AUG02/wong.html.

Wong, H., and Wong, R. 2004a. A Well-Oiled Learning Machine. Gazette Article. Teachers.net. http://teachers.net/wong/MAR04.

Wong, H., and Wong, R. 2004b. *The first days of school: How to be an effective teacher.* Mountain View, CA: Harry K. Wong Publications.

Wong, H., and Wong, R. 2005. The First Ten Days of School. Gazette Article. Teachers.net. http://teachers.net/wong.

CHAPTER 9

Discipline through Same-Side Win-Win Strategies

Authoritative Input

■ Spencer Kagan, Patricia Kyle, and Sally Scott / Win-Win Discipline

CHAPTER PREVIEW

The primary goal of Win-Win Discipline is to help students develop long-term, self-managed responsibility. This is accomplished by taking student needs strongly into account, recognizing that disruptive behavior is merely students' ineffective attempts to meet certain unfulfilled needs. Responsible behavior grows when teacher and student work together to cocreate effective discipline solutions, which include tactics for the moment of disruption, for follow-up, and for long-term results. Through this approach, students gradually develop self-management, responsibility, and other autonomous life skills.

Fundamental Hypothesis of Win-Win Discipline

Quality classroom discipline, where students manage themselves responsibly, is best achieved when teacher and students work together cooperatively from the same side to find a common ground in dealing with behavior problems that occur in the classroom.

Win-Win Discipline

Win-Win Discipline enables students and teachers to work together closely to find acceptable solutions to behavior problems. In the process, concerns of everyone involved are addressed and resolved satisfactorily. Everyone benefits or "wins"; hence, the label *Win-Win Discipline*.

About Spencer Kagan, Patricia Kyle, and Sally Scott

Spencer Kagan, a clinical psychologist, educational consultant, and former professor of psychology, now specializes in researching and developing discipline strategies and life skills training. His company, Kagan Publishing and Professional Development, produces a number of products and programs, many of which have to do with Win-Win Discipline. Information on Kagan and his company can be obtained from the website www .KaganOnline.com.

Patricia Kyle, school counselor, school psychologist, and university professor, also researches and writes about classroom discipline. She is coordinator of the School Psychology program at the University of Idaho and can be reached by email at pkyle@ rmci.net.

Sally Scott is a school administrator and teacher trainer. She has been the lead trainer in Win-Win Discipline since its inception. National and international educators consider Scott's school a "must-see school." She can be contacted by email at sscott@ washoe.k12.nv.us.

The Goal of Win-Win Discipline

Win-Win Discipline considers disruptive behavior to be a starting point for helping students become more responsible and self-directing. To make the process effective, Kagan, Kyle, and Scott advise teachers to provide a positive learning environment, interesting curriculum, and engaging instruction. Further, they are asked to create a "we" approach in which students and teacher work together on the same side and toward the same end. Discipline tactics that are harmonious with students' needs and states of mind are organized and employed.

Over time, the win-win process empowers students to make behavior choices that serve them beneficially and that are compatible with the interests of the class. At the same time, students develop certain life skills that serve them advantageously throughout their lives. Disruptive students are not viewed as "bad kids," but rather as individuals who are attempting, albeit ineffectively, to meet their personal needs. Thus, to say that a student is misbehaving is simply to say that the student is making poor choices in meeting his or her needs. Kagan, Kyle, and Scott present a parable that conveys the basic philosophy of Win-Win Discipline:

Two women are standing on a bank of a swift river. In the strong current, flailing about, desperately struggling to stay afloat, a man is carried downstream toward them. The women both jump in, pulling the man to safety. While the brave rescuers are tending the victim, a second man, also desperate and screaming for help, is carried by the current toward them. Again the women jump into the river to the rescue. As they are pulling out this second victim, they spot a third man flailing about as he is carried downstream toward them. One woman quickly jumps in to save the latest victim. As she does, she turns to see the other woman resolutely walking upstream. "Why aren't you helping?" she cries. "I am," states the other. "I am going to see who is pushing them in!" (Kagan, 2001, p. 50)

The parable suggests that teachers have a fundamental decision to make when dealing with discipline problems. They can either wait and try to deal with each discipline problem as it erupts, or they can be proactive, see the places from which discipline problems arise, and do something about conditions at that point. With the first choice, they are doomed to treat an unending stream of symptoms. With the second choice, they cure the cause of the problem by teaching students how to behave responsibly rather than disruptively.

The Premises of Win-Win Discipline

Kagan, Kyle, and Scott set forth the premises of Win-Win Discipline as follows (2004, p. 2.3):

- The ultimate goal of discipline is not to end disruptions, but to teach autonomous responsibility.
- Almost all disruptions can be categorized into four types, ABCD (aggression, breaking rules, confrontations, and disengagement).
- Disruptions almost always spring from one of seven student positions, which can be thought of as currently existing motives, emotions, or states of mind. Those positions are attention-seeking, avoiding failure, being angry, control seeking, being energetic, being bored, and being uninformed.
- Positions are neither right nor wrong, but simply a fact of the universal human condition.
- Teachers should never accept disruptive behaviors, but we always accept and validate student positions.
- In attempts to meet the needs associated with given positions, students sometimes engage in disruptive behaviors.
- If teachers respond proactively to the four behaviors and seven positions, they can prevent most of the disruptive behavior that would otherwise occur.

Key Elements in Win-Win Discipline

The following are the major elements in Win-Win Discipline. As you read further, you will learn more about these elements and see how they interact.

- *Three Pillars of Win-Win Discipline.* **Three Pillars** form the strength of Win-Win Discipline. They are (1) *same side,* meaning students, teachers, and parents are all working together on the same side to enhance the school experience for everyone; (2) *collaborative solutions,* meaning students and teachers collaborate when identifying problems and proposing solutions; and (3) *learned responsibility,* which results from continually emphasizing self-management and autonomous proactive life skills.

■ *Preventive measures.* Win-Win Discipline gives detailed attention to what teachers can do, in advance, to keep class disruptions to a minimum. Preventive measures reduce disruptive behavior, making it easier for students to meet their needs in the classroom.

■ *ABCD disruptions.* There are four categories of disruptive behavior that teachers must deal with. The **ABCD of disruptive behavior** include aggression, breaking rules, confrontations, and disengagement.

■ *Student positions.* **Student positions** are composites of attitudes, perceptions, and emotions that exist in individual students at any given time. We can think of them as states of mind that may lead to different kinds of disruptive behavior. They can change from moment to moment. As noted previously, the seven student positions are: attention-seeking, avoiding failure, being angry, being control seeking, being energetic, being bored, and being uninformed. When a student disrupts the class, he or she is said to be "coming from" one or more of the positions. When students misbehave, the teacher uses clues and certain indicators to identify the position the student is coming from. How the teacher intervenes in disruptive behavior is determined, in part, by the position the student is in at the time.

■ *Class rules.* Win-Win Discipline requires the use of **class rules,** but does not view them as teacher imposed. Rather, class rules are agreements worked out cooperatively by teacher and students. Kagan, Kyle, and Scott say to keep rules simple, limit them to a maximum of five, and write them on a poster for display in the room. They say further that all students must understand the rules clearly, which means they should be carefully taught by the teacher and then practiced until they seem natural. Kagan, Kyle, and Scott add that some teachers prefer to use only one rule, such as: *"In our class we agree to foster our own learning, help others learn, and allow the teacher to teach."* The class posts the agreements in the room for easy reference. Some classes call the agreements "The Way We Want Our Class to Be." Because students formulate and choose responsible alternatives, they do not feel the rules are imposed on them, hence, they are less likely to oppose them. Although rules (or agreements) naturally vary from class to class, here are some typical examples:

> *Ready rule.* Come to class ready to learn.
> *Respect rule.* Respect the rights and property of others.
> *Request rule.* Ask for help when needed.
> *Offer rule.* Offer help to others.
> *Responsibility rule.* Strive to act responsibly at all times.

■ *Moment-of-disruption structures.* These structures specify strategies that teachers apply at the moment students misbehave. Win-Win Discipline provides approximately twenty such structures. Examples are Picture It Right (If we were at our very best right now, how would we look?), Make a Better Choice (I want you to think of a better choice to make right now), and To You . . . To Me (To you, this lesson may be boring; to me, it is important because . . .). You will see later that particular sets of strategies are designed for each of the seven positions. It is important, therefore, that teachers be able to identify the student position before applying a corrective tactic.

■ *Follow-up structures.* Students normally require time and repeated experiences to develop responsibility. Follow-ups are designed to help in this process. Four types of follow-ups are available for use when it is clear that the student needs further assistance: (1) establishing new preventive procedures or re-establishing existing preventive measures; (2) establishing moment-of-disruption procedures for the next disruption; (3) implementing a follow-up structure, such as a same-side chat or exploring responsible thinking; and (4) offering training in a life skill such as self-control or personal relations.

■ *Life skills.* Life skills, such as anger management and self-motivation, are extremely important, not only in the classroom but in all aspects of life. They are given much attention in Win-Win Discipline. They are often called into play after preventive and moment-of-disruption structures are in place and functioning properly.

How Win-Win Discipline Works

The following is a brief overview of how Win-Win Discipline works. Before class begins, do all you can to eliminate conditions that might lead to misbehavior. Cooperatively with your class decide how class members are to conduct themselves. When misbehavior occurs (it will usually be aggression, breaking rules, confrontation, or disengagement), identify which of the seven students positions (attention-seeking, avoiding failure, being angry, control seeking, being energetic, being bored, or being uninformed) the student seems to be coming from. Then, in a cooperative manner, identify and apply an appropriate structure that will help the student behave more responsibly, now and in the future.

Before the Class Begins

Preventing Disruptive Behavior

Most classroom misbehavior can be prevented if the teacher makes certain provisions in advance. Kagan, Kyle, and Scott emphasize preventive measures built into

- An interesting and challenging *curriculum*
- *Cooperative activities* that allow students to work together meaningfully
- An *interesting, stimulating teacher* who adapts the curriculum to student interests and needs

Learn How to Identify Student Positions

As you have seen, Kagan, Kyle, and Scott list seven student positions that often lead to disruptive behavior. The positions are considered to be *normal and acceptable*. When students become disruptive, you need to be able immediately to correctly identify and then acknowledge or otherwise validate the student's position. For example, if it is evident a student is bored, you might say, "I can tell you are bored. We all get that way at times, when we are not interested in a topic." You should then be prepared to apply a moment-of-disruption structure to help the student. You will learn more about such structures presently.

Anticipate Types of Disruptive Behavior

The seven student positions can easily foster four types of disruptive behavior—aggression, breaking rules, confrontation, and disengagement. Please note that while student positions are considered acceptable, these disruptive behaviors are considered *unacceptable*. However, you must realize that unacceptable behavior represents students' attempts to meet personal needs—attempts that are ineffective. Win-Win Discipline corrects this situation by helping students make better decisions that lead to acceptable behavior.

Commit to Always Applying the Three Pillars of Win-Win Discipline

When misbehavior occurs in the class, seize the moment as an opportunity for teaching your students how to make better behavior choices. The tactics for doing so are embedded in the Three Pillars of Win-Win Discipline: (1) a same-side approach by teacher, students, and parents working together toward building responsible behavior; (2) collaboration by teacher and students in co-creating immediate and long-term discipline solutions; and (3) helping students make responsible choices rather than creating disruptions in the classroom.

Each of these three pillars employs certain **discipline structures** for teachers to use when students make poor behavior choices. The structures are designed for use at three different points: the moment of disruption, for follow-up, and for working toward long-term solutions.

During Instruction and Other Class Interactions

Assume that during a cooperative work group situation, Samuel, a new boy in class, disrupts the class by standing up and calling over to Duwahn in another group. This violates one of the class rules that teacher and students have formulated jointly. Samuel may or may not know that this behavior is inappropriate. What does the teacher, Mr. Alistair, do? Kagan, Kyle, and Scott suggest the following:

1. Quickly look beyond the misbehavior to identify the *position* Samuel is coming from. Let's suppose Samuel's position is identified as "being uninformed."
2. Apply a *moment-of-disruption structure* suited to Samuel's position. Mr. Alistair says, "Samuel, because you are a new member of our class, you may have forgotten our rule against calling out in class. Can we take just a moment to review it so you will know next time?"
3. It is not likely that more need be said, but if necessary Mr. Alistair can use a *follow-up structure* to help Samuel learn to make better behavior decisions. He decides to use a same-side chat with Samuel to help the boy understand why there is a rule against calling out. In the chat, Mr. Alistair will help Samuel identify an alternative behavior that would be acceptable.

More on Types of Disruptive Behavior—ABCD

We have seen that Kagan, Kyle, and Scott see disruptive student behavior occurring in four types—aggression, breaking rules, confrontation, or disengagement. We have noted that the type of behavior suggests the type of intervention the teacher should use.

Aggression

Taking hostile actions toward others is called **aggression**. It may occur physically, verbally, or passively. Physical aggression includes hitting, kicking, biting, pinching, pulling, and slapping. Verbal aggression includes verbal put-downs, swearing, ridiculing, and name-calling. Passive aggression involves stubbornly refusing to comply with reasonable requests.

Breaking rules

Students may break class rules for a variety of reasons, as when they are angry, bored, full of energy, desirous of attention, attempting to avoid failure, wanting to control, not understanding what is expected, or not having the ability to follow the rule. Common examples of rule-breaking behavior include talking without permission, making weird noises, chewing gum, passing notes, being out of seat, and not turning in work.

Confrontations

Confrontations are power struggles among students or between students and teacher to get one's way or strongly argue one's point. Examples of confrontational behavior include refusing to comply, complaining, arguing, and giving myriad reasons why things are no good or should be done differently. When students don't get their way, they often pout or make disparaging remarks about the task or teacher.

Disengagement

Students may disengage from lessons for a variety of reasons. They may have something more interesting on their minds, feel incapable of performing the task, or find the task too difficult or boring. Passive disengagement includes not listening, working off task, not finishing work, acting helpless, or saying "I can't." Active disengagement includes put-downs, excessive requests for help, and comments such as "I've got better things to do" or "It would be better if . . . ."

More on Student Positions and Associated Misbehavior

We have seen that a position is a state of mind and body that disposes the student to act in certain ways. When students seek to meet the needs inherent in a given position, they sometimes disrupt the class. Teacher and students can work together to understand the positions, identify the needs associated with them, and devise ways for students to meet those needs in a nondisruptive manner.

The art of using Win-Win Discipline is to identify the position from which misbehavior emanates. You then communicate *acceptance* of the student position while *refusing to accept* the disruptive behavior it engenders. As explained earlier, student positions are not to be considered negative; they simply reflect students' needs or condition at the time they act out. Disruptive behavior springs from unmet needs inherent in student positions. Effective teachers try to gain the student's perspective in order to understand and deal with what is prompting students' behavior, and they remember that every disruption is an opportunity for helping students learn to behave more responsibly.

Intervention Strategies for Types of Disruption

Kagan, Kyle, and Scott present numerous tactics for dealing with disruptive behavior that is associated with the various student positions. Here is a sample of what they suggest:

For Attention-Seeking

Most individuals want to know others care about them, and when they feel they are not being cared about, they often seek attention. Students wanting attention may interrupt, show off, annoy others, work slower than others, ask for extra help, or simply goof off. Instead of the positive results the student is hoping for, attention seeking further annoys and disrupts. Teachers usually react to it by nagging or scolding, which causes students to stop the behavior temporarily but not for long.

Dealing with Disruptions That Come from Attention-Seeking. Positive interventions teachers can use at the *moment of disruption* for attention seeking include physical proximity, hand signals, I-messages, personal attention, appreciation, and affirmation. If attention seeking is chronic, teachers can ask students to identify positive ways of getting attention. They can *follow up*, if necessary, by meeting with students and discussing with them their need for attention and how it might be obtained in a positive manner. Suggested strategies for *long-term solutions* include focusing on the interests of the student and building self-concept and self-validation skills.

For Avoiding Failure

We all have been in situations where we rationalize our inadequacies in order to avoid pain or embarrassment. No one likes to fail or appear inept. The student who says, "I don't care about the stupid math quiz, so I won't study for it," knows that it is more painful to fail in front of others than not to try at all and, therefore, will rationalize the failure as lack of caring.

Dealing with Disruptions That Come from Avoiding Failure. Win-win teachers help students find ways to work and perform without feeling bad if they aren't first or best. For the moment of disruption, teachers can encourage students to try, assign partners or helpers, or reorganize and present the information in smaller instructional pieces. *For follow-up and long-term strategies,* ask students how responsible people might deal with fear of failure. As necessary, include peer support, showing how mistakes can lead to excellent learning, and Team Pair Solo, a structure in which students practice first as a team and then in pairs before doing activities alone.

For Being Angry

Everyone experiences displeasure and at times expresses it angrily. Anger is a natural reaction to many situations that involve fear, frustration, humiliation, loss, and pain. Angry students may go to the extreme because they are unable to express themselves in acceptable ways.

Dealing with Disruptions That Come from Being Angry.   Teachers don't like to deal with angry students. When doing so, they may experience feelings of hurt or indignation. Their immediate reaction often is to isolate the student or retaliate. However, these reactions do nothing to help students better manage their anger. Win-Win Discipline provides several structures to help teachers handle angry disruptions, including asking students to identify responsible ways of handling anger, providing cool down and think time, and tabling the matter. *Long-term interventions* include conflict resolution conferences, class meetings, and practice in skills of self-control.

For Control Seeking

We all want to feel in charge of ourselves and be able to make our own choices, but doing so has negative as well as positive ramifications. On the negative side, control-seeking students may engage in power struggles with the teacher and, when challenged, argue or justify their actions. Teachers usually do not respond well to such behavior. Their reaction is to fight back to keep students from taking the upper hand.

Dealing with Disruptions That Come from Control Seeking.   For the *moment of disruption*, Kagan, Kyle, and Scott suggest that teachers acknowledge the student's power, use Language of Choice (a structure where teacher provides students with choice, "You may either . . . or . . ."), or provide options for how and when work is to be done. For *follow-up* they may need to schedule a later conference or class meeting to discuss the situation, solicit student input concerning what causes students to struggle against the teacher, and consider how the struggle can be avoided. Long-term strategies include involving students in the decision-making process and working with them to establish class agreements concerning challenging the teacher.

For Overly Energetic Students

At times students have so much energy they simply cannot sit still or concentrate. A few students remain in this condition a good deal of the time, moving and talking incessantly.

Dealing with Disruptions That Come from Being Energetic.   If energetic behavior becomes troublesome, teachers can, at the *moment of disruption*, provide breaks into the lessons, provide time for progressive relaxation, remove distracting elements and objects, and channel energy productively. *Follow-up strategies* include teaching a variety of calming strategies and providing activities for students to work off energy in a positive manner. *Long-term solutions* include managing energy levels during instruction and connecting students' interests to the instruction.

For Bored Students

Students who act bored show they are not enjoying and do not want to participate in the curriculum, instruction, or activities at a given time. Boredom is communicated through body language, lack of participation, and being off task.

Dealing with Disruptions That Come from Being Bored. To help bored students at the *moment of disruption,* teachers can restructure the learning task, involve students more actively, and infuse timely energizers. As *follow-up,* they may talk privately with the students and assign them helping roles such as gatekeeper, recorder, or coach. For *long-term solutions,* teachers can provide a rich, relevant, and developmentally appropriate curriculum that involves students actively in the learning process and emphasizes cooperative learning and attention to multiple intelligences.

For Uninformed Students

Sometimes students respond or react disruptively because they simply don't know what to do or how to behave responsibly. Disruptions stemming from being uninformed are not motivated by strong emotions, but by lack of information, skill, or appropriate habit. Although these disruptions are not emotional or volatile, they are frustrating to teachers.

Dealing with Disruptions That Come from Being Uninformed. To determine whether students know what is expected, at the *moment of disruption* the teacher should gently ask students if they know what they are supposed to do. If they don't, you can reteach them at the time. If they only need support, let them work with a buddy. *Follow-up strategies* include more careful attention to giving directions, modeling, and practicing the responsible behavior. *Long-term solutions* include encouragement and focusing on the student's strengths.

More on Responding in the Moment of Disruption

Once the win-win philosophy of same-side collaboration has been internalized, students who disrupt usually need only a reminder to get back on track. This can be done by referring to the chart on which rules are posted and asking, "Are we living up to the way we want our class to be?" If more is required, the teacher might use a structure such as Picture It Right, which asks students to picture how they would like the class to be and verbalize what they need to do to make it that way. Win-Win Discipline provides a number of such structures for use at the moment of disruption. The purpose of these activities is not to obtain conformity to rules, but rather to help everyone internalize a process of seeking out mutually satisfying solutions that take needs into account. In summary, the teacher should, at the moment of disruption:

- End the disruption quickly and refocus all students back to the lesson.
- If necessary, acknowledge the student position.
- If necessary, communicate that the disruptive behavior is unacceptable.
- If necessary, work with the student to find solutions that are mutually satisfactory.

Occasionally for persistently disruptive behavior, teachers may have to use more prescriptive structures, including applying consequences such as apology, restitution, or loss of activity. These consequences are then built into the offending student's **personal improvement plan**. The suggested sequence for applying consequences is as follows:

1. *Warning*. A warning is given to the student. If more is needed, then . . .
2. *Reflection time*. The student is given time to think about the disruptive behavior and its improvement. If more is needed, then . . .
3. *Personal improvement plan*. The disruptive student formulates a personal improvement plan to develop responsible ways of meeting needs. If more is needed, then . . . .
4. *Phone call to parent or guardian*. If more is needed, then . . .
5. *Principal's office visit*.

More on Follow-Ups and Long-Term Goals

Kagan, Kyle, and Scott (2004) suggest the following long-term goals in association with the various student positions:

Student Position	Long-Term Needs and Goals
Attention-seeking	Student needs self-validation
Avoiding failure, embarrassment	Student needs self-confidence
Being angry	Student needs self-control
Control seeking	Student needs self-determination
Being energetic	Student needs self-direction
Being bored	Student needs to self-motivate
Being uniformed	Student needs to self-inform

Win-Win Discipline offers a progression of follow-up structures to help students reach these long-term goals. Here are some of those structures, progressing from less directive to more directive.

Same-Side Chat

Through discussion, teacher and students get to know each other better and come to see themselves as working on the same side toward better conditions for all.

Responsible Thinking

Activities are used to direct students to reflect on three considerations: (1) their needs and others' needs, (2) how they treat others, and (3) how they conduct themselves. As a responsible thinking activity for following up disruptive behavior, students can be asked to consider three questions:

1. What if everyone acted that way? (How would our class be if everyone acted that way?)
2. How would I like to be treated? (Did I treat others the way I would like to be treated?)
3. What would be a win-win solution? (What would meet everyone's needs?)

Reestablish Expectations

Discuss and if necessary reteach expectations concerning rules, procedures, and routines. This strengthens knowledge, understanding, acceptance, application, and adherence to expectations.

Identify Replacement Behavior

Teachers guide students to generate, accept, and practice responsible behavior that they can use in place of disruptive behavior.

Establish Contracts

Contracts are written agreements in which teacher and individual students clarify and formalize agreements they have reached. Contracts sometimes increase the likelihood that the student will remember, identify with, and honor the agreement.

Establish Consequences

Consequences are reserved as a last resort and are used only when all other follow-up efforts have failed. Consequences are conditions that teacher and students have agreed to invoke when students misbehave. Consequences should be aligned with the Three Pillars of Win-Win Discipline: They begin with same-side orientation; they are established through teacher–student collaboration; and they are instructive, aimed at helping students learn to conduct themselves with greater personal responsibility. Consequences may call for responsible thinking, apology, or restitution. When the behavior disrupts or harms others and responsible thinking is not enough, students may need to *apologize* to those they have offended. Genuine apologies have three parts: (1) a statement of regret or remorse, (2) a statement of appropriate future behavior, and (3) the request for acceptance of the apology. Students may also need to make *restitution*, which means taking care of physical or emotional damage that was done. This is a tangible way of taking responsibility and dealing with the consequences of inappropriate choices, and it has the potential to "heal the violator," as well.

Promoting Life Skills

A major goal of Win-Win Discipline is the progressive development of what Kagan, Kyle, and Scott call "life skills" that help people live more successfully. Examples of life skills are self-control, anger management, good judgment, impulse control, perseverance, and empathy. Teachers are urged to work on these skills through the curriculum as well as when responding to students at the moment of disruption, following-up, and seeking long-term solutions. Kagan, Kyle, and Scott say that by fostering these life skills, teachers can avoid ineffective approaches that end a disruption but leave students just as likely to disrupt again in the future. Here are some illustrations:

- A student puts down another student. The recipient of the put-down, having been publicly belittled, has the impulse to retaliate to give back a put-down or even initiate a fight. If the offended student has acquired the life skills of self-control, anger management, and/or good judgment, he or she can move away from a potential discipline situation.

■ A student is finding an assignment difficult. She is tempted to avoid a sense of failure by saying to herself and others, "This assignment is stupid." To the extent the student has acquired self-motivation, pride in her work, and perseverance, a discipline problem is averted.

■ A student is placed on a team with another student he does not like. He is tempted to call out, "Yuck! Look who we are stuck with!" To the extent the student has acquired relationship skills, cooperativeness, empathy, and kindness, a discipline problem is averted.

Parent and Community Alliances and Schoolwide Programs

Partnerships and alliances that include teachers, parents, and community assist greatly in helping students learn to make responsible behavior choices. Parents appreciate and support teachers who handle disruptive behavior in a positive manner and guide their child toward responsible behavior. Parents' input, support, follow-through, and backup strengthen the likelihood of responsible student behavior. Ongoing teacher–parent communication is essential in this regard. The degree of cooperation depends largely on how teachers reach out to parents. Rather than give up when parents are reluctant to work with them, teachers should continue to invite them to be actively involved in the process.

Win-Win Discipline provides many helpful suggestions for teacher–parent communication and interaction. Contact with parents should be made during the first week of school. Letters sent home, class newsletters, class websites, and emails are efficient ways to connect with parents. Phone calls are effective, although they take considerable time. Parent nights and open houses offer person-to-person communication opportunities. Conferences can be used to show parents they are valued as allies and may at times encourage parents to serve as mentors and tutors. Schoolwide programs, such as assemblies and incentive programs, encourage whole school involvement. The broader community can become involved through field trips, guest speakers, apprenticeships, and adopting and working with day care and senior centers.

Initiating Kagan, Kyle, and Scott's Win-Win Discipline

Ideally, implementation of Win-Win Discipline in the classroom should begin before the first day of school, with the teacher making advance preparation of procedures, routines, and curriculum materials associated with each of the seven positions. However, if that is not possible, Win-Win Discipline can be put in place at any time. The concept and procedures must be taught, but they are learned quickly. Once learned, maintenance of the program is relatively easy. In keeping with Kagan, Kyle, and Scott's suggestions, here is how you can introduce Win-Win Discipline to your students.

Begin by setting the tone for a win-win climate in your classroom. Let the students know that the class will be built on the Three Pillars of Win-Win Discipline—same side, collaborative solutions, and learned responsibility. You might say something like this:

This is our class, and with all of us working together we will create a place where each person feels comfortable and all of us can enjoy the process of learning. As your teacher, I have a responsibility to create an environment where this can happen, but I need your help to make it work. Each of you must know that you are an important member of this class, with important responsibilities, and that you can help make the class a pleasant place to be. One of your main responsibilities is to help us create a positive learning atmosphere where everybody's needs are met. To accomplish this, we all must work together. I suggest that we begin by creating an agreement about how we will treat each other in this class.

Kagan, Kyle, and Scott suggest creating class agreements as follows: Begin by constructing a chart with the headings "Disruptive Behavior" and "Responsible Behavior," and subheadings under each of "Say" and "Do." Tell the students: "Let's name some of the disruptive things people say and do when they want attention." Record their responses. Then ask the class to name some of the responsible things people say and do for attention. Again, record their responses. Continue this process for each of the seven positions.

When you have reasonable lists, ask students, "How do you feel about these lists? Would you be willing to adopt the responsible behaviors as our class agreement? Can we agree to avoid the disruptive behaviors?" It is essential that students believe their opinions and cooperation are valued. Tell them, "You and I need to be on the same side and work together to create a classroom we all enjoy where everyone can learn. You will always be included in the decision-making process. You will be able to have your say. We will learn and practice skills that are important for being citizens in a democratic society. Choosing responsible behavior will be one of the most important things we will learn."

During the first weeks, use activities that strengthen the concept of the Three Pillars. This reassures students that discipline will not be done to them but will happen *with* them. In collaboration with the class, you might decide on preferred classroom procedures, discuss discipline structures and their purposes, develop follow-ups and logical consequences, and solicit student input on some curriculum decisions. You can do all this in a series of class meetings. You also can show students how you will help them turn disruptive behavior into good learning situations. That is where reflection, follow-up, and long-term structures come into play. Remember that during the first weeks you will need to begin establishing alliances with parents.

Summary Review of Kagan, Kyle, and Scott's Advice

Many ideas are suggested in Win-Win Discipline. The following summary is provided to help you tie them together.

Discipline is not something you do to students. It is something you help students acquire. Any disruptive behavior that interrupts the learning process can become an important learning opportunity. The aim of discipline is to help students learn to meet their needs in a nondisruptive, responsible manner.

When developing an approach to discipline, use the Three Pillars of Win-Win Discipline: same-side, collaborative solutions, and learned responsibility. Teacher and student must be on the same side, working toward the same goal. They share responsibility for creating discipline solutions that help students conduct themselves more responsibly now and in the future.

Win-Win Discipline identifies four types of disruptive behavior: aggression, breaking rules, confrontation, and disengagement (the ABCD's of disruptive behavior). Those behaviors spring from one or more of the seven student positions: attention-seeking, avoiding failure, being angry, control seeking, being energetic, being bored, and being uninformed. The teacher should validate the student's position as being natural and understandable. However, the disruptive behavior is not accepted. By identifying the student position that leads to the disruptive behavior, teachers are better able to select appropriate discipline responses.

Teachers help students see how to meet their needs through behavior that is acceptable. This is accomplished by maintaining students' dignity while encouraging students to identify behavior that would be acceptable under the circumstances. Teachers openly express genuine caring for students, validate student positions, and provide support in establishing responsible alternatives to disruptive behavior. Students who participate in the learning process and help create their own discipline solutions become more likely to make responsible choices in the future.

The ultimate goals of Win-Win Discipline are for students to become able to manage themselves, meet their needs through responsible choices, and develop life skills that serve them well in the future. Win-Win Discipline is not just a strategy for ending disruptions, but also one that teaches autonomous responsibility and other skills that transfer to life situations. Potential discipline problems are less likely to occur when students experience engaging curriculum and instruction.

Teachers are advised to seek parent and community alliances and create schoolwide programs for dealing with disruptive behavior. When parents, teacher, and students collaborate in creating solutions—when they all see themselves as being on the same side—students become more likely to make responsible choices.

KEY TERMS AND CONCEPTS EMPHASIZED IN THIS CHAPTER

Three Pillars	class rules	confrontations
ABCD of disruptive behavior	discipline structures	personal improvement plan
student positions	aggression	

SELECTED SEVEN—SUMMARY SUGGESTIONS FROM KAGAN, KYLE, AND SCOTT

1. Base your discipline program on the Three Pillars of Win-Win Discipline: same-side, collaborative solutions, and learned responsibility.

2. Do what you can to prevent the occurrence of misbehavior. Students seldom misbehave if needs associated with their positions are met. Therefore, the best way to prevent misbehavior is by structuring the class to meet the needs associated with the seven positions.

3. Involve students in making decisions about class matters including behavior and discipline. Strive to establish win-win solutions to problems so that everyone benefits.

4. Remember that disruptions offer prime conditions for students to learn responsible behavior and a number of other valuable life skills.

5. When a student disrupts, respond according to the type of disruption, the position from which it springs, and the history of disruptive behavior of the student.

6. Do your best to involve parents in your efforts to help students conduct themselves more responsibly.

7. Always maintain focus on the ultimate goal of Win-Win Discipline, which is for students to become able to manage themselves effectively.

CONCEPT CASES

Case 1: Kristina Will Not Work

Kristina, a student in Mr. Jake's class, is quite docile. She socializes little with other students and never disrupts lessons. However, despite Mr. Jake's best efforts, Kristina will not do her work. She rarely completes an assignment. She is simply there, putting forth no effort at all. *How would Kagan, Kyle, and Scott deal with Kristina?*

Kagan, Kyle, and Scott would advise Mr. Jake to do the following: Mr. Jake would identify Kristina's disruptive behavior and ask behavior-specific questions. He also would identify and help Kristina acknowledge her position. Mr. Jake might ask Kristina how she feels about the work, determining if it is too difficult for her (leading to avoidance of failure), or not interesting (leading to boredom). If the work is too difficult for Kristina, and her position is avoiding, or if she doesn't know how to do the work, he might say quietly, "I really want to help you be successful, Kristina. I see this work is not getting finished. None of us wants to tackle something we know will be too hard for us. The best thing to do if something is too hard is to break it into smaller pieces, mastering a part at a time. Another good strategy is to work on the difficult pieces with someone else. What suggestions do you have that will help you be successful?" Together they come up with possible solutions and then, if they agree that Kristina could benefit by working with a partner on smaller pieces, Mr. Jake may ask, "Would you like to work on this section with Danielle before moving on?" Throughout the interaction, Mr. Jake is attempting to help Kristina find a nondisruptive way to meet her needs. But more importantly, Mr. Jake is helping Kristina internalize a process of validating her own needs and seeking responsible rather than disruptive ways to fulfill them. As follow-up, Mr. Jake might focus on her success by saying something like, "Kristina, I knew you could do this if we tried making the pieces smaller." His long-term solutions will include further encouragement and individual attention to Kristina's strengths.

Case 2: Sara Cannot Stop Talking

Sara is a pleasant girl who participates in class activities and does most, though not all, of her assigned work. She cannot seem to refrain from talking to classmates, however. Her teacher, Mr. Gonzales, has to speak to her repeatedly during lessons, to the point that he often becomes exasperated and loses his temper. *What suggestions would Kagan, Kyle, and Scott give Mr. Gonzales for dealing with Sara?*

Case 3: Joshua Clowns and Intimidates

Joshua, larger and louder than his classmates, always wants to be the center of attention, which he accomplishes through a combination of clowning and intimidation. He makes wise remarks, talks back (smilingly) to the teacher, utters a variety of sound-effect noises such as automobile crashes and gunshots, and makes limitless sarcastic comments and put-downs of his classmates. Other students will not stand up to him, apparently fearing his size and verbal aggression. His teacher, Miss Pearl, has come to her wit's end. *Would Joshua's behavior be likely to improve if Win-Win Discipline were used in Miss Pearl's classroom? Explain.*

Case 4: Tom Is Hostile and Defiant

Tom has appeared to be in his usual foul mood ever since arriving in class. On his way to sharpen his pencil, he bumps into Frank, who complains. Tom tells him loudly to shut up. Miss Baines, the teacher, says, "Tom, go back to your seat." Tom wheels around, swears loudly, and says heatedly, "I'll go when I'm damned good and ready!" *How would Tom's behavior be handled in a Win-Win classroom?*

QUESTIONS AND ACTIVITIES

1. In your journal enter notes from Kagan, Kyle, and Scott's model that you might wish to include in your own system of discipline.

2. To what extent do you feel you could put Win-Win Discipline into effect in your classroom? What portions do you believe you could implement easily? What portions do you believe might present difficulty?

3. Win-Win Discipline rests on Three Pillars—same side, collaborative solutions, and learned responsibility. How would you go about communicating these key principles to students?

4. In what ways are curriculum, instruction, and management linked to preventing discipline problems? How might each help with the moment of disruption, follow-up, and long-term solutions?

YOU ARE THE TEACHER

Middle School World History

Your third-period world history class is comprised of students whose achievement levels vary from high to well below average. You pace their work accordingly, ask them to work cooperatively, and make sure everyone understands what they are supposed to do. For the most part you enjoy the class, finding the students interesting and refreshing. Your lessons follow a consistent pattern. First, you ask the students to read in groups from the textbook, then you call on students at random to answer selected questions about the material. If a student who is called on is unable to answer a question, the group he or she represents loses a point. If able to answer correctly, the group gains a point. For partially correct answers, the group neither receives nor loses a point. For the second part of the period, the class groups do something productive or creative connected with the material they have read, such as making posters, writing a story, doing a skit, or the like. As appropriate, these efforts are shared with members of the class.

Typical Occurrences

You call on Hillary to answer a question. Although she has been participating, she shakes her head. This has happened several times before. Not wanting to hurt Hillary's feelings, you simply say, "That costs the group a point," and you call on someone else. Unfortunately, Hillary's group gets upset at her. The other students make comments under their breath. Later, Clarisse does the same thing that Hillary has done. When you speak with her about it, she replies, "You didn't make Hillary do it." You answer, "Look, we are talking about you, not Hillary." However, you let the matter lie there and say no more. Just then Deonne comes into the class late, appearing very angry. He slams his pack down on his desk and sits without opening his textbook. Although you want to talk with Deonne, you don't know how to

approach him at that time. Will is in an opposite mood. Throughout the oral reading portion of the class, he has continually giggles at every mispronounced word and at every reply students give to your questions. Will sits at the front of the class and turns around to laugh, seeing if he can get anyone else to laugh with him. He makes some "oooh" and "aaah" sounds when Hillary and Clarisse decline to respond. Although most students either ignore him or give him disgusted looks, he keeps laughing. You finally ask him what is so funny. He replies, "Nothing in particular," and looks back at the class and laughs. At the end of the period, there is time for sharing three posters students have made. Will makes comments and giggles about each of them. Clarisse, who has not participated, says, "Will, how about shutting up?" As the students leave the room, you take Deonne aside. "Is something wrong, Deonne?" you ask. "No," Deonne replies. His jaws are clenched as he strides past you.

Conceptualizing a Strategy

If you followed the suggestions of Kagan, Kyle, and Scott, what would you conclude or do with regard to the following?

1. Preventing the problems from occurring in the first place.

2. Putting an immediate end to the undesirable behavior.

3. Involving other or all students in addressing the situation.

4. Maintaining student dignity and good personal relations.

5. Using follow-up procedures that would prevent the recurrence of the misbehavior.

6. Using the situation to help the students develop a sense of greater responsibility and self-control

REFERENCES

Kagan, S. 2001. Teaching for character and community. *Educational Leadership*, 59(2), 50–55.

Kagan, S. 2002. What is Win-Win Discipline? *Kagan Online Magazine* 1(15). www.KaganOnline.com.

Kagan, S., Kyle, P., and Scott, S. 2004. *Win-win discipline*. San Clemente, CA: Kagan Publishing.

Kagan, L., Scott, S., and Kagan, S. 2003. *Win-Win discipline course workbook*. San Clemente, CA: Kagan Publishing.

CHAPTER 10

Discipline through Dignity and Hope for Challenging Youth

Authoritative Input
■ Richard Curwin and Allen Mendler / Discipline with Dignity

CHAPTER PREVIEW

Dignity refers to respect for life and oneself. Discipline with Dignity is designed to help teachers maintain a positive classroom learning environment by emphasizing student dignity and providing a genuine sense of hope to students who are otherwise likely to drop out of school. The approach offers no magical fix for behavior problems, but does provide tools that lead to solid, long-term solutions to chronic misbehavior, including violence. Discipline with Dignity is for use with all students, but in recent years Curwin and Mendler have determined that it is especially helpful in bringing about positive change in students considered to be difficult to manage.

Fundamental Hypothesis of Discipline with Dignity

Misbehavior does not become a significant problem in classrooms that maintain student dignity and provide genuine hope for and expectation of success.

The Nature and Practice of Discipline with Dignity

Almost always, students who are particularly difficult to manage feel that their personal dignity is constantly under threat; moreover, they have little belief that they will ever be successful in school, or even that school has anything of value for them. However, most of these students can be reclaimed through tactics that enhance their dignity and provide a sense of hope for school success.

About Richard Curwin and Allen Mendler

Richard Curwin and Allen Mendler write and consult widely in matters related to discipline and working with challenging youth. Curwin, a university professor and private consultant, began his teaching career in a seventh-grade class of boys whose behavior was seriously out of control. That experience led him toward a career specialization in school discipline. His articles have appeared in *Educational Leadership; Reclaiming Children and Youth; Instructor, Parenting, and Learning.* Mendler, a school psychologist and psychoeducational consultant, has worked extensively with students and teachers at all levels. His articles have appeared in many journals, including *Educational Leadership, Kappan, Learning, Reclaiming Children and Youth,* and *Reaching Today's Youth.*

Curwin and Mendler attracted national attention with their 1988 book *Discipline with Dignity,* which has been updated a number of times. In 1992 Curwin published *Rediscovering Hope: Our Greatest Teaching Strategy,* in which he explained how to improve the behavior of students who are difficult to control and who are otherwise likely to fail in school. In 1997 Curwin and Mendler published *As Tough as Necessary: Countering Violence, Aggression, and Hostility in Our Schools,* in which they provide suggestions for working with hostile, aggressive students. They followed in 1999 with *Discipline with Dignity for Challenging Youth,* designed to help teachers work productively with students with especially difficult behavioral problems. More recently, Allen Mendler published *Connecting with Students* (2001), and Richard Curwin published *Making Good Choices: Developing Responsibility, Respect, and Self-Discipline in Grades 4–9* (2003). Curwin and Mendler's website is www.disciplineassociates.com.

Curwin and Mendler ask teachers first to understand that helping students learn to behave acceptably in school is an essential part of teaching. They urge teaches to do everything possible to instill hope and promise of success, especially in students who chronically misbehave. The way to do so is by always interacting with students in a helpful manner that preserves their dignity, while making sure that no discipline tactic interferes with their willingness to learn.

All students misbehave at one time or another, usually for inconsequential reasons, such as fun or expedience. Some misbehave for more serious reasons, however, including "gaining a measure of control over a system that has damaged their sense of dignity" (Curwin 1992, p. 49). They seek to experience that control by refusing to comply with teacher requests, arguing and talking back to the teacher, tapping pencils and dropping books, withdrawing from class activities, and overtly acting out hostility and aggression. As Curwin puts it, these students have found that they can't be good at learning but they can be very good at being bad, and that by doing so they can gratify their needs for attention and power. They are usually at risk for failure in school, and they usually find others like themselves with whom to bond, which encourages further misbehavior.

Teachers dread dealing with students whose behavior is so unacceptable they not only disrupt learning but threaten others. Such behavior makes teachers feel trapped and overwhelmed. Curwin and Mendler have provided realistic help for working with such students and for reducing behavior that is hostile, aggressive, and violent.

A Four-Phase Plan for Schools and Educators

Curwin and Mendler suggest a four-phase plan for educators to help students move toward values-guided behavior. The plan can be used effectively in single classrooms, although Curwin and Mendler believe it produces even better results when used throughout the entire school. The four phases in the plan are (1) identifying the core values that the class or school holds and wishes to emphasize, (2) creating rules and consequences based on the core values identified, (3) modeling the values continually during interactions with students and staff members, and (4) using no interventions that violate the core values. Here are suggestions they offer within each of the four phases.

Identify the Core Values

Faculty, staff, students, and parents work together to specify a set of **core values** that shows how they want individuals in the class or school to conduct themselves and relate to each other. A set of core values might include statements such as the following (1997, p. 24):

- School is a place where we solve our problems peacefully.
- School is a place where we protect and look out for one another, rather than hurt or attack one another.
- School is a place where we learn we are responsible for what we do.
- School is a place where we learn that "my way is not the only way."

Create Rules and Consequences

Rules are needed to govern classroom behavior; those rules should be based on the school's stated values. Whereas the values state broad intentions, rules say exactly what one should and should not do. This can be seen in the following examples (1997, p. 31):

Value	Rule
School is a place where we protect and look out for one another, rather than hurt or attack one another.	No put-downs allowed.
School is a place where we solve our problems peacefully.	Keep your hands and feet to yourselves.

Model the Values

It is essential that teachers and administrators continually model behaviors that are in keeping with the school values. Teachers must express their emotions nonviolently, use positive strategies to resolve conflict with students, and walk away when they receive put-downs from students. Curwin and Mendler (1997, p. 32) suggest that teachers, individually or in staff meetings, write on paper how they want students to express their anger and how they want classroom conflicts to be resolved. Teachers should then teach their students these techniques and make sure they use them, as well.

Use No Interventions that Violate Core Values

Teachers everywhere tend to use their past experiences when responding to student misbehavior. Their responses often take the form of threats, intimidation, and making examples of students. Responses of these types fail to model behavior consistent with school values and tend to produce further conflict. Threats, for example, destroy student comfort in the classroom. If carried out vengefully, they produce a backlash of resentment. If threats are not carried out, student behavior worsens, calling for still more dire threats, which, in turn, cannot be carried out. Students conclude that it is all right to threaten others, because they see the teacher modeling that behavior. Such a cycle is broken by showing students the dangers of threats and teaching them alternative behaviors.

The same applies to intimidation and using students as examples—familiar tactics of a majority of teachers years ago and still evident in many classrooms. When teachers intimidate students, students may cower (or may not); the students, in turn, become more likely to treat others in the same way. It is also self-defeating to reprimand one student as an example for others. The humiliation felt by the disciplined student produces a permanent effect. The primary goal of interventions is to help students learn more responsible behavior. This cannot be accomplished through hurtful tactics, but instead, through modeling positive, nonviolent behavior when intervening in student behavior, and through helping students use such behavior in their interactions with others.

Preparing Oneself in Advance

It is helpful for teachers to prepare themselves in advance for misbehavior they might encounter. Curwin and Mendler suggest doing the following (1997, p. 71):

- Write down things students do or say that you find irritating.
- Determine why students do those things. What basic needs are they trying to meet? What motivates them?
- What do you presently do when students say or do irritating things?
- Are your current tactics effective in solving the problem?
- What response strategies can you think of that address the reasons for the irritating behavior while at the same time model behavior consistent with school values?
- Practice the strategies beforehand and then put them into practice at the next opportunity.

Working with Students Who Are Behaviorally at Risk of Failure

Behaviorally at risk refers to students whose willful behavior severely inhibits learning and puts them in danger of failing in school. These are the students teachers consider to be out of control—turned off, angry, hostile, irresponsible, disruptive, or withdrawn. They are commonly said to have "attitude problems." They make little effort to learn, disregard teacher requests and directions, and instigate trouble in the classroom.

The exact percentage of students considered to be behaviorally at risk is not known, but as of October 2000 in the United States, there were 612,900 public school students enrolled in alternative schools for students considered to be too dangerous or disruptive to remain in regular schools. That figure represented 1.3 percent of the public school population (National Center for Education Statistics, 2001b). Most of those schools were at the secondary level. Some educators estimate that about 5 percent of all school students are probably behaviorally at risk of failure in school.

Richard Curwin and Allen Mendler (1992) have taken a special interest in these students. They say the students behave as they do because they have low self-concepts in relation to school and little or no hope of being successful there. They associate with and are reinforced by students similar to themselves. Curwin and Mendler emphasize that the term *at risk* refers solely to behavior, not to the nature of the student, saying, "It is what students do under the conditions they are in, not who they are, that puts them at risk" (Curwin 1992, p. xiii).

Students who are behaviorally at risk are difficult to control for several reasons. They usually, though not always, have a history of academic failure. Unable to maintain dignity through achievement, they protect themselves by withdrawing and acting as if they don't care. They have learned that it feels better to misbehave than to follow rules that provide no payoff. Curwin (1992) illustrates this point.

> Ask yourself, if you got a 56 on an important test, what would make you feel better about failing? Telling your friends, "I studied hard and was just too stupid to pass" or, "It was a stupid test anyway, and besides I hate that dumb class and that boring teacher?" (p. 49)

When their dignity has been repeatedly damaged in school, students make themselves feel better by lashing out at others. As they continue to misbehave, they find themselves systematically removed from opportunities to act responsibly. When they break rules, they are made to sit by themselves in isolation. When they fight, they are told to apologize and shake hands. In such cases they are taken out of the very situations in which they might learn to behave responsibly. Curwin (1992) makes the point as follows:

> No one would tell a batter who was struggling at the plate that he could not participate in batting practice until he improved. No one would tell a poor reader that he could not look at any books until his reading improved. In the same way, no student can learn how to play in a playground by being removed from the playground, or how to learn time-management skills by being told when to schedule everything. Learning responsibility requires participation. (p. 50)

The importance of personal dignity in the lives of students who are at risk can hardly be overstated. In their book, *Discipline with Dignity* (2001), Curwin and Mendler point out that students with chronic behavior problems see themselves as losers and have stopped trying to gain acceptance in normal ways. In order to maintain a sense of dignity, those students tell themselves it is better to stop trying than to continue failing, and that it is better to be recognized as a troublemaker than be seen as stupid. Students try to protect their dignity at all costs. Teachers must take pains, therefore, to keep dignity intact and bolster it when possible. Curwin (1992) advises

> We must . . . welcome high risk students as human beings. They come to school as whole people, not simply as brains waiting to be trained. Our assumptions about their social behavior need to include the understanding that their negative behaviors are based on protection and escape. They do the best they can with the skills they have under the adverse conditions they face. . . . When they are malicious, they believe, rightly or wrongly, that they are justified in defending themselves from attacks on their dignity. (p. 27)

It is very difficult for most teachers to remain understanding and helpful when students behave atrociously. A steady diet of defiant hostility makes many teachers become cynical, and they give up trying to help students. Some who face such behavior on a daily basis leave teaching because they don't feel its rewards justify the distress they must endure. However, Curwin and Mendler believe teachers can help most students who are at risk to become reasonably successful in school. What those students need is a renewed sense of hope and help and opportunity to learn how to accept responsibility. Teachers can often restore hope simply by treating students with respect while making instruction more interesting and worthwhile. Curwin and Mendler urge teachers to do the following:

- Always treat your students with dignity. Respect them as individuals, show concern for their needs, and understand their viewpoints.
- Don't allow your discipline tactics to interfere with student motivation. Any discipline technique that reduces motivation to learn is self-defeating.
- Emphasize responsibility rather than obedience. Obedience means "do as you are told." Responsibility means "make the best decision possible."

Disciplining Students Who Are Difficult to Control

Traditional methods of discipline are relatively ineffective with students who are behaviorally at risk. These students have grown immune to scolding, lecturing, sarcasm, detention, extra writing assignments, isolation, names on the chalkboard, or trips to the principal's office. It does no good to tell them what they did wrong, nor does it help to grill them about their failure to do class work or follow rules. They already doubt their ability, and they know they don't want to follow rules. Sarcastic teacher remarks, because they attack student' dignity, only make matters worse. Students who are at risk need no further humiliation. Punishment destroys their motivation to cooperate. They see no reason to commit to better ways of behaving and, therefore, do not achieve the results teachers hope for.

How, then, should teachers help these students learn to behave more responsibly? Curwin and Mendler set forth principles and approaches they consider significantly more effective than the discipline approaches normally used. They acknowledge that dealing with students who chronically break rules is never easy and admit that the success rate is far from perfect, but they claim it is possible to produce positive changes in 25 to 50 percent of students considered to be out of control. Curwin (1992, pp. 51–54) encourages teachers to base their discipline efforts on the following principles:

1. *Dealing with student behavior is an important part of teaching.* Most teachers do not want to deal with behavior problems, but their attitudes change when they adopt the conviction that being a professional means doing whatever they can to help each individual student. Teachers can look on misbehavior as an ideal opportunity for teaching responsibility. They should put as much effort into teaching good behavior as they put into teaching content.

2. *Always treat students with dignity.* Dignity is a basic need that is essential for healthy life. Its importance is preeminent. To treat students with dignity is to respect them as individuals, show concern for their needs, and understand their viewpoints. Effective discipline does not attack student dignity but instead offers hope. Curwin and Mendler advise teachers to ask themselves the following question when reacting to student misbehavior: "How would this strategy affect my dignity if a teacher did it to me?"

3. *Good discipline must not interfere with student motivation.* Any discipline technique is self-defeating if it reduces motivation to learn. Students who become involved in lessons cause few discipline problems. Poorly behaved students usually lack motivation to learn what is being offered them. They need encouragement and a reason to learn. Curwin suggests that teachers, when about to deal with misbehavior, ask themselves this question: "What will this technique do to motivation?"

4. *Responsibility is more important than obedience.* Curwin differentiates between obedience and responsibility as follows: Obedience means doing as you are told. Responsibility means making the best decision possible. Obedience is desirable in matters of health and safety, but when applied to most misbehavior it is a short-term solution against which students rebel. Responsibility grows, albeit slowly, as students engage in sorting out facts and making decisions. Teachers should regularly provide such opportunities.

Rules and Consequences

Curwin and Mendler believe in establishing class rules and invoking consequences if students break those rules. Those consequences can be of three different types, called logical, conventional, and generic.

Logical consequences are those in which students must make right what they have done wrong. The consequence is logically related to the behavior. If they make a mess, they must clean it up. If they willfully damage material, they must replace it. If they speak hurtfully to others, they must practice speaking in ways that are not hurtful.

Conventional consequences are those commonly used by most teachers, such as time-out and removal from the room. These consequences are seldom logically related to the behavior in question; therefore, they should be modified to increase student commitment. When teachers invoke time-out, instead of banning the student for a specified length of time, they should say something like "You have chosen time-out. You may return to the group when you are ready to learn."

Generic consequences are reminders, warnings, choosing, and planning that are invoked when misbehavior is noted. Often, simple *reminders* are enough to stop misbehavior: "We need to get this work completed." *Choosing* allows students to select from three or four options a plan for improving their behavior. *Planning*, which Curwin (1992, p. 78) calls the most effective consequence that can be used for all rule violations, requires students to plan their own solution to a recurring behavior problem. Planning indicates that the teacher has faith in students' competence. That faith often engenders a degree of student commitment. The process involves the student's making a plan of positive action that specifies the steps the student will follow. It should be written, dated, and signed.

Curwin (1992, pp. 79–80) suggests a number of additional considerations related to consequences.

- Always implement a consequence when a rule is broken.
- Select the most appropriate consequence from the list of alternatives, taking into account the offense, situation, student involved, and the best means of helping that student.
- State the rule and consequence to the offending student. Nothing more need be said.
- Be private. Only the student(s) involved should hear.
- Do not embarrass the student.
- Do not think of the situation as win-lose. This is not a contest. Do not get involved in a power struggle.
- Control your anger. Be calm and speak quietly, but accept no excuses from the student.
- Sometimes it is best to let the student choose the consequence.

An **insubordination rule** should be established that will remove the student from the classroom should he or she refuse to accept an assigned consequence.

Preventing Escalation

When teachers respond to student misbehavior, students often dig in their heels. A contest of wills then ensues, with neither side willing to back down. Curwin and Mendler remind teachers it is not their duty to win such contests but to do what they can to help the student. This requires keeping the channels open for rational discussion of problem behavior. That cannot be done if the teacher humiliates, angers, embarrasses, or demeans the student. This point is critical in working with high-risk students, who are predisposed to respond negatively. Curwin (1992) suggests that teachers do the following toward **preventing escalation** of incipient conflicts:

- Use active listening. Acknowledge and/or paraphrase what students say without agreeing, disagreeing, or expressing value judgment.
- Arrange to speak with the student later. Allow a time for cooling off. It is much easier to have positive discussions after anger has dissipated.
- Keep all communication as private as possible. Students do not want to lose face in front of their peers and so are unlikely to comply with public demands. Nor do teachers like to appear weak in front of the class. When communication is kept private, the chances for productive discussion are much better because egos are not so strongly on the line.
- If a student refuses to accept a consequence, invoke the insubordination rule. Don't use this provision until it is clear the student will not accept the consequence.

Dealing with Aggression, Hostility, Violence, and Conflict

Curwin and Mendler note that students are becoming increasingly aggressive, hostile, and violent, and are doing so at an earlier age. Teenagers are two and a half times more likely to experience **violence** than people over age 20. Curwin and Mendler say the increase in violence has occurred in part because society has been rewarding and punishing students in school, home, and community rather than teaching them values—such as that it is wrong to intimidate others, hurt them physically, or destroy their property. A large number of students who use violence lack a sense of compassion or remorse and, thus, do not respond to normal discipline techniques. This makes it especially difficult for teachers to work with them productively.

Curwin and Mendler have addressed this problem in their 1997 book *As Tough As Necessary: Countering Violence, Aggression, and Hostility in Our Schools.* They point out that by "as tough as necessary" they do not mean a zero-tolerance stance. Instead, the mean using "a variety of ways to help aggressive, hostile, and violent children learn alternatives to hurting others" (p. ix). They contend that "behavior change among hardened, antisocial, and angry students cannot result simply from offering more love, caring, and opportunities for decision making" (p. 16). They say that if schools are to deal with violence, they must adopt schoolwide approaches that (1) teach students how, when threatened or frustrated, to make nonviolent choices that serve them more effectively than do violent choices; (2) model for students nonhostile ways of expressing anger, frustration, and impatience; and (3) emphasize the teaching of values that relate to cooperation, safety, altruism, and remorse.

Curwin and Mendler suggest several strategies for teachers and students to use when they encounter violence. These strategies are designed to help everyone calm down, decide how to proceed, and take positive steps. Teachers should teach the procedures to students and model them in practice. The following are a few of the many techniques suggested (1997, pp. 94–118):

- *Use the six-step solution.* (1) Stop and calm down. Wait a moment, take a deep breath, and relax. (2) Think. Quickly explore options and foresee what will happen if you use them. (3) Decide what you want to have happen. (4) Decide on a second solution in case the first doesn't work. (5) Carry out the solution you deem best. (6) Evaluate the results. Have you accomplished what you hoped? Will you use the tactic again in similar circumstances?
- *Solve my problem.* First, name the problem, indicating specifically what somebody has said or done. Second, say what you would like to have happen. Third, say what you will do to make those things happen. Fourth, make a backup plan to use if the first one doesn't work. Fifth, carry out the plan.
- *Learn to have patience.* As we grow up we learn that our needs can't always be met when we'd like, and that often we have to wait. If we don't learn to have patience, we will feel frustrated and angry because we are not getting what we want when we want it. Learning to be patient requires practice in such areas as walking away from a fight, waiting in line with a smile, and remaining calm when somebody cuts in line.
- *Wear an invisible shield.* Pretend you are wearing an invisible shield that deflects all bad thoughts and unkind words. It makes you immune to them. You cannot be hurt as long as you are wearing it.
- *Use words that work.* Instead of being provoked into retaliation, practice the following to stop almost all attacks against you: (1) speaking politely, using words such as *please* and *thank you*; (2) asking if you have done something that has upset the other person; and (3) apologizing if you have offended the person.
- *Plan for confrontations.* List five situations you recall in which people got into a dispute. Next to each, write down strategies you think would bring the situation calmly to a close. Practice what you would say and do if you found yourself in one of these situations.

Teachers who agree with approaches to deter violence still ask the legitimate question, "What, specifically, do I do when . . . ?" In answer to that question, Curwin and Mendler provide many concrete suggestions concerning the best teacher responses when students misbehave, such as (1997, p. 66)

- Use privacy, eye contact, and proximity when possible. Speak privately and quietly with the students. This preserves their dignity and takes away the likelihood of their fighting back.
- Indicate to the student politely but clearly what you want. Use the words *please* and *thank you* (e.g., "Bill, please go to Mr. Keene's room. There's a seat there for you. Come back when you are ready to learn. I hope that doesn't take very long. Thank you, Bill.")
- Tell the student that you see a power struggle brewing that will not be good for anyone. Defer discussion to a later time. (e.g., "Juan, you are angry and so am I. Rather than have a dispute now, let's calm down and talk later. I'm sure we can help each other out after we cool off. Thanks a lot.")

Dealing with Bullying and Hate Crimes

Note: Whereas most of the contents of this chapter are drawn from the works of Curwin and Mendler, the information in this section comes mainly from Barbara Coloroso (2003) and John Hoover and Pam Stenhjem (2003).

Bullying and hate crimes seldom put the perpetrators in danger of failing in school, but they often have devastating effects on students and seriously trouble teachers. **Bullying** is defined as intentionally and repeatedly committing hurtful acts against others. It is a daily occurrence in most schools. It may consist of physical aggression, sexual aggression, name-calling, threatening, taunting, intimidating, or shunning. Four kinds of bullying are common:

1. *Physical bullying.* Including punching, poking, strangling, hair pulling, beating, biting, kicking, and excessive tickling.
2. *Verbal bullying.* Including hurtful name-calling, teasing, and gossip.
3. *Emotional bullying.* Including rejecting; terrorizing; extorting; defaming; humiliating; blackmailing; rating/ranking of personal characteristics such as race, disability, ethnicity, or perceived sexual orientation; manipulating friendships; isolating; ostracizing; and exerting peer pressure.
4. *Sexual bullying.* Including many of the actions listed above as well as exhibitionism, voyeurism, sexual propositioning, sexual harassment, physical contact, and sexual assault.

Among middle school students, one in four is bullied on a regular basis, while one in five admits to bullying others. About one in seven says he or she experienced severe reactions to the abuse.

Acts of bullying usually occur away from the eyes of teachers or other responsible adults. As perpetrators go undetected, a climate of fear develops that affects victims adversely. Grades may suffer because attention is deflected away from learning. Fear may lead to absenteeism, truancy, or dropping out. If the problem persists, victims occasionally resort to drastic measures, such as fighting back, carrying weapons, and occasionally suicide.

Bystanders and peers of victims can suffer harmful effects as well. They may be afraid to associate with the victim for fear of lowering their own status or of receiving retribution from the bully. They may not report bullying incidents because they do not want to be called a snitch, a tattler, or an informer. Some experience feelings of guilt or helplessness for not standing up to the bully on behalf of their classmate. They may feel unsafe, with loss of control and inability to take action.

Hate crimes are similar to bullying, but are related to a dislike of other races, ethnic groups, or religions. They typically involve intimidation, harassment, bigoted slurs or epithets, force or threat of force, and vandalism.

The incidence and effects of bullying and hate crimes are grossly underreported. Educators, family members, and children concerned with violence prevention must be concerned with hate crimes and their linkage to other violent behaviors. Excellent suggestions for limiting and dealing with bullying and hate crimes are found in *Preventing Bullying: A Manual for Schools and Communities.* (U.S. Department of Education, 1998), and in Barbara Coloroso's 2003 book, *The Bully, the Bullied, and the Bystander: How Parents and Teachers Can Break the Cycle of Violence.* Here are a few of the many suggestions provided in those two resources.

- Schedule regular classroom meetings during which students and teachers engage in discussion, role-playing, and other activities to reduce bullying and hate crimes.
- Involve parents or guardians of bullies and victims of bullying and hate crimes. Listen receptively to family members who report bullying. Establish procedures whereby such reports are investigated and resolved expeditiously.
- Form friendship groups or other supports for students who are being victimized by bullying or hate crimes.
- Closely supervise students on the grounds and in classrooms, hallways, restrooms, cafeterias, and other areas where bullying occurs. Immediately intervene in all bullying incidents.
- Post and publicize clear behavior standards, including rules against bullying, for all students. Consistently and fairly enforce such standards.
- Establish a confidential reporting system that allows students to report victimization. Keep records of the incidents.
- Provide students with opportunities to talk about bullying and hate crimes. Enlist their support in defining bullying as unacceptable behavior.
- Involve students in establishing classroom rules against bullying. Such rules may include a commitment from the teacher not to ignore incidents of bullying.
- Develop an action plan to ensure that students know what to do when they observe an episode of bullying.
- Don't try to mediate a bullying situation. The difference in power between victims and bullies may cause victims to feel further victimized by the process.

Helping Students Regain Hope

Teachers can do a great deal to help students who are victimized or at risk regain a **sense of hope.** Hope is the belief that things will be better in the future. It inspires us, provides courage and incentive to overcome barriers, and helps us live more meaningfully. Students who are behaviorally at risk have, for the most part, lost hope that education will serve them. Curwin and Mendler contend that such students can be helped to regain hope and that as they do so their behavior will improve. This can be accomplished, they say, by making learning much more interesting and worthwhile. If students are to get involved in the learning process, they need something to hope for, something that will make their efforts seem worthwhile. Learning activities become successful when students see they build competence in matters the students consider important (Curwin 1992, p. 25).

Learning must not only be made attractive but, as mentioned, must bring success as well. Students who are behaviorally at risk will not persevere unless successful, despite the initial attractiveness of the topic. To ensure success, teachers can explore ways to redesign the curriculum, encourage different ways of thinking, provide for various learning styles and sensory modalities, allow for creativity and artistic expression, and use grading systems that provide encouraging feedback without damaging the students' willingness to try.

Motivating Students Who Are Difficult to Manage

There is no set of techniques that automatically motivate students who are difficult to manage. Certain tactics, however, can yield positive results for many. Students who are behaviorally at risk have the same general needs and interests as other students, but they have encountered so much failure that they have turned to resistance and misbehavior to bolster their egos. Curwin (1992, pp. 130–144) makes the following suggestions for increasing motivation among all students, and especially those who are behaviorally at risk:

- Select for your lessons as many topics as you can that have personal importance and relevance to the students.
- Set up authentic learning goals—goals that lead to genuine competence that students can display and be proud of.
- Help students interact with the topics in ways that are congruent with their interests and values.
- Involve students actively in lessons. Allow them to use their senses, move about, and talk. Make the lessons as much fun as possible. Lessons needn't be easy if they are important and enjoyable.
- Give students numerous opportunities to take risks and make decisions without fear of failure.
- Show your own genuine energy and interest in the topics being studied. Show that you enjoy working with students. Try to connect personally with them as individuals.
- Each day, do at least one activity that you love. Show pride in your knowledge and ability to convey it to your students. Don't be reluctant to ham it up.
- Make your class activities events students look forward to. Make them wonder what might happen next.

Making Changes in Yourself

Most teachers have to work at times with students who are unusually defiant, hostile, stubborn, offensive, or unmotivated. To help those teachers be more successful, Curwin and Mendler (1999) developed an approach called Dignity with Discipline for Challenging Youth. A cornerstone of the approach is helping teachers make changes *in themselves* that enable them better to meet the needs of their students. You have seen that Discipline with Dignity urges teachers to treat all students in a dignified manner while emphasizing responsibility. For working with challenging students, Curwin and Mendler add or reemphasize these suggestions:

- Adopt the stance that teachers are responsible for teaching all students and that all students are worthy of our best effort.
- Take comfort in knowing that you can help difficult students move toward better behavior in all aspects of life.
- Think of discipline as instruction for such behavior change.
- Learn to identify the reasons for misbehavior and address those reasons in your classes by teaching students to identify and deal with them.
- Develop a repertoire of effective discipline strategies and use them patiently and persistently.
- Develop discipline tactics for each of three categories: *crisis* (e.g., fights), *short term* (stopping misbehavior while preserving dignity of teacher and student), and *long term* (working to meet the needs of students over time). Effective crisis strategies call for specific plans of action you will take when crises arise. Short-term strategies include I-messages, PEP (privacy, eye contact, proximity), PEP notes or cards with words or phrases of appreciation or correction, privacy 3-step (privately set a limit, offer a choice, or give a consequence), and LAAD tactics (listening, acknowledging, agreeing, deferring action).
- Remove or limit the causes of misbehavior.
- Use affirmative rather than negative labels (e.g., "sticks up for himself" rather than "defiant," or "has yet to find the value in lessons" rather than "lazy").
- Create a caring classroom.
- Teach students self-control.
- Teach students to have concern for others.
- Set clearly defined limits on behavior.
- Teach conflict-resolution skills that students can use.
- Help students network with peers, older students, staff members, volunteers, and mentors.
- Always look for a common ground when dealing with troublesome students.
- Maintain the conviction that all students can change.
- Accept the challenge to stay personally involved with each student without taking personally any of their obnoxious, irritating, disruptive, or hurtful behavior.
- Remember that 70 percent of school misbehavior has its roots at home rather than at school and it is our obligation to break the cycle of hostility and aggression by not retaliating in kind.
- Always strive for responsible student behavior rather than mere obedience. Do this by establishing sensible limits on behavior and allowing students choices within these limits, such as writing or drawing as a way of expressing anger. Help students learn from the consequences of their behavior and in the process develop a commitment to change. In all cases, place more emphasis on motivation than on discipline.
- Use tactics that tend to overcome student resistance. Such tactics include personal interest, personal interaction, kindness, helpfulness, encouragement, acknowledgment of effort, and use of challenge rather than threat. Evaluate each strategy you consider against the following:

Does it promote dignity or humiliation?
Does it teach responsibility or obedience?
Does it motivate students to learn?
Does it foster commitment?

Putting Curwin and Mendler's Ideas into Practice

Suppose you teach a class that contains several chronically misbehaving students, and you feel the Curwin and Mendler model can help you work with them more effectively. How do you make their suggestions operational? To begin, base your efforts on the following four principles:

1. *Student dignity must always be preserved.* When faced with threat, students, especially those who chronically misbehave, use antisocial behavior to counter it. You must guard against threatening students' dignity, even when they threaten yours.
2. *Dealing with misbehavior is one of the most important parts of teaching.* You are in the classroom to help your students. Those whose behavior puts them at risk of failure especially need your help, though their behavior may suggest that they want nothing to do with you. The best thing you can do for them is find ways to encourage prosocial behavior.
3. *Lasting results are achieved only over time.* There are no quick-fix solutions to chronic misbehavior, but by finding ways to motivate students and help them learn, you will enable many to make genuine improvement.
4. *Responsibility is more important than obedience.* You must be willing to put students into situations where they can make decisions about matters that concern them, be willing to allow them to fail, and then help them try again. progressively, they will learn to behave in ways that are best for themselves and others.

Mendler and Curwin (1999 pp. 13–16) further identify twelve points that provide functionality to their Discipline with Dignity.

1. Let students know what you need.
2. Provide instruction at levels that match students' abilities.
3. Listen to what students are thinking and feeling.
4. Use humor.
5. Vary your style of presentation.
6. Offer choices.
7. Refuse to accept excuses.
8. Legitimize behavior you cannot stop.
9. Use hugs and pats when communicating with students.
10. Be responsible for yourself and allow students to be responsible for themselves.
11. Accept that you will not be successful in helping every student.
12. Start fresh every day.

As for specific actions, when you first meet your students, spend as much time as necessary discussing goals for the class, interesting topics and activities you will provide, and class behavior that will enhance enjoyment and accomplishment for everyone. In those discussions, class rules and consequences should be agreed to. It is important that students contribute to those decisions and agree to abide by them. Then provide lessons that are structured to keep students active while allowing success. Emphasize topics and activities that students find interesting, rather than trying to drag the class perfunctorily through the standard curriculum. Display your own energy, enjoyment of learning, and pride in teaching. They will affect students positively and your willingness to help students without confrontation will slowly win them over.

Curwin and Mendler (2005) want you to remember and practice the following:

1. The most effective discipline technique at your disposal is making every student feel welcome and important.
2. Spend plenty of time at the beginning helping students get to know you, understand the nature and value of the class, and understand how they are expected to behave.
3. When students withdraw, give them an even bigger invitation.
4. Discipline responses require a two-stage approach: stabilize the behavior and teach behaviors that bring greater success.
5. Model ways of expressing anger effectively.
6. When you take something away from students, give them something back.
7. Eventually you must face students who misbehave. At that time, provide them limits and choices.

KEY TERMS AND CONCEPTS EMPHASIZED IN THIS CHAPTER

dignity	conventional consequences	violence
core values	generic consequences	bullying
behaviorally at risk	insubordination rule	hate crimes
logical consequences	preventing escalation	sense of hope

SELECTED SEVEN—SUMMARY SUGGESTIONS FROM CURWIN AND MENDLER

1. Safeguard and support student dignity in all class matters. Students make every effort to preserve dignity, and those efforts sometimes become misbehavior.

2. Do what you can to foster students' sense of hope that they will benefit from education. Students who have lost hope usually don't care how they behave.

3. Approach discipline as a very important part of teaching. It can teach students how to conduct themselves in ways that bring success in life.

4. Work toward long-term solutions to behavior problems. Short-term solutions are rarely effective.

5. Focus on student responsibility, not obedience, as the primary goal of discipline.

6. Use personal attention and good teaching as the major avenues to success with students who are chronically disruptive.

7. Prepare yourself to respond effectively to students who are hostile, disobedient, and inconsiderate.

CONCEPT CASES

Case 1: Kristina Will Not Work

Kristina, in Mr. Jake's class, is quite docile. She never disrupts class and does little socializing with other students. But despite Mr. Jake's best efforts, Kristina rarely completes an assignment. She doesn't seem to care. She is simply there, putting forth virtually no effort. *How would Curwin and Mendler deal with Kristina?*

Curwin and Mendler would suggest the following: Consider that Kristina's behavior might be due to severe feelings of incapability. She may be protecting herself by not trying. Relate to Kristina as an individual. Chat with her informally about her life and interests. Find topics that interest Kristina and build some class lessons around them. Assign Kristina individual work that helps her become more competent in her areas of special interest. Have a private conversation with Kristina. Ask for her thoughts about how you could make school more interesting for her. Show her you are interested and willing to help. As Kristina begins to work and participate, continue private chats that help her see herself as successful.

Case 2: Sara Cannot Stop Talking

Sara is a pleasant girl who participates in class activities and does most, though not all, of her assigned work. She cannot seem to refrain from talking to classmates, however. Her teacher, Mr. Gonzales, has to speak to her repeatedly during lessons, to the point that he often becomes exasperated and loses his temper. *What suggestions would Curwin and Mendler give Mr. Gonzales to help with Sara's misbehavior?*

Case 3: Joshua Clowns and Intimidates

Joshua, larger and louder than his classmates, always wants to be the center of attention, which he accomplishes through a combination of clowning and intimidation. He makes wise remarks, talks back (smilingly) to the teacher, utters a variety of sound-effect noises such as automobile crashes and gunshots, and makes limitless sarcastic comments and put-downs of his classmates. Other students will not stand up to him, apparently fearing his verbal and physical aggression. His teacher, Miss Pearl, has come to her wit's end. *What do you find in Curwin and Mendler's work that might help Miss Pearl deal with Joshua?*

Case 4: Tom Is Hostile and Defiant

Tom has appeared to be in his usual foul mood ever since arriving in class. On his way to sharpen his pencil, he bumps into Frank, who complains. Tom tells him loudly to shut up. Miss Baines, the teacher, says, "Tom, go back to your seat." Tom wheels around and says heatedly, "I'll go when I'm damned good and ready!" *How would Curwin and Mendler have Miss Baines deal with Tom?*

ACTIVITIES

1. In your journal, enter ideas from Discipline with Dignity that contribute to the five principles of building a personal system of discipline.
2. In small groups, conduct practice situations in which classmates play roles of students who make hurtful comments to you, the teacher. Begin with the examples given here and explore new ones you have seen or think might occur. Take turns being the teacher and responding to the comments in some of the ways Curwin and Mendler suggest.

Example 1
Teacher: Jonathan, I'd like to see that work finished before the period ends today.

Jonathan: [Sourly] Fine. Why don't you take it and finish it yourself if that's what you want?
Teacher:

Example 2
Teacher: Desirée, that's the second time you've broken our rule about profanity. I'd like to speak with you after class.
Desirée: No thanks. I've seen enough of your scrawny tail for one day.
Teacher:

Example 3
Teacher: Marshall, I'd like for you to get back to work, please.

Marshall: [Says nothing, but makes a face, rolls his eyes, and turns his palms up. Other students snicker.]

Teacher:

Imagine additional occurrences and use them for practice. Strive to deescalate the confrontations without becoming defensive, fighting back, or withdrawing your request.

3. One of Curwin and Mendler's suggestions is to make your class activities events that students look forward to. Make them wonder what might happen next. For a selected grade level, brainstorm ways of complying with this suggestion.

4. Many suggestions were made for anticipating and dealing with violent, aggressive, or hostile behavior. What would you do to prepare yourself for situations involving such behavior?

YOU ARE THE TEACHER

Continuation High School Photography Lab

You teach photography lab, an elective class, in a continuation high school attended by students who have been unsuccessful for behavioral reasons in regular high school settings. Many of the students want to attend this particular school because it is located in what they consider their turf. Some of the students are chemically dependent and/or come from dysfunctional homes. The photography lab class enrolls fifteen students, all of whom are on individual study contracts.

Typical Occurrences

As students begin work, you busy yourself with a number of different tasks such as setting out needed materials, giving advice on procedures, handing out quizzes for students who have completed contracts, examining photographs, and so forth. You see Tony sitting and staring into space. You ask him if he needs help. He shrugs and looks away. You ask him if he has brought his materials to work on. He shakes his head. You tell Tony he can start on a new part of his contract. He doesn't answer. You ask what's the matter. When Tony doesn't respond, Mike mutters, "He's blasted, man." At that moment, you hear heated words coming from the darkroom. You enter and find two students squaring off, staring each other down. You ask what the problem is but get no reply. You tell the boys to leave the darkroom and go back to their seats. Neither makes the first move. As tension grows, another student intervenes and says, "Come on, you can settle it later. Be cool." You call the office and inform the counselor of the incident. The boys involved hear you do so and gaze at you insolently. The class settles back to work,

and for the remainder of the period you circulate among them, providing assistance, stifling horseplay, urging that they move ahead in their contracts, and reminding everyone that they only have a limited amount of time in which to get their work done. From time to time you glance at Tony, who does no work during the period. You ask Tony again if something is bothering him. He shakes his head. You then ask him if he wants to transfer out of the class, since it is elective. Tony says, "No, man, I like it here." "That's fine," you say, "but this is not dream time. You do your work, or we will find you another class. You understand?" "Sure, I understand." You turn away, but from the corner of your eye you are sure you see Tony's middle finger aimed in your direction.

Conceptualizing a Strategy

If you followed the suggestions of Richard Curwin and Allen Mendler, what would you conclude or do with regard to the following?

1. Preventing the problem(s) from occurring in the first place.

2. Putting a clear end to the misbehavior now.

3. Involving other or all students in addressing the situation.

4. Maintaining student dignity and good personal relations.

5. Applying follow-up procedures that would prevent the recurrence of the misbehavior.

6. Using the situation to help the students develop a sense of greater responsibility and self-control.

REFERENCES

Coloroso, B. 2003. *The bully, the bullied, and the bystander: From preschool to high school: How parents and teachers can help break the cycle of violence.* New York: HarperResource.

Curwin, R. 1992. *Rediscovering hope: Our greatest teaching strategy.* Bloomington, IN: National Educational Service.

Curwin, R., and Mendler, A. 1988. *Discipline with dignity.* Alexandria, VA: Association for Supervision and Curriculum Development. Revised editions 1992, 1999, 2001. Upper Saddle River, NJ: Merrill.

Curwin, R., and Mendler, A. 1997. *As tough as necessary. Countering violence, aggression, and hostility in our schools.* Alexandria, VA: Association for Supervision and Curriculum Development.

Curwin, R., and Mendler, A. 2005. Practical Discipline Guidelines. www.disciplineassociates.com/dwd.htm.

Hoover, J., and Stenhjem, P. 2003. Bullying and Teasing of Youth with Disabilities: Creating Positive School Environments for Effective Inclusion. www.ncset.org/publications/viewdesc.asp?id=1332.

Mendler, A., and Curwin, R. 1999. *Discipline with dignity for challenging youth.* Bloomington, IN: National Education Service.

CHAPTER 11

Discipline through Self-Restitution and Moral Intelligence

Authoritative Input
- Diane Gossen / Discipline through Self-Restitution
- Michele Borba / Building Moral Intelligence

CHAPTER PREVIEW

This chapter presents two approaches to helping students develop more desirable behavior. The first is Diane Gossen's work on discipline through self-restitution, an approach that provides a needs-satisfying environment in which students who have behaved inappropriately are encouraged to reflect on their behavior, identify the need that prompted it, and create new ways of behaving indicative of the responsible people they want to be. Gossen's approach emphasizes helping students learn how to make things right within themselves, as well as with whomever or whatever they have offended or damaged with their behavior.

The second, Michele Borba's approach to helping students grow in moral intelligence, involves (1) the ability to distinguish right from wrong, (2) the establishment and maintenance of strong ethical convictions, and (3) the willingness to act on those convictions in an honorable way. As students increase in moral intelligence, they become more able to direct themselves and their classroom behavior improves.

Part 1. Diane Gossen
RESTITUTION SELF-DISCIPLINE

Fundamental Hypothesis of Self-Restitution

Self-restitution, which involves regular reflection on personal behavior, helps students learn to profit from mistakes and become better able to conduct themselves in harmony with their needs and inner sense of morality.

Self-Restitution Theory

Gossen (2005) calls attention to three things that have remained unchanged in schools over recent decades: discipline continues to be the number one concern of teachers, violence among youth is increasing, and research indicates that students need a school environment that satisfies needs and is free from fear and coercion. She points out that over a hundred studies show that punishments and rewards are not effective in promoting desirable classroom behavior because they discourage student reflection on personal behavior, thus stifling the development of moral and emotional intelligence. She warns that any system of learning that makes use of heavy authority, threats, rules, punishments, or rewards will, over the long run, only perpetuate the behaviors we are trying to eliminate.

To help resolve the discipline problem, Gossen contributes her program, Discipline through Self-Restitution, an approach that provides a needs-satisfying environment in which students who have behaved inappropriately are encouraged to reflect on their behavior, identify the need that prompted it, and create a new way of behaving that is indicative of the responsible person they want to be. Gossen credits some of the main concepts in her program to child-rearing practices she observed in Canadian aboriginal families—practices that are rooted in internal self-discipline.

Gossen's approach does not focus on student faults or mistakes, but instead helps students learn how to make things right within themselves, as well as with whomever or whatever they have offended or damaged with their behavior. In this process, students deal with their own behavior shortcomings while genuinely committing themselves to better behavior in the future. The main characteristics of the **restitution** healing process are (Gossen, 2004)

1. Not a payback, which repairs a harm, but rather a *pay-forward*, which provides an avenue to becoming a better person
2. Meets the needs of the offended person, but more importantly, meets the needs of the offender and is restorative and healing

About Diane Gossen

Diane Chelsom Gossen is the author of *Restitution: Restructuring School Discipline* (1992) and *It's All About We: Rethinking Discipline Using Restitution* (2004). She has worked on Restitution Theory with hundreds of school systems in Canada, the United States, and many other countries. In 2001, Gossen received the YWCA Women of Distinction Award in the Lifetime Achievement category. She served as creative consultant to the award-winning video series on classroom management, *Monday—Marbles and Chalk,* and was featured in the *Journal of Education's* video titled *Dealing with Disruptive and Unresponsive Students.* She taught school in Canada and elsewhere for several years, has held faculty positions in two Canadian universities, and for 25 years was a senior faculty member of the Institute for Reality Therapy. Other books by Diane Gossen include: *My Child Is a Pleasure* (1988) and *Creating the Conditions: Leadership for Quality School* (with Judy Anderson, 1995). Gossen's website is www.realrestitution.com.

3. Provides a means for dealing with root causes of problems
4. Focuses on solutions and restores and strengthens relationships
5. Operates through invitation, not coercion
6. Teaches persons to look inside themselves, identify the need behind problematic behavior, and visualize the kind of person they want to be
7. Creates solutions to problems and restores the offender to the group

In short, self-restitution creates conditions whereby an individual can repair mistakes affecting self and others and return to the group strengthened.

The Restitution Triangle and How It Is Used

The **restitution triangle** (see Figure 11.1) helps us understand more easily how the self-restitution process works.

We can follow the self-restitution process by beginning at the base of the triangle. The first step in helping a student who has offended is to *stabilize* the student's identity by removing fear or anger so learning can take place. This is done by saying things to the student such as, "It's okay to make a mistake. You are not the only one. We can solve this problem."

The next step is shown on side 2 (left side) of the triangle. Here we help students understand that people always do things for a reason and usually they are doing the best

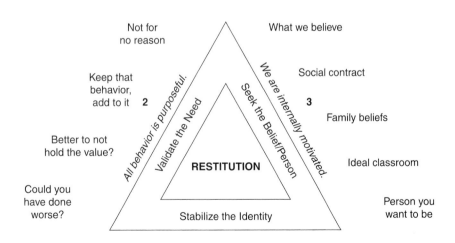

FIGURE 11.1 The Restitution Triangle

Source: Gossen (2004, p. 36). Reprinted by permission.

they know how, under the circumstances. To help the student see that the behavior was not the worst possible choice, we ask questions such as, "Is there a worse thing you could have done? Why would that have been worse?" This helps students see that their behavior was not as bad as it might have been, and it lifts their guilt so they can think. Then we explain that most behavior occurs when a person senses a need that is not being met. (In previous class discussions we would have reviewed needs that often precipitate behavior, such as the need for safety from threat, for a sense of belonging as a member of the class, for love or esteem from others, for having fun, for a sense of freedom, or for having some control over our lives.) We review the needs and ask, "Do you think any of those needs might have led you to do what you did?" The student is given time to reflect and reply.

Then we move to the right side of the triangle where we encourage the student to tap into more ideal pictures of behavior, with comments or questions such as, "Think about the kind of person you want to be. What beliefs do you and your family have that concerns [the problem]? What is our class agreement about this matter?" These questions and comments are always made in a calm tone, never in a confrontational or guilt-producing manner. The effect is to stimulate the student to reflect on the behavior and judge it against the image of the person he or she would like to be. The restitution process stabilizes the self-identify of the offending student, validates the behavior as related to a genuine need, and helps the student identify a way to meet the need in keeping with his or her inner sense of morality. It does not shame the student, but brings a sense of relief, produces a feeling of hope, and helps the student create a solution to the problem.

The Least Coercive Road

Gossen believes that self-restitution is most effective when teachers relate to students in a manner she refers to as the **least coercive road.** She says (2002) that when teachers are having a difficult job in the classroom, it is usually because they are trying to make students do what they don't want to do. Because students naturally resist being made to do anything, the coercive approach virtually never produces a true inner change in behavior. Moreover, the process is extremely draining on teachers, leaving them disheartened, fatigued, and anxious. Gossen says if you want students to become responsible for their own behavior, and if you recognize that it is your job to provide a rich environment in which students learn because they *want to,* use self-restitution with the least coercion possible. That, she says, will bring you the satisfaction that comes from your students' enjoying school and developing inner self-discipline.

The least coercive road is installed and maintained through four steps, each of which employs certain "tools."

1. *Open Up the Territory.* Use the tools "Does it really matter?" and "Yes, if . . ."
2. *Establish the Social Contract.* Use the tools "What we believe in" and "The social contract."
3. *Establish Limits.* Use the tools "My job, your job" (or the modifications "The teacher I want to be" and "The Student you want to be") and "Bottom lines."
4. *Teach Students How to Make Self-Restitution.* Use "Manager of restitution."

Open Up the Territory—Maximizing Freedom

The first step in the Least Coercive Road is to reduce the number of interventions you make into your students' behavior. By reducing the number of interventions, you "open up the territory" for students to have more freedom to explore options, make choices, and learn from the process, which in turn leads to responsible behavior. Reducing interventions does not mean adopting a laissez-faire, permissive approach to teaching. Rather, it calls on teachers to identify and address only what they believe is truly important in class behavior. The two tools Gossen suggests for helping open up the territory are "Does it really matter?" and "Yes, if . . .".

Does It Really Matter?

If we find ourselves continually trying to control students, we should ask ourselves, "Does what they are doing really matter?" For example: **Does it really matter** if . . . He sits with his feet on the floor? She chews gum? Everyone is silent when working? She does her homework? Two students want to exchange seats? Gossen says we should not intervene in any behaviors of that type unless we can give students a plausible reason for doing so. She says teachers can decide if a behavior really matters by asking themselves

- What are my personal and my family beliefs about this sort of behavior?
- What do I believe about how learning occurs? Will this affect learning?
- What do I want for my students long after they have left my class?

Gossen suggests we place strong limits only on behavior that pertains to safety, proper function of the class, or other matters about which we have especially strong convictions.

Yes, If . . .

The second tool useful for opening up the territory is called "**Yes, if** . . ." When you find yourself too frequently responding to student requests with "No" or "No, because," consider changing to a positive response that guides the student toward desirable behavior. Suppose a student asks, "Can I sharpen my pencil?" Your normal reply is, "No, this is not the time." A better alternative would be to say, "Yes, if you will wait until I finish my directions." Gossen urges teachers to say yes as often as possible. When no is the response you need to give, provide a reason and stick to it.

Establish the Social Contract—Building a Sense of Belonging

As you begin to "open up the territory," take steps to gain student willingness to work with you collaboratively to establish and maintain a better class. This process leads to a **social contract** between you and your students concerning how you want to be when together. A common goal for each of us is to be an effective member of the group. Almost all students want to be part of the group, and they easily understand that the class functions better when everyone pulls together. To reach this goal, we must determine how to get our needs met without interfering with the needs of others.

Discussions that center on group values and class agreements increase involvement between teacher and students and allow students to accept some responsibility for how the class is to function.

What We Believe In

Class members should spend time exploring and discussing their beliefs regarding the kind of person they want to be, individually and as a member of the group. You can begin this process by asking students to think, draw, or write about the kind of friend they want to be, the kind of student, the kind of team member, or the kind of individual. They might think about a relative or friend they greatly admire and specify what that person does that they find laudable. After allowing them to discuss their ideas, you can next ask them to think about the kind of class they would like to be, including how they would like to work together, conduct themselves, help each other, and enjoy their experience together. These activities produce a list of qualities students agree on. Point out that those qualities indicate the values students hold, or what they believe in. Then you can ask them how they think the class could be conducted so they experience those positive qualities.

Social Contract

As the students reflect further, ask them if they can suggest ways of conducting themselves that will support the values they have identified—that is, how they can behave in order to enjoy the kind of class they have envisioned. This leads to agreements concerning desirable and undesirable behavior, formalized as the class social contract.

Establish Limits—Clarifying Personal Power

Membership in a group requires that individuals give up some personal freedom in exchange for benefits obtained from group membership. Students are helped to realize that duties accompany membership in social relationships. For example, one such duty would be managing themselves in a manner that does not interfere unduly with others' needs. Each of us wants predictability, enjoyment, and a degree of power in our lives. These qualities can be attained through class agreements that indicate responsibilities and include bottom lines beyond which behavior is not acceptable. These agreements bring about a shift in balance of responsibility for classroom demeanor. As students assume a portion of the load, and as they identify and accept their responsibilities, the class begins to function more effectively.

My Job, Your Job

To clarify teachers' and students' view of how they should function in the class, you may find it helpful to identify the expected class roles, or jobs of teacher and students. These role specifications should be established jointly by teacher and students, with examples that show what *is* expected, and what is *not* expected of each. This helps students understand who is responsible for what. Originally, Gossen (1993, p. 85) depicted "My job, your job" as follows:

My Job Is To . . .
Teach
Answer questions
Explain different ways
Go at a pace you can learn
Manage the class
Enforce rules
Care

Your Job Is To . . .
Learn
Ask if you don't understand
Keep on trying
Tell teacher if the pace is too fast
Follow the rules
Communicate needs
Listen to teacher and other school people

My Job Is *Not* To . . .
Take abuse
Babysit
Do students' jobs or work

Your Job Is *Not* To . . .
Do the teacher's job
Decide for another student
Discipline other students

When students interfere with a job to be done, it is suggested that the teacher ask, "What's the rule?" or "What's your job?" Doing so moves attention from the problem to the solution and avoids debate and excuses. If the student doesn't know the rule or won't say it, state it yourself and ask, "Can you do that?" When the student complies, say "Thank you, I appreciate it." This type of exchange involves monitoring and redirection of behavior, and is vastly preferable to lecturing or moralizing.

Gossen (2005) reports that "My job, your job" has resonated strongly with teachers, but she believes it is important to explain *why* we hold those expectations. If we want to move this activity to self-discipline, it is not reasonable to expect students to support a plan that conflicts with their needs or beliefs. Accordingly, Gossen now suggests that teachers think in terms of "My personal job as a manager" and "The Teacher I want to be," while asking students to think in terms of "My personal job as a student" and "The student I want to be." These are ideal pictures, beyond the original "My job, your job" which tended to promote compliance.

Teacher I Want to Be
Asks, "How can I best teach you?"

Says and believes, "It's OK to make a mistake—that is how we learn."

Talks about needs of teacher and students.

Models self-restitution and uses the self-restitution triangle.

Seeks to understand others.

Has fun teaching.

Student I Want to Be
Learns new things and thinks for self.

Learns self-restitution.

Identifies own needs and recognizes those of others.

Has fun learning.

Thinks about the ideal person to be.

Helps make and maintain a social contract with the class.

Teacher I *Don't* Want to Be
Tells you what to think.

Does your work for you.

Criticizes or shames you.

Student I *Don't* Want to Be
Tells you what I think you want to hear.

Says "sorry," but only to get off the hook.

Watches the clock.

Bottom Lines

Rules are used to impose *external control*. Their contract of employment usually requires that teachers apply sanctions for tardiness, incomplete work, and antisocial behaviors. Even in restitution, a teacher may have to fall back to rules, but their first choice is to use restitution, which involves beliefs that are used to develop students' *internal control*. Beliefs are not used to coerce students or impose guilt. Any student may decide not to be a moral, cooperative person or decide not to learn. We can't change their internal decision. We can only say what we will do if they take this route.

The **bottom line** refers to the point beyond which a student is not allowed to transgress without consequences. Usually, we can prevent students from crossing the bottom line by using redirection or role-related comments (e.g., "What is your job?"). When a student does go beyond the bottom line, the teacher must apply the consequences specified in the class rules. Even then, consequences are to be used sparingly.

Self-Restitution—Making Things Right and Healing Oneself

Self-restitution is more than simple repayment. It always takes two things into account— making amends to the victim and helping offenders heal themselves. Restitution is not the same as forgiveness. Forgiveness is bestowed by the victim and offers relief, but does not build character in the offender. In contrast, self-restitution says to students, "What are you going to do to fix what was done wrong, and how are you going to become more like the person you want to be? Think about it."

Understand and Teach Self-Restitution

The restitution process and the restitution triangle both rest on the following principles (Gossen, 2004, p. 45):

- We respect each individual's view of the world.
- We create conditions of safety and space for reflection so the brain can take in and evaluate information and create moral meaning.
- We minimize rewards and punishments, which inhibit the development of self-discipline.
- We develop internal moral sense and focus on harmony, rather than conformity.
- We uphold bottom lines on behavior consistently and publicly so students feel safe in the classroom.

We tie these principles back to our beliefs and help students understand why we have these principles. Offenders *look inside themselves* and explore questions such as, "What do I believe about how people should treat each other?" "How would I want to be treated in this same circumstance?" "What are my family values concerning this topic?" "Do I hold those values?" "What kind of person do I want to be?" "What would it look like, sound like, and feel like if I were being that kind of person?" When teachers put these questions to offending students, the teachers should say, "No need to answer me. But do answer yourself. We can't change our lives unless there is honesty within." Let the students have time to reflect on these questions.

Because restitution seeks to *identify the basic need behind the problem*, you must help your students understand that we all have needs for love, power, freedom, fun, and survival, and that our behavior, acceptable or unacceptable, is associated with one or more of those needs. When students offend, ask them if they can identify the need behind their behavior as well as other students' needs with which the behavior might have interfered. Focusing on needs reduces combativeness, thus **collapsing the conflict** that might otherwise exist, and it helps find solutions that work for all involved.

In summary, restitution has power to repair an immediate wrong and to lead to improved behavior in the future. It stabilizes the offending person with the reassurance that making a mistake is OK. It meets the needs of the person who is offended, as well as the person who has committed the offense. It strengthens the offenders with new skills. The process of restitution is an invitation, not a demand. When you use it, students need time to reflect. The process cannot be rushed. You can tell it is working when students become able to describe their behavior, evaluate it, make choices related to it, and come up with plans that benefit themselves as well as those they have offended.

Function as a Manager of Restitution

Teachers are of greatest help to students when they serve as **managers of restitution.** In this role they ask misbehaving students to work with them to invent solutions to problems. They do not punish or coerce, nor do they remove offending students from the group. Instead, they help them remain in the group with strengthened capability. As mentioned earlier, managers ask students questions such as "What do we believe?" "Do you believe it?" "If you believe it, do you want to fix it?" "If you fix it, what does it say about you?" In this manner you do something *with* the student, rather than *to* the student, thus allowing the student to take responsibility for the behavior and correct it.

Part 2. Michele Borba
BUILDING MORAL INTELLIGENCE

Fundamental Hypothesis
of Moral Intelligence

Moral intelligence, comprised of seven essential virtues that can be taught and developed, controls students' ability to deal effectively with ethical and moral challenges they encounter in school and elsewhere.

Moral Intelligence and the Foundations of Character

Moral intelligence can be understood as (1) the ability to distinguish right from wrong, (2) the establishment and maintenance of strong ethical convictions, and (3) the willingness to act on those convictions in an honorable way. Moral intelligence is the foundation of what we call "good character," and it grows with experience. As students bring their moral intelligence to higher levels, they become more self-directing and their classroom behavior improves.

Borba (2001) depicts moral intelligence as consisting of universal virtues of "goodness," seven of which enable a student to act properly and resist pressures that can damage his or her character. The seven **essential virtues** are empathy, conscience, self-control, respect, kindness, tolerance, and fairness. Borba refers to the first three as the **moral core**. The virtues can be taught in school through a five-step process that will be explained later. Descriptions of the seven virtues follow, with some of Borba's comments. For each virtue, Borba provides examples of what people say and do that reflect the virtue.

Empathy

Empathy is the capacity to relate to the feelings of others. Without empathy, moral intelligence cannot develop fully. At present, a number of societal conditions are hindering the development of empathy in the young, such as parents who are absent or emotionally

About Michele Borba

Michele Borba, a former teacher and recipient of the *National Educator Award*, is an educational consultant who has presented keynotes and workshops on moral education and other topics to over one million participants in North America, Europe, Asia, and the South Pacific. Her proposal to end school violence and student bullying was signed into California law (SB1667) in 2002. She appears regularly on TV and NPR talk shows including *Today, The View, Fox & Friends, MSNBC, The Early Show, Canada AM, Talk of the Nation, Ronn Owen KGO,* and *Focus on the Family*. She has been interviewed by numerous publications including *Newsweek, U.S. News & World Report,* the *Chicago Tribune,* the *Los Angeles Times, Parenting,* and *Child,* and serves as an advisor to *Parents* magazine. Her article publications have appeared in *Redbook, Parents,* and *Family Circle,* and she is author of twenty-one books, including *Building Moral Intelligence,* cited by *Publishers' Weekly* as "among the most noteworthy of 2001," and *Parents Do Make A Difference,* selected by *Child Magazine* as Outstanding Parenting Book of 1999. Her latest book is *Nobody Likes Me, Everybody Hates Me: The Top 25 Friendship Problems and How to Solve Them* (2005a). Information on her publications and seminars can be accessed through her websites, www.moralintelligence.com and www.micheleborba.com.

unavailable to children; overabundant media images of suffering, which dull sensitivity; boys being discouraged from expressing their feelings; and abuse of children by peers and adults. To counteract these negative influences, Borba urges teachers to (1) Develop an empathic, caring relationship with students, listen to them with empathy, help them develop stronger emotional vocabularies, and tell them stories or scenarios that promote empathetic reaction; (2) create a caring, prosocial moral learning environment; (3) use stories and situations to enhance sensitivity to the feelings and perspectives of others; (4) provide meaningful and concrete hands-on activities that develop empathy for other persons' points of views or situations; and (5) use discipline techniques that show empathy for the feelings of the student. She says (2001, p. 19) that people who are empathetic often do the following:

- Notice when people are hurting and experience something of what they feel.
- Try to console or comfort others who are in pain.
- Mirror the facial expressions of people in distress.

People who are empathetic often say things such as:

- "You look upset."
- "I think I understand how you must feel."
- "I'm happy for you."

Conscience

Conscience refers to the ability to comprehend the right or wrong of one's actions. Borba believes there is a crisis of conscience in the world today, as evident in the rise in youth violence, peer cruelty, stealing by the young, cheating, sexual promiscuity, and substance abuse. Borba suggests a number of things you can do to help reverse the decline in public and individual conscience: (1) set clear class expectations and standards based on your core moral beliefs; (2) create a context for moral growth, featuring teacher modeling; (3) teach, cultivate, and reinforce virtues that strengthen conscience while providing a guide for behavior; (4) help students understand how moral conscience develops and show them how reparation can turn moral wrongs into moral rights; and (5) use meaningful moral dilemmas presented in context (e.g., historical, scientific, or literary issues, current events, peer interactions) to promote students' moral reasoning . Borba (2001, p. 53) says people with conscience often do the following:

- Act the way they know is right.
- Refuse to be swayed by others who wish to do wrong.
- Ensure they can be trusted to do what they say they will.

People with a conscience say things like:

- "You can count on me."
- "This isn't right. Let's do something else."
- "I'm sorry. It was my fault."

Self-Control

Borba suggests that the lack of self-control evident in society today is made worse by factors such as over-worked and stressed-out parents, early child abuse and trauma, glorification of out-of-control behavior in entertainment, and over reliance on chemical mollification in place of self-constraint. Borba suggests a number of conditions that can promote growth in self-control: (1) adults giving priority to and modeling self-control; (2) encouraging students to become their own internal motivators by seeking to do the "right thing" when confronting temptation; (3) showing students specific ways to control urges and think before acting, accomplished through anger management, self-control in stress situations, and a three-part formula that includes *think, stop, act right,* (4) providing ongoing opportunities for students to practice self-control strategies and transfer the techniques to the real world to be used without teacher prompting. Borba (2001, p. 81) says individuals with self-control usually

- Maintain control of themselves when angry or upset.
- Behave well even when no one is watching.
- Plan what they will do and then follow through.

People with self-control often say things such as:

- "I'd really like to go with you, but I have to study."
- "I need to calm down. I'm feeling upset."
- "I understand the rule and I won't break it."

Respect

Lack of respect is rampant in most segments of society, manifested in the decline in civility, rise of vulgarity, fall of the Golden Rule, disrespect for authority, and low respect for children. Borba makes a number of suggestions for dealing with disrespect, such as, (1) Discuss, model, and teach the differences between respect and disrespect. Act toward students in ways that show them respect and talk regularly with them about the meaning and practice of respect. (2) Work to increase student respect for authority and squelch rudeness. Eliminate disrespect by consistently targeting the misbehavior and specifically teaching new, respectful "replacer" behaviors. Use signals to call attention to sassiness, back talk, whining, vulgarity, and other types of disrespect. (3) Emphasize and expect good manners and courtesy. Help students learn the basic manners that enable them to function productively in society. Teach students to say *please* and *thank-you* and increase the repertoire of respectful behaviors. (4) Involve peers in creating a respectful learning environment and reinforcing each other's prosocial, respectful behaviors. Borba (2001, p. 131) says respectful people often do the following:

- Refrain from talking back, whining, or sassing.
- Listen without interrupting.
- Interact carefully with others' belongings.

Respectful people often say things such as:

- "Excuse me."
- "I didn't mean to interrupt."
- "I understand you feel differently."

Kindness

The crisis of unkindness in today's world is being worsened by lack of good modeling by parents and adults, lack of encouragement for children to behave with kindness, influence of unkind peers, and general desensitization to kindness. To counter this crisis, teachers can do the following: (1) Teach the meaning and value of kindness, help students understand that kindness begins with them, and explicitly teach students what kind behaviors look and sound like. (2) Establish a zero tolerance for mean and cruel behavior at school, including putting clearly spelled-out procedures in place to stop bullying. (3) Encourage kindness at school and point out its positive effects. Ask students to behave with kindness in all situations and point out the difference it makes. (4) Provide meaningful, concrete activities for children to experience and practice "being kind and receiving kindness" such as Random Acts of Kindness or Service Learning. Borba (2001, p. 163) says kind people often

- Offer to help someone in need.
- Show concern when someone is treated badly.
- Refuse to take part in ridiculing others.

Kind people often say things such as:

- "How can I help you?"
- "Are you new? Would you like to join us?"
- "I really appreciate your thoughtfulness."

Tolerance

The crisis in tolerance we are experiencing today is the result of factors such as a lack of moral monitoring in the young, accessibility of internet hate sites, racially charged video entertainment aimed at youth, hate music, and stereotypes displayed on television and motion pictures. To counter this crisis, Borba suggests that teachers (1) model and teach about tolerance, (2) draw attention to and discourage intolerant comments and practices, and (3) instill an appreciation for diversity. Borba (2001, p. 199) says tolerant people often do the following:

- Focus on what they have in common with others, rather than their differences.
- Refuse to take part in activities that make fun of people who are different.
- Refuse to exclude certain students from activities.

People who are tolerant may be heard to say

- "We don't know her, so let's not make fun of her."
- "Would you like to join our team?"
- "I'd like to know more about her."

Fairness

The degree of fairness in the way we treat others is being worsened by a breakdown of role models and an over emphasis on competition, so that winning at any cost becomes paramount. This decline can be countered by teachers who discuss fairness with students, unfailingly demonstrate fairness, avoid making comparisons among students, help students show respect for their competitors, and limit the excessively strong emphasis on winning. Borba (2001, p. 235) says that fair people

- Play by the rules and don't try to change them midstream.
- Keep an open mind and listen to all sides.
- Compromise so everyone gets a fair share.

People who are fair are often heard to say

- "Let's find a way to make things fair."
- "Let's take turns. You go first."
- "Let's consider both sides of the story."

Reasons for Building Moral Intelligence

You may be asking yourself whether trying to develop moral intelligence is worth all the effort it requires. For Borba, there is no doubt. She insists that by helping students develop higher moral IQs, we can promote significant improvement in the following:

1. *Good character.* The foundation to good character, or "moral intelligence" consists of the seven virtues explained in the preceding section. Those virtues form students' character and are the principles that guide their behavior.
2. *Ability to think and act appropriately.* Character is evident in one's thoughts and actions. Moral intelligence teaches the specific moral habits that help students think and conduct themselves ethically. High moral intelligence does not occur spontaneously, but can be taught by teachers who intentionally model, nurture, reinforce, and teach its essential qualities. Without such guidance, students are at risk of becoming ever more insensitive, dishonest, aggressive, uncivil, cruel, hateful, and unjust.
3. *Protection against "toxic" influences in society.* Toxic influences such as cruelty, drugs, and self-centeredness are so entrenched in society that it is impossible to shield students from them. Moral IQ can serve as a compass that helps students develop and stand by deep-seated convictions and resist influences contrary to good character.

4. *Crucial life skills.* Moral IQ incorporates skills students need for resolving conflicts, empathizing, knowing right from wrong, asserting themselves, controlling anger, learning tolerance, negotiating fairly, communicating respectfully, cooperating, using self-control, sharing, and knowing right from wrong. These skills come into play in all life arenas.

5. *Good citizens.* The most important measure of a nation is not its gross national product, its technological genius, or its military might, but rather the character of its people. The seven virtues within moral intelligence provide the bedrock of good citizenship and responsible living.

6. *Resistance to temptation.* Moral intelligence enables students to resist the appeal of insidious vices such as dishonesty and gaining unfair advantage.

7. *Prevention of violence and cruelty.* The best protection against violence and cruelty is found in the core values of moral intelligence.

8. *Good behavior.* Moral IQ incorporates the essential moral virtues that enable students to be decent, caring, and respectful. These seven virtues become a template for creating students' character, guiding their actions, and earning them reputations as good, caring human beings.

9. *Shaping moral destinies.* Moral growth is a developmental process that is ongoing throughout one's life. The beliefs and habits it promotes become the ethical foundations of behavior in all aspects of life.

Fostering Moral Intelligence

As we have seen, Borba believes the schools offer the best venue for developing sound character in the young. Moral intelligence grows as improvements are made in students' character traits, and schools hold the key to that improvement. There are few other places where the young can learn the value of responsibility, caring, respect, and cooperation, or where they can observe adults displaying those traits consistently.

People sometimes question whether good character and desirable morality can be taught, but Borba reminds us that that since character traits are learned, at least in part, they can certainly be taught. Borba's book Building Moral Intelligence contains well over a thousand strategies to help students develop or deal with peer pressure, bullying, anger management, disrespect, self-control, fair play, sensitivity to others, strengthening conscience, negotiation skills, peaceful confrontation, kindness, tolerance, conflict resolution, self-reliance, empathy, generosity, impulse control, responsibility, calm, group harmony, stereotypes, compromising, negotiating, sharing and taking turns, decision making, motivation, respectfulness, and courtesy. Borba explains a five-step approach to teaching moral values that teachers can easily incorporate into the daily curriculum.

Accentuate a Character Trait or Virtue

The first step in working to improve a character trait is to draw it strongly to students' attention over time. A different character trait can be emphasized each month. The process works best if all personnel at the school are modeling and reinforcing the same trait. As each character trait is introduced, a student campaign committee can create banners, signs, and posters to hang up around the school to convince students of the trait's merit. For example, students can make a poster about responsibility that says, "Responsibility: It means I'm doing what is right for myself and others and I can be counted on." Character assemblies can be held at school, with attention drawn to character through public announcements ("It's perseverance month! Remember to work your hardest and not give up!") and new screen savers each day about the character trait.

Tell the Meaning and Value of the Trait

The second step to teaching a character trait is to convey to students exactly what the trait means and why it is important and relevant to their lives. Explain the trait to your students, in keeping with their realm of experience, as if they have never been exposed to the trait. Borba lists some ways of doing this. For example, in a story, locate an episode that exemplifies the trait. Read it aloud and ask, "How did the main character demonstrate perseverance? How did that make the other characters feel?" Or ask students to find current news articles that describe people demonstrating the trait. To confirm the value of the trait, you might begin each day with a brief review of a real world event in which the trait was displayed.

Whenever you see or hear a student displaying the targeted trait, take a moment to point out specifically what the student did that demonstrated the trait. "Alex, that was respectful because you waited until Jill was finished before you spoke." Be sure to share your beliefs about the trait; it helps students if they can hear why you feel the trait is important. If you are targeting respect, for example, you might tell students how strongly you feel about avoiding negative talk about others.

Teach What the Trait Looks and Sounds Like

There is no perfect way to teach the trait, but *showing* the behavior is always more effective than just talking about it. When you discuss a trait, model it as well and perhaps role-play it with a student. Borba cautions us against making the assumption that students understand the actions and words of character traits. They may not have been exposed to them, so we must look for ways to provide examples explicitly and implicitly. For instance, students could identify the specific behaviors of the character trait using video clips (e.g., Atticus Finch as an example of integrity in *To Kill a Mockingbird*); literature (e.g., Julius Caesar for fortitude); historical models (e.g., Gandhi for fairness); science (e.g., Thomas Edison for perseverance); as well as actual current events in their school, community, or world. This helps students see what the trait looks and sounds like. You can also ask students to create skits involving the trait and enact them in class.

Provide Opportunities to Practice the Moral Habits of the Trait

Students should be provided frequent opportunities to practice the moral habits or behaviors that comprise the character trait. Borba says it usually takes 21 days of practice before a new behavior is acquired. She makes three suggestions for reviewing student efforts and progress in the trait: (1) Make or obtain character videotapes that allow students to watch demonstrations of the trait and analyze what they have seen. (2) Have students keep reflection logs over the time the trait is being emphasized and write at least one action they did each day to demonstrate the trait. (3) Assign character homework that asks students to practice the skill at home with their family and record the results.

Provide Effective Feedback

Finally, as you teach appropriate behaviors, be sure to reinforce students as they improve: "You're on the right track. Keep it up" or "Almost, but this is what to do instead." If you see students failing to demonstrate the trait, draw their attention to the behavior: "What you did was not right, but this is what you can do next time." Students benefit from immediate behavior correction, so ask them to redo any incorrect behavior immediately, if possible.

Fostering Prosocial Behavior

As students conduct themselves in accordance with the essential virtues of moral intelligence, they naturally display good manners and improved behavior. However, they often benefit from still more instruction in prosocial behavior. Borba (2001, pp. 152–153) provides a list of "Eighty-Five Important Manners Kids Should Learn." The following are a few examples from her list:

- *Essential polite words.* Please, thank you, excuse me, I'm sorry, May I? Pardon me. You're welcome.
- *Meeting and greeting others.* Smiles and looks at the person. Shakes hands. Says hello. Introduces self. Introduces other person.
- *Conversation manners.* Starts a conversation. Listens without interrupting. Uses a pleasant tone of voice. Knows how to begin and end a conversation.
- *Sports manners.* Plays by the rules. Shares equipment. Provides encouragement. Doesn't brag or show off. Doesn't argue with referee. Congratulates opponents. Doesn't complain or make excuses. Cooperates.
- *Anywhere and anytime.* Doesn't swear. Doesn't belch audibly. Doesn't gossip. Covers mouth when coughing.

Space does not permit listing all of Borba's suggestions for prosocial behavior. Other suggestions have to do with hospitality, table manners, visiting manners, telephone manners, and manners toward older people. They are presented in her 2001 book *Moral Intelligence.* To access Borba's ideas on a number of closely related topics, consult her website, www.micheleborba.com.

The Relation of Moral Intelligence to Classroom Discipline

Borba wants teachers to understand that successful discipline depends strongly on creating a moral learning community in the classroom—an environment where students feel safe and cared about. In that environment the teacher connects with students, shows care for them, and models essential character traits. Given that environment, most approaches to discipline work well, but without it, no approach to discipline works well.

As for proper behavior, Borba emphasizes that teachers today simply cannot assume that students know how to behave properly. She emphasizes this point in her books *No More Misbehavin'* (2003) and *Don't Give Me That Attitude* (2004), explaining that you cannot allow misbehavior to persist or it becomes an attitude that weakens the character of the student. The teacher must target the specific behaviors that damage respectful classrooms and student character, such as vulgarity, meanness, bullying, and disrespect. Students must replace them with acceptable behavior. The replacement behavior is then tracked until it becomes internalized, which takes approximately 21 days. Virtues are made up of behavior and moral habits. You can't teach behavior through posters or vocabulary drill. If you want to change behavior, you must teach specific behaviors.

Discipline in classes that emphasize character building involves direct interaction between teacher and students who have behaved inappropriately. This **four-step approach to discipline involves** the following: respond, review, reflect, and make right. Suppose Juan and Eddie get into a fight just outside the classroom. The teacher quickly goes through the four steps.

1. *Respond.* Stay calm and listen. Find out what happened: "Tell me what happened." "Why did you do it?" "What did you think this would accomplish?"

2. *Review.* Explore why the behavior was wrong: "Tell me what the rules are in the class." "Why do you think I called you over?" Briefly review the rules or your behavior expectations: "Fighting is not allowed in this class." "We don't solve our problems by fighting."

3. *Reflect.* Quickly go over the effects of the behavior and any impact it may have on the victim: "How do you make each other feel when you fight?" "What do you believe others think of you?" "Do you want to think of yourself as a person who tries to solve problems by fighting, or do you want to think of yourself as someone who can reason things out?" Ask questions that guide the student to empathize with or gain the perspective of the victim: "How do you think your friend feels?" "If you were in her shoes what do you think she'd like to say to you about what happened?" The student could even be required to write (or draw) the situation from the other person's point of view.

4. *Make right.* Help students atone for wrongs they have done. A good way to do so is to encourage offending students to make reparation of some sort, something more than an apology and promise not to do it again. Perhaps Juan and Eddie can work

together on a project, such as making a chart for the class that lists alternatives to fighting.

This intervention process may take a bit of time until you get used to it, but remember that the emphasis is on character building, not quickly applied consequences.

KEY TERMS AND CONCEPTS EMPHASIZED IN THIS CHAPTER

Diane Gossen's Self-Restitution
restitution
restitution triangle
least coercive road
"Does it really matter?"
"Yes, if . . . "
social contract
rules

bottom line
collapsing the conflict
managers of restitution

Michele Borba's Moral Intelligence
moral intelligence
essential virtues

moral core
four-step approach to
  discipline

SELECTED EIGHT—SUMMARY SUGGESTIONS FROM GOSSEN AND BORBA

Diane Gossen

1. Give up trying to make students do anything. Adopt an approach, consistent with student needs, that entices and invites cooperation. Strive for the least coercive road without becoming permissive.

2. Establish a social contract with your class, specifying what the class believes in. Use that contract as the foundation of your discipline system.

3. Clarify teacher and student roles in the classroom and expect teachers and students to take responsibility for the roles that apply to them.

4. Use restitution in the more serious instances of classroom misbehavior, as a means of helping students strengthen themselves.

Michele Borba

1. Make character building a central part of your discipline system and include it in your curriculum. Create a moral learning community where students know how to behave and want to behave because they feel safe, respected, and cared about. Become a living example to your students of solid character.

2. Do not assume students know how to behave appropriately: Explicitly show them how to do so. Directly teach the seven virtues and point out examples of people displaying virtuous behaviors, giving students examples to emulate.

3. Involve students in creating their class rules and expectations. Choose the four to eight most important rules (your "core class values") and write them in the language of virtues, such as, "Use self-control by keeping your hands and feet to yourself." "Be responsible by being in class on time and having your work completed." Post them as visual reminders.

4. When students misbehave, remind them of class expectations. Ask if they are being the kind of people they want to be. Ask what they plan to do to improve their behavior. Keep students accountable for their behavior so they recognize they have choices concerning their actions and that actions have consequences.

CONCEPT CASES

Case 1: Kristina Will Not Work

Kristina, a student in Mr. Jake's class, is quite docile. She socializes little with other students and never disrupts lessons. However, despite Mr. Jake's best efforts, Kristina will not do her work. She rarely completes an assignment. She is simply there, putting forth no effort at all. *What would Michele Borba and Diane Gossen suggest to help Kristina and Mr. Jake?*

Assuming that Mr. Jake is sure Kristina is able to do the work and will be attempting to determine why she is having difficulty, Borba might involve the class in a discussion about conscience and perseverance. In that discussion she would ask students to reflect on concepts such as doing the right thing, being responsible, and letting others know you can be counted on to do your part. (It is essential that the teacher create a caring relationship with the child, is aware of those students who are underachieving, and can identify what seems to be triggering the behavior.) Mr. Jake would show concern and empathy for Kristina and make occasional private comments to her, such as, "Do you know what you are supposed to do in this activity?" "Do you understand why it needs to be done?" "Do you think you can do your part?" As Kristina improves, Mr. Jake may make comments such as, "You made a good effort today. Thank you for that."

Diane Gossen would have Mr. Jake make sure class activities were appealing and consistent with student needs. Previously, he would have established a social contract with the class that specifies what the class believes in, including giving their best effort. If Kristina finds the activity unpleasant, Mr. Jake might change it for her, following her suggestions. Then, as Kristina begins to work, Mr. Jake might compliment and encourage her. Neither Gossen nor Borba would consider that Kristina's situation calls for consequences. Encouragement and support are what she needs.

Case 2: Sara Cannot Stop Talking

Sara is a pleasant girl who participates in class activities and does most, though not all, of her assigned work. She cannot seem to refrain from talking to classmates, however. Her teacher, Mr. Gonzales, has to speak to her repeatedly during lessons, to the point that he often becomes exasperated and loses his temper. *What suggestions would Diane Gossen and Michele Borba give Mr. Gonzales for dealing with Sara?*

Case 3: Joshua Clowns and Intimidates

Joshua, larger and louder than his classmates, always wants to be the center of attention, which he accomplishes through a combination of clowning and intimidation. He makes wise remarks, talks back (smilingly) to the teacher, utters a variety of sound-effect noises such as automobile crashes and gunshots, and makes limitless sarcastic comments and put-downs of his classmates. Other students will not stand up to him, apparently fearing his size and verbal aggression. His teacher, Miss Pearl, has come to her wit's end. *Would Joshua's behavior be likely to improve if Borba's or Gossen's techniques were used in Miss Pearl's classroom? Explain.*

Case 4: Tom Is Hostile and Defiant

Tom has appeared to be in his usual foul mood ever since arriving in class. On his way to sharpen his pencil, he bumps into Frank, who complains. Tom tells him loudly to shut up. Miss Baines, the teacher, says, "Tom, go back to your seat." Tom wheels around, swears loudly, and says heatedly, "I'll go when I'm damned good and ready!" *How would Gossen or Borba have Miss Baines deal with Tom?*

QUESTIONS AND ACTIVITIES

1. Write notes in your journal concerning ideas from Gossen and Borba that you might want to include in your personal system of discipline.
2. By yourself or with others, see if you can combine Gossen's Self-Restitution Theory and Borba's Moral Intelligence into a unified approach to class management. Share your conclusions with the class.

3. How might you use Gossen's and Borba's suggestions in a class of unruly teenagers? Do the approaches offer what is needed, individually or combined, to manage a class of disruptive students? Discuss with class members.

YOU ARE THE TEACHER

Second Grade

You teach second graders in a highly transient neighborhood. You receive an average of one new student each week, and those students typically remain in your class for fairly short lengths of time before moving elsewhere. Most are from somewhat dysfunctional homes, and their poor behavior, including aggression, boisterousness, and crying, seems to reflect many emotional problems.

A Typical Occurrence

The morning bell rings, and students who have been lined up outside by an aide enter the classroom noisily. You are speaking with a parent who is complaining that her son is being picked on by others in the class. When finally able to give attention to the class, you see that Ricky and Raymond have crawled underneath the reading table, while a group of excited children is clustered around Shawon who has brought his new hamster to share with the class. Two girls are pulling at your sleeve, trying to give you a note and lunch money. You have to shout above the din before you can finally get everyone seated. Several minutes have passed since the bell rang. Having lost much of your composure, you finally get the reading groups started when you suddenly remember that an assembly is scheduled for that morning. You stand up from your reading group and exclaim, "We have an assembly this morning! Put down your books and get

lined up quickly! We are almost late!" Thirty-one students make a run for the door, pushing and arguing. Rachael, a big, strong girl, shoves Amy and shouts, "Hey, get out of the way, stupid!" Amy, meek and retiring, begins to cry. You try to comfort Amy while Rachael pushes her way to the front of the line. During the assembly, Ricky and Raymond sit together. They have brought some baseball cards and are entertaining the students seated around them. When the first part of the assembly performance is over, they boo loudly and laugh instead of applaud. Under the school principal's stern eye, you separate Ricky and Raymond, but for the rest of the performance they make silly faces and gestures to each other, causing other students to laugh. When you return to the classroom, certain that the principal will speak to you about your class's behavior, you try to talk with the students about the impropriety of their actions. You attempt to elicit positive comments about the assembly, but several students say it was dumb and boring. The discussion has made little progress before recess time. You sigh and direct the students to line up, reminding them again to use their best manners. As they wait at the door, Rachael is once again shoving her way to the head of the line.

Conceptualizing a Strategy

If you followed the suggestions of Diane Gossen or Michele Borba, what would you do to improve conditions in your classroom? Outline your strategy.

REFERENCES

Borba, M. 1999. *Parents do make a difference: How to raise kids with solid characer, strong minds, and caring hearts.* San Francisco: Jossey-Bass.

Borba, M. 2001. *Building moral intelligence: The seven essential virtues that teach kids to do the right thing.* San Francisco: Jossey-Bass.

Borba, M. 2003. *No more misbehavin': 38 difficult behaviors and how to stop them.* San Francisco: Jossey-Bass.

Borba, M. 2004. *Don't give me that attitude! 24 rude, selfish, insensitive things kids do and how to stop them.* San Francisco. Jossey-Bass.

Borba, M. 2005a. *Nobody likes me: everybody hates me: The top 25 friendship problems and how to solve them.* San Francisco: Jossey-Bass.

Gossen, D. 1988. *My child is a pleasure.* Saskatoon, SK, Canada: Chelsom Consultants Limited.

Gossen, D. 1992. *Restitution: Restructuring school discipline.* Chapel Hill, NC: New View Publications.

Gossen, D. 2002. What do you want? Student behavior. *γA! Magazine for Middle Level Educators.* 3(3).

Gossen, D. 2004. *It's all about we: Rethinking discipline using restitution.* Saskatoon, SK, Canada: Chelsom Consultants Limited.

Gossen, D., and Andersen, J. (1995). *Creating the conditions: Leadership for quality schools.* Chapel Hill, NC, New View Publications.

Gossen, D. 2005. Diane Gossen on Restitution. www.realrestitution.com.

The William Glasser Institute. 2005. Control Theory. www.wglasser.com/whatisct.htm.

CHAPTER 12

Discipline through Raising Student Responsibility

Authoritative Input
■ Marvin Marshall / Discipline without Stress

CHAPTER PREVIEW

This chapter presents Marvin Marshall's approach to classroom discipline, which he has constructed around the concept of student responsibility. Marshall believes that behavior problems at school gradually disappear when students are shown how to conduct themselves responsibly and are empowered to do so through being allowed to make certain behavior choices. Marshall shows teachers how to encourage desirable behavior in their classrooms by helping students understand the value of responsible behavior. He describes how four levels of social development are taught to students and used in the process.

Fundamental Hypothesis of Marshall's Raise Responsibility System

Desirable classroom behavior is best achieved by promoting responsibility—rather than obedience—and by articulating expectations and then empowering students to reach those expectations.

The Nature and Practice of the Raise Responsibility System

Raising responsibility as a means of ensuring positive classroom behavior is a main theme in Marvin Marshall's 2001 book, *Discipline without Stress, Punishments, or Rewards: How Teachers and Parents Promote Responsibility & Learning.* To help teachers work with students in a more positive manner, Marshall provides an easily implemented strategy called the Raise Responsibility System, which he characterizes as follows:

About Marvin Marshall

Marvin Marshall is an international speaker and former teacher, counselor, and adminis-trator, with experience at all levels of public education. Currently, he devotes himself to writing, speaking, and assisting with staff development in schools. His suggestions about classroom discipline have appeared in various venues, including Phi Delta Kappa's *Fostering Social Responsibility* (1998), his book titled *Discipline without Stress, Punish-ments, or Rewards: How Teachers and Parents Promote Responsibility & Learning* (2001), and his monthly electronic newsletter titled *Promoting Responsibility & Learning*, which is available free of charge via email from www.MarvinMarshall.com (his home site), www.AboutDiscipline.com (a discussion about the disadvantages of using rewards and punishments to change behavior), and www.DisciplineWithoutStress.com (table of con-tents and online posting of sections from his book).

- Promoting responsibility, rather than obedience
- Relying on internal motivation, rather than external motivation
- Proactive, rather than reactive
- Noncoercive, rather than coercive
- Empowering, rather than overpowering
- Positive, rather than negative
- Reflective, rather than impulsive
- Establishing positivity, choice, and reflection as life-long practices

The system calls on teachers to do three things: (1) *teach* students about four levels of social development and relate the levels to behavior and learning; (2) *check for understanding*, when students behave inappropriately; and (3) provide g*uided choices* if disruptions continue. A major tactic in Marshall's approach is called *elicitation* (also referred to as "authority without punishment"), which brings misbehavior to an end and helps students develop a procedure for behaving appropriately. Later in the chapter, we will explore these elements further.

Theories of How to Manage Others

Marshall refers to Theory X and Theory Y, proposed by Douglas McGregor (1960), as con-trasting views of how to manage people. **Theory X** holds that people dislike work, try to avoid it, and must be directed, coerced, controlled, or threatened with punishment to do their work. **Theory Y** holds that people will work gladly if their tasks bring satisfaction, and they will exercise self-direction, self-control, and personal responsibility in doing so. You will see that Marshall's Raise Responsibility System is concordant with Theory Y.

Moving toward Responsible Behavior

Marshall maintains that although students are generally inclined to behave responsibly, they often do not, either because they don't know how or because peer pressure or lack of self-control overrides their better judgment. What can teachers do? Marshall advises them to begin establishing a classroom that is conducive to good relationships. This is done by weaving three simple practices into teachers' daily communications with students. Marshall (2005e) calls the three practices *positivity, choice,* and *reflection* and says their power lies in their ability to make school a place where students and teachers like to be.

Positivity is an emotion of optimism focusing on the upside of things. Being around optimistic people makes us feel better, whereas being around negative people has the opposite effect. When someone treats us nicely or says something complimentary to us, we tend to feel good. When someone remarks how fine the day is, we tend to see it in the same way. If students see you being positive in your outlook and dealings with others, rather than negative and faultfinding, they like that and are pleased to be in your class.

Unfortunately, students often perceive teachers and schools in a negative light. Marshall says this occurs because teachers unwittingly set themselves up as enforcers of rules rather than as encouragers, mentors, and role models. They aim at promoting obedience, without realizing that obedience has no energizing effect on students. In fact, mere obedience distances students into apathy, indifference, resistance, and even defiance. Marshall advises teachers to strive for a positive outlook and positive ways of speaking, and to encourage students to do the same.

Choice empowers students by offering them options. Marshall (2005b) reports the following comments he received from a school administrator:

> I began to experiment with giving choices to students. When speaking to students about their behavior at recess, in the lunchroom, or on the bus, I would try to elicit from them what choices they had and how they could make better choices. If a consequence were needed, we would talk together about some of the choices. I would usually start with, "What do you think we should do about the situation?" When I was satisfied with the student's choice, I would say, "I can live with that." The process worked every time and I would wonder at its simplicity.

Reflection is a process of thinking about one's own behavior and judging the effectiveness of what one does. Such reflection is necessary for changing behavior for the better. Although we can control others by imposing some activity or consequence, we cannot change how they think, want to behave, or will behave after our presence is no longer felt. They can only change themselves when they see a good reason for doing so. Usually, teachers try to change students' inappropriate behavior by requesting obedience or making demands coupled with coercion. What we should do instead is establish expectations and influence students in a noncoercive manner, by empowering them to reach our expectations. One of the best ways to do this is to ask students questions that prompt them to think about how they are behaving. The resultant reflection often sets in motion a positive change in behavior. Encourage students to ask themselves questions such as, "If I wanted to be successful in this class right now, what would I be doing?" In most cases, the answer will be apparent to them and they will move toward that behavior.

The Hierarchy of Social Development, Its Value, and How It Is Used

Marshall believes that by helping students understand levels of social development and what they entail, we can help them conduct themselves more responsibly. To facilitate the process, he has articulated a **hierarchy of social development,** which consists of four levels:

1. *Level A: Anarchy.* When functioning at this lowest level of social development, students give no heed to expectations or standards. They have no sense of order or purpose and they seldom accomplish anything worthwhile in class.

2. *Level B: Bossing, Bullying, Bothering.* When functioning at this level, students are bossing, bullying, or bothering others without consideration of the harmful effects of their actions. At this level, students only obey the teacher or others when authority is used. In effect, they are saying to the teacher, "We are unable to control ourselves. We need you to boss us." Marshall says sharing this concept with students has a profound effect on how they behave.

3. *Level C: Cooperation, Conformity.* When functioning at this level, students conform to expectations set by the teacher or others and are willing to cooperate with them. Here, motivation comes strongly from external influences, including peer pressure, that at times may be irresponsible. Discussing and reflecting on the concept of external motivation helps students understand and resist such influences.

4. *Level D: Democracy, Taking the Initiative to Act Responsibly.* Democracy and responsibility are inseparable. When functioning at this level, students take the initiative to do what is right and proper—that is, they behave responsibly without having to be told to do so. They do this because of internal motivation associated with an understanding of what is expected, which prompts them to take the initiative to do what they feel to be the right thing. Marshall suggests explaining to students that democracy requires citizens to make decisions for themselves, rather than having decisions made for them, as is the case in dictatorships. Democracy requires that people do the right thing because they believe it is best for themselves and for the people around them.

Marshall says that Level C behavior is acceptable in school. However, he asks teachers and students to aim at Level D, where students are motivated to make good decisions about their personal behavior, regardless of circumstances, personal urges, or influence from others.

To see how the hierarchy of social development is used to help students reflect on their behavior, suppose two boys are talking together audibly while another student is making a class report. The teacher quietly asks the disruptive boys, "At what level is that behavior?" They think for a moment and answer, "Level B." Their misbehavior typically ceases at that point, and their minds turn toward behavior at a higher level. This happens because reflection leads the boys to immediately see how they can behave in a more responsible manner.

Value of the Hierarchy

Marshall says that once students understand the hierarchy, their attention turns to self-control and thence to social responsibility. He describes a number of attributes that give power to the hierarchy. The hierarchy enables teachers to separate the act from the actor, the deed from the doer. Without that separation, students become overly defensive about their behavior when asked to correct it. The hierarchy helps students realize they are constantly making choices, both consciously and unconsciously. It helps them understand

and deal with peer pressure. It fosters internal motivation to behave responsibly. It promotes good character development without calling attention to personal values, ethics, or morals. It serves as a vehicle for communication that uses the same conceptual vocabulary for youths and adults. The hierarchy encourages students to help keep their classroom conducive to learning rather than only relying on the teacher to do so. It raises awareness of individual responsibility. It empowers students by helping them analyze and correct their own behavior. It serves as an inspiration to improve. It encourages mature decision making. It fosters understanding about internal and external motivation. The hierarchy promotes self-management and doing the right thing, even when no adult is around or when no one else is watching.

Teaching the Hierarchy to Students

Marshall (2001, pp.70–80) describes activities useful in teaching students the names and characteristics of the four levels. Some examples include visualizing each level and then drawing a picture of it, describing it in writing, describing it orally to others, and listening to others' examples of applying the levels to what goes on in school. He explains that by using these various modalities and illustrations, the four levels become pictures in students' minds. He argues that the pictures in our minds drive behavior. They drive us toward those activities we believe will bring satisfaction or pleasure and away from those we believe will bring displeasure or pain. He urges teachers to emphasize that the major difference between the acceptable levels of C and D is the source and nature of the motivation. Level C is behaving responsibly because of adult directions and may involve rewards and punishments. However, at that level students remain overly susceptible to peer influence, which at times can be counterproductive to responsible behavior. Level D is being responsible without being asked, told, rewarded, or punished. On Level D, students *take the initiative* to do the right thing because they believe it is best for the class, the school, and themselves.

You might wonder how well students can understand these levels and relate them to real life. Brief excerpts from "A Letter Worth Reading" provide commentary on that question. The letter was sent to Marvin Marshall by a teacher using the Raise Responsibility System (Marshall, 2005a).

> Just this week we had a discussion with our students about how they could use their understanding of the four levels of development to help themselves become better readers. We talked about our 30-minute "Whole School Read" time that we participate in each morning. We had the children come up with scenarios of what it would look like if someone were operating at each of the four levels. Students were able to clearly describe conduct at each level.
>
> At Level D, the students described that a person would be using reading time each morning to really practice reading. They wouldn't have to have an adult directly with them at all times; they would keep on task simply because they know what is expected of them. They would read and reread sections of their book because they know that by doing so they will become better readers. The motivation would be INTERNAL. They wouldn't be wasting any time watching the teacher in hopes of being specially noticed as "someone

who was reading," and they wouldn't rely on an adult to keep them on task. Instead they would be reading in an effort to become the best reader that they could be.

The children discussed further that Level D is where people take the initiative to do things that are truly going to pay off for them—what is right or appropriate. People at this level *motivate themselves* to work and achieve. The results are long lasting and powerful. These people put in the necessary effort to become good readers and therefore can get a lot of enjoyment from reading. Because they get enjoyment, they keep reading and therefore become even better readers. People at this level feel good about themselves because they experience improvement and are aware that it is a result of choices that they have consciously made.

It is amazing to see the results of discussions such as these. That night, without any suggestion or prompting on my part, our poorest reader in the class went home and read his reader over and over again. Although his parents are kind people, they haven't understood the importance of nightly reading for their child despite many conversations with us. That night they watched as their little boy independently read and reread his reader. Both the parents and little boy could see the dramatic improvement in his ability to read. They experienced the powerful impact that internal desire, coupled with one night of true effort, could have on someone's skill at reading. He came back to school the next day bursting with pride and determination to practice more and more so that he could move on to a new, more difficult reader. It only took one more night of practice, and he was able to do that.

For additional cases of how the hierarchy promotes learning in reading, mathematics, spelling, physical education, and other areas, see "Samples of Hierarchies for Promoting Learning" (Marshall, 2005g).

Focus on Internal Motivation

Internal motivation is in effect when individuals behave in ways they believe will bring them pleasure or satisfaction. Marshall places great emphasis on internal motivation. He clarifies that although humans are influenced by many factors, all motivation takes place *within* a person. We hear an outstanding speaker, are motivated to take action, and then refer to the person who prompted our action as a great motivator. Technically speaking, however, the person only *stimulated* us. In both thought and speech, our language is such that we simply do not refer to people as "stimulators." We call them "motivators" and refer to what they do as "motivation." Stimulators can be very influential, however. Few people are born with an innate desire to consider the effect of their actions on others, but they learn to do so when stimulated by role models who cause them to reflect on their own behavior. In that manner, they learn to share and show consideration for others.

External motivation, on the other hand, is in effect when individuals behave in ways that are aimed at gaining approval or avoiding discomfort. The prompt that instigates action comes from outside the person. External motivation has been dominant in school. It is evident when teachers direct, cajole, admonish, criticize, and use rewards and punishments to make students behave in certain ways. Although students usually comply with teacher exhortations, they only do so to avoid discomfort or gain approval. Marshall believes those external pressures are the main causes of stress and poor relations in the classroom.

Twenty-Five Tactics to Stimulate Students to Behave Responsibly

To help students increase their reliance on internal motivation, Marshall suggests a number of tactics teachers can use to stimulate students to behave responsibly and put forth effort to learn. They include the following:

1. *Think and speak with positivity.* People learn and perform better when they feel good, but sometimes we make students feel bad because they perceive a negative tone in our communication with them. If we approach people and situations in a positive manner, we enjoy ourselves more and are more likely to have our students respond in similarly positive ways. By helping students think in positive terms, we reduce stress, improve relationships, and help them become more successful.

2. *Use the power of choice.* We all have the power to choose some of our responses and attitudes to situations, events, impulses, and urges. The optimist perceives that choices are available; the pessimist perceives a lack of choice. The power of choice-response thinking gives students control and engenders responsibility, helping them move away from seeing themselves as victims of life events. Regardless of age, each of us likes to feel we have control over our lives. When we are encouraged to make choices, we sense that control. Consider offering your students a number of choices in school activities, including homework. Offering choices is one of the most effective approaches to influence behavioral change because it is noncoercive and gives hope, feelings of control, and ownership.

3. *Emphasize the reflective process.* Thinking reflectively increases positivity and choice and, when applied to one's behavior, can lead to self-evaluation and correction, which are necessary ingredients for growth and change. Ask questions of students and encourage them to ask themselves questions, especially about their chosen behavior. The questioning process jump-starts the thinking process. When students ask themselves "What?" and "How?" their alertness and interest increase.

4. *Control the conversation by asking questions.* One way for the teacher to be in control and to direct conversations is to ask questions. Here, the word *control* refers to the conversation, not to a student's behavior. When someone asks you a question there is a natural inclination to answer it. It is in this sense that the person who does the asking controls the conversation or situation. Therefore, if you find yourself in a reactive mode in a discussion or argument and you want to move into a proactive mode and regain control, ask a question of your own. For example, a student asks you, "Why do we have to do this assignment?" Instead of answering, redirect the conversation by simply asking, "Do you feel there is another way we can learn this information more easily?" When students complain, you are likely to get good results by asking, "What can I do to improve the situation, and what can you do?"

5. *Create curiosity.* Marshall says curiosity may be the greatest of all motivators for learning. Much of the learning we do on our own occurs because of curiosity. Marshall suggests presenting a problem or a challenge to students and allowing them to grapple with it at the beginning of a lesson. Their involvement in attempting to figure something out naturally engenders curiosity, which is one of the best ways to motivate students to learn.

6. *Create desire to know.* Allow some time at the beginning of each lesson to talk about what the lesson offers. Students always want to know what's in it for them. Point out how new knowledge, skills, and insights can make life more enjoyable. Also show students how the new knowledge can help them solve problems, make better decisions, get along better with others, and live life more effectively.

7. *Use acknowledgment and recognition.* Acknowledgment and recognition help students feel affirmed and validated. Such a simple comment as, "I see you did well on that," fosters reflection and feelings of competence, as does a comment such as, "Evelyn raises an interesting question, one that applies to what we've been exploring."

8. *Encourage students.* One of the most effective techniques for stimulating students is to let them know you believe they can accomplish the task before them. With many students, a word of encouragement following a mistake is worth more than a great deal of praise after a success. Emphasize that learning is a process and no one can learn something and be perfect at the same time. Doing something in a particular way and not being successful is a valuable way of learning. It should be seen as a learning experience, not as a failure. (See Marshall, 2005f, "Reducing Perfectionism.")

9. *Use collaboration.* Allow students to work together cooperatively. Generally speaking, cooperation is a much better teaching tactic than is competition, which is a great motivator for improving performance, but not for learning. Competing with others is not effective for youngsters who never reach the winner's circle. Students who never feel successful would rather drop out than compete. Instead of competition, allow students to work together, preferably in pairs. Even a very shy student will participate with one other person. (See Marshall, 2005d, "Collaboration for Quality Learning.")

10. *Get yourself excited.* You can't expect others to get excited about what you are teaching if you are not excited about it yourself. Show enthusiasm for the lesson. When lecturing, use a little more animation than when you are conversing, facilitating, or reviewing.

11. *Foster interpersonal relationships.* Connecting with your students on a one-on-one basis is extremely valuable, but helping them connect with each other one-on-one can be even more valuable. Sometimes allow students an opportunity to socialize for short periods before learning activities begin. Relationships are extremely important to young people. One good method for improving relationships is to have students use an activity called "Think, pair, and share" at the end of a lesson.

12. *Use variety.* Variety spices up topics that students might otherwise find tedious. A myriad of visual, auditory, and manipulative techniques can be employed in teaching. These include charts, cartoons, models, parts of films, videos, PowerPoint creations, overhead transparencies, listening to music, recording music, rapping, creating verse, creating rhythms, physical movements, enacting the roles of characters in stories or events, large group discussions, case studies, and working with small groups or buddies.

13. *Stress responsibility rather than rules.* Consider calling behaviors you expect in class "responsibilities" rather than "rules." If you find that any of the 'responsibilities' you expect of students are actually procedures, rather than matters of personal conduct, teach the appropriate procedure and have students practice until they can do it correctly.

When you write and post responsibilities, make sure the word *no* does not appear in them. Every expectation or responsibility should be stated in positive terms.

14. *See situations as challenges, not problems.* If we help students take a positive approach and view situations as *challenges* rather than as problems, we help them deal better with what life brings. This also helps students feel they have some control over their lives rather than being victims of circumstance. Emphasize to students that they can use adversity as a catalyst to becoming better, stronger, wiser, and more capable in dealing with the challenges of life.

15. *Use listening to influence others.* It is surprising how strongly we can influence students simply by listening to them. In fact, the more we are open to students, the greater our influence is. One tactic for developing our listening ability is to pretend we are doing the talking for the other person. This causes us to set aside some of our views and redirect some of our impulsive reactions. Also, we should ask **reflective questions** rather than continually lecturing. Learning to listen and to ask evaluative questions takes practice. As with any skill, practice brings improvement.

16. *Be careful about challenging students' ideas.* Very few people like to have their ideas and beliefs challenged. No one likes being put on the defensive. Instead of challenging, ask questions such as, "How did you come to that interesting conclusion?" or "An alternative point of view is (such and such). Have you ever considered that viewpoint?"

17. *Avoid telling students what to do.* No one likes being told what to do. Regardless of how admirable our intentions might be, when we tell someone to do something, they often perceive it as criticism or an attempt to control. Rather than telling, phrase your idea as a suggestion, such as, "You may want to consider doing that later and focusing on the current lesson now." You can also try using a reflective question that is stated as if you were curious, such as, "What would be the long-term effect of doing that?" Three more questions you will find useful are: "Is there any other way this could be handled?" "What would a responsible action look like?" and "What do you think a highly responsible person would do in this situation?"

18. *Raise your likeability level.* Most teachers want students to like them. Many believe they can make that happen by trying to be friends with student. They may decide, for example, to let students call them by their given name, rather than the more traditional surname. There is much to be said for a friendly demeanor, but personal friendship is not what students need or even want most from teachers. Encouragement and empowerment are more effective in causing students to like you. If you practice the three principles of positivity, choice, and reflection, your students will like you very much.

19. *Empower by building on successes.* Great teachers know that learning is based on motivation and students are best motivated when they can build on existing interests and strengths. That doesn't mean we should ignore the negative or disregard what needs improvement. But students are more likely to achieve success through their assets, not their shortcomings. The more they are successful, the more they are willing to put effort into areas that need improvement. This is especially true for students at risk who have negative perceptions of their school achievements and, therefore, of school in general.

20. *Nurture students' brains.* Marian Diamond is an internationally known neuroscientist who has studied mammalian brains for decades. She and Janet Hopson are the authors of *Magic Trees of the Mind: How to Nurture Your Child's Intelligence, Creativity, and Healthy Emotions from Birth through Adolescence.* In that book Diamond and Hopson (1998) recommend that teachers do the following:

■ Provide a steady source of positive emotional support for students.
■ Stimulate all the senses, though not necessarily all at the same time.
■ Maintain an atmosphere free of undue pressure and stress but suffused with a degree of pleasurable intensity.
■ Present a series of novel challenges that are neither too easy nor too difficult for the students.
■ Allow students to select many of their instructional activities because each brain is unique.
■ Offer opportunities for students to assess the results of their learning and modify it as they think best.
■ Provide an enjoyable atmosphere that promotes exploration and fun of learning.
■ Allow time for students to reflect and let their brains assimilate new information.

21. *Emphasize the four classical virtues.* The **four classical virtues** are prudence, temperance, fortitude, and justice. Prudence is making proper choices without doing anything too rash. Temperance is remaining moderate in all things, including human passions and emotions. Fortitude is showing courage in pursuit of the right path with strength and conviction, despite the risks in doing so. Justice refers to ensuring fair outcomes based on honesty. Through the ages, philosophers have contended that these four virtues help people meet challenges more effectively and find greater satisfaction in life. Marshall believes we can do no better for our students than to pass on this wisdom from former generations.

22. *Tutor a few students every day.* Tutoring students one-on-one is the easiest, quickest, and most effective way of establishing personal relationships with students.

23. *Hold frequent classroom meetings.* Classroom meetings provide excellent opportunities for all members of the class to work together. These meetings are good for resolving challenges that confront the whole class and for helping individual students deal with certain problems. (See Marshall, 2005c, "Classroom Meetings.")

24. *Resolve conflict in a constructivist manner.* When people are involved in conflict, ask each of them what they are willing to do to resolve the situation. Get across the notion that we can't force other people to change, but we can influence them to change through what we do and through changes we are willing to make in ourselves.

25. *Establish trust.* Relationships with others are extremely important to students, especially those who are at risk and those from low income families. Students who do not value school will be motivated to put forward effort only for a teacher they trust and who cares about them and their interests. Trust in the classroom also involves feelings of emotional and psychological safety. To establish optimal trust, employ the three principles of positivity, choice, and reflection.

How to Intervene when Misbehavior Occurs

Although we can control student behavior temporarily, we cannot control how or what students think or the way they *want* to behave. We must realize that teachers are seldom successful in bringing about behavior change through force. But when teachers *empower* students, classroom behavior becomes more self-directed and considerate, resulting in a better educational experience for everyone, with less stress for teacher and students.

You have seen how the hierarchy of social development can be used to empower students. It provides a reference for students to identify their level of behavior, reflect on it, and move toward a more responsible level. Let's suppose a student behaves inappropriately and the teacher needs to intervene. How should the intervention be done? The following three steps indicate how the teacher should proceed. They assume the hierarchy has been taught and students understand how it applies in the classroom.

Step 1. Use an Unobtrusive Tactic

Suppose Syong is annoying Neri. Before saying anything to Syong, you would prompt her to stop by using an unobtrusive technique, such as facial expression, eye contact, hand signal, moving near to Syong, changing voice tone, thanking students for working, saying, "Excuse me," or asking students for help. Marshall (2001, pp. 90–93) offers twenty-two unobtrusive visual, verbal, and kinetic techniques that may be useful.

Step 2. Check for Understanding

If the unobtrusive tactic doesn't stop Syong's misbehavior, check to see if she understands the level of her chosen behavior. Use a neutral, unemotional tone of voice and phrase the question as, "Syong, which level are you choosing?" Or, "Syong, reflect on the level you have chosen." No mention is made of the nature of the behavior or what Syong is doing, but only the level of chosen behavior. This helps prevent a natural self-defense that often leads to a confrontation. Without the hierarchy—which separates the student from the student's inappropriate behavior—a teacher may ask, "What are you doing?" This too often leads to a confrontational situation, especially if Syong responds, "Nothing." However, asking, *"On what level is that behavior?"* prompts not only acknowledgement but also self-evaluation. You are not attacking Syong; you are separating her as a person from the inappropriate behavior, something educators often talk about but find difficult to do.

Step 3. Use Guided Choice

This procedure is designed to stop the disruption, provide the student a responsibility-producing activity to encourage self-reflection, and allow the teacher to return promptly to the lesson. It is crucial to understand that when providing **guided choices,** the teacher does so by *asking* the student, *not telling.* This reduces confrontation, minimizes stress, and helps preserve student dignity.

Marshall (2001, pp. 102–104) suggests several options for use at various grade levels. In the example we have explored, Syong has probably stopped misbehaving and has selected a more responsible way of behaving. However, if an unacceptable level of behavior continues—such as continuing to bother Neri—you should move to using authority without punishment. If time permits, have a discussion with Syong that would begin something like the following: "You realize that every time you choose to act on an inappropriate level, you are allowing yourself to be a victim of your impulses. Do you really want to be a victim? If not, let's come up with a procedure you can use to redirect that impulse when you have it again. When you have a procedure to rely on, you are in control and not a victim of your impulses."

Working with Syong individually during a lesson would take time away from the lesson. For that reason, you might plan to work with her at a more convenient time. In the meantime, you can place an essay form on Syong's desk and quietly offer *three* choices, such as, "Do you prefer to complete the form in your seat, in the rear of the room, or in the office?" On the form, Syong writes about the following:

What did I do? (Acknowledgment)
What can I do to prevent its happening again? (Choice)
What will I do? (Commitment)

Guided choice options should be adjusted in accordance with the grade level, the individual student, and the class. Before responding to the form, the student is asked two questions: 1) "Do you know the reason the form was given to you?" and (2) "Do you think it is personal?" Students understand that the form was given because he or she behaved on an unacceptable level and the teacher needs to quickly resolve the disruption and return to the lesson. The form allows you to use teacher authority in a nonpunishing way. Asking a student to reflect is not classified as punishment. After the student responds to the second question, the teacher (of grades six and above), asks, "What would you like me to do with the form?" Students generally respond, "Throw it away." Although some teachers keep the forms, Marshall recommends tearing it up in front of the student and placing it in the wastepaper basket to show the student to leave the class without negative feelings.

It is very unlikely that Syong, having completed the essay form, will continue to bother others, but teachers always want to know what to do in case a student continues to misbehave. Marshall suggests the following:

Step 4. Make a Self-Diagnostic Referral

Before moving to a more in-depth reflective form, Syong is given the essay form to complete a second time. If this procedure is not effective, then a **self-diagnostic referral** is given, which contains items such as the following:

- Describe the problem that led to writing this.
- Identify the level of behavior.
- Explain why this level of behavior is not acceptable.
- On what level should a person act in order to be socially responsible?
- If you had acted on an acceptable level, what would have happened?
- List three solutions that would help you act more responsibly.

Marshall advises keeping the completed referrals on file for the entire year, because they might be useful in discussions with parents or the administration.

Step 5. Give an Additional Self-Diagnostic Referral

If Syong continues to bother other students, assign an additional referral to complete, in the same manner as the first. Then mail a copy of the first and second referrals to Syong's parents or guardian, together with a brief note explaining the problem.

Step 6. Give a Final Self-Diagnostic Referral

If Syong continues to behave on an unacceptable level, assign a third and final self-diagnostic referral. Mail a copy along with copies of the first two referrals and both notes to parents. The final note indicates to parents that you have exhausted all positive means of fostering social responsibility and will refer future disruptions to the administration. Marshall points out that in all these cases, it is the *student who has identified the problem and proposed positive solutions.* All the teacher does is write brief notes to parents and mail them copies of the student's self-diagnostic referrals. The student has done most of the thinking and planning, which gives ownership to the student—a necessary ingredient for lasting change. Marshall notes that the last few steps rarely, if ever, need to be used.

Note: Before you use the preceding approach, explain it to your building administrator. This informs the administrator so (1) he or she is not caught off guard by parent questions and (2) your approach receives official sanction from the administrator.

Initiating the Raise Responsibility System in the Classroom

The Raise Responsibility System is implemented by doing the following: First, decide how you will teach the four levels so students understand how they apply in the classroom. Some teachers initially think that students will get confused using Levels D, B, C, and A because many schools use A, B, C, and D for grading. Marshall says experience has shown that even very young students understand the context of levels of social development and are not confused by the same letters being used in reverse for grades.

Second, explain the system to your administrator for approval. Prepare communication to send to parents when you are ready to implement the system. Here is a form letter that Marshall (2005h) suggests:

> Dear Parent(s) or Guardian(s):
>
> Our classroom houses a small society. Each student is a citizen who acts in accordance with expected standards of behavior.
>
> With this in mind, rewards are not given for expected behavior—just as society does not give rewards for behaving properly. Also, irresponsible behavior is seen as an opportunity for growth, rather than for punishment.
>
> Our approach encourages students to exercise self-discipline through reflection and self-evaluation. Students learn to control their own behavior, rather than always relying on the teacher for control.

We want our classroom to be encouraging and conducive to learning at all times. In this way, young people develop positive attitudes and behavioral skills that are so necessary for successful lives.

Sincerely,

(Teacher)

Third, plan to teach procedures, rather than relying on rules. Teach students the hierarchy of social development through hands-on activities and scenarios in which students share examples of the four levels in the classroom, in other areas in the school, and in their personal lives. Have discussions about how students felt when they were told to do something (Level C) and how they felt when they took the initiative to do the right thing without being asked (Level D). Have students compare their feelings. Marshall contends that from such comparisons students realize that taking the initiative to do what is right is the most satisfying of rewards. Post the hierarchy on your classroom Internet site so parents and students can refer to it. Include examples of how the hierarchy can be referred to in various skill areas, on the playground, in the cafeteria, and on field trips. When a student misbehaves, follow the sequence of phases described previously; that is, ask the student to identify the level of chosen behavior and then elicit a procedure to help students redirect impulses. If time does not allow for a private conversation, use the forms as indicated. At another time have students discuss the advantages and disadvantages of punishments and rewards. Use their comments as a platform for explaining why you do not use punishment or rewards in your classes. Marshall presents his views regarding use of external approaches at www. AboutDiscipline.com.

Marshall relates that some teachers and parents initially object to the terms *anarchy* and *bullying* used in the hierarchy of social behavior. He urges you to understand—and explain to parents, if necessary—that the hierarchy does not teach either anarchy or bullying, but helps explain that when anarchy and chaos exist, someone or some group will take control and make the rules for all others. He contends that this is how societies operated before 1776 when the Declaration of Independence articulated a new world view: "We hold these truths to be self-evident. . . . That to secure these rights, *governments are instituted among men, deriving their just powers from the consent of the governed."* Before this concept became operational and spread around the world, societies were granted their rights from the person who held power. This is the concept behind Level B. Once parents understand that anarchy and bossing, bullying, and bothering are unacceptable levels of behavior, they become supporters and particularly appreciate your teaching the differences between external and internal motivation, Levels C and D, respectively.

Summary of the Raise Responsibility System

The following material summarizes Marshall's Raise Responsibility System and indicates how it is used in the classroom:

The Marvin Marshall Teaching Model

I. Classroom Management versus Discipline

The key to effective classroom management is teaching and practicing procedures. This is the teacher's responsibility. Discipline, on the other hand, has to do with behavior and is the student's responsibility.

II. Three Principles to Practice

1. **Positivity**
Teachers practice changing negatives into positives. "No running" becomes "We walk in the hallways." "Stop talking" becomes "This is quiet time."

2. **Choice**
Choice-response thinking is taught—as well as impulse control—to redirect impulsive behavior so students are not victims of their own impulses.

3. **Reflection**
Since a person can only control another person temporarily and because no one can actually change another person, asking *reflective* questions is the most effective approach to actuate change in others.

III. Teaching the Raise Responsibility System (RRSystem)

1. **Teaching the Hierarchy (Teaching)**
The four levels in the hierarchy are taught to students. They engender a desire to behave responsibly and put forth effort to learn. Students differentiate between internal and external motivation—and learn to rise above inappropriate peer influence.

2. **Checking for Understanding (Asking)**
During a disruption, the teacher has the student reflect on the *level* of chosen behavior. This immediately stops inappropriate behaviors.

3. **Using Guided Choices (Eliciting)**
If disruptions continue, a consequence or procedure is *elicited* from the student to redirect the inappropriate behavior. This approach is in contrast to the usual coercive approach of *imposing* a "logical consequence" or a punishment.

IV. Using the Raise Responsibility System to Increase Academic Performance

Using the hierarchy for review *before* a lesson and for reflecting *after* a lesson increases effort and raises academic achievement.

Raise Responsibility Self-Analysis

If you decide to use the Raise Responsibility System, you may find the following questions helpful in evaluating your progress. You may wish to discuss them with your students to get their perspective, as well.

1. Are you *teaching the procedures* you expect of your students?
2. Are you *communicating in a positive manner* with your students?

3. Are your students made aware that they continually make choices, some consciously but most unconsciously and that the *choices they make largely determine their happiness and success* in school and life?

4. Do you always *give your students choices* concerning behavior that shows responsibility—preferably three choices?

5. Have you carefully taught, and have your *students adequately learned the ABCD* levels of social development?

6. When disruptions occur, do you ask questions in a noncoercive, nonthreatening manner that *prompts student reflection and self-evaluation* of behavior?

7. If disruptive behavior continues, do you *elicit a procedure or consequence* from the student for redirecting future impulsive behavior?

8. Do you use the hierarchy to *promote a desire* in students to put forth effort in learning?

KEY TERMS AND CONCEPTS EMPHASIZED IN THIS CHAPTER

raising responsibility	reflection	reflective questions
Theory X	hierarchy of social	four classical virtues
Theory Y	development	guided choices
positivity	internal motivation	self-diagnostic referral
choice	external motivation	

SELECTED SEVEN—SUMMARY SUGGESTIONS FROM MARVIN MARSHALL

1. Establish trusting and empowering relationships with students by using positivity, choice, and reflection.

2. Teach procedures for everything you want students to do. Don't assume students know the procedures automatically.

3. Explain the levels of social development to raise student expectations. Differentiate between the two levels of unacceptable behavior and the two levels of acceptable behavior. Ask students to reflect on their chosen levels at various times. This prompts them to consciously aim toward Level D.

4. Also use the hierarchical structure in subject areas to prompt students to want to put forth effort for their learning.

5. Weave tactics for increasing responsibility into your normal teaching routines.

6. When working with students, avoid the thinking behind Theory X, which assumes your students dislike school and must be directed, coerced, controlled, and threatened before they will do their work. Simply remember that no student comes to school to deliberately fail or to get into trouble. Use Theory Y, which assumes your students will put forth proper effort because they have good feelings and relationships and find their tasks bring satisfaction. If you practice the three principles of positivity, choice, and reflection, your students will begin to exercise self-direction, self-control, and personal responsibility.

7. Remember that although you can control students temporarily through rewards, threats, and punishments, those tactics will not make a lasting change in the way students think or behave when an adult is not present. Teaching obedience often engenders resistance and rebellion. However, when you promote responsibility, you will get obedience as a natural by-product.

CONCEPT CASES

Case 1: Kristina Will Not Work

Kristina, a student in Mr. Jake's class, is quite docile. She socializes little with other students and never disrupts lessons. However, despite Mr. Jake's best efforts, Kristina will not do her work. She rarely completes an assignment. She is simply there, putting forth no effort at all. *How would Marshall deal with Kristina?*

Marshall would classify this as a *learning challenge, not as a behavior problem.* He would not attempt to force Kristina to learn, knowing that he could not force her even if he wanted to. To learn or not to learn is Kristina's choice. He has seen that she is capable of learning and reassures her of this fact. If she chooses to put forward the effort to learn, she will feel more competent, enjoy herself more, and be happier. But this is her choice. Accordingly, Marshall would attempt to establish a positive relationship by sharing with her his belief in her competency. He would then find out what Kristina likes to do and weave into the assignments some activities that would capitalize on her interests. He would continually check with her to see how she is doing and, thereby, communicate his interest in her. He would suggest that what she chooses to do or not do affects her more than anyone else and that she will not gain any satisfaction if no effort is put forth. He may also refer to the hierarchy in the following manner: (1) Ask Kristina to identify the level of her behavior. (2) Ask her how a responsible person would behave in this circumstance. (3) Positively reiterate his belief that Kristina is capable. (4) Provide Kristina with a few guided choices. (5) Ask her to self reflect on her subsequent behavior and future decisions.

Case 2: Sara Cannot Stop Talking

Sara is a pleasant girl who participates in class activities and does most, though not all, of her assigned work. She cannot seem to refrain from talking to classmates, however. Her teacher, Mr. Gonzales, speaks to her repeatedly during lessons, to the point that he often becomes exasperated and loses his temper. *What suggestions would Marshall give Mr. Gonzales for dealing with Sara?*

Case 3: Joshua Clowns and Intimidates

Joshua, larger and louder than his classmates, always wants to be the center of attention, which he accomplishes through a combination of clowning and intimidation. He makes wisecrack remarks, talks back (smilingly) to the teacher, utters a variety of sound-effect noises such as automobile crashes and gunshots, and makes limitless sarcastic comments and put-downs of his classmates. Other students will not stand up to him, apparently fearing his size and verbal aggression. His teacher, Miss Pearl, has come to her wit's end. *Would Joshua's behavior be likely to improve if Marshall's techniques of noncoercion and reflection were used in Miss Pearl's classroom? Explain.*

Case 4: Tom Is Hostile and Defiant

Tom has appeared to be in his usual foul mood ever since arriving in class. On his way to sharpen his pencil, he bumps into Frank, who complains. Tom tells him loudly to shut up. Miss Baines, the teacher, says, "Tom, go back to your seat." Tom wheels around, swears loudly, and says heatedly, "I'll go when I'm damned good and ready!" *How would Marshall have Miss Baines deal with Tom?*

QUESTIONS AND ACTIVITIES

1. In your journal enter ideas from the Raising Responsibility System you might want to incorporate into your personal system of discipline.

2. Describe your overall impression of Marshall's Raise Responsibility System. What do you see as its strengths and shortcomings? How easily do you feel it could be used in the classroom? How well do you think it can stop aggressive misbehavior?

3. With a fellow student, practice asking the reflective questions and giving the guided choices Marshall suggests for identifying level of behavior and behaving at Level B or Level C.

4. With a fellow student, discuss the key terms used in Marshall's model, concerning meaning and application.

YOU ARE THE TEACHER

High School American Literature

You teach an eleventh-grade one-semester course in American literature. The course is required for graduation. Among your thirty-three students are eight seniors who failed the course previously and are retaking it. The students at your school are from affluent middle-class families, and many of them are highly motivated academically. But at the same time, there is a significant number who have little interest in school aside from the opportunity to socialize. Your teaching routine proceeds as follows: First, you begin the period with a three-question quiz over assigned reading. The quiz focuses on facts such as names, places, and description of plot. Second, when the quiz papers are collected, you conduct a question-and-discussion session about the assigned reading. You call on individual students, many of whom answer, "I don't know." Third, you have the class begin reading a new chapter in the work under study. They take turns reading orally until the end of the period. The remainder of the assignment not read orally is to be completed as homework.

A Typical Occurrence

The students enter your classroom lethargically and begin taking the quiz from questions you have written on the board. You notice that many of their answers are simply guesses. You see that Brian, who has already failed the class and must pass it now in order to graduate, doesn't know the answers to any of the questions. You say, "I can tell that many of you didn't read your assignment. What's going on?" When oral reading begins, you notice that Brian does not have his copy of *Huckleberry Finn*, the work being studied. This is nothing new. You lend Brian a spare copy. Brian follows along in the reading for a while and then begins doodling on a sheet of paper. You call on him to read. He cannot find the place. You say, "Brian, this is simply unacceptable. You have failed the class once; fail it

again now and you know you don't graduate." Brian does not look up but says, "Want to make a bet on that?"

"What?"

"I guarantee you I'll graduate."

"Not without summer school, you won't!"

"That's okay by me. That will be better. This class is too boring, and the assignments are too long. I've got other things to do besides read this stupid story. Who cares about this anyway? Why can't we read something that has to do with real life?"

You are offended and reply, "You couldn't be more wrong! Other students enjoy this work, and it is one of the greatest books in American literature! There is nothing wrong with the book! What's wrong, Brian, is your attitude!"

Brian's eyes are hot, but he says nothing. His book remains closed. You struggle through the final 10 minutes of class. The bell rings and Brian is first out the door.

Conceptualizing a Strategy

If you followed the suggestions of Marvin Marshall, what would you conclude or do with regard to the following?

1. Preventing the problem(s) from occurring in the first place.

2. Putting an immediate end to the inappropriate behavior.

3. Involving other or all students in addressing the situation.

4. Maintaining student dignity and good personal relations.

5. Applying follow-up procedures that would prevent the recurrence of the misbehavior.

6. Using the situation to help the students develop a sense of greater responsibility and self-control.

REFERENCES

Diamond, M., and Hopson, J. 1998. *Magic trees of the mind: How to nurture your child's intelligence, creativity, and healthy emotions from birth through adolescence.* New York: Dutton.

Marshall, M. 1998. *Fostering social responsibility.* Bloomington, IN: Phi Delta Kappa.

Marshall, M. 2001. *Discipline without stress, punishments, or rewards: How teachers and parents promote responsibility & learning.* Los Alamitos, CA: Piper Press.

Marshall, M. (Monthly since August, 2001). *Promoting Responsibility & Learning: The Monthly Newsletter.* www.MarvinMarshall.com.

Marshall, M. 2005a. A Letter Worth Reading. www
.marvinmarshall.com/aletterworthreading.html.

Marshall, M. 2005b. A Principal's Experience. www
.marvinmarshall.com/principal.htm.

Marshall, M. 2005c. Classroom Meetings. www
.disciplinewithoutstress.com/sample_chapters.html.

Marshall, M. 2005d. Collaboration for Quality Learning.
www.disciplinewithoutstress.com/sample_chapters
.html.

Marshall, M. 2005e. Promoting Positivity, Choice, and
Reflection.   www.MarvinMarshall.com/promoting_
positivity.htm.

Marshall, M. 2005g. Samples of Hierarchies for Promoting
Learning. www.marvinmarshall.com/hierarchy.htm.

Marshall, M. 2005h. Implementing the Raise Responsibility
System (part 6). www.marvinmarshall.com/newsletter/
promotingresponsibility_7-05.htm.

McGregor, D. 1960. *The human side of enterprise*. New York:
McGraw-Hill.

CHAPTER 13

Discipline through Careful Teacher Guidance and Instruction

Authoritative Input
■ Ronald Morrish / Real Discipline

CHAPTER PREVIEW

This chapter presents Ronald Morrish's ideas concerning classroom discipline. Morrish contends that today's popular discipline systems are inefficient because they expect students to make many decisions they are not yet ready to make, resulting in an overabundance of negotiating and haggling between teacher and students. His approach, which he calls Real Discipline, teaches students right from wrong, expects students to comply with adult authority until they are able to make decisions effectively, and then encourages them to make choices about behavior when they are sufficiently mature and experienced to do so effectively.

Fundamental Hypothesis of Real Discipline

Students do not enter school knowing how to behave responsibly, nor do they learn self-discipline from experience alone. To acquire these essential skills, they need supportive guidance from enlightened, caring teachers.

About Ronald Morrish

Ronald Morrish was a teacher and behavior specialist in Canada for 26 years before becoming an independent consultant in 1997. He now devotes his efforts to writing, giving conference presentations, conducting professional development programs, presenting courses for teachers, and working with parent groups and child care providers around the world. He has authored three books. The first, *Secrets of Discipline* (1997), was also produced as a video. In *Secrets of Discipline,* Mr. Morrish discusses twelve keys for raising responsible children without engaging in deal making, arguments, and confrontations. His second book, *With All Due Respect* (2000), focuses on improving teachers' personal discipline skills and building effective discipline within schools through a team approach. In 2003, he published *FlipTips,* a mini-book of discipline tips and maxims excerpted from his books and presentations. Morrish can be contacted through his website, www.realdiscipline.com.

Morrish on Discipline Gone Wrong

Ronald Morrish (2005) concurs with other authorities that school discipline is an ever-growing problem, as students become increasingly defiant and manipulative. He places part of the blame on undesirable trends in society, but assigns much of it to currently popular discipline practices that, he believes, allow students to make too many choices about how they will conduct themselves in school. He reminds us that for over a quarter of a century behavior experts have claimed that plentiful choice leads to student self-esteem, responsibility, and motivation to achieve. The teacher's role in the process has been to encourage good choices and discourage poor ones. That approach has failed, Morrish contends, for three reasons. First, it does not demand proper behavior from students, but instead allows them, if they wish, to make self-defeating choices and accept the consequences. Such a system is only effective with students who care about consequences. Second, it requires teachers to bargain and negotiate to get students to cooperate in school. Third, it doesn't teach students how they are expected to behave.

Morrish contends that when given full latitude, students make many choices that educators have difficulty living with. We want our students to know right from wrong and behave accordingly, but today's discipline generally teaches them to do not what is "right," but whatever is advantageous at a particular point in time, basing their decisions on whether they can live with the consequences. The overall result is that students too often choose to underachieve in school, engage in high-risk behaviors, contribute little or nothing to the school environment, and use violence and intimidation in dealing with others. These facts, says Morrish, clearly show that discipline based on student choice is not producing the results we have expected.

Morrish feels teachers have been sidetracked into focusing on behavior management rather than "real discipline." He makes a clear distinction between the two but stresses that both are needed. Management is about making the learning environment functional, keeping students on task, and minimizing disruptions. It attempts to deal with whatever behavior students bring to school. Management is certainly important, but does not, by itself, help students develop responsible behavior. **Real Discipline,** on the other hand, teaches students how to behave properly. It requires they show courtesy and consideration. It teaches needed social skills and trains students to work within a structure of rules and limits. It does these things while protecting students from self-defeating mistakes they would otherwise make.

Real Discipline

Morrish calls his approach Real Discipline, and he believes it will restore proper behavior to today's schools. Morrish explains that Real Discipline is not a new theory, but an organized set of techniques that great teachers and parents have used for generations to teach children to be respectful, responsible, and cooperative. It emphasizes careful teacher guidance to ensure that children learn how to conduct themselves appropriately. As Morrish (1997) puts it:

Real Discipline is a lot more than simply giving choices to children and then dealing with the aftermath. We have to teach them right and wrong. We have to teach them to respect legitimate authority. We have to teach them the lessons that have been learned by others and by ourselves. Then, and only then, will we enjoy watching them develop into adults. (p. 33)

These provisions are necessary because in their early years, children are impulsive and self-centered. To develop into contributing members of society, they must learn to cooperate, behave responsibly, and show consideration for others. Sometimes they have parents and role models who teach them these things. Too often these days, they do not. Children who are overly indulged and never called to account for their behavior remain self-centered. They grow up concerned only with their own needs, without regard for those of others. They want things their way, cooperate in school only when they feel like it, and are seldom considerate of teachers and fellow students. For many, abusive language and bullying are the rule of the day.

In part, this situation has developed because we live in a society that stresses individual rights and freedom. We hold those rights and freedoms dear, but we have lost sight of personal responsibility, without which rights and freedom mean little. Personal responsibility is too important to leave to chance. We must live in accordance with requirements that put constraints on individual freedom. We do this in exchange for life that is safer, more secure, and more orderly.

Morrish believes students should have choices, but only when they are prepared to deal with them. Otherwise, the choices they make are too often detrimental rather than beneficial. Students do not know, innately, how to make responsible choices. Before they can do so, they must develop two things—a degree of compliance and respect for authority. Yet, many of today's discipline programs immediately give students a strong voice in deciding on class rules and personal conduct. That does little to help students learn to live by rules, because it permits them to do as they please.

Maxims Regarding the Mindset for Real Discipline

In 2003, Morrish published a small, spiral-bound book called *FlipTips,* containing comments and maxims from his various publications and presentations. They clarify the mindset toward discipline that Morrish would like teachers to acquire. Here are a few of the tips that illustrate Morrish's ideas on discipline (some wording has been slightly changed, but meaning is intact).

- Discipline is a process, not an event.
- Discipline is about giving students the structure they need, not the consequences they seem to deserve.
- Discipline comes from the word *disciple,* not the word *ogre.* It's about teaching and learning, not scolding and punishing.
- Discipline isn't what you do when students misbehave. It's what you do so they won't.

- Discipline isn't about letting students make their own choices. It's about preparing them for the choices they will be making.
- Don't let students make choices that are not theirs to make.
- Train students to comply with your directions. Compliance precedes cooperation. If you bargain for compliance now, you'll have to beg for it later.
- Always work from more structure to less structure, not the other way around.
- To prevent major behavior problems, deal with all the minor behavior problems.
- Students learn far more from being shown how to behave appropriately than from being punished.
- The best time to teach a behavior is when it isn't needed, so it will be there when it is needed.
- If you teach students to be part of the solution, they're less likely to be part of the problem.
- When dealing with adolescents, act more like a coach and less like a boss.
- A single minute of practicing courtesy has more impact than one hour of lecturing on the importance of it.
- To stop fights, stop put-downs. Verbal hits usually precede physical hits.
- Discipline should end with the correct behavior, not with a punishment.
- Today's practice is tomorrow's performance.
- Rapport is the magical ingredient that changes a student's reluctance to be controlled into willingness to be guided.

Real Discipline's Three-Phase Approach

Rather than approach discipline from the perspective of choice, Real Discipline asks teachers to guide students through three progressive phases—training, teaching, and managing. Each of these **three phases of Real Discipline** is aimed at a particular goal and relies on a certain set of strategies. Let's see what these phases entail.

Phase 1. Training for Compliance

This first phase is organized to train students to accept adult authority and comply with it automatically. Basic **compliance** should initially be taught as a *nonthinking activity.* Nonthinking activities are habits you don't have to reflect on or make choices about, such as stopping at red lights or saying "thank you" when people do something nice for you. Students should be carefully trained how to pay attention, follow directions, and speak respectfully, to the point that they do these things automatically, or habitually.

Compliant classroom behavior is taught through direct instruction and close supervision. If you want students to raise their hands before speaking, tell them what you expect and show them how to do it. Then have them replicate the act and practice it until it becomes habitual. When students make mistakes, they are shown again how to do the act properly and, again, practice it. Morrish says to start small, and you will see a general attitude of compliance grow out of many small compliances.

Morrish observes that although compliance is extremely important, it receives virtually no attention in other popular programs of discipline. He finds this strange in light of the fact that compliance helps students conduct themselves properly and provides the basis for later decision making. Compliance is based on the fundamental recognition that there are effective ways of behaving in civilized societies, with limits to what people do. Therefore, in compliance training, teachers address all misbehavior. They do not overlook small misbehaviors, as they are advised to do in many discipline programs. Overlooking small misbehavior is necessary in those other programs, Morrish says, because of the excessive time required for explaining, negotiating, and tending to consequences. As a result, teachers are advised to "pick your battles," and "don't sweat the small stuff." Accordingly, teachers may allow students to lie on their desks during opening routines, talk during announcements, throw their jackets in a corner instead of hanging them up, and wander around the room instead of getting ready to work.

Such behaviors may seem unimportant, but should never be overlooked. They are poor habits that easily expand to poor overall behavior. If you walk by students who are doing something wrong and you say nothing, they interpret that as meaning you don't care; the next thing you know they are engaged in even more unacceptable misbehavior. Don't get the idea you can't manage such behavior, but do understand it is not corrected by scolding or doling out consequences. Instead, your best approach is to tell students what you want them to do and then insist they do it properly. When they do something wrong, have them do it right. This is how you establish good practices and habits in your classes. Students get the picture quickly

Morrish asks teachers to train their students to comply with rules, limits, and authority. **Rules** indicate how students are to behave. An example of a rule is, "Show courtesy and respect for others at all times." Limits specify behavior that will not be allowed. An example of a limit is, "No name-calling in this room." **Authority** refers to power that has been assigned to certain individuals. By custom and law, a teacher is given legitimate authority to control and direct students in school. They should use this authority to set and maintain standards of conduct.

Rules and Compliance

Just as we need rules for structure and predictability in everyday living, so we also need rules for classroom behavior. Teachers need to make the rules; there is no need to ask students if they agree with them. Students are supposed to learn rules, not determine them. Therefore, teach students why we have rules and why they are made by people in positions of authority. Explain the rules to students and take their opinions into account, but don't pretend they are helping decide what the class rules are to be.

Morrish cautions that you really don't have rules unless you can enforce them. Thus, when you establish rules, you must make a commitment to ensuring they are obeyed. Your enforcement should be consistent, even for misbehavior that seems incidental, such as carelessly dropping rubbish on the floor or talking during quiet study time. As noted earlier, small infractions tend to build up into large infractions.

Morrish says **insistence** is the best strategy for enforcing rules. Punishment is rarely needed. You must be absolutely determined that students will do what you want them to. You must be willing to persist until they do so. You should develop the mindset that once you give an instruction, there is no question about students' doing what you say. Morrish does not say that punishment should never be used, but he does point out that punishment cannot teach cooperation or responsibility and that it sometimes produces bad side effects. However, punishment can do two things well. First, it can teach that "*No* means no," a message students need to learn quickly. Second, punishment can bring misbehavior to a stop when other methods can't.

Limits and Compliance

As with rules, limits on behavior are set and enforced by teachers, in accordance with established standards. Teachers do not negotiate those limits with students. Morrish says the first secret of good discipline is: *Never give students a choice when it comes to limits.* You set limits in many ways, formally and informally. For example, as students arrive at your classroom, you may say in a friendly but businesslike tone, "Line up at the door, please" "Hang up your jackets, please" or "Get ready for work immediately." You state limits firmly: "No fighting" or "No swearing in this room." Students do not have a say in these matters. If there are questions about the limits you should select a time and explain the reasons behind them, but in no case are students allowed to ignore your directions. Your word is final.

Morrish laments that limits in today's classrooms are often compromised by bargaining between teacher and students. He notes that the more teachers agree to give students special privileges in exchange for behaving properly, the more students are likely to misbehave. That is because bargaining does not produce the results teachers expect. Teachers expect that once the bargaining is done, students will assess the possible outcomes of their behavior choices and make good choices accordingly. However, for students the main effect of this process is not better choice making, but feeling as if everything in the class is decided through bargaining. All bargaining does is give students power in decisions they are not adequately prepared to make.

Authority and Compliance

Morrish acknowledges that it makes many teachers uneasy when they are asked to train their students for compliance. They fear automatic compliance will make their students passive, submissive, and unable to think for themselves. Morrish believes, however, that today's discipline gives students too much freedom of choice, not too little. What we need, says Morrish, is a balance, which is achieved thorough the three phases of Real Discipline.

Morrish insists we need to reestablish teacher authority in the classroom, and he reminds teachers where their authority comes from—from legality and custom. The power of teacher authority comes from teachers' knowing their job, knowing why they are setting limits, and knowing what they expect their students to learn. It is conveyed by tone of voice, choice of words, and the way one presents oneself. Teachers should clearly communicate what they expect of students and then accept nothing less. They should make clear that no negotiation is involved. They do this without threatening or raising their voices. They simply say, with authority in their voice, "This is what you must do. This is the job you are here for. Now let's get on with it" (1997, p. 65).

If, in this process, students question your authority, tell them, "It is my job." If they challenge your right to make demands, tell them, "It is my job." Morrish says don't worry if your students don't like some of the things you expect them to do. It is respect you need at this point, not appreciation. Appreciation will come later, provided respect comes first.

Phase 2. Teaching Students How to Behave

The second phase in Real Discipline focuses on teaching students the skills, attitudes, and knowledge needed for cooperation, proper behavior, and increased responsibility. You set the class rules and quickly teach them through explanation, demonstration, practice, and corrective feedback. Students understand the need for rules, and they will comply with them if they accept your authority. This process teaches students to be courteous, work and play together harmoniously, resolve conflicts, set personal goals, organize tasks, and manage time. Most teachers erroneously think students will somehow learn those skills from experience. You can't wait for experience to teach them these things, even if experience was capable of that.

Today's students must be taught what to do, if you are to have order and acceptable behavior in your classes. The best way to teach behavior skills is through direct instruction and carefully supervised practice. When students fail to comply with expectations, don't scold or punish them. Simply have them redo the behavior in an acceptable manner and continue to practice it.

Phase 3. Managing Student Choice

The third phase of Real Discipline is called choice management. It helps students move toward greater independence by offering them more and more choices as they show capability for handling them. One basic requirement in making choices is that students must take into account the needs and rights of other students and school personnel. You must ensure they do so. Today's popular discipline approaches place heavy emphasis on student choice, but they do little to establish compliance and set limits that would prepare students to make choices effectively.

Morrish explains that choice management also requires specification of who has the right, or duty, to make a particular choice. Teachers have to make certain choices, whereas students can be allowed to make others. As a rule of thumb, if students don't care about the outcome of a particular goal, they should not be allowed to make choices about it. To illustrate, most people assume that students who do poor class work should receive low marks that will motivate them to do better in the future. This may work for some highly motivated students, but it does nothing for those who don't care and are perfectly willing to accept the low grades. If Mary indicates she doesn't care about her performance in important class matters, you should say to her, "That's okay, Mary, because I do care and that's why this is my choice. Someday, when you care about it as much as I do, it will become your choice" (Morrish, 1997, p. 101). Suppose Mary has handed in poor work. You say the following: "Mary, your work is disorganized and incomplete. I'm not accepting it. Take it back, please, and fix it up. I'll mark it when it is done properly" (Morrish, 1997, p. 105).

Teachers must make decisions for students like Mary until those students begin sincerely to care about quality and completeness. The teacher should never suggest that Mary can choose to do poor work if she wants to. Morrish says this is one area where we truly need to get back to basics, meaning we should expect students to do quality work and accept nothing less. Morrish reiterates (1997, p. 106): Schools are not democracies. Teachers must be willing to make the decisions that are theirs to make.

When you encounter a student like Mary, you continue to work toward the major goal of Real Discipline, which is to help the student become self-disciplined and to conduct him- or herself properly even when you are not present. This is not likely to occur in discipline systems where students learn they can do what is advantageous rather than what is right. Morrish (1997, pp. 93–94) relates a classroom incident that epitomizes self-discipline. To paraphrase Morrish:

> I was visiting a combination grade 2/3 class when the teacher told her students she would be leaving the classroom for a few minutes. The students were to continue working quietly. She asked them, "What does this mean you need?" Hands were raised. A student answered, "Self-discipline." The teacher continued, "What does self-discipline mean?" Another student answered, "It means we behave when you're not with us, exactly the same way we behave when you are standing right next to us." The teacher and I both left the room but I stopped in the hallway to watch the students from a distance. The students continued to work as if the teacher were in the room with them. Later I asked the teacher how she had accomplished that result. She said she had the class practice the skill from the first day. She would stand next to them and ask them to show their best behavior. Then she challenged them to continue behaving that way as she moved farther and farther away. Before long the students had learned how to maintain their behavior when the teacher left the room.

But if students misbehaved when the teacher was out of the room, what should she do? Morrish says she should first ask the students "What happened?" When they told her, she would follow with, "Would you have made the same decision if I had been standing right next to you?" Usually the students will say, "No." Then the teacher asks, "Why do you need me standing next to you for you to make a good decision?"

As students become older and move toward independence, Real Discipline is already at work teaching them three things about making independent choices: First, that independence requires balancing personal rights with personal responsibility; second, that the rights and needs of others must be taken into account; and third, that students should look at every unsupervised situation as an opportunity to demonstrate personal responsibility. Morrish points out that independence isn't "doing your own thing"; it's doing what's right when you are on your own.

Planning the Discipline Program

Real Discipline requires teachers to be proactive. They should anticipate problems, prevent as many as possible, and carefully prepare for any that might occur. Morrish (2000) guides teachers through eleven steps in organizing their discipline system.

1. *Decide in advance how you want your students to behave.* Think through matters such as the following: how students will demonstrate courtesy, the words and tone of voice

they will use, how they will speak to you, what other signs of courtesy they will show, how they will treat visitors, how they will welcome new students to the class, how they will listen to you and other students and how they will contribute to discussions, how they will help substitute teachers, what they will do when upset or when they disagree with you or others, how they will respond to other students who need assistance, how they will deal with losing, how they will comply when you tell them what to do, how they will respond when you correct them, and how they will behave when you step out of the room.

2. *Design the supporting structure.* When you have in mind how you want students to behave, design a structure that will support your goals. This structure will have mostly to do with procedures, such as how students will enter and exit the room, what they will do when arriving late, how they will handle completed work, how they request assistance, what they should do about missed assignments, what they should do if they finish work early, what they should do if the teacher does not appear on time, how they will learn class rules and enforcement procedures, and what the specific limits on behavior are.

3. *Establish a threshold for behavior at school.* You must not allow students to bring negative behaviors from home and community to the class. You must create a clear separation between inside of school and outside of school. Say to students, "You're now at school. Remember how you behave when you are here." Then enforce the courtesy, rules, and work habits required in your class.

4. *Run a two-week training camp.* Good teachers work hard on discipline expectations and procedures during the first two weeks of the year or term. They use this time to establish clear limits, expectations, routines, appropriate behavior, and compliance. Morrish maintains that the investment you make in discipline during the first two weeks of school will determine how the rest of the school year unfolds. This does not suggest you overlook academic work. In the early stages, academic work is a lower priority than proper behavior, but as students acclimate to Real Discipline, academic work moves to highest priority.

5. *Teach students how to behave appropriately.* Morrish believes that students should be taught any skills that are required for school success, including how to behave in school assemblies, on school buses, and in the school cafeteria. They need to learn how, and why, to dress appropriately for school. (They should consider school to be their workplace.) They should be taught how to treat new students and be good role models for younger students. In addition, Morrish (2000, pp. 94–103) presents "Ten Great Skills" you should teach your students. The skills, which overlap some of Morrish's suggestions presented earlier, are shown here in abbreviated form:

- *Courtesy.* Teach students how to greet others, say "please" and "thank you," listen when others speak, and acknowledge good effort by others.
- *How to treat substitute teachers.* Teach students to behave for others just as they would for you. Show them how to welcome others and help them.
- *Conflict prevention.* Help students recognize events that lead up to various incidents and then problem-solve alternative ways of avoiding the conflict. Teach them how to respond to teasing and avoid people and situations that provoke trouble.

- *Self-discipline.* Work to help your students understand they should make the same behavior decisions when you are not there as when you are present. Talk about various hypothetical behavior situations. Ask how your students would behave if you were there. Ask if they can commit to that same behavior when you are not beside them.
- *Concentration.* Help students learn to ignore distractions. Give them practice by having them maintain concentration when a selected student makes noise or speaks to you.
- *Being part of the solution rather than part of the problem.* Teach students how to do such things as helping classmates with learning, stopping someone from teasing, keeping students from fighting, and keeping the classroom and school grounds neat. Congratulate them when they do those things. When you see them fail to do so, ask them why they didn't help.
- *Thinking about others.* Children are self-centered and have to be taught to take others into account. Ask students to try to help someone every day. Periodically, call on them to identify others who helped them.
- *Perseverance.* Students won't ordinarily persevere at tasks that are difficult or boring, unless they have to. Speak with them about the importance of completing tasks. Have them complete something you assign every day and do not allow them to quit or change tasks.
- *Being a good role model for younger students.* Students learn many of their behaviors by watching people older than they, such as siblings, friends, parents, and teachers. Teach students to try to make a positive impression on younger students. Ask them to consider the effects of their words, jokes, body language, and conversational topics. Ask them to model compliance with school routines.
- *Being a good ambassador for your class and school.* Help students understand they are ambassadors for their school and class. When they behave well in public, people notice and conclude the students come from a good school and good family. Ask students to conduct themselves in that manner, to bring credit to themselves, the school, and their parents.

6. *Set the stage for quality instruction.* Discipline cannot succeed in an environment where students must endure boring, tedious lessons and activities. You must make your classes interesting and worthwhile. Ask questions that force students to expand their thinking. Increase the amount of hands-on activities. Make use of group learning activities. Include activities based on sports, music, drama, and crafts. Ask students to make presentations to the class and to younger students. Approaches such as these keep students interested and involved, which concomitantly reduces the incidence of misbehavior.

7. *Provide active, assertive supervision.* Good discipline requires that you take certain steps to forestall misbehavior. Remind students of rules and expectations ahead of time. Remind them of limits that might apply. Be specific and don't over-verbalize. Govern and correct small misbehaviors. Reinforce good social skills when you see them. Move briskly around the classroom. Talk briefly with various students if it does not interrupt their work. Let everyone see your presence. Move with a sense of purpose. Make eye contact with students.

8. *Enforcing rules and expectations.* Consequences for poor behavior are not very effective in getting students to conduct themselves properly. Yet, most teachers believe consequences are the basis of enforcement and use them as warnings. Students may or may not behave properly as a result. It is the teacher's ability to *require* good behavior that determines success. You must be willing to establish your natural authority and take charge of students. There is no game playing involved. Don't let them decide whether to comply with rules. Don't allow them to call you by your first name, talk back, run around the room, or throw things at each other. Teachers worry that some students will confront them about expectations and rule enforcement. You can avoid this by beginning with small infractions associated with courteous language or cleaning up after themselves. When they learn to comply on small matters, they will continue to do so with large matters. Meanwhile, connect with your students on a personal basis. Listen to them and take their concerns into account. Capitalize on their interests. Be understanding and supportive when a student is going through a hard time. Establish rapport, but combine it with insistence.

9. *Focus on prevention.* Real Discipline goes to lengths to prevent misbehavior. Discipline isn't as much what you do to students when they misbehave, as it is what you do in advance so they won't misbehave. Use the suggestions presented earlier for making classes interesting and engaging. Do not allow verbal put-downs. Discuss potential behavior situations with students and devise ways of avoiding the problems.

10. *Set high standards.* In Real Discipline, underachievement is not a student choice. It is the teacher's responsibility to see that it doesn't occur. Don't accept underachievement in any form, whether academic or social. When students do something inadequately or improperly, have them do it over again. Challenge your students and get them excited about improving everything they do in school.

11. *Treat parents as partners.* Keep parents informed about serious incidents and repetitive misbehavior involving their child, but don't worry parents with minor matters—take care of those in class. When you need to communicate with parents, do so personally if possible. Don't send notes. Suggest ways they might help the student do better in school, but never suggest punishment. Talk *with* parents, not down to them. Assure them you and they want the same thing—success for their child—and that you want to work together with them to make that happen.

Developing Teacher–Student Relationships

Teacher relationships with students are the single most important factor in classroom discipline. They determine how cooperative students will be and how they understand discipline and teacher expectations. Two teachers using identical discipline tactics may get vastly different results, simply because of the way students react to them personally. When students like their teacher and believe he or she likes and wants to help them, they will abide by most requests. If they do not like the teacher, they will be less than enthusiastic about cooperating.

If you can establish positive relationships with your students, they will understand that your discipline requirements are for their personal benefit as well as for the benefit of the class as a whole. They will understand that rules improve safety, security, and proper treatment. Students want to please teachers they like, and not disappoint them. Most teachers can establish this sort of relationship with their classes by emphasizing the following:

- *Consistently focus on the positive.* Look for things students do right, rather than things they do wrong. Show a genuine sense of understanding when they make mistakes and, in a positive manner, try to help them do better. It is much better to help than to criticize.

- *Wipe the slate clean after students make mistakes.* Deal with the mistake in a positive manner and move on. Don't hold grudges; they don't help in any way. The important thing is what the student does now, so help plan for success today and in the days to come.

- *Don't back away from discipline.* Students don't often say they appreciate discipline. They don't like having to obey rules, and they don't enjoy practicing appropriate behavior. Nevertheless, they understand that discipline is a teacher's role and they expect it. They will even appreciate it, especially later. They interpret the time and effort you expend as signs of concern for them.

- *Lead the way.* Students learn more from watching what you do than from hearing what you say. Model civilized behavior and attitudes. Listen to students. Speak kindly to them. Be helpful and give credit when it is due.

- *Never use humiliation in correcting misbehavior.* Morrish says teachers use humiliation more than they imagine, frequently unintentionally, as when they scold students in front of their friends or display work to show how it could have been done better. Whenever students need to be corrected, show them how to behave properly and have them practice until the behavior becomes habitual.

- *Don't accept mediocrity.* Some teachers never set adequate standards of learning and behavior for their classes, believing it better to befriend students to make them more cooperative. Standards are essential, however, if students are to recognize success and maintain their determination to improve. If you willingly accept mediocrity, that is what you will get. Your standards tell students you believe they are bright and sensitive enough to learn and behave properly.

Consequences in Real Discipline

Morrish believes that consequences, when structured and applied properly, help students learn to conduct themselves properly. First and foremost, consequences should show students how to behave correctly. When students speak discourteously, the consequence is for them to stop and speak again in a proper manner. Consequences are also applied when a student continues to push at the boundary of acceptable behavior. In that event, apply a consequence that stops the behavior. This is most often done to indicate clearly that "*no* means no."

Morrish says you should explain consequences and their use to your students, adjust them to students' level of development, and always try to use them to promote learning. He provides examples of such consequences (Morrish, 2000, p. 66).

- *Compensation.* Have the student do something positive to make up for negative behavior. This might include making the victim of bad behavior feel better or the school look better.
- *Letter writing.* Have the offending student write a letter to the person who was offended, including a statement of commitment for better behavior in the future.
- *Improvement plan.* Have the student make a plan for handling the situation better in the future. Keep track to ensure the student follows through.
- *Teach younger children.* Have the offending student write and illustrate a story about the incident to read to younger children, emphasizing what was done wrong and what was learned from the experience.

About Motivation and Rewards

Many experts in school discipline assert that we can't *make* students do anything—that the best we can do is provide an environment so appealing that students will engage in activities naturally. Certainly we can entice students much of the time, but it is ridiculous, says Morrish, to believe we cannot make students do anything. He insists that the very purpose of discipline is to make students do what they don't want to do. He points out that students ordinarily do not want to obey rules, don't want to stay quiet, don't want to do homework, don't want to study for tests, and so forth. The reason we discipline students is to help them learn to set aside their natural desires and accept educators' plans for helping them succeed in life.

Real Discipline does not rely on high natural motivation. Instead, it teaches students how to persevere and work through activities that are not especially appealing. To the extent you can make instructional activities interesting, please do so, and everyone will enjoy school more, including you. But when that is not possible, don't shy away from teaching students what they need to know, even when lessons are tedious.

Morrish also advises teachers to forego continually praising and rewarding students for doing what is expected of them in school. He says that occasional rewards are fine, because they give special recognition when it is needed, but that rewards are overused today, and students often see them as ends in themselves. You do have some powerful rewards at your disposal, but they are not stickers, points, or special privileges. Rather, they are what you always have with you—your personal attention and approval.

Praise is the reward teachers most often dispense. But we must be cautious of that, too. Teachers often fall into the habit of giving indiscriminate praise. As Morrish says, they spread it on as thick as jam on toast. Beyond a certain point, praise actually reduces motivation while increasing dependency. Students develop healthier attitudes when teachers reserve praise for work and behavior that is truly deserving of recognition.

Don't Promote Self-Indulgence

Many educators believe low self-esteem is the root cause of behavior problems. Morrish does not agree. He acknowledges that students who do poorly in school and get into trouble often have low self-esteem, whereas those who do well tend to have high self-esteem. But self-esteem does not determine success or failure. It is the other way around—success in school or lack thereof helps determine self-esteem. If you are competent and successful, you think better about yourself than if you are incompetent and unsuccessful.

Morrish goes on to say that teachers who work hard to build student self-esteem may actually do more harm than good, especially if they never allow failure, never put pressure on students to excel, and permit students to express themselves freely without fear of rebuke. They remove students from the helpful criticism that normally follows serious misbehavior. As a result, students become more self-indulgent. They gradually lose their sense of shame and begin to rationalize their misdeeds with explanations such as "I just felt like it. It made me feel good." As Morrish (1997) puts it:

> In the real world, the most likely result of attempting to raise self-esteem directly is that children will feel much better about themselves while they continue to misbehave.
>
> Genuine self-esteem does not grow in students who are allowed to do as they please. Rather, it comes from increased competence in academic and social matters and the ability to overcome obstacles. If we teach students academic and social skills, if we hold high expectations for them, we will see them come to think well of themselves, based on the reality of positive competence. The real hallmark of self-esteem is one's balanced view of personal competence in relation to the surrounding world. (p. 121)

When Students Fail to Comply

Occasionally a student may fail to comply with your directions or may, in the heat of the moment, revert to other inappropriate behavior. Suppose one of your students has behaved discourteously toward you in class. Many teachers, if the infraction is serious enough, will send the offending student to time-out for an indefinite period before allowing the student to rejoin the class. That does nothing positive for the student. Instead of time-out, you should insist on a **do-over.** Have the student repeat the behavior in an acceptable manner. If a student speaks to you in a disrespectful manner, tell him or her to start over and do it courteously this time. The same procedure applies any time a student fails to follow directions or comply with class standards.

Many teachers make the mistake of using "if-then" statements, such as, "If you speak to me in that manner again, then you will be going to the principal's office." Teachers should not use such statements with misbehaving students. They should give students no choice in the matter. They should say, "We don't speak that way in this class. Start over." Most of the time, that is all you need to do. Remember, your most important and powerful tool is insistence. You must convey to students they have no choice but to do as you instruct. Morrish says that students who are never required to act appropriately seldom will.

If a student still refuses to do as you direct, repeat your instruction in a serious tone of voice. If that doesn't work, use a mild punishment such as time-out to get across the message that you mean what you say. Then after a short time, bring the student back to the task correctly. The discipline procedure does not end with the time-out, however. The student is still expected to show proper behavior. Only positive practice ensures that result. Morrish says that most of the time when we punish students, it was unnecessary. We only needed to have them redo their behavior correctly.

Moving to Real Discipline

Morrish maintains that Real Discipline is the best approach for teaching the skills and attitudes students need in the twenty-first century. He wants us to teach students to be responsible, cooperative, courteous, and productive. He wants students to respect rules, authority, and the rights and needs of others. And he wants us to teach them how to make good choices as they develop the foundation for doing so.

Doing these things, Morrish contends, requires that we move in a new direction in discipline. We have tried to befriend students, treat them as equals, let them help make decisions, and make them happy. We thought they would respond in kind, but they haven't. It is now clear that this approach doesn't work. Instead, we should concentrate on training students so they can work well within the structures required by society. That means we must impose limits on self-defeating behavior so students can develop properly.

We have a job to do, and it takes time. There are no shortcuts. We need to look at discipline not as an event, but as a process that leads to cooperative and responsible behavior. Each day we should strive to help students do better than they did the day before. We should insist on it. Whether students seem to appreciate our efforts is of no major importance. The important thing is for them to respect our decisions.

Initiating Real Discipline in the Classroom

From the beginning, communicate to your students that, by training and profession, you are committed to providing a classroom in which they can learn easily, without threat or put-downs, and where everyone, teacher and students alike, courteously and willingly does the jobs expected of them. Tell them about duties in the class—what your job is and what their job is. You might explain that your role is to provide a quality learning environment, teach students the best you can, and treat everyone with respect and courtesy, and that their role is to follow your directions, do the best they can to learn, and treat everyone with respect and courtesy. Indicate how you will steadfastly help them make the most of their opportunities to learn. Inform them, using examples, why it is necessary they follow your directions every time. Show them how you will teach directions for simple activities, such as beginning work when entering the classroom and handing in homework or class assignments. Project an image of friendly authority. Then introduce the rules of behavior for the class. Discuss the rules thoroughly, making plain how the rules help everyone learn things they need to know in life. Tell the students you will insist they follow the rules, but you will teach them how to do so and always help them. Follow through and have students practice proper behavior. During the first days of school, ask in advance if students remember the rules for beginning work, having only school materials on their desks, and so forth.

KEY TERMS AND CONCEPTS EMPHASIZED IN THIS CHAPTER

Real Discipline
three phases of Real
  Discipline

compliance
rules
authority

insistence
do-over

SELECTED SEVEN—SUMMARY SUGGESTIONS FROM RONALD MORRISH

1. Strive for a balanced approach to discipline that includes student compliance, teaching of acceptable behavior, and gradual introduction of student choice.

2. Set and consistently enforce class rules that provide for safety, courtesy, work expectations, and good learning conditions.

3. Think in terms of prevention, the best way to reduce misbehavior.

4. Establish and maintain good personal relations with all your students.

5. Carefully teach students how you expect them to behave.

6. Don't bargain with students when it comes to standards of classroom behavior.

7. Use insistence and do-over as your main discipline tactics.

CONCEPT CASES

Case 1: Kristina Will Not Work

Kristina, a student in Mr. Jake's class, is quite docile. She socializes little with other students and never disrupts lessons. However, despite Mr. Jake's best efforts, Kristina will not do her work. She rarely completes an assignment. She is simply there, putting forth no effort at all. *What would Ronald Morrish suggest to help Kristina and Mr. Jake?*

    Morrish would have Mr. Jake remind Kristina of the class rule about everyone doing their best to learn. He would insist that Kristina begin her work and follow through. Mr. Jake might need to stand beside her to help

her get started. He would not punish her, but would continue to press her to comply with the assignment. He might ask questions such as, "Do you know what you are supposed to do in this activity?" "Do you understand why it needs to be done?" and "Can I count on you to do your part?" As Kristina improves, Mr. Jake might make comments to her such as, "You made a good effort today. I can see you are trying. Thank you for that." If more intervention was required, Morrish would consider assigning Kristina to the school's study hall or keeping her in the classroom for additional time (a productive extension of her day, rather than a punitive detention). He might also have her create a daily plan for accomplishing her school work, involve her parents in the process, or assign an older student to mentor her.

Case 2: Sara Cannot Stop Talking

Sara is a pleasant girl who participates in class activities and does most, though not all, of her assigned work. She cannot seem to refrain from talking to classmates, however. Her teacher, Mr. Gonzales, has to speak to her repeatedly during lessons, to the point that he often becomes exasperated and loses his temper. *What suggestions would Ronald Morrish give Mr. Gonzales for dealing with Sara?*

Case 3: Joshua Clowns and Intimidates

Joshua, larger and louder than his classmates, always wants to be the center of attention, which he accomplishes through a combination of clowning and intimidation. He makes wise remarks, talks back (smilingly) to the teacher, utters a variety of sound-effect noises such as automobile crashes and gunshots, and makes limitless sarcastic comments and put-downs of his classmates. Other students will not stand up to him, apparently fearing his size and verbal aggression. His teacher, Miss Pearl, has come to her wit's end. *Would Joshua's behavior be likely to improve if Morrish's techniques were used in Miss Pearl's classroom? Explain.*

Case 4: Tom Is Hostile and Defiant

Tom has appeared to be in his usual foul mood ever since arriving in class. On his way to sharpen his pencil, he bumps into Frank, who complains. Tom tells him loudly to shut up. Miss Baines, the teacher, says, "Tom, go back to your seat." Tom wheels around, swears loudly, and says heatedly, "I'll go when I'm damned good and ready!" *How would Ronald Morrish have Miss Baines deal with Tom?*

ACTIVITIES

1. Make entries in your journal concerning ideas from Morrish's Real Discipline that you might wish to include in your personal system of discipline.

2. Many schools are using discipline programs that combine the suggestions from Ronald Morrish and Harry Wong. Do you feel the two approaches are a natural fit? Explain, with examples. Share your conclusions with the class.

3. Ronald Morrish makes some interesting contentions about the role of student choice in discipline. Outline your understanding of his points and indicate whether you agree with them, and why. Discuss your conclusions in class.

YOU ARE THE TEACHER

High School Biology

You teach an advanced placement class in biology to students from middle- to upper-income families. Most of the students have already made plans for attending college. When the students enter the classroom, they know they are to go to their assigned seats and write out answers to the daily questions you have written on the board. After that, you conduct discussions on text material that you assigned students to read before coming to class. During the discussion, you call randomly on students to answer questions and require them to support their answers with reference to the assigned reading. Following the discussion, students engage in lab activity for the remainder of the period.

A Typical Occurrence

You have just begun a discussion about the process of photosynthesis. You ask Sarolyn what the word *photosynthesis* means. She pushes her long hair aside and replies, "I don't get it." This is a comment you hear frequently from Sarolyn, even though she is an intelligent girl. "What is it you don't understand?" "None of it," she says. You say, "Be more specific! I've only asked for the definition!" Sarolyn is not intimidated. "I mean, I don't get any of it. I don't understand why plants are green. Why aren't they blue or some other color? Why don't they grow on Mercury? The book says plants make food. How? Do they make bread? That's ridiculous." You gaze at Sarolyn for a while, and she back at you. You ask, "Are you finished?" Sarolyn shrugs. "I guess so." She hears some of the boys whistle under their breath; she obviously enjoys their attention. You say to her, "Sarolyn, I hope some day you will understand that this is not a place for you to show off." "I hope so, too," Sarolyn says. "I know I should be more serious." She stares out the window. For the remainder of the discussion, which you don't handle as well as usual, you call only on students you know will give proper answers. The discussion completed, you begin to give instructions for lab activity. You notice that Nick is turning the valve of the gas jet on and off. You say to Nick, "Mr. Contreras, would you please repeat our rule about the use of lab equipment?" Nick drops his head and mumbles something about waiting for directions. Sarolyn says calmly, "Knock it off, Nick. This is serious business." She smiles at you. After a moment, you complete your directions and tell the students to begin. You walk around the room, monitoring their work. You stand behind lab partners Mei and Teresa, who are having a difficult time. You do not offer them help, believing that advanced placement students should be able to work things out for themselves. But as they blunder through the activity, you find yourself shaking your head in disbelief.

Conceptualizing a Strategy

If you followed the suggestions of Ronald Morrish, what would you conclude or do with regard to the following?

1. Pinpointing the problems in your class.
2. Preventing the problems from occurring in the first place.
3. Putting an end to unwarranted misbehavior.
4. Maintaining student dignity and good personal relations.
5. Using the situation to help the students develop a sense of greater responsibility and self-control.

REFERENCES

Morrish, R. 1997. *Secrets of discipline: 12 keys for raising responsible children.* Fonthill, ON, Canada: Woodstream Publishing.

Morrish, R. 2000. *With all due respect: Keys for building effective school discipline.* Fonthill, ON, Canada: Woodstream Publishing.

Morrish, R. 2003. *FlipTips.* Fonthill, ON, Canada: Woodstream Publishing.

Morrish, R. 2005. What is Real Discipline? www.realdiscipline.com.

CHAPTER **14**

Discipline through Synergy and Reducing Causes of Misbehavior

Authoritative Input
■ C. M. Charles / The Synergetic Classroom

CHAPTER PREVIEW

This chapter presents C. M. Charles's views on the role that synergy—a mutually energizing phenomenon—can play in making classroom discipline more effective and pleasant for everyone. Charles contends that discipline programs are most effective when they (1) make provisions for meeting student needs, (2) emphasize conditions and activities that students find attractive, (3) eliminate or minimize conditions and activities that students generally dislike, and (4) foster ethics and trust among members of the class. In this chapter, Charles explains how discipline approaches of this type can be organized and implemented in the classroom.

Fundamental Hypothesis of Synergetic Discipline

Good classroom behavior is best established by teachers and students cooperating to meet individuals' needs in the classroom, minimize the causes of misbehavior, and, when appropriate, energize the class for greater enjoyment and easier learning.

The Nature and Practice of Synergetic Discipline

Synergetic Discipline is the behavior management portion of **Synergetic Teaching,** a way of teaching and working with students that produces quality learning and responsible behavior, while removing much of the job stress teachers normally experience. Synergetic Teaching and Discipline involve developing same-side cooperation between teacher and students, attending to known causes of misbehavior, focusing on student needs, energizing the class, and minimizing mistakes teachers sometimes make in relating with students. One of the strengths of Synergetic Teaching is its ability to increase motivation and enjoyment for everyone. No coercive measures are involved. Teachers gain the willing

About C. M. Charles

C. M. Charles began his career as a public school teacher and later held faculty appointments at the University of New Mexico, Teachers College Columbia University, Pepperdine University, Universidade do Maranhao, Brazil, and San Diego State University, where he is now Professor Emeritus. He directed innovative programs in teacher education at San Diego State and five times received outstanding professor and distinguished teaching awards. He served on various occasions as advisor in teacher education and curriculum to the governments of Peru and Brazil. He has authored twenty-seven books that have attracted wide audiences internationally, with translations into several foreign languages. Those having to do most directly with school discipline are *Teachers' Petit Piaget* (1972), *The Synergetic Classroom: Joyful Teaching and Gentle Discipline* (2000), *Essential Elements of Effective Discipline* (2002), *Classroom Discipline: Today's Best Strategies and Tactics* (2008), and *Building Classroom Discipline* (ninth edition, 2008).

Author's Note: This chapter contains many of my personal views on discipline. I include my views here for two reasons: First, many people have written over the years asking for my personal ideas about discipline and how I would implement them in the classroom. I think they—and you, if you are among them—deserve that consideration. Second, I believe strongly in the value of three of the main elements of Synergetic Discipline that are not given much attention in other discipline programs: (1) limiting the conditions that are known to foster student misbehavior; (2) using synergetic activities to energize the class, when appropriate to do so; and (3) identifying what might be called "teacher misbehavior" that requires attention. Synergetic Discipline is not a commercial program, nor am I affiliated with Synergetic Discipline in any way. If you are interested in Synergetic Discipline, you can find more information about it on my website, www.teacherweb.com/ca/sdsu/charles.

cooperation of students by meeting their needs in a helpful manner, communicating effectively, and treating students with respect. This is done within a sense of community that emphasizes ethical behavior.

Synergy and Synergetic Discipline

Synergy is a phenomenon in which two or more people (or other entities) interact in a manner that builds mutual energy. Among humans, that condition often leads to increased productivity, creativity, satisfaction, and enjoyment. This effect is seen when students get caught up in group spirit and strong sense of purpose, as typically occurs in athletic competitions, science fairs, dramatic productions, and the like. Teachers note that during episodes of synergy, discipline problems are largely nonexistent.

The following is a brief description of how you can implement Synergetic Teaching and Discipline in your classroom; the remainder of this chapter explains these suggestions further:

1. Invite your students sincerely to work with you in maintaining an interesting, inviting program for learning, one that is free from fear and based on personal dignity and consideration for others.

2. Involve your students in discussing the details of your discipline plan and listen to suggestions they might have. Make sure they understand what it involves, what their responsibilities are, and what your responsibilities are.
3. Discuss and demonstrate conditions that elevate class spirit and energy. Ask the class continually to help identify topics and activities they find appealing.
4. Discuss student (and teacher) misbehavior, how it is manifested, why it is detrimental to learning, and the factors that are known to foster it. Ask students to work with you to eliminate or reduce those factors.

Establishing Conditions that Elevate Class Spirit and Energy

Synergetic Teaching depends on maintaining student interest and good personal relations. All of us seek out people, places, objects, situations, and activities we like. Similarly, we avoid people, places, objects, situations, and activities that we dislike. The following paragraphs focus on what students typically like and dislike and what you should do accordingly. This information is distilled from contributions made by Steve Biddulph (1997), Cynthia Mee (1997), William Glasser (1998a, 1998b), Jean Piaget (2001), Harry Wong (2001), and a number of experienced teachers and school administrators.

Discuss and Take into Account Student Needs

Briefly discuss with your class the predominant needs we all share. Go through the following list of **basic student needs** and reassure students that you will take these needs fully into account in the class. (Of course, adjust the discussion to your students' developmental level.)

- *Security.* A sense of safety without worry
- *Hope.* The belief that school is worthwhile and success is possible
- *Dignity.* Feeling respected and worthwhile
- *Belonging.* Feeling a part of things, being valued, and having a place in the class
- *Power.* Having some control of and input into events in the class
- *Enjoyment.* Finding pleasure in activities that are stimulating or rewarding
- *Competence.* Becoming able to do many things well, including the expected schoolwork

Point out that both students and teachers become uncomfortable when these needs are not being met at school, and that their discomfort reduces enjoyment, learning, and willingness to try their best. Reassure your students that you will reduce or eliminate topics and activities they clearly do not like or that affect them adversely, and that you will not permit anything in the class to damage their sense of safety and security. The same will be true for their sense of belonging and hope.

Emphasize Class Conditions and Activities Students Are Known to Like

Inform your students that with their help you will strive for the following in the classroom:

- A teacher who is friendly, interesting, helpful, and supportive
- Camaraderie—enjoyable associations among class members
- Students understanding the importance of what they are asked to learn
- Interesting topics to learn about that are intriguing and worthwhile
- Enjoyable instructional activities
- Opportunity for, and likelihood of, success and accomplishment
- Attention that is drawn tactfully to student accomplishments

Also discuss with students some of the things they normally dislike in school, as listed below. Indicate that you will guard against this things. Note, however, that some students do not object to all of these activities or conditions—you might wish to ask their opinions about them. Also ask students about situations in which some of these conditions might be necessary.

- Sitting still for long periods
- Keeping quiet for long periods
- Working by oneself
- Not knowing why something is being taught or learned
- Memorizing facts for tests
- Completing lengthy writing assignments
- Doing repetitive work
- Completing long reading assignments
- Engaging in individual competition in which there is little or no chance of winning
- Having little or no choice in activities, assignments, or assessment

Work to Develop Class Ethics and Trust

Ethics refers to doing what one believes to be the honorable thing in all situations. Ethical student behavior should be a prime goal of education, and ethical *teacher* behavior, needed as a model for students to emulate, is essential for building **trust** in the class. Students see teachers as ethical and trustworthy if they are invariably kind, considerate, helpful, fair, and tactfully honest. Trust is essential in Synergetic Discipline, as it enables teachers and students to count on each other for support and fair treatment.

Emphasize and Use Your Personal Charisma

Charisma is an aspect of personality that attracts others. Students greatly enjoy charismatic teachers and flock to them. Charisma seems to emerge from a blend of talent, experience, knowledge, and understanding of others, and it is made evident in how people react to each other. We can all increase our level of charisma and display it through personal charm, friendliness, enthusiasm, and helpfulness.

Improve the Quality of Communication in Your Classroom

Except for trust, no element of synergy is more important than communication. The type of communication that contributes most to synergy is verbal give-and-take between teacher and students. It involves listening sensitively, showing genuine interest, and speaking encouragingly rather than arguing, moralizing, or giving unsolicited advice.

Make Use of Coopetition

Coopetition, pronounced "co-opetition," refers to members of groups cooperating together in order to compete against other groups. Coopetition is not given a great deal of direct attention in teaching, but it contributes powerfully to synergy. In school, it is exemplified in team athletic events and other performances and competitions. Coopetition can be incorporated into almost all areas of the curriculum. Generally speaking, students respond to it more enthusiastically than to any other activity.

Resolve Class Problems and Conflicts Amicably and Productively

A class **problem** is a situation or condition that affects the class seriously enough to require attention, whereas a **conflict** is a strong disagreement between students or between teacher and student.

How to Address Problems

Suppose students in a high school geometry class are troubled by a heavy load of homework. Or suppose a middle school teacher is greatly embarrassed when the principal visits and finds the room very untidy. When such situations hinder teaching or learning, for any reason, they should be addressed immediately. The teacher, sensing the problem, might say, "Class, something is going on that I think we need to talk about." The problem is then clarified, possible solutions are sought, and a solution is selected and tried.

How to Address Conflicts

Conflicts are interpersonal situations characterized by strong disagreements, which may or may not include misbehavior. If the individuals involved do not know how to find a peaceful solution, they tend to fight each other verbally, or sometimes physically. Conflict threatens personal dignity, which is strongly defended. Examples of conflict situations include disputes over who won a contest, who is entitled to play with a toy, whether work was turned in on time, and whether work has met the standards expected. Conflict is best resolved through a win-win approach in which both sides feel most of their concerns are being properly addressed. To resolve conflicts in your class, do the following:

- Make sure all individuals involved have the opportunity to express their concerns.
- Insist that all comments, observations, and suggestions are presented in a courteous manner.
- Encourage both sides to be open and honest, but tactful.
- Encourage each person to try to see things from the other's point of view.
- Keep attention focused on areas of agreement between the disputants.
- Help disputants formulate solutions as joint agreements.
- Do not allow students to argue back and forth, defend themselves, or debate.

Addressing the Causes of Student Misbehavior

The single best way to limit misbehavior is to do what you can to prevent it from occurring. This is done by attending, proactively, to the known **causes of misbehavior,** meaning conditions that tend to foster inappropriate behavior. Generally speaking, we can identify twenty-five causes of (or conditions that promote) student behavior. Those causes lead to thirteen types of student behavior usually identified as misbehavior, inappropriate behavior, or irresponsible behavior. The thirteen types of student misbehavior are *inattention, apathy, needless talk, moving about the room without permission, annoying others, disruption, lying, stealing, cheating, sexual harassment, bullying and fighting, malicious mischief,* and *defiance of authority.* In the paragraphs that follow, many causes of such misbehavior are reviewed. Teachers can control most of the causes, which are grouped here in accordance with where they seem to reside or originate.

Causes of Misbehavior that Reside in Individual Students

Nine causes of misbehavior reside within individual students: unmet needs, thwarted desires, expediency, urge to transgress, temptation, inappropriate habits, poor behavior choices, avoidance, and egocentric personality.

Unmet Needs

In the classroom, students continually try to meet needs related to security, belonging, hope, dignity, power, enjoyment, and competence. When any of these needs is not being satisfied, students become unsettled, distracted, and more inclined to misbehave.

Teacher Action. By observing students and talking with them, you can identify most student needs and help students meet them in an acceptable manner.

Thwarted desires

When students fail to get something they want badly, they may complain, become destructive, sulk, pout, or act out.

Teacher Action.   Tell students you can see they are troubled or distracted. Ask if there is anything you can do to help. Be sympathetic, but don't dwell on the problem. Try to get them interested in something else.

Expediency

Students always look for ways to make their lives easier and more enjoyable. They take shortcuts, conveniently forget what they are supposed to do, look for ways to get out of work, and intentionally break rules.

Teacher Action.   Expedient behavior is seldom a problem in classes that are interesting and enjoyable, but it appears often in classes that are dull and boring. Hold discussions about expediency and its troublesome effects. Ask students why they sometimes take the easy way, such as reading book summaries or reviews rather than the assigned book, rushing through a writing assignment, or copying others' ideas. If they are comfortable enough to answer honestly, they will probably say they do so because they don't like the work, don't see the point in it, or don't want to spend time on it. Ask them what would encourage them to give their best effort. Listen to their suggestions and make use of them if you can.

Urge to Transgress

All of us feel the urge to transgress rules and regulations and we often do so, knowing there is a chance we will get caught or even harm ourselves or others. Students succumb to this urge frequently, especially when class activities are not appealing, and they cheat, take shortcuts, tell lies, break class rules, and annoy others, seemingly for no beneficial purpose at all.

Teacher Action.   Discuss this urge, its effects, and how it can be controlled sensibly. Discuss the reasons for rules, including how they equalize opportunity, reduce potential harm, and help us live together harmoniously. If students are old enough, ask if they understand what ethics, ethical conduct, and personal character mean. Ask why they think ethical people are so widely admired.

Temptation

Students regularly encounter objects, situations, behaviors, and people they find powerfully attractive. This phenomenon is evident in association with music and lyrics, desirable objects, ways of speaking, styles of clothing, lifestyle, and cheating on tests and assignments. Although pursuit of these temptations can result in mild or severe misbehavior, students nevertheless find them so attractive they will occasionally do, adopt, mimic, acquire, or associate with them, even though forbidden to do so.

Teacher Action. With your students, discuss and analyze temptation, seeking to understand why certain objects, styles, and opportunities are so seductive. Help students foresee the undesirable consequences of following disapproved styles and manners. Help them clarify the lines that separate the approved from the disapproved and reinforce their resolve to resist factors that are likely to harm them.

Inappropriate Habits

Inappropriate habits are ingrained ways of behaving that violate established standards and expectations. Jason uses profanity at school. Maria is discourteous and calls others names. Larry shirks his assignments. Some of these habits are learned in school, but most become established in the home or community.

Teacher Action. Bring inappropriate habits to students' attention without pointing a finger at anyone. Discuss their harmful effects and, if necessary, have students practice desirable alternatives to habits such as name-calling, teasing, verbal put-downs, cheating, lying, and disregard for others.

Poor Behavior Choices

The behaviors students use in attempting to meet their needs are sometimes acceptable, sometimes not. Levels of acceptability may not be clear to students. Alicia, trying to get attention, annoys others so much they avoid her. Alan, seeking an increased sense of power, refuses to do what his teacher requests.

Teacher Action. Alicia and Alan need to understand that their behavior choices are detrimental to themselves or others. To help students such as Alicia and Alan, ask the class: "What are some of the things you have seen students do to [get attention, be acknowledged, get better grades than they deserve, get out of work, become members of groups, etc.]? Does their behavior usually get them what they want? What could those students do that would probably bring better results?"

Avoidance

No one likes to face failure, intimidation, ridicule, or other unpleasant situations and treatment. One way to escape them is to avoid situations where they might occur, but in school we can't always do that. Consider Norona, who refuses to participate in a group assignment. Her refusal seems to show disrespect for the teacher, but in reality, she is intimidated by her peers and doesn't want them to think she is inept.

Teacher Action. To help students such as Norona behave advantageously in circumstances they dislike, show them how to face unpleasant situations and work through them. Rather than singling out Norona, ask the following in a group discussion: "Are there things you try to avoid in school, such as people, events, or activities you find frightening or embarrassing? Which of those things could best be dealt with through avoidance (e.g., a clique that is maligning other students)? Which of those things cannot be dealt with through avoidance (e.g., giving an oral report in front of the class)? What is the worst thing that can happen in class if we make a mistake? Can mistakes help us learn? What could a person do to reduce fear of mistakes or unpleasant situations?" Consider exploring these ideas in pairs, then small groups, then the class as a whole.

Egocentric Personality

Students with egocentric personalities focus primarily on themselves, believe they are superior to others, and think they do little wrong. Most classes contain one or more such students.

Teacher Action.   To help these students behave more appropriately, ask questions such as the following in class discussions: "Are the needs and interests of all students important, or do only certain students deserve attention? Is one person often entirely right and everyone else entirely wrong? Is everyone entitled to an equal opportunity in the class? How should you and I react to a person who always wants to dominate, be first, be right, and quarrel with those who don't agree?" Make sure the proffered suggestions are positive in nature, not negative.

Causes of Misbehavior that Reside in Class Peers and Groups

Two significant causes of misbehavior reside in class peers and groups—provocation and group behavior. Here are suggestions for dealing with them.

Provocation

A great amount of school misbehavior results from students' provoking each other through petty annoyance, put-downs, sarcastic remarks, and aggression or bullying. Heather is trying to study, but Art's incessant chatter frustrates her to the bursting point. Marty calls Jerry a name and Jerry responds hotly. Randall is trying to pay attention but Larry keeps poking him in the back with a pencil.

Teacher Action.   Provocation often produces strong emotions that reduce self-control and increase combativeness. Discuss this phenomenon with your class. Ask: "Can you name some things people say or do that upset you so much you want to retaliate? How do you feel when this happens? If you retaliate, is it likely to improve the situation or make it worse? What might you do that would resolve the incident peacefully? Is provoking others or bullying them consistent with the class character we are trying to build? Would you act that way if the teacher were standing beside you?"

Group Behavior

Students often succumb to peer pressure or get caught up in group emotion, and as a result may misbehave in ways they would not if they were by themselves. It is difficult for students to disregard peer pressure, easy for them to get swept up in group energy and emotion, and easy for them to justify their misbehavior as only what others were doing. Because Kerry and Lee want to look cool to their peers, Kerry defaces school property, and

Lee bullies a weaker member of the class, even though Kerry and Lee would not do those things if by themselves.

Teacher Action.   Try the following techniques to discuss this phenomenon with your class:

- Tell the class about some event in which a friend of yours, let's say Sarah, behaved badly just because others were doing so. Indicate that Sarah is now very embarrassed about her behavior and wishes no one knew about it.
- Ask your students if they know any stories like Sarah's they can share, without mentioning names the class might recognize. (Tell them they must not mention family matters or members—doing so is a sure way to get parents upset at you.) If they share stories, guide the class in analyzing one or two of them. If they don't contribute a story, have a fictional one ready for their consideration. After hearing or recounting the story, ask questions such as the following:

> Is the behavior something the person will be proud of later?
>
> Why do you suppose the person behaved that way? (e.g., for fun, comradeship, to test limits, to be seen as clever or "cool")
>
> What do you think the long-term results will be for the person? (e.g., an unpleasant story to remember, regret, guilt, getting caught, being found out, worry, disappointing one's family, possible punishment, living with knowing you did the wrong thing)
>
> How do you think the possible benefits compare with the probable harmful effects?
>
> Once you do something you are ashamed of, is there any way to make amends?
>
> How can you stay away from, or keep out of, group activities that are unlawful, unethical, or against the rules?

Causes of Misbehavior that Reside in Instructional Environments

Four causes of misbehavior reside in instructional environments and all can be corrected easily—physical discomfort, tedium, meaninglessness, and lack of stimulation.

Physical Discomfort

Students often become restless when made uncomfortable by inappropriate temperature, poor lighting, or unsuitable seating or workspaces.

Teacher Action.   Attend to comfort factors in advance and ask students about them. Make corrections as necessary.

Tedium

Students are likely to begin to fidgeting after a while when an instructional activity requires them to pay close attention for a long time, especially if the topic is not appealing.

Teacher Action.   Break the work into shorter segments or add something that increases the interest level.

Meaninglessness

Students grow restless when required to work at topics they do not comprehend or for which they see no purpose.

Teacher Action.   Make sure the topic is meaningful to students—that they understand it and see its relevance and importance in their lives.

Lack of Stimulation

Students take no interest in the lesson when the topic and learning environment provide little that is attractive or otherwise stimulating.

Teacher Action.   Select topics and activities in which students have natural interest. When that is not possible, introduce elements students are known to enjoy, such as novelty, mystery, movement, competition, group work, and role-playing.

Causes of Misbehavior that Reside in Teachers and Other School Personnel

We must honestly recognize that teachers sometimes misbehave in the classroom. Other personnel at school do so as well, including administrators, librarians, clerical staff, health personnel, cafeteria personnel, custodial personnel, and family members working in the school. The following ten factors within school personnel sometimes promote student misbehavior:

Poor Habits

Personnel in the schools have sometimes unknowingly acquired counterproductive ways of speaking to or dealing with students. They may have become set in these ways.

Teacher Action.   Watch closely to see how students react to you and other school personnel. Do they seem friendly? Wary? Eager to cooperate? Reticent? If they are reticent, fearful, uncooperative, or unfriendly, analyze the situations you observe and see if you can determine the problem. Correct your own behavior, should that be necessary, but be careful about approaching colleagues with criticism.

Unfamiliarity with Better Techniques

Some educators have not had occasion to learn some of the newer, more effective ways of teaching and relating with today's students.

Teacher Action.   If you feel you might be less than well-informed, ask students about things school people do that they really like. Notice what popular teachers at your school do, and don't be reluctant to request ideas from them. Your school may keep a library of professional books and journals. You can also access dozens of sites through the Internet that present outstanding ideas and suggestions.

Presenting Poor Models of Behavior

At times all of us are inconsistent, irresponsible, and short on self-control, and we sometimes treat students with discourtesy or disregard. We can't expect to be perfect, but we must realize that when we treat students poorly—which is to say, in ways we would not want to be treated—we not only damage relationships but also encourage students to imitate our poor behavior.

Teacher Action.   Always be the best model you can for your students, who watch you very closely and often pattern their behavior after yours (especially when you misbehave). If you do anything inappropriate, call attention to it, explain why it was wrong, and apologize if necessary.

Showing Little Interest in or Appreciation for Students

We sometimes fail to show interest in students or appreciation for them as individuals, despite knowing they want our attention. If we disregard them repeatedly, students become hesitant or may disruptively seek our attention.

Teacher Action.   Give each student as much personal attention as possible. Greet them personally, exchange a friendly word, show you are aware of their difficulties, try to help them feel at ease, and acknowledge their progress.

Succumbing to Personal Frustration

Some educators are beaten down from continually having to deal with misbehavior or inconsiderate parents. The stress may make it difficult for them to work with students in a kind, helpful manner.

Teacher Action.   Educators often experience intense frustration from trying unsuccessfully to force students to comply with their expectations. Force does not work. Replace it with encouragement and enticement and you will see your students become cooperative, willing to learn, and considerate. Go out of your way to communicate with parents and show appreciation for their child.

Succumbing to Provocation

Students may do and say things intentionally to get under your skin, hoping to see you become upset and befuddled and perhaps lose self-control.

Teacher Action.   Do not allow students to provoke you. When they try to do so, disregard their comments and actions and proceed as if nothing has happened. If you feel it necessary to respond, say, "Something is causing violations of our agreement about being considerate of others. I don't understand why. Is there something we can do to fix the problem?"

Providing Ineffective Guidance and Feedback

In the absence of guidance and feedback, students sometimes do not understand what is expected of them, how much progress they have made, or how they can improve.

Teacher Action.   Make sure students understand clearly what they are supposed to do and how they should do it. During and after assigned activities, tell students what they have done well or poorly and indicate how they can improve. Ask them for their opinions about the activity and their efforts.

Using Ineffective Personal Communication

Some educators are not adept at communicating with students on a personal level. This may cause students to become uneasy and reticent.

Teacher Action.   Speak regularly with students in a friendly way. Students want you to know their names and exchange pleasantries with them. They sometimes want to know your views on various matters, and want to tell you theirs. This provides them a measure of personal validation. Avoid comments that hurt feelings or dampen enthusiasm. Say things that increase optimism and bolster confidence. Build students up when you can, but do so honestly.

Failure to Plan Proactively

Many educators do not plan ahead adequately to foresee potential problems. Then, when unexpected events occur, they are unable to respond effectively.

Teacher Action.   Think carefully about problems that might arise in class or about possible student reactions to topics, lessons, your requests, or unexpected events. By anticipating potential difficulties, you can avoid most problems and can prepare yourself to deal with whatever might eventuate. Think through what you will do when people are injured or become suddenly ill, grow defiant, or get into fights. Decide what you will do and say if an unauthorized visitor approaches you, if a parent berates you, if the class moans when you make an assignment, and so forth. Determine how you can respond decisively to such eventualities, yet maintain positive relationships.

Using Coercion, Threat, and Punishment

Students don't like to be forced to do anything and they don't like to be threatened. If you treat them abrasively, they keep a watchful eye on you, fearful of being scolded, embarrassed, or demeaned, and will very likely develop negative attitudes toward you and school.

Teacher Action.   Give up coercion and threat and replace them with considerate helpfulness, personal attention, and good communication.

Recognizing and Correcting Teacher Misbehavior

Despite our dedication and concern for students, teachers sometimes do or say things that provoke antagonism, inhibit student progress, and leave the class dispirited. Five types of **teacher misbehavior** should be acknowledged: *inducing fearfulness, denigrating students, being demanding and abrasive, presenting poor models of behavior,* and *not making classes interesting and worthwhile.* When we misbehave in these ways, it is usually because we are fearful of losing control of our classes or because we simply do not know how to use positive tactics that work well. Do what you can to make sure you are not guilty of such misbehavior. Think back at the end of each day and judge yourself against the misbehaviors listed above. If you need to improve, work on one of the behaviors each day until you get it right. Tell your students what you are doing and ask for their feedback.

Establishing a Discipline Plan with Your Class

On the first day of class begin discussing with your students how the class is to function and how members can conduct themselves to achieve greatest personal and class benefit. Tell your students that everyone, including you, is expected to show consideration for others in the class and not do or say anything that will hurt others' feelings or interfere with their work. You should have already thought through a desirable discipline approach carefully, but rather than presenting your plan as a fait accompli on the first day, lead students into it gradually by asking a series of questions, adjusted to their maturity level. When done as suggested here, the process requires six short sessions that, ideally, should begin the first day of class and be completed in six consecutive days. Expect to use about 10 minutes per session for young children, and about 15 minutes for older students. Consider having your students sit in a closed circle and explain that a circular seating arrangement will be used when the class needs to have class meetings to discuss matters that concern everyone.

Session 1

Begin to establish rapport with your students. Smile. Look into their faces. Tell them you are pleased to see them and are looking forward to working with them. Tell them you want to discuss with them some ideas for making the class enjoyable and useful, but first you want to begin getting acquainted with them. Call their names and ask if you have pronounced them correctly. Tell students just a little bit about yourself, including your special interests and why you became a teacher. Then tell the students you'd like to learn more about them. Using the class roster, call on a few individual students. As appropriate to their age, ask a question or two about siblings, pets, hobbies, and special interests. Call on as many as time allows and end the session by saying you will get to know all of them very soon.

Session 2

Tell the students you are dedicated to helping them learn and have an enjoyable time in school. To make sure that happens, you would like to hear their ideas about some matters that might make the school year more enjoyable. Ask the following and take notes on a chart (e.g., on an easel or overhead display):

- Ask what some of the things are that they like best about school. List their comments on the left side of the chart. They will probably mention playing, being with friends, sports, art, and music. Some may mention plays, concerts, and athletics.
- Ask what they like, specifically, about each of the things you've written on the chart. Write these notes on the right side of the chart.
- Ask if they think any of the things they've mentioned might be possible in this class. Circle the things they indicate.

Thank them for their contributions and tell them you will do what you can, with their help, to make the class as they would prefer it to be, although there are many things the school requires that are outside your control.

Session 3

Give feedback concerning the suggestions students made in Session 2. Before the meeting, revise the chart to indicate the suggestions you consider appropriate for the class. Ask students if they have further thoughts or suggestions. Turn to a fresh page or new transparency and elicit comments about the kind of teacher they prefer.

- Ask if they have had a teacher they really enjoyed or respected (ask them not to mention names). Have the students indicate what that teacher did that made such a good impression. They will say things such as nice, interesting, helpful, fair, and good sense of humor. They may also mention favorite activities and special teacher talents. Write the traits they mention on the left side of the chart.
- Review the traits with the class. Ask for examples, such as what is meant by "helpful" or "really fun." Make these notes on the right side of the chart.
- Tell students that all teachers and all students are different, but that as much as you can, you will try to be the kind of teacher they prefer. Tell them you will think more about their comments and will give them feedback at the next session. Thank them for their helpfulness.

Session 4

Show students a clean chart of the preferred traits they have identified in teachers. Ask if they have additional comments. Tell them you have been thinking about how you can be the kind of teacher they want. If you know you can't do so in every respect, tell them so, and why. Next, draw students out about how they feel they should behave in the class.

- Ask students to think of a classmate who has behaved in class in ways they admired or appreciated (ask them not to mention names). Have them tell what the student was like or what he or she did. List the descriptions on the left side of a clean chart.
- When several behaviors have been listed, go back and ask students *why* they appreciated those behaviors. Make notes accordingly.
- Now ask students how they like for other members of a class to treat them. Make notes. Go back and once more ask *why*.
- Next, ask what kind of behavior they most appreciate from other students when they are working together on assignments. Ask why and make notes.
- Finally, ask students if they understand the meaning of *personal responsibility* and what it involves. Discuss that concept briefly. Ask them if they think it would be possible to have, in this classroom, the kinds of responsible behavior they have discussed. Thank them for their input and tell them you will review their suggestions at the next session.

Session 5

Provide a review of behaviors the students have indicated they like and appreciate. Ask if they have further comments.

- Now ask what they *dislike* fellow students doing in class. Ask if they have any ideas *why* students behave in ways others do not like. (If they do not, mention a few of the major causes of misbehavior.)
- Then ask if they have ideas about what we, as a class, can do to keep those unwanted behaviors from occurring—that is, how we can prevent them.
- Ask students if they feel they have control over how they, themselves, behave in the class. Follow with, "What makes you decide whether to behave responsibly or irresponsibly?" Ask them if they feel they can almost always behave responsibly in class, for their own sake and for the good of the class.

Thank the students for their input and tell them you will provide feedback later.

Session 6

Ask students to respond to a summary you have made of their suggestions. Show them a display that lists their contributions concerning (1) things students like best in school, (2) traits appreciated in teachers, (3) behaviors appreciated in classmates, and (4) behaviors disliked in classmates. Once you have done that, show them an outline of the discipline plan you wish to implement in the classroom. Indicate where their suggestions fit into the plan. It is suggested that your plan make specific mention of:

- Desirable and responsible teacher behavior
- Desirable and responsible student behavior
- Things that will be done to remove or limit "causes" of misbehavior
- What you will do to help students behave responsibly when they have made behavior mistakes (have behaved irresponsibly)

Ask the class what they think of the plan and if they can commit themselves to living with its stipulations. Thank them for their cooperation. By the next day, have the discipline plan outlined and printed. Give a copy to each student and ask them to share the plans with parents or guardians. Also prepare a chart of the plan and post it in the classroom.

Intervening When Students Misbehave

Synergetic Discipline emphasizes prevention of misbehavior, but it can also deal effectively with misbehavior when it occurs. For your consideration, four types of interventions are presented here, sequenced from mildest to strongest. You might wish to consider them, modifying them in your mind to suit a particular age of students.

First Intervention

Subtly remind students of expected behavior. Do this with physical proximity, eye signals, or facial expressions. If these reminders don't work, point to the chart that shows responsible behavior and say, "Class, let's please remember what it means to behave responsibly."

Second Intervention

If it seems advisable, identify what you believe is causing the misbehavior. The cause may be apparent, as when students seem to find the lesson boring and therefore disengage from it, or it may be obscure, as when Jason and Nathan continue an emotional dispute that originated outside the classroom. Even if you think you know the cause, check with students to obtain their view. For example, ask, "Is this too boring for you?" or "Boys, is there a problem I can help you with?" or "Something is causing us to be inconsiderate of others. What do you suppose is causing that? Can we fix it? What can we do that would show greater responsibility?" Then address the cause if you can. You can usually remove it easily if it resides in activities, classroom, or teacher behavior. You can minimize its effects when it involves student needs, simply by trying to provide what students are seeking. It is more difficult to limit causes that have to do with egocentric personalities. You can say privately, "Jason, something is causing you to call out and disrupt the lesson. That makes it difficult for me to teach and for other students to learn. Can you help me understand what is causing you to do that so we might make things better for you?"

Third Intervention

Ask the misbehaving student to suggest how he or she might behave in a more responsible manner. If there is any hesitation on the student's part, make a direct suggestion, such as, "Let's keep our hands to ourself. Will you do that for me, please?" or "Let's start again and find a more responsible way of acting. May I show you once more what is expected of you? Thank you."

Fourth Intervention

If the misbehavior involves, or leads to, a confrontational dispute, help those involved identify the cause of the disagreement and work together to find a solution. *If the confrontation is between students,* as when Jason and Nathan are speaking angrily to each other, consider the following: Ask, "Boys, this is disturbing the class. Can you work the problem out between yourselves, or do you need my help?" If they say they can work it out, ask them if they can keep their dispute from affecting the class. If the boys can't resolve the matter, get together with them at a suitable time and in a nonthreatening manner to help them. Consider the following:

- Ask each to tell you calmly what is troubling them. (Explain that you need to hear each person clearly, so they should not interrupt or argue while the other is talking.)
- Ask Jason what he would like for Nathan to do differently. Nathan listens carefully.
- Ask Nathan what he would like for Jason to do differently. Jason listens carefully.
- Ask each of the boys if he feels he could do part, or most, of what the other wants.
- If they agree on a possible solution, thank them and leave it at that. If they cannot reach a solution, ask them if they'd mind having the class discuss the matter to learn more about resolving disputes considerately.
- If they agree to that, bring up the matter at the next class meeting. If they decline permission, say, "Boys, it is not good for any of us in the class when bad feelings exist. How can we resolve this matter so both of you feel all right? What ideas do you have?" If they reach a settlement, thank them. If they can't, say," I'm disappointed we can't settle this matter so both of you feel all right. But since we can't, I need to ask you to control yourselves, for the sake of the class." It is unlikely that the conflict negotiations will ever reach this point; the boys will agree to a solution earlier in the process.

If the conflict is between you and a student, consider the following: When you are helping a misbehaving student, your efforts will seldom lead to conflict provided you treat the student with consideration. If conflict occurs, you need to deal with it in a way that brings resolution while preserving positive feelings. Suppose Melissa has once again failed to do her homework. You ask her kindly if there is a problem that is preventing her from complying with the class expectation. Your question strikes a nerve and Melissa retorts, "There wouldn't be a problem if you didn't assign this stupid stuff!" What do you do? Consider saying, "Melissa, can you help me understand why you feel the homework is stupid? I'd like your opinion because I want it to be helpful to your progress. What can you suggest that would help make it better?" Melissa may apologize, say nothing, come back with another snide remark, or give you a suggestion. If she says nothing or remains uncooperative, consider saying, "Now is not a good time for us to discuss the matter. Perhaps we can do so later, just the two of us. Could you meet with me for a minute or two at [name a time and place]?" When you meet, tell her you are willing to listen if she has something she needs to talk about. If she declines, assure her you are interested in her views and are always ready to help. If Melissa apologizes or explains her feelings or talks about some other problem in her life that is probably her real cause of concern, consider saying, "Thank you, Melissa, for informing me. If I can make some changes in the homework or otherwise help with your situation, I'd like to do so. I'll listen to any suggestions you might have."

KEY TERMS AND CONCEPTS EMPHASIZED IN THIS CHAPTER

Synergetic Discipline
Synergetic Teaching
synergy
basic student needs

ethics
trust
charisma
coopetition

problem
conflict
causes of misbehavior
teacher misbehavior

SELECTED SEVEN—SUMMARY SUGGESTIONS FROM SYNERGETIC DISCIPLINE

1. Do what you can to make your class responsive to and compatible with student needs.

2. Energize your class through interesting activities, good communication, and your personal charisma.

3. Involve students in identifying and reflecting on desirable and responsible behavior in the classroom.

4. Address causes of misbehavior, identify them, and discuss them with your students. Explore with students how the causes can be minimized and behavior improved.

5. Guard against teacher misbehavior that induces fearfulness, denigrates students, or presents poor models of behavior.

6. Teach students how to resolve conflicts on their own.

7. When misbehavior occurs, deal with it in a helpful, nonconfrontive manner. Show continual willingness to try to correct whatever is troubling the students.

CONCEPT CASES

Case 1. Kristina Will Not Work

Kristina, a student in Mr. Jake's class, is quite docile. She socializes little with other students and never disrupts lessons. However, despite Mr. Jake's best efforts, Kristina will not do her work. She rarely completes an assignment. She is simply there, putting forth no effort at all. *How would Charles deal with Kristina?*

Charles would advise Mr. Jake to do the following: First, Mr. Jake should quickly appraise Kristina's efforts and general demeanor, to see if he can determine why Kristina is not working. Then in a quiet, friendly tone, he might say, "Kristina, I see this work is not getting done. We have agreed that we will always try to do our best in this class. Is there something about the assignment that bothers you?" If she indicates a difficulty, such as the work being too hard or a lack of understanding, Mr. Jake could reply, "What do you think might help?" or "Is there something I could do to help you get started?" Kristina will most likely begin working. If she does not,

Mr. Jake could say, "Kristina, I think this work is important and I want to help you get it done. Would you like to try [lists two options, such as working with another student to complete the assignment or doing an alternative assignment]?" In the unlikely possibility this still doesn't get Kristina started, Mr. Jake might say, "Kristina, I want to do everything possible to help you enjoy the class and learn successfully. I know I can't make you learn if you don't want to. Frankly, I'm not sure what to suggest now. Can you think of anything?" If she cannot, ask if she would allow the class to discuss the situation in a class meeting, as a way to make it easier for every student to learn.

Case 2. Sara Cannot Stop Talking

Sara is a pleasant girl who participates in class activities and does most, though not all, of her assigned work. She cannot seem to refrain from talking to classmates, however. Her teacher, Mr. Gonzales, has to speak to her repeatedly during lessons, to the point that he often becomes exasperated and loses his temper. *What suggestions would Charles give Mr. Gonzales for dealing with Sara?*

Case 3. Joshua Clowns and Intimidates

Joshua, larger and louder than his classmates, always wants to be the center of attention, which he accomplishes through a combination of clowning and intimidation. He makes wise remarks, talks back (smilingly) to the teacher, utters a variety of sound-effect noises such as automobile crashes and gunshots, and makes limitless sarcastic comments and put-downs of his classmates. Other students will not stand up to him, apparently fearing his size and verbal aggression. His teacher, Miss

Pearl, has come to her wit's end. *Would Joshua's behavior be likely to improve if synergetic discipline were used in Miss Pearl's classroom? Explain.*

Case 4. Tom is Hostile and Defiant

Tom has appeared to be in his usual foul mood ever since arriving in class. On his way to sharpen his pencil, he bumps into Frank, who complains. Tom tells him loudly to shut up. Miss Baines, the teacher, says, "Tom, go back to your seat." Tom wheels around, swears loudly, and says heatedly, "I'll go when I'm damned good and ready!" *How would Tom's behavior be handled in a synergetic classroom?*

QUESTIONS AND ACTIVITIES

1. In your journal, add information from this chapter that you might wish to include in your personal system of discipline.

2. To what extent do you feel you could put synergetic teaching and discipline into effect in your classroom? What portions do you believe you could implement easily? What portions do you believe might be difficult?

3. Synergetic Discipline does not punish students for misbehavior nor does it apply penalties or other measures to try to force student compliance. Do you think students will take advantage of Synergetic Disci-

pline's softer nature, that they will disregard the teacher because they have no fear of the consequences? Is there anything in Synergetic Discipline that would prevent their doing so?

4. If you introduce Synergetic Discipline as Charles suggests, a few days might pass before students know exactly what is expected of them in the discipline system. Charles suggests you stress personal consideration until the plan is presented to students. Can you think of two or three other things you might do to keep students from misbehaving during the first days of class?

YOU ARE THE TEACHER

Shortly before school begins, a new girl, Mei, is brought into the class. She speaks very little English and is crying. She tries to run out of the classroom but is stopped by the aide. When you ring your bell, the students know they are to sit on the rug, but those already at the play area do not want to do so. You call them three or four times, but finally have to get up and physically bring two of them to the rug. As the opening activities proceed, you repeatedly ask students to sit up. (They have begun rolling around on the floor.) Kinney is pestering the girl next to him. Twice, you ask him to stop. Finally, you send

him to sit in a chair outside the group. He has to sit there until the opening activities are finished, then he can rejoin his group for the first rotation at the art table. As soon as the groups get under way, you hear a ruckus at the art table, which is under the guidance of Mrs. García, a parent volunteer. You see that Kinney has scooped up finger paint and is making motions as if to paint one of the girls, who runs away squealing. Mrs. García tells him to put the paint down. Kinney replies, "Shut up, you big fat rat!" You leave your group and go to Kinney. You tell him, "You need time-out in Mrs. Sayres's room (a first grade next door to your kindergarten)." Kinney, his hand covered with blue paint, drops to the floor and refuses to move. He calls you foul names. You leave him there, go to the phone, and call the office for assistance. Kinney gets up, wipes his hand on a desk and then on himself, and runs out the door. He stops beside the entrance to Mrs. Sayres's room. When you follow, he goes inside and sits at a designated table without further resistance. You return to your group. They sit quietly and attentively but do not speak. You are using a Big Book on an easel, trying to get the students to repeat the words you pronounce, but with little success. When it is time for the next rotation, you go quickly to Mrs. Sayres's room and bring Kinney back to the class. He rejoins his group. As you begin work with your new group, you see Rey and Duy at the measuring table pouring birdseed on each other's heads. Meanwhile, the new girl, Mei, continues sobbing audibly.

Conceptualizing a Strategy

If you followed the suggestions of C. M. Charles, what would you conclude or do with regard to the following?

1. Preventing the problem(s) from occurring in the first place.

2. Addressing the problems now.

3. Involving students in addressing the situation.

4. Maintaining student dignity and good personal relations.

5. Using the situation to help the students develop a sense of greater responsibility and self-control.

REFERENCES

Biddulph, S. 1997. *Raising boys.* Sydney, Australia: Finch Publishing.

Charles, C. 1974. *Teachers' petit Piaget.* San Francisco: Fearon.

Charles, C. 2000. *The synergetic classroom.* Boston: Allyn & Bacon.

Charles, C. 2002. *Essential elements of effective discipline.* Boston: Allyn & Bacon.

Charles, C. 2008. *Classroom discipline: Today's best strategies and tactics.* Boston: Allyn & Bacon.

Glasser, W. 1998a. *The quality school: Managing students without coercion.* New York: HarperCollins.

Glasser, W. 1998b. *The quality school teacher.* New York: HarperCollins.

Mee, C. 1997. *2,000 voices: Young adolescents' perceptions and curriculum implications.* Columbus, OH: National Middle School Association.

Piaget, J. 2001. *The psychology of intelligence.* London: Routledge & Kegan Paul.

Wong, H. 2001. *Selection of tips for teachers.* www.glavac.com/harrywong.htm.

CHAPTER 15

Formalizing Your Personal System of Discipline

Throughout this book, you have been encouraged to explore various philosophical, theoretical, and practical views on discipline. It has been suggested that you select from those views the ideas and practices you find most appealing and then organize them into a personal system of discipline aligned with the needs of your students and compatible with your needs and preferences. This chapter will help you construct your personal system of discipline. It begins by asking you to reflect on your philosophy of discipline, your theory of discipline, and your views on the practical application of discipline. It then provides suggestions for completing your personal system of discipline.

Reflecting on a Philosophy of Discipline

Edward Savage, a high school math teacher who recently retired, was asked about the views he had on discipline when he first began teaching in 1961, and specifically whether at that time he had a particular philosophy or theory of discipline. He shook his head and said, "No, I don't think I ever thought about a philosophy or theory of discipline. If you are asking how I approached discipline, well . . . my methods changed over the years, but I knew when students were behaving improperly and so did they, and I stopped them from doing it. I don't think I was tyrannical. They knew how they were supposed to act in class. Lots of students want to see what they can get away with. When my students were out of line I asked them to stop, and they usually did. Sometimes if they kept at it I gave them detention or made them do extra work. I had confrontations with students occasionally, which left me feeling pretty bad afterward." Prompted again about philosophy and theory of discipline, Mr. Savage said, "No, I really am not sure what that means. What do you mean by that?"

Your philosophy about any matter—life, education, politics, teaching, what have you—summarizes what you believe to be true, good, and correct about that matter, as well as what might become false, bad, and incorrect about it. Mr. Savage had a philosophy of discipline, but had never had occasion to think about it or articulate it. Had he done so, he might have found a more fruitful and comfortable way of working with students. To help use your **philosophy of discipline** to advantage, consider the following questions:

1. What is classroom misbehavior and why does it require attention?
2. What is the purpose of discipline and what results do we want it to achieve?

In Chapter 1, classroom misbehavior was defined as any behavior that, through intent or thoughtlessness, interferes with teaching or learning, threatens or intimidates others, or oversteps society's standards of moral, ethical, or legal behavior. It was suggested that such behavior requires attention because it often disrupts learning and interferes with the development of self-control and effective personal relations. In order to do the best you can for your students, you must help them learn to choose responsible behavior that serves them well while not interfering with the rights of others, and of course you must maintain a classroom climate that is conducive to learning. The purpose of discipline is to help all students learn more easily, relate better with others, and become more self-directed and responsible.

Reflecting on a Theory of Discipline

If asked to describe class discipline, most people would say it is what teachers do to make students behave themselves in school. But to establish optimal systems of discipline, teachers need a more encompassing view of it, including not only its purpose, but also the elements it comprises and how those elements function to improve behavior while maintaining dignity and motivation. Consider these two questions. Your responses to them reflect your theory of discipline.

3. What are the essential components of a good discipline system?
4. How do the components work together or influence each other?

Your **theory of discipline**—meaning what it involves and how it works—ties back to your philosophy of discipline. If you believe, as did Mr. Savage, that the purpose of discipline is to make students behave themselves in class, your theory contains only two main elements—expectations (or rules) and enforcement. Teachers who adhere to this philosophy, and many still do, often tell their students exactly what kinds of misbehavior they will not tolerate. They are ready to take actions that students find unpleasant if students misbehave. Favorite control tactics usually include scowling, scolding, lecturing, moralizing, and punishing.

If your philosophy sees the goal of discipline as helping students get along with each other, and if you believe students misbehave mainly because they are unable to satisfy their desire for belonging, your theory of discipline incorporates four main elements: (1) what "getting along well" and "sense of belonging" mean and how they affect each other, (2) the kinds of misbehavior students are likely to engage in when they fail to experience a sense of belonging, (3) conditions that will provide the sense of belonging students crave, and (4) what you can do to help students who misbehave find a genuine sense of belonging in the class.

If your philosophy holds that misbehavior has many identifiable causes, that students misbehave when a range of needs goes unmet, and that student behavior improves when those causes of misbehavior are limited or removed, your theory of discipline will contain a number of elements, such as: (1) student needs that must be considered; (2) behavior that best serves the interests of individuals and the group; (3) factors that often cause students to violate class expectations; (4) preventive steps you can take to remove or limit the causes of misbehavior; (5) strategies for fostering trust and ethical qualities in the class, and among members of the class, especially between you and your students; and (6) dignified interventions that can be used to deal with misbehavior in a helpful manner.

Reflecting on the Practice of Discipline

Here we move to a consideration of how you want your system of discipline to work in the classroom. Your preferences derive logically from your philosophy and theory of discipline. Consider the following two questions. Your responses reflect your beliefs about the **practice of discipline.**

5. What will you do to prevent or limit the occurrence of misbehavior?
6. How can you react most effectively when students misbehave?

A balanced program of discipline gives attention to four important matters: (1) teaching students how to conduct themselves in a desirable manner, (2) preventing misbehavior by attending proactively to conditions that might foster it, 3) supporting students' efforts to conduct themselves responsibly, and (4) intervening when students behave inappropriately—in a manner that helps them find success and positive personal relations.

The Instruction Aspect of Discipline

The instruction aspect of discipline involves teaching students how to conduct themselves considerately and responsibly in various class routines and activities. You might recall that this tactic, stressed by Harry Wong and others, calls on teachers to model, demonstrate, and have students practice the behaviors expected of them.

The Prevention Aspect of Discipline

The prevention aspect of discipline entails removing, in advance, the known causes of misbehavior or limiting their effects to the extent possible. Any misbehavior you prevent saves you many minutes of instructional time and helps you and your students maintain good personal relations and positive attitudes toward school and learning. All in all, you can prevent most misbehavior by attending to the following:

Treatment of Students
- Show students that each is a valued member of the class.
- Give personal attention to each student as often as possible.
- Never threaten students or back them into a corner.

Trust and Responsibility

■ Develop bonds of trust with students, through helpfulness and fair treatment.
■ Help students understand the importance of responsibility. Give them responsibility for making decisions and help them see that we all make mistakes as a natural part of learning.

Communication

■ Learn students' names quickly and chat with each student often.
■ Always speak respectfully; don't preach to students, speak derisively, or use sarcasm.
■ Use I-messages rather than you-messages when discussing problems.

Instruction

■ Make instructional activities as interesting and worthwhile as possible.
■ Give constant attention to students' needs for security, hope, enjoyment, and competence.
■ Always ask yourself how you can most help your students at any given moment.

Teacher Personality

■ Present yourself as enthusiastic, energetic, and eager to help.
■ Tactfully share information about your life, aspirations, and interests.
■ Always be a model of kindness, consideration, and good manners.

Class Agreements

■ Involve your students in discussions concerning class expectations, instruction, and behavior.
■ Encourage students to view the discipline plan as a code that safeguards them and guides the class.
■ Think of misbehavior not just as a violation of expectations, but also as an opportunity to learn a better way of behaving.

The Support and Intervention Aspects of Discipline

The support aspect of discipline refers to what teachers do to help students maintain self-control. The intervention aspect refers to what teachers do when students break class rules or behave irresponsibly. Despite teachers' diligent efforts to prevent misbehavior, students will still misbehave, sometimes for reasons outside the teacher's control and sometimes as willful transgressions of class expectations. Suppose Jon gets up and wanders around the room, bothering others when he is supposed to be working. What do you do? Here are some possibilities:

■ You can simply ask Jon to return to his seat and complete his work. That might be all that is needed.
■ You can address the cause of Jon's misbehavior, which might be boredom, frustration, desire for attention, poor habits, or self-centeredness. If you can identify the cause, you can remove or limit it. The models of discipline analyzed in earlier chapters suggest numerous tactics for preventing boredom and fatigue, teaching charismatically,

managing lessons to maintain student attention, building students' sense of responsibility, and holding students accountable for learning. Those tactics all touch on known causes of misbehavior.

■ You can provide direct assistance to Jon. You might talk with him and see if he identifies a problem with which he might need help. If he does so, you can do what is required to deal with it, or at least show understanding and empathy. If he says there is no problem, you might ask for his cooperation so the lesson can continue without further disruption. You might also consider altering the lesson by shortening it or changing activities, or arranging for Jon to work with another student. Any intervention you use with Jon should stop the misbehavior, help him choose to behave acceptably, and ensure he maintains a positive attitude. You can usually accomplish this by speaking to him in a kindly, respectful manner.

Other Considerations in the Practice of Discipline

Student Response

Overall, students do not respond well to forceful discipline tactics, but they do appreciate and profit from tactics that are considerate and helpful.

Students Becoming Restive

Even the most accomplished teachers expect at some point to see their students begin to fidget, doodle, look out the window, smile or gesture to each other, whisper, and otherwise indicate they are disengaging from the lesson. You can limit such behavior by making your instructional activities especially interesting and interacting personally with different students during the lesson, when appropriate to do so.

You should try to remain attentive to all members of the class all the time. Your students become aware of this, and your eye contact or physical proximity is usually enough to keep them on task. You might move to the student involved and ask a question about the work in progress. (Meanwhile, ask yourself if the lesson is interesting enough to hold student attention much longer.) You may need to make a comment such as, "Class, I'll really appreciate it if you can stick with the lesson for five more minutes." If they like and trust you, they will probably comply. If they don't comply, you might ask, "Class, I see that the lesson is not holding your attention. What seems to be the trouble?" Based on their comments, you might make modifications that resolve the problem.

Students Thoughtlessly Breaking Class Agreements

Most of the time when students transgress class agreements they do so unintentionally or without malice by talking, calling out, moving about, goofing off, or failing to complete their work. What do you do in those cases? Some suggestions include:

■ Use body language such as eye contact, physical proximity, and attention.
■ Remind the students of the class expectations they have discussed and agreed to.
■ Stop the class and say, "This lesson doesn't seem to be holding your attention. What might I do to make it better for you?"

- Stop the class and say, "We seem to have a problem here. What do you think we can do to resolve it?"
- Don't draw undue attention to the students who are offending, but rather to the undesirable behavior.
- Conduct class meetings to discuss ongoing incidents and explore solutions. Be careful not to single out individual students. Your objective is to help them improve.

All of these tactics are effective. It is for you to decide which is best in your circumstance. Remember that it is self-defeating to scold or deride the offending students. You and they will both be better off if you can help them abide by class rules willingly.

Students Misbehaving Seriously

The vast majority of student misbehavior is benign. Although it interferes with learning, wastes time, and annoys the teacher and perhaps other students, it can be dealt with fairly easily. Occasionally, however, students behave in ways considered immoral, outrageous, or violent. These behaviors range from lying and cheating to stealing, sexual immorality, bullying, cruelty, aggression, and violence. Because these behaviors affect the class strongly, you should carefully think through how you will respond to them. Before matters of this type occur, hold a class meeting and explain to your students that there are certain kinds of behavior that are so serious they will certainly cause problems if they occur. Mention the kinds of behaviors you are concerned about, such as bullying, fighting, profanity and verbal abuse, sexual harassment, and malicious damage to the classroom. Indicate that although you don't expect the behaviors to appear in the class, you feel it is important to bring them out in the open. That way, everyone can be mindful of them and guard against them.

Indicate to the class what you will probably do in response, if such behavior occurs. Let them know you will do your best to conceal your distress and maintain your composure, and that you will talk with offending students privately, or to the entire class if all are affected. Consider saying something along these lines: "This is a serious problem. I'd like us to resolve it together. Let's try. But if we can't, I'll need to ask for help from the vice principal."

Meanwhile, begin working immediately toward positive solutions with the students involved. Show your willingness to help them move toward behavior that serves them and the class productively. Later, bring the topic up for discussion in class meetings, provided it is not a private matter.

You can usually handle lying, cheating, stealing, and sexual transgressions without having to call for expert assistance. Sexual innuendo and harassment should be squelched immediately. Without attacking the individuals involved, point out what is occurring and why it is forbidden in the classroom. If the behavior continues, speak with the culpable individual privately and explain once more why those acts are not permitted in the class or school. Remind yourself that your goal is not to punish but to help. Ask the individual to meet with you privately so you can explain your concern more frankly. Some students will admit what they've done; others will deny it. Don't try to make students admit wrongdoing. Don't threaten them or use logic in trying to persuade them, and never insist they apologize. When you talk with an offending student, explain your perception of the situation. Ask students if they understand why behaving in that way causes others to lose trust in them and stop wanting to associate with them. Ask them if they can think of more responsible ways of behaving. Assure offending students that you want to help them learn and become the best persons they can. Show them kind personal attention. Go out of your way to be helpful. This is as much as you can realistically do. If it does not resolve the problem, you should inform the school counselor or administrator and let that person take over from there.

For behavior that is threatening, dangerous, or wantonly cruel—such as severe bullying, intimidation, fighting, or possession of weapons or dangerous substances—be ready to call for help immediately. You are not expected to deal with those situations on your own. Some authorities suggest including a "severe clause" in class agreements, which makes clear to students that dangerous or threatening behavior will result in immediate notification of the school administrator and removal from the classroom. From that point, the matter moves out of your hands and into those of persons with special training. To make sure what you are expected to do in such circumstances, discuss the matter with your school administrator.

Helping Students Behave More Responsibly

The dream of all teachers is to work with students who behave responsibly because they feel it is the proper thing to do. As you may recall, Marvin Marshall makes responsible behavior the cornerstone of his approach to discipline. Many years ago, Rudolf Dreikurs made "social interest" a prime ingredient in his scheme of classroom discipline. He sought to help students see that they prospered individually when the class prospered as a whole. He pointed out that the best way for students to help themselves is to help the class function well. Social interest can be developed through making joint decisions, assuming personal responsibility, developing a sense of community, and producing class synergy, as described in the following paragraphs.

Making Joint Decisions.   Students like to have a sense of power in the classroom. When power is not available to them, they sometimes try to seize it inappropriately. Wise teachers proactively give students power by involving them in helping make selected decisions that affect the class. This gives students a feeling of being in control and makes them more likely to comply with expectations. When they see that what benefits the class also benefits them personally, they become more inclined to work for the betterment of the class.

Assuming Responsibility.   Students desire freedom and power but often do not understand that responsibility is tied to them. Teachers, wanting to give students more responsibility, often put them in charge of keeping the room tidy, managing the media or science equipment, helping take care of plants and pets, and so forth. This is one kind of responsibility, certainly, and it does contribute to group concern for the class. There is, however, a more important kind of responsibility. It involves accepting the results of one's actions and learning from them. When students are allowed to make decisions about selected class matters, they must be helped to understand they must deal with the results of their decisions. They need to see, too, that they can learn from poor decisions and thus do better in the future. Mr. Abrams always stands ready to help the class overcome difficulties. He allows them to make decisions, but when they do poor work he does not accept it or excuse them. This same principle applies when students work in groups and become aware that some students are not doing their part. The students must assume responsibility for working things out. Mr. Abrams will help them find ways to do so, but the working-through process is up to them. In this manner the class begins to realize that they have a collective responsibility to help maintain a classroom in which everyone can learn and contribute.

Developing a Sense of Community.   Involvement in decision making and acceptance of responsibility helps build a sense of community in the class. Alfie Kohn has done much to advance the concept of classes as communities, a concept many authorities in discipline have adopted. Kohn describes class community as a place where students feel valued and connected to each other and think in terms of "we" instead of "I." He says when students' personal needs are met, they show increased tendency to help meet their classmates' needs rather than remaining preoccupied with their own.

Developing Synergy.   Teachers have long recognized the value of group spirit, where students reach high levels of energy and involvement. It is usually evident in athletic contests, school plays, concerts, and other productions. Most teachers have experienced it in the classroom, as well, and know it provides a time of happy learning and joyful teaching, with a low incidence of irresponsible behavior. However, teachers have not understood very well what causes this condition or how they can make it occur.

Class synergy occurs when members of a class begin, through interest or excitement, to feed psychic energy to each other. When the energy level becomes high enough, students work together eagerly. They communicate, cooperate, share resources, and find pleasure in the process. Learning occurs rapidly. Good will predominates, and misbehavior disappears. Synergy is most likely to occur in the presence of trust, teacher charisma, good communication, high interest, group enterprise, and considerate human relations. Although synergy can occur without all those elements in place, it cannot be made to occur reliably when certain elements are absent, especially trust, communication, charisma, and interest.

The Five Principles and Your Personal System of Discipline

To begin organizing your personal system of discipline, take a moment to refresh yourself on the following five principles that were introduced in Chapter 1. They concern the following, which you can use as a framework for your system of discipline:

1. What must you do to ensure you are thoroughly professional in the ways you present yourself and interact with others?
2. What kinds of behavior do you wish to see in your students, now and in the future?
3. What emotional and moral qualities will you promote in the classroom to help your students develop into the kinds of people you hope they will be?

4. What provisions will you make to encourage and enable your students to conduct themselves in a responsible manner?

5. What tactics will you use to intervene effectively when common disruptions, neurological-based behaviors, or serious actions occur in your classroom?

Thoughts from Students Preparing Themselves to Be Teachers

The following paragraphs are selected excerpts from reflections submitted by three New Mexico State University students preparing to become teachers. Which of the five principles can you identify in their comments? The selections were provided by Professor Eileen VanWie and are included with the students' permission.

Alison K. Pryor on Developing Respect in the Classroom

I call my discipline approach the Pryor R-E-S-P-E-C-T Plan for Classroom Management (Responsibility, Excellence, Self-control, Participation, Encouragement, Civility, and Trust). It is designed to make the class run smoothly while at the same time developing character traits that serve students well now and in the future.

I introduce my program with a discussion of *respect*. Students discuss how we show respect for others and why we do so and they practice respectful behavior. This theme is stressed in class, on the school grounds, and with school personnel. From that point, we progress to the consideration of responsibility, excellence, self-control, participation, encouragement, civility, and trust. I model these qualities in my interactions with students and require they show them in their behavior, as well.

Rachel Space on Relating to and Connecting with Students

I work to create a more democratic classroom by involving students closely in class matters. We do a great deal of group work and together have decided on procedures for assigning grades and dealing with students who break class rules or don't keep agreements about class assignments. My students love being a part of this process. They know I value their opinions.

To understand my students better, I conduct two one-on-one meetings with each student during the semester. In those meetings we explore the students' feelings about the class in general and their plans for their final project. This makes students feel more a part of things and it gives me a better understanding of their progress.

In school, I conduct myself professionally, follow all of the rules the students must follow, treat everyone with respect, and never behave hypocritically. I ask students to help me maintain a safe, orderly classroom and continue their good behavior outside the class. I do what I can to help each student enjoy achievement and fulfillment.

Manuel Vigil on How He Presents Himself

I endeavor to be a professional role model. I treat others with dignity and show respect for my colleagues and students. At the same time, I challenge my students to excel, intellectually and behaviorally. I work to display a charismatic personality with good humor, which helps students enjoy the class.

Overall, I model the sort of personal behavior I want to see in my students. I am intent on helping them learn to show respect and courtesy for one another. If I see students disrespecting each other I interrupt the behavior and explain why it is wrong and how any of us should treat other individuals. I help students learn to make amends for serious misbehavior and embrace and welcome differences among class members. I make my classroom warm and welcoming, with a climate of trust. I involve students in class decisions and take them seriously, encouraging them to speak their minds while understanding that people have different points of view. I make the curriculum relate to students' lives as much as I can and involve parents in helping support my work with their children. I try to make sure they understand the important role they play in their children's education.

Two Sample Discipline Plans from Teachers in Service

Many different approaches to discipline are effective in the classroom, varying from teacher directed to collaborative. Almost any approach to discipline can be organized to emphasize helpfulness and positive relations with students. You are entitled to devise a plan of discipline that you consider best for you and your students. The following examples are two of many possibilities. They are not presented as exemplary models for you to emulate, but merely to show how two experienced teachers organized procedures that suited them best in their situations. The first emphasizes rules of behavior, supported by positive and negative consequences. The second emphasizes student–teacher cooperation and focuses on preventing misbehavior.

Sample 1. An Approach That Emphasizes Rules and Consequences

Many teachers use discipline plans that feature rules and consequences. Teachers who use such plans believe the teacher should be firmly yet sensitively in control and should ensure that everyone behaves as expected in the classroom. They feel their approach cuts down on disruptions and allows students to learn in an environment free from worry. Discipline plans of this type usually contain the following:

- *Rules.* A set of rules indicates what students are allowed and not allowed to do in class. The teacher is responsible for establishing the rules, but discusses them carefully to make sure students understand their rationale supporting the rules and the procedures for enforcing them.
- *Consequences.* Consequences are attached to the rules and made plain to students. Positive consequences are pleasant experiences that students enjoy when they follow

the rules. Negative consequences are unpleasant conditions that students experience when they break the rules.

- *Implementation and maintenance.* Students are taught how they are expected to behave, and a series of steps is established for applying the consequences. Parents are informed about the rationale, expectations, rules, consequences, and procedures of enforcement. Teachers change aspects of their programs when the need to do so becomes evident.

This approach has served hundreds of thousands of teachers for a great many years and is still widely used, although it is not as popular as it once was. To see how a present-day teacher uses the rules-consequences-procedure protocol, adjusted to her needs, examine the following program developed by third-grade teacher Deborah Sund.

Deborah Sund's Third-Grade Discipline Program

Deborah Sund had been teaching for two years when she devised this program. She wanted to provide a clear structure for behavior expectations while at the same time meeting everyone's needs. Ms. Sund clarifies her students' needs, her own needs, and her special dislikes, then builds her discipline system so all are taken into account.

My Students' Needs

- To learn interesting and useful information, especially that which promotes skills in reading, math, and language
- A learning environment that is attractive, stimulating, free from threat, and conducive to productive work
- A teacher who is helpful, attentive, and kind
- The opportunity to interact and work cooperatively with other students
- To be accepted and feel part of the group
- To learn how to relate to others humanely and helpfully
- To have the opportunity to excel

My Own Needs

- Orderly classroom appearance: good room arrangement; neatly stored materials; interesting, well thought-out displays
- Structure and routines: a set schedule that provides security, but that also allows flexibility and improvisation when needed
- Attention and participation: students pay attention to directions and speakers and participate willingly in all instructional activities
- Situationally appropriate behaviors: quiet attention during instruction, considerate interaction during group activities
- Enthusiasm from me and my students
- Warmth as reflected in mutual regard among all members of the class
- Positive, relaxed classroom environment reflecting self-control, mutual helpfulness, and assumption of responsibility

My Dislikes

- Inattention to speaker, teacher, other adult, or class member
- Excessive noise: loud voices, inappropriate talking and laughing
- Distractions: toys, unnecessary movement, poking, teasing, and so on
- Abuse of property: misusing, wasting, or destroying instructional materials
- Unkind and rude conduct: ridicule, sarcasm, bad manners, and physical abuse

Class Rules.   When I first meet my students, I explain that it is very important for us to have a class where everyone feels safe and is not worried about how others will treat them—where they can be happy and enjoy what we learn. I explain that to make that possible, I have prepared a list of rules for how we are to act. I explain the rules and give examples of what students do when they follow the rules, and what they might do when they break the rules. I involve them in the discussion and have them practice correct ways of conducting themselves. I also tell them about some things I don't want them to do, and I show them examples to make sure they understand. I also demonstrate the prompts, cues, hints, and other assistance I will give students to help them abide by the rules, which are:

1. Be considerate of others at all times. (Speak kindly. Be helpful. Don't bother others.)
2. Do our best work. (Get as much done as possible. Do work neatly, to be proud of it. Don't waste time.)
3. Use quiet voices in the classroom. (Use regular speaking voices during class discussions. Speak quietly during cooperative work. Whisper at other times.)
4. Use signals to request permission or receive help. (I explain the signal systems for requesting assistance, movement, restroom pass.)

Positive Consequences.   I emphasize that I will always try to show I am pleased when students follow the rules we have agreed to. I tell them the following:

- Mostly I will give them smiles, winks, nods, and pats when they are behaving well.
- Sometimes I will say out loud how pleased I am with the way they are working or behaving toward each other.
- Once in a while, when the whole class has behaved especially well, I will give them a special privilege (e.g., go early to recess, do one of their favorite activities, see a video).
- From time to time I will send a complimentary note to their parents, or call their parents and comment on how well they are doing.

Negative Consequences.   When discussing the class rules, I ask students what they think should happen when someone breaks a rule. They usually suggest punishment. I tell them that because I want them always to be as happy as possible, I don't want to punish them. I say that instead of punishment, I will do the following:

- Give them "pirate eyes" or a stern glance with disappointed or puzzled expression.
- Remind them when a rule is being broken: "I hear noise" or "Some people are not listening."

- When necessary, tell them exactly what they are doing wrong: "Gordon, you did not use the signal. Please use the signal."
- When necessary, separate them from the group until they can conduct themselves properly.
- As a last resort, contact their parents for help.

To Prevent Misbehavior. I discuss with my students a number of things I will do to help them want to behave properly, such as:

- Show respect for each student as entitled to the best education I can provide.
- Look for the positive and enjoyable qualities in each student.
- Take time to know each student better on a personal level.
- Each day assess students' feelings and discuss them if necessary.
- Talk with students in ways that imply their own competence, such as, "Okay, you know what to do next."
- Involve them in clarifying rules and assuming responsibility for proper behavior.
- Keep a good room environment to prevent their feeling strained, tired, or inconvenienced (e.g., proper lighting, temperature, traffic patterns, attractiveness).
- Emphasize, model, and hold practice sessions on good manners, courtesy, and responsibility.
- Provide a varied, active curriculum with opportunities for physical movement, singing, interaction, and times of quiet.
- Communicate with parents in the following ways:
  1. Post messages on our Internet site outlining expectations and the discipline system.
  2. Occasionally make short, positive phone calls to parents.
  3. Send home with children notes concerning good work and behavior.
- End each day on a positive note, with a fond good-bye and hope for a happy and productive tomorrow.

Intervening When Students Misbehave. When students begin to misbehave, I do the following:

- Move close to the student.
- Show close attention to the student's work.
- Modify the lesson or activity if it seems to be causing difficulty.
- Invoke the negative consequences that we have agreed to.

Sample 2. An Approach That Emphasizes Prevention and Teacher–Student Cooperation

The following approach emphasizes preventing misbehavior through meeting student needs and building personal relationships. The rationale for this approach is that it promotes a greater sense of satisfaction and enjoyment in the class, while removing student resentment and reluctance to cooperate. Plans of this sort emphasize the following:

- Attending continually to students' needs for security, hope, acceptance, dignity, power, enjoyment, and competence.
- Communicating effectively and regularly with students and their parents.
- Making sure to give all students attention, encouragement, and support.
- Making class activities consistently enjoyable and worthwhile.
- Ensuring that all students accept responsibility and experience success.
- Establishing agreements about how everyone will interact and behave.
- Discussing and practicing manners, courtesy, and responsibility.
- Involving all students meaningfully in the operation of the class.
- Dealing with misbehavior by attending to its causes.

Teachers who employ this discipline approach feel it allows them to relate with students in a way that builds positive relationships with relatively little stress. Gail Charles uses a discipline plan that incorporates many of these qualities.

Gail Charles's Discipline Plan—Eighth-Grade English

The following narration is in Gail Charles's words:

> I have been teaching for 25 years. For many of those years, my students misbehaved much more than I thought they should, and I tried to control their misbehavior with scowls, reprimands, lectures, threats, and detentions. My students grudgingly behaved well enough to learn most of what I intended, but I'm sure they felt under siege. I know I did, and the effort it required left me continually frustrated and exhausted.
>
> A few years ago I began to understand that I am more effective and enjoy my work more when I organize the curriculum to accommodate and embrace the needs of my adolescent students and work cooperatively with them. While I still provide a challenging curriculum, I have switched from a coercive to a collaborative way of teaching. I now try to guide, encourage, and support students' efforts rather than endlessly push and prod. The result has been fewer power struggles, more success, and happier students and teacher.

Winning My Students Over.   My students want to feel part of the group. They want to feel accepted and valued by each other and especially by me. They want to feel safe, so I forbid all ridicule and sarcasm. I've never ridiculed a student, but sorry to say, I have spoken sarcastically many times when struggling against students who defied my rules. I no longer use sarcasm or allow students to belittle each other in any way.

I give my students a voice in class matters and listen to them sincerely. I allow them to make decisions about where they sit and with whom they wish to work. I do this as part of trying to make learning enjoyable. They like to work with each other, participate, talk, and cooperate.

Meeting My Needs.   We discuss the importance of making classwork enjoyable, and I tell my students that the class needs to be enjoyable for me, too. I tell them up front that I want the tone in the class to be positive, with everyone showing patience, tolerance, good manners, and mutual respect. I tell them that I want them to be enthusiastic and do the best work they can. I say I need their attention and that I want them to help care for materials and keep the room clean. I promise to treat them with respect, and they usually reciprocate.

Rules and Student Input.   I have learned to request and make use of student input concerning expectations, operating procedures, and codes of conduct. When I meet a new class, I discuss their needs and mine and focus on how we can meet those needs and make our class productive. I give students power to make many decisions and I respect what they say.

Together we write a plan for how we will work and behave in the class. Because I want students to make thoughtful suggestions, I ask them, for their first homework assignment, to think back on previous years in school and write brief responses to the following:

1. When have you felt most successful in school?
2. What did the teacher do to help you feel successful?
3. What kinds of class activities have you found most helpful and enjoyable?
4. What suggestions do you have for creating a classroom in which all can work, learn, and do their best?

The next day I organize students into small groups to share and discuss what they have written. Volunteers present each group's responses, which I list on the overhead projector. Occasionally I may add a suggestion of my own. We then streamline, combine, reword, and sometimes negotiate until we reach a set of agreements we think will serve us best. Before the next class, I type up the agreements and ask each student and his or her parent to sign, indicating their support. I do this for each of my five classes.

Prevention.   In all my class activities, I try to interact personally with every student. It is not easy to forge relationships with 160+ students, but I try to do so in order to show I "see" and like them. At the beginning of the year I write a letter to my students introducing myself and telling a bit about my family, hobbies, interests, and goals. I ask them to do the same so I can know them better. I keep a birthday calendar to remember student birthdays. I try to comment on new hairstyles, new outfits, or how great a now brace-free set of teeth looks. I chaperon field trips and dances, supervise the computer writing lab after school, and make myself available for conversation before and after school. These little things mean a lot to students.

For their part, many students like to involve themselves in the workings of the classroom. I provide them tasks such as classroom librarian, bulletin board designer, plant caretaker, and class secretary. Their involvement makes them feel important and useful.

Interventions.   With the collaborative plan in place, I have few discipline problems and little difficulty dealing with those that occur. Most often, a simple reminder is all that is needed to get students back on track. For the occasional student who repeatedly misbehaves despite our agreements, I ask the counselor to set up a meeting with the student's parent and, sometimes, with other teachers. We discuss the problem and explore how it can be resolved. Very occasionally, a student may behave in a dangerous manner or prevent my teaching. When that happens, I call the vice-principal for assistance.

Finalizing Your Personal System of Discipline

As you begin sketching out your personal approach to discipline, consider making use of the five principles for a personal system of discipline that were introduced in Chapter 1 and repeated earlier in this chapter. Those principles are embodied in the first five of the six following steps and will help you construct a balanced, complete system of discipline tailored to your needs. (The sixth step is to decide how you will introduce your system in the classroom.)

Step 1. Specify How You Will Present and Conduct Yourself

State your conclusions concerning what you must do to present and conduct yourself in a professional and ethical manner, in accordance with legal considerations. A few reminders are that you

- Must exercise due diligence over students
- Shall not intentionally expose students to embarrassment or disparagement
- Shall not disclose information about students obtained in the course of professional service unless disclosure serves a compelling professional purpose or is required by law

In addition to the NEA stipulations, professionalism requires you to do the following:

- Dress professionally, as an adult in a professional situation.
- Use appropriate language for the educational setting, with correct speech patterns and complete avoidance of obscenities.
- Treat others with respect and courtesy.

Step 2. Specify the Behavioral Goals for Your Students

Clarify the social, emotional, and moral learning students need in order to interact respectfully, now and in the future. Compare your views with the following reminders:

- Show positive attitude.
- Behave considerately toward others.
- Take initiative.
- Show self-direction.

- Make a strong effort to learn.
- Assume personal responsibility for behavior.

Step 3. Describe the Classroom Conditions You Will Provide

List the physical and psychological classroom conditions you can provide to help students do their work peacefully and develop into the kinds of people you hope they will be. You might wish to consider the following reminders:

- Comfortable physical environment
- Sense of community
- Positive attention
- Good communication
- Consideration for others
- Trust
- Interesting activities
- Student knowledge of expectations
- Continual helpfulness
- Preservation of dignity
- Minimizing causes of misbehavior
- Teacher charisma
- Student involvement in decisions about the class

Step 4. Specify How You Will Help Students Conduct Themselves Appropriately

Explain what you will do to encourage students to do quality work, relate well with others, and conduct themselves in a responsible manner. You might wish to refer to the following list of reminders:

- Help students meet their needs.
- Involve students in discussing and planning aspects of the class program, including behavior, interactions, instructional activities, and preferences.
- Identify and minimize conditions that lead to misbehavior.
- Teach students how to follow necessary routines and procedures.
- Give each student personal attention as often as possible.
- Develop trust with and among class members.
- Seek to energize the class when doing so seems appropriate.
- Select instructional topics and activities students enjoy and find rewarding.
- Use congruent communication and I-messages in speaking with students.
- Encourage student initiative and responsibility.
- Seek parental support for the class program.
- Teach students to use win-win methods for resolving problems and conflicts.
- When students misbehave, help them assume responsibility for correction and self-restitution; use established interventions that preserve personal dignity

Step 5. Indicate How You Will Intervene When Misbehavior Occurs

Clarify supportive actions you will take when common disruptions, neurological-based behaviors, or serious actions occur or appear imminent in your classroom. You might wish to consider the following reminders:

- Show interest in the student's work and ask cheerful questions, make favorable comments, or provide hints.
- Catch students' eyes, send private signals, or move closer to students.
- Provide a light challenge: "Can you get five more problems done before we stop?"
- Ask students if they are having difficulty; ask what you might to do help.
- If the work is boring or too difficult, restructure it or change the activity.
- For more serious infractions, follow procedures that have been clearly established in advance, with student involvement and approval. (Indicate what those procedures might involve.)
- Talk with offending students calmly and respectfully. Don't lecture, threaten, impugn their dignity, or back them into a corner. Always try to help the student and the class.
- Teach students how to use win-win conflict resolution. If they have disputes, ask them to try to resolve their conflict.
- Conduct the interventions in a consistent manner. Don't give in to student wheedling or begging. Remind them that everything will be all right so long as they behave responsibly and show consideration for others. Use mistakes as learning opportunities, from which to make fresh starts.

Step 6. Think Through and Write Out How You Will Introduce and Explain the System to Your Students

Consider doing the following:

- Write, in outline form, what you will say, show, demonstrate, explain, and discuss with students when introducing your system. This may include indicating the behavioral goals for the class, a description of how you want the class to function, how you will relate to students, and how you want them to relate to you and each other so everyone has an opportunity to flourish in comfort and safety.
- Indicate how you will provide topics and activities for learning that bring interest, excitement, and competence to your students' lives.
- Specify and show on a chart the roles or jobs of teacher and students that will lead to the goals your program is designed to achieve.
- Identify behaviors and procedures you want students to understand clearly and describe how you will have students practice sufficiently to familiarize themselves with expectations. You might either state these behaviors and procedures in advance or lead students through a process in which they help you identify appropriate and inappropriate behavior for the class. This activity should culminate in a brief set of agreements concerning how students and teacher are to behave, together with what

will be done to help students (and teacher) behave more appropriately if class agreements are violated.

■ Specify what you will do to inform your school administrator and students' parents or guardians about your discipline approach. Indicate what you will do to enlist and maintain parental support.

Your Formula for Success Is in Your Hands

When you have successfully done what was indicated in the six preceding steps, you will have developed a system of discipline that will provide success and satisfaction for you and your students. You can confidently gain students' respect and cooperation through establishing personal relations with them, tending to their concerns, supporting their efforts, and helping them overcome obstacles. Of course, both you and your students will make mistakes—perhaps many at first. But mistakes will not deter you or them. As we have noted many times, mistakes are a natural part of the educational process and provide effective springboards toward higher levels of competence. When you make mistakes, learn from them. Ask your students to do the same. Ask them to work together with you. Reassure them you will always help them the best you can. The resultant attitude of cooperation will allow you to make full use of your teaching skills and will help ensure an educational experience of high quality for everyone involved.

KEY TERMS AND CONCEPTS EMPHASIZED IN THIS CHAPTER

philosophy of discipline   theory of discipline   practice of discipline

The following are terms featured in the models of discipline and supporting chapters in this book. When appropriate, authorities who originated or helped popularize the term are indicated.

ABCD of disruptive behavior (Kagan, Kyle, and Scott): Aggression, breaking rules, confrontations, disengagement.

Active listening (Gordon): Listener showing obvious attention by providing responses to what speaker is saying.

Affective disorders: Disorders that affect mood or feeling, such as bipolar disorder.

Aggression (Kagan and others): Behavior in which hostility or unwanted attention is directed toward others.

Anxiety disorders: Emotional disorders that involve fear and extreme uneasiness.

Appraising reality (Redl and Wattenberg): Having students recognize what they are doing wrong.

Appreciative praise (Ginott): Praise that expresses gratitude or admiration for effort.

Assertive response style (the Canters): Responding to student behavior in a helpful manner while insisting that class rules be followed.

Assertive teachers (the Canters): Teachers who clearly, confidently, and consistently reiterate class expectations and attempt to build trust with students.

Attention: *See* Attention-seeking.

Attention-deficit hyperactivity disorder (ADHD): Disorder characterized by inattentiveness, impulsive behavior, and hyperactivity.

Attention-getting mechanisms (Albert): Tactics such as pencil tapping, showing off, calling out, and asking irrelevant questions, used to get attention from teacher and peers.

Attention-seeking (Dreikurs): A mistaken goal of student behavior, involving disruption and showing off, to gain attention from the teacher and other students.

Authority (Morrish): A teacher quality that has a positive effect on discipline.

Autism spectrum disorder: A range of disorders in which individuals fail to develop normal speech patterns or personal relationships.

Autocratic classrooms (Dreikurs and others): Classrooms in which teachers demand cooperation, dominate, and criticize.

Backup system (Jones): The planned action teachers take when students misbehave seriously and refuse to comply with positive teacher requests; often means being sent to the principal's office.

Barriers to relationships (Nelsen and Lott): Teacher behaviors that are disrespectful and discouraging to students.

Basic needs: Psychological requirements for normal functioning.

Basic student needs (Charles): Security, belonging, hope, dignity, power, enjoyment, and competence.

(Dreikurs): Belonging.

(Glasser): Survival, belonging, control, freedom, fun.

Behavior: The totality of one's physical and mental activities.

Behavior management: Organized efforts to get students to behave in particular ways.

Behavior modification (Skinner's followers): The use of Skinnerian principles of reinforcement to control or shape behavior.

Behaviorally at risk (Curwin and Mendler): Students whose behavior prevents their learning and puts them in serious danger of failing in school.

Bell work (Jones): Work that students do to begin a class period that does not require instruction from the teacher, such as reading, writing in journals, or completing warm-up activities.

Belonging (Dreikurs; Glasser; Albert): A basic human need for legitimate membership in groups, with attendant security and comfort.

Bipolar disorder: A mental health diagnosis characterized by alternating cycles of euphoria and depression.

Body carriage (Jones): Posture and movement that indicate to students whether the teacher is well, ill, in charge, tired, disinterested, or intimidated.

Body language (Jones): Nonverbal communication transmitted through posture, eye contact, gestures, and facial expressions.

Boss teachers (Glasser): Teachers who set the tasks, direct the learning activities, ask for little student input, and grade student work. (Contrasted with Lead Teachers.)

Bottom line (Gossen): The level beyond which misbehavior will not be accepted.

Brain injuries, nontraumatic: Cerebral injuries resulting from disrupted blood flow to the brain (as in strokes), or from tumors, infections, drug overdoses, and certain medical conditions.

Brain injuries, traumatic: Cerebral injuries resulting from blows or other physical damage to the brain, incurred during events such as accidents, sporting events, assaults, or birth.

Builders of relationships (Nelsen and Lott): Teacher behaviors that show respect for and give encouragement to students.

Bullying: Students systematically inflicting physical or emotional harm on other students.

Causes of misbehavior (Charles): Factors known to foster misbehavior, such as boredom and threat to personal dignity. Charles identifies twenty-five such factors, most of which can be minimized or eliminated from the classroom.

Charisma, teacher (Charles): Teacher personal allure that attracts student attention and cooperation.

Choice (Marshall): An element used in helping students learn to conduct themselves more responsibly. Marshall emphasizes "empowerment through choice."

Choice Theory (Glasser): Theory that we all choose how to behave at any time, cannot control anyone's behavior but our own, and all behavior is purposeful in meeting basic needs.

Circle of friends (Albert): Organized relationships that help all students feel they belong and are interconnected with others.

Class code of conduct (Charles; Albert; and others): Agreements or codes formalized by teachers and students that indicate how class behavior, instruction, and other matters are to occur.

Class rules: Written code that specifies acceptable and unacceptable behavior in the classroom.

Classroom meetings (Glasser; Nelsen and Lott; and others): Meetings held in the classroom for communication and addressing and solving problems.

Classroom structure (Jones): Classroom organization, including room arrangement, class rules, class routines, chores, and the like.

Collaborative rule setting (Gordon): A procedure in which teachers and students work together to establish rules for making the classroom safe, efficient, and harmonious.

Collapsing the conflict (Gossen): A tactic for deflating conflict between teacher and students.

Communication roadblocks (Gordon): Ways teachers speak to students, such as moralizing and preaching, that tend to shut down communication.

Compliance (Morrish): Students coming routinely to abide by teacher requests and directions—an important element in Morrish's approach to discipline.

Compliant behavior: Calm student acquiescence to teacher expectations, held as a main purpose of discipline by many teachers.

Conduct disorder: A mental heath diagnosis in which students breach society's moral constraints.

Confer dignity (Ginott; Curwin and Mendler): Respecting students by putting aside their past history, treating them considerately, and being concerned only with the present situation.

Conflict (Gordon and others): A problem situation, such as a dispute, that involves a strong clash of wills.

Confrontation (Kagan, Kyle, and Scott): One of four basic types of classroom misbehavior featured in Win-Win Discipline.

Congruent communication (Ginott): A style of communication in which teachers acknowledge and accept students' feelings about situations and themselves.

Connecting habits (Glasser): Seven things teachers do that help foster strong relations with students—caring, listening, supporting, contributing, encouraging, trusting, and befriending.

Consequences: Penalties or rewards that are applied when rules are violated or complied with.

Conventional consequences: Consequences ordinarily provided in the classroom, such as disapproval and reprimand.

Constant reinforcement: Reinforcement provided every time the individual behaves in the desired manner.

Constructivist theory: A theory of school learning which holds that students cannot receive knowledge directly from teachers but must construct it from experience.

Coopetition (Charles): Cooperation by members of a group that are engaged in competition against other groups.

Coping mechanisms: Ways students deal with situations they find unpleasant—examples include fleeing, fighting, clamming up, and resisting passively.

Core values: What the school or class believes in.

Corrective actions: Steps taken by the teacher to stop student misbehavior.

Democratic classroom (Dreikurs): Classroom in which teachers give students responsibility and involve them in making decisions.

Dignity (Ginott; Curwin and Mendler): Respect for oneself and others.

Discipline

(Charles): (1) What teachers do to help students conduct themselves appropriately in class. (2) Also used to refer to the quality of student conduct or teacher control in class.

(Jones): Teacher efforts to engage students in learning in the most positive, unobtrusive fashion possible.

Discipline hierarchy (the Canters): Levels of consequences and the order in which they are imposed within the period or day.

Discipline structures (Kagan, Kyle, and Scott): Discipline tactics used to deal with various types of disruptive behavior.

Does it really matter? (Gossen): A question teachers should ask themselves when mild "misbehavior" is noted in the classroom.

Door openers (Gordon): Comments or other teacher acts that encourage students to communicate about themselves or problems they are experiencing.

Do-over (Morrish): A tactic in which teachers ask students to repeat, in a correct manner, a behavior that has not been acceptable.

Dyslexia: A mental health diagnosis characterized by difficulties in word recognition, spelling, word decoding, and occasionally with the phonological (sound) component of language.

Economic disadvantage: Conditions of students living in poverty that may interfere with expected educational progress.

Eight building blocks for classroom meetings (Nelsen and Lott): Eight suggestions for establishing and conducting effective classroom meetings.

Encouragement (Dreikurs): Showing belief in students and stimulating them to try, as distinct from praising students for their accomplishments.

Essential virtues, seven (Borba): Empathy, conscience, self-control, respect, kindness, tolerance, and fairness, all of which can and should be taught in school.

Ethics: Behavior considered in terms of what is right and what is wrong.

Evaluative praise (Ginott): Praise that expresses judgment about students' character or quality of work. Considered to be detrimental by Ginott and various other authorities.

External motivation: Synonymous with extrinsic motivation. Motivation from outside the individual.

Fetal alcohol spectrum disorder: A mental health diagnosis in which students show poor impulse control, poor judgment, lack of common sense, and learning difficulties. Caused by alcohol consumption by the mother during pregnancy.

Five A's of connecting (Albert): Acceptance, attention, appreciation, affirmation, and affection.

Five principles for a personal system of discipline (Charles): Developing your professionalism, clarifying your goals for students, establishing optimal classroom conditions, helping students accept responsibility for their behavior, and intervening helpfully when misbehavior occurs.

Four classical virtues (Marshall): Prudence, temperance, justice, and fortitude. Should be emphasized in the process of helping students develop desirable behavior.

Four R's of consequences (Albert): Consequences should be related to the misbehavior, reasonable, respectful, and reliably enforced.

Four-step approach to discipline (Borba): Respond, review, reflect, and make right.

General rules (Jones): General rules of behavior that apply at all times, as distinct from specific rules related to certain activities.

Generic consequences: The usual consequences teachers provide following student behavior, such as approval or disapproval.

Genuine discipline (Ginott): That which leads to student self-control and responsibility.

Genuine goal of class behavior (Dreikurs; Albert): Belonging, a fundamental desire to acquire a sense of place and value in a group.

Genuine incentives (Jones): Incentives that truly motivate students to work or behave appropriately, as contrasted with vague incentives such as "become a better person."

Graceful exits (Albert): Things teachers can do to distance themselves gracefully from confrontations with students who are very upset.

Grandma's rule (Jones): "First eat your vegetables, then you can have your dessert," or, "First finish your work, then you can do something you especially enjoy."

Group alerting (Kounin): Quickly getting students' attention to advise them of what they should be doing or do next.

Group concern (Jones): A condition in which every student has a stake in the behavior the group uses to earn preferred activity time.

Group dynamics (Redl and Wattenberg): Psychological forces that occur within groups and influence the behavior of group members.

Guided choices (Marshall): Eliciting from students a consequence or procedure to help redirect inappropriate or impulsive behaviors.

Hate crimes: Crimes committed against people because of their race, culture, or fundamental beliefs.

Helpless handraising (Jones): A condition in which a student sits with hand raised, not working unless the teacher is hovering nearby.

Hidden asset, teacher's (Ginott): Sincerely asking students, "How can I help you?" Showing willingness to help any given student at any given moment.

Hierarchy of social development (Marshall): A hierarchy of four levels used to help students reflect on their chosen behaviors. From lowest to highest, the four levels are: (A) anarchy, (B) bossing/bullying, (C) cooperation/conformity, and (D) democracy (inseparable from responsibility). Levels A and B are unacceptable in the classroom. Level C is the expected level of behavior and is essential for a civil society. Level D connotes taking the initiative to do the right thing without supervision.

Hostile response style: Teacher interaction with students that is abrasive or confrontive.

Hostile teachers (the Canters): Teachers who are rigid, demanding, and unfriendly.

I-messages (Ginott; Gordon): Teachers' expressing their personal feelings and reactions to situations without addressing student behavior or character. For example, "I have trouble teaching when there is so much noise in the room."

Inadequacy, displaying (Dreikurs): A mistaken goal of behavior in which the individual feigns inadequacy or inability to perform a task.

Incentive (Jones): Something outside of the individual that can be anticipated and that entices the individual to act.

Inner discipline (Coloroso): A desirable condition in which individuals control their own behavior and make responsible decisions.

Insistence (Morrish): A discipline tactic to be used when students appear reluctant to comply with directions.

Insubordination rule (Curwin and Mendler): If a student does not accept the consequence for breaking a class rule, then he or she will not be allowed to participate with the class until the consequence is accepted.

INTASC: The Interstate New Teacher Assessment and Support Consortium that has described competencies teachers require for professional teaching.

Interior loop (Jones): A classroom seating arrangement with wide aisles that allows teachers to move easily among students at work.

Intermittent reinforcement (Skinner): Reinforcement provided occasionally, not on a fixed schedule.

Internal motivation (Marshall): Motivation to be responsible, rooted in ethics and values.

Invite cooperation (Ginott): Encouraging and enticing students into activities and giving them choices, rather than demanding their participation.

I-statements: Statements that begin with "I" and tell how the speaker feels. The same as I-messages.

Laconic language (Ginott): Brevity of teacher's comments about misbehavior. For example, "This is work time."

Lead teachers (Glasser): Teachers who involve students in exploring topics and activities for learning. Lead teachers also provide necessary help and encourage students to do quality work.

Learning communities (Kohn): Classrooms in which students and teachers pursue topics of interest and actively support each other in their efforts to learn.

Learning disabilities (LD): Unusual difficulties students exhibit in learning certain subjects in school. A mental health diagnosis, not simply teacher observation or opinion.

Least coercive road (Gossen): A discipline strategy in which teachers use the least amount of coercion (of student behavior) that still allows the class to function effectively.

Living in poverty: *See* Economic disadvantage.

Logical consequences (Dreikurs): Conditions invoked by the teacher that are logically related to behavior students choose. For example, making amends for what one has done wrong.

Manager of restitution (Gossen): A teacher role in behavior management.

Massive time wasting (Jones): A condition Jones found prevalent in classrooms where discipline was not done efficiently.

Misbehavior: Behavior that is inappropriate for the setting or situation in which it occurs.

(Charles): Any behavior that, through intent or thoughtlessness, interferes with teaching or learning, threatens or intimidates others, or oversteps society's standards of moral, ethical, or legal behavior.

(Gordon): An adult concept in which a student's behavior causes a consequence that is unpleasant to the teacher.

Misbehavior, teacher (Charles): *See* Teacher misbehavior.

Misbehavior, types of

(Charles): Inattention, apathy, needless talk, moving about the room, annoying others, disruption, lying, stealing, cheating, sexual harassment, aggression and fighting, malicious mischief, and defiance of authority.

(Coloroso): Mistakes (unintentional), mischief (intentional light misbehavior), and mayhem (more serious misbehavior).

(Dreikurs; Albert): Attention-seeking, power seeking, revenge seeking, and feigned helplessness.

(Kagan, Kyle, and Scott): Aggression, breaking rules, confrontation, and disengagement.

Mistaken goals (Dreikurs; Albert): Goals of attention, power, revenge, and avoidance of failure that students seek in the mistaken belief they will bring positive recognition and sense of belonging.

Momentum (Kounin): Refers to teachers' getting activities started promptly, keeping them moving ahead, and bringing them to efficient transition or closure.

Moral core (Borba): The first three—empathy, conscience, and self-control—of Borba's seven essential virtues.

Moral intelligence (Borba): The ability to distinguish right from wrong, the establishment and maintenance of strong ethical convictions, and the willingness to act on those convictions in an honorable way.

Neurological-based behavior (NBB): Behavior associated with compromised neurological functioning, often outside the control of the student.

Neurological differences: Notable variations in student behavior, believed to be the result of differences in cerebral functioning.

No-lose method of conflict resolution (Gordon): An approach that finds a mutually acceptable solution to a disagreement, so that neither party is made to feel a loser.

Nonassertive response style (the Canters): Teacher responses that let students get by with misbehavior in the classroom.

Nonassertive teachers (the Canters): Teachers who take a passive, hands-off approach in dealing with students.

Noncontrolling methods (Gordon): Discipline in which teachers invite and encourage proper behavior, rather than using demands or threats.

Nonverbal communication (Jones): Communicating with students via body language.

Omission training (Jones): An incentive plan for an individual student who, by cutting down on undesired behavior, can earn preferred activity time for the entire class.

Oppositional defiant disorder: A mental health diagnosis in which students regularly oppose and defy the teacher and others.

Overlapping (Kounin): Refers to teachers' attending to two or more issues in the classroom at the same time.

Ownership of behavior problem

(Coloroso): Students taking responsibility for their actions so they can work out appropriate solutions.

(Gordon): The person who is troubled by a situation is said to "own the problem."

Participatory classroom management (Gordon and others): An operating procedure in which teachers share power and decision making with their students.

Passive listening (Gordon): A communication tactic, consisting only of listening, that encourages students to communicate.

People first language: Referring to the person first, then the person's condition (e.g., "students with dyslexia" rather than "dyslexic students").

Permissive classrooms: Classrooms in which teachers do not attempt to establish or maintain acceptable standards or student effort or conduct.

Personal improvement plan (Kagan, Kyle, and Scott): A plan devised cooperatively between teacher and student, to help curtail the student's disruptive behavior.

Personal system of discipline (Charles): How you will present and conduct yourself at school, the goals and aspirations you have for your students, the classroom conditions you want to maintain, how you will work individually or cooperatively with students to help ensure appropriate behavior, and how you will intervene when misbehavior occurs or appears imminent.

Perspective taking (Kohn): Doing one's best to see and understand a situation from another person's point of view.

Philosophy of discipline: The beliefs one has about the nature, purpose, and value of discipline.

Positive influence (Gordon): Influence teachers exert in a positive manner to encourage students to conduct themselves more appropriately.

Positive recognition (the Canters): Giving sincere personal attention to students who behave in keeping with class expectations.

Positivity (Marshall): Maintaining an inclination toward optimism.

Posttraumatic stress disorder: A mental heath diagnosis in which students have been adversely affected emotionally by witnessing or hearing about traumatic events.

Poverty, in: Describes any member of a family that has to spend more than one-third of its disposable income for food adequate to meet the family's nutritional needs.

Power (Albert): A basic student need for control, satisfied when students are given significant duties in the class and are allowed to participate in making decisions about class matters.

Power seeking behavior (Dreikurs; Albert): Behaviors such as temper tantrums, back talk, disrespect, and defiance that students use to try to show they have power over the teacher.

Practice of discipline (Charles): How discipline is put into effect and conducted in the classroom—follows from one's philosophy and theory of discipline.

Pragmatic discipline (the Wongs): An approach to discipline organized from best practices of teachers, rather than from a particular theory.

Praxis: A series of tests published by Educational Testing Service for assessing the competency levels of teachers.

Preferred activity time (PAT) (Jones): Time allocated for students to engage in activities of their preference; used as an incentive to encourage responsible behavior.

Preventing escalation of conflicts (Curwin and Mendler): Employing tactics such as allowing a cool-off period or rescheduling classwork for a more appropriate time.

Preventive I-messages (Gordon): I-messages teachers can use to influence students to behave more appropriately in the future. Such messages convey no blame.

Problem (Gordon): A situation that causes discomfort for someone.

Procedures (the Wongs): Detailed instructions that show students how to perform all activities in class—a procedure that eliminates most discipline problems.

Punishment

(Coloroso): Psychologically harmful consequences applied by teachers to students; likely to provoke resentment and retaliation.

(Dreikurs): Action taken by the teacher to get back at misbehaving students and show them who is boss.

(Redl and Wattenberg): Planned, unpleasant consequences, not physical, the purpose of which is to change behavior in positive directions.

(Skinner): Supplying aversive stimuli, a process that may or may not result in behavior change.

Quality curriculum (Glasser): A program of study that emphasizes excellence in learning that students consider useful.

Quality education (Glasser): Education in which students acquire knowledge and skills that the students themselves see as valuable.

Quality learning (Glasser): Learning in which students attain high competency in knowledge and skills they judge to be important in their lives.

Quality schoolwork (Glasser): Learning activities centered on knowledge and skills that students find important and engaging; students refine their work product until it reaches a high level of excellence.

Quality teaching (Glasser): Instruction in which teachers help students become proficient in knowledge and skills the students consider important. This is usually done via "lead teaching."

Rage: Extreme behavior, sometimes exhibited by students with neurological-based behavior (NBB), manifested as an explosion of temper that occurs suddenly with no real warning and may turn violent.

Rage cycle: Progression of rage through five phases—pre-rage, triggering, escalation, rage, and post-rage.

Raising responsibility (Marshall): Helping students move toward increased personal responsibility—a key element in improving student self-control and self-direction.

Real Discipline (Morrish): An approach to discipline that makes use of teacher insistence and careful teaching of expectations and procedures.

Reconciliation (Coloroso): A human relations skill in which individuals who have been in dispute take steps to resolve and smooth over their differences.

Reflection (Marshall): Thinking critically about one's own behavior, a valuable component in developing greater responsibility.

Reflective questions (Marshall): Questions posed to students to help them make better behavioral choices and assume responsibility.

Resolution (Coloroso): Ironing out the problem, one of the follow-up steps in dealing with misbehavior.

Restitution (Gossen; Coloroso): Repairing or replacing damage done in irresponsible behavior—one of the steps in resolving the problem.

Restitution triangle (Gossen): A triangle graphic that helps explain and guide the steps involved in the restitution process.

Revenge seeking (Dreikurs; Albert): A mistaken goal toward which students sometimes turn when thwarted in their desire to find acceptance in the group.

Routines (the Wongs): Detailed instructions that show students how to carry out various tasks in the classroom.

Rules: Statements that specify how students are to behave.

Sane messages (Ginott): Teacher messages that address situations rather than students' character.

Satiation (Kounin): Getting all one can tolerate of a given activity, resulting in frustration, boredom, or listlessness.

Say, See, Do teaching (Jones): A teaching method of repeated short cycles of teacher input, each followed by student response. Keeps students attentive and involved.

Self-control: *See* Self-discipline.

Self-diagnostic referral (Marshall): A self-diagnosis done by a student who has violated class rules and submitted as a plan for improvement—includes description of what was done wrong and the steps that will be taken to improve.

Self-discipline (Dreikurs; Albert; others): Self-control, which grows out of freedom to make decisions and having to live by the consequences.

Self-discipline, teacher's (Ginott): Teacher self-control, of paramount importance in helping students conduct themselves appropriately.

Sense of hope (Curwin): The belief that things will get better in the future, or that present tasks will be worthwhile. Many students have lost a sense of hope concerning the value of education.

Sensory integration dysfunction (SID): Irregularities in the process we use to take in information from our senses, organize the information, interpret it, and respond to it.

Seven deadly habits (Glasser): Seven things teachers do that damage relationships with students—criticizing, blaming, complaining, nagging, threatening, punishing, and rewarding.

Shaping behavior (Skinner): The process of using reinforcement to produce desired behavior in students.

SIR (Glasser): An acronym standing for the process of self-evaluation, improvement, and repetition, used to promote quality.

Situational assistance (Redl and Wattenberg): Providing help to students who, because of the difficulty of the task, are on the verge of misbehaving.

Six-D conflict resolution plan (Albert): A six-step tool for helping resolve matters under dispute.

Smoothness (Kounin): Absence of abrupt changes or interruptions by the teacher that interfere with students' activities or thought processes.

Social contract (Curwin and Mendler): The agreement concerning rules and consequences that teacher and students construct to govern behavior in the classroom.

Social interest (Dreikurs): The concept that one's personal well-being is dependent on the well-being of the group. This encourages individuals to behave in ways that benefit the group.

Specific rules (Jones): Classroom rules that detail specifically what students are to do and how they are to do it.

Student needs

(Charles): Security, belonging, hope, dignity, power, enjoyment, competence.

(Dreikurs; Albert): Belonging.

(Glasser): Security, love and belonging, control, freedom, fun.

Student positions (Kagan, Kyle, and Scott): Conglomerates of factors that leave students uninformed or dispose them to seek attention, show anger, avoid failure, become bored, seek control, or be overly energetic.

Student rights (the Canters): The right to be treated with respect and have teachers who do all they can to promote student success.

Student roles (Redl and Wattenberg): Roles students assume in the classroom, such as instigator, clown, leader, and scapegoat.

Successive approximation (Skinner): Behavior that, through reinforcement, moves progressively closer to the desired goal.

Support buddies (the Wongs): Students assigned to help or support each other.

Support groups (the Wongs): Groups of students who help and support each other.

Supporting student self-control (Redl and Wattenberg): Teachers' doing things that help students maintain self-control when they are on the verge of misbehaving.

Synergetic Discipline (Charles): Discipline that removes most causes of misbehavior and energizes the class.

Synergetic Teaching (Charles): Teaching in a manner that energizes the class. Done by putting in place combinations of elements known to produce heightened classroom energy.

Synergy (Charles): A heightened state of energy that can occur when two or more entities feed energy to each other.

Teacher misbehavior (Charles): Anything teachers do in the classroom that adversely affects learning or human relations, or that is unprofessional in any way.

Teacher rights (the Canters): Opportunity to teach in a professional manner, without interruption by students and with the backing of administrators and parents.

Teacher roles (Redl and Wattenberg): Various roles students expect teachers to play, such as surrogate parent, arbitrator, disciplinarian, and moral authority.

Teachers at their best (Ginott): Teachers, when using congruent communication that addresses situations rather than students' character, invites student cooperation, and accepts students as they are.

Teachers at their worst (Ginott): Teachers, when they name-call, label students, ask rhetorical questions, give long moralistic lectures, and make caustic remarks to their students.

Theory of discipline: An overall explanation of the elements that comprise discipline and how they work together to produce particular outcomes.

Theory X and Theory Y (Marshall): Theories of managing people. Theory X holds that people must be directed and controlled, while Theory Y holds that people should be encouraged and given responsibility.

Three C committee (Albert): A school committee whose purpose is to think of ways to help all students feel more capable, connected, and contributing.

Three C's (Albert): Albert's prescription for ensuring student sense of belonging in the class: feel capable, connect with others, and contribute to the class.

Three phases of Real Discipline: (1) Training for compliance, (2) teaching students how to behave, and (3) managing student choice.

Three Pillars of Win-Win Discipline (Kagan, Kyle, and Scott): Teacher and students on the same side, sharing responsibility, and emphasizing behavior that meets student's needs in a nondisruptive manner.

Three R's of reconciliatory justice (Coloroso): Restitution, resolution, and reconciliation.

Three R's of solutions (Nelsen and Lott): Solutions for correcting misbehavior that are related to what was done wrong, respectful of the persons involved, and reasonable.

True discipline: Defined by most authorities as inner discipline; self-discipline; self-control.

Trust (Charles and others): Confidence between teachers and students that the teacher is working in the students' best interests and will not harm them, while students are making genuine effort and are showing responsible self-control. Necessary for synergy and desirable in all aspects of teaching.

Value system: Overall, what members of particular cultures and segments of society believe to be right, proper, and worthwhile, and, conversely, what they believe to be wrong, improper, and of no worth.

Violence (Curwin and Mendler): Verbal abuse, physical threat or action against a person, or damage done maliciously to the property of another person.

Visual instruction plan (VIP) (Jones): Picture prompts that guide students through the process of the task or performance at hand.

Who owns the problem (Gordon): Persons bothered by a particular situation are said to "own the problem."

Why questions (Ginott): Counterproductive questions that teachers put to students, asking them to explain or justify their behavior (e.g., "Why did you . . . ?").

Withitness (Kounin): The teacher's knowing what is going on in all parts of the classroom at all times.

Work the crowd (Jones): Moving about the class while teaching and interacting with students.

Yes, if . . . (Gossen): A tactic to help teachers be more positive in their interactions with students. To be used in place of "No, because . . ."

You-messages (Ginott; Gordon): Teacher messages that attack students' character, such as "You are acting like barbarians." These messages are put-downs that can convey heavy blame and guilt.

BIBLIOGRAPHY

Acorn, S., and Offer, P. (Eds). 1998. *Living with brain injury: A guide for families and caregivers.* Toronto: University of Toronto Press.

Albert, L. 1996. *Cooperative discipline.* Circle Pines, MN: American Guidance Service.

Albert, L. 2003. *A teacher's guide to cooperative discipline.* Circle Pines, MN: American Guidance Service.

Amen, D. 2001. *Healing ADD: The breakthrough program that allows you to see and heal the six types of attention deficit disorder.* New York: G.P. Putnam's Sons.

American Academy of Child and Adolescent Psychiatry. 2004a. Child Psychiatry Facts for Families: Recommendations, Help and Guidance from the AACAP. http://pediatrics.about.com/library/bl_psych_policy_statements.htm.

American Academy of Child and Adolescent Psychiatry. 2004b. Children with Oppositional Defiant Disorder. www.aacap.org/publications/factsfam/72.htm.

American Academy of Child and Adolescent Psychiatry. 2004c. Teen Suicide. www.aacap.org/publications/factsfam/suicide.htm.

American Academy of Pediatrics. 2004. Fetal Alcohol Syndrome. www.aap.org/advocacy/chm98fet.htm.

Ascher, C. 1991. School programs for African American males. ERIC Digests. ED334340. www.ericdigests.org.

Attention Deficit Disorders Association, Southern Region, ADD/ADHD. 2002. www.adda-sr.org/BehaviorManagementIndex.htm.

Baruth, L., and Manning, M. 1992. *Multicultural education of children and adolescents.* Boston: Allyn & Bacon.

Bempechat, J. 2001. Fostering high achievement in African American children: Home, school, and public policy influences. http://eric-web.tc.columbia.edu/monographs/ti16_index.html.

Benard, B. 1997. Drawing forth resilience in all our youth. *Reclaiming Children and Youth,* 6(1): 29–32.

Biddulph, S. 1997. *Raising boys.* Sydney, Australia: Finch Publishing.

Borba, M. 2001. *Building moral intelligence.* San Francisco: Jossey-Bass.

Borba, M. 2003. *No more misbehavin': 38 difficult behaviors and how to stop them.* San Francisco: Jossey-Bass.

Borba, M. 2004. *Don't give me that attitude! 24 rude, selfish, insensitive things kids do and how to stop them.* San Francisco: Jossey-Bass.

Borba, M. 2005. *Nobody likes me: everybody hates me: The top 25 friendship problems and how to solve them.* San Francisco: Jossey-Bass.

Borba, M. 2005. Various articles posted on the Borba website. www.micheleborba.com.

Butterfield, R. 1994. Blueprints for Indian education: Improving mainstream schooling. ERIC Digests. ED372898. www.ericdigests.org.

Cajete, G. 1986. Science: A Native American perspective (A Culturally Based Science Education Curriculum). Ph.D. dissertation. San Diego, CA: International College/William Lyon University.

Canter, L., and Canter, M. 1976. *Assertive Discipline: A take-charge approach for today's educator.* Seal Beach, CA: Lee Canter & Associates. The second and third editions of the book, published in 1992 and 2001, are entitled *Assertive Discipline: Positive behavior management for today's classroom.*

Canter, L., and Canter, M. 1993. *Succeeding with difficult students: New strategies for reaching your most challenging students.* Santa Monica, CA: Lee Canter & Associates.

Centers for Disease Control and Prevention. 2004. Alcohol Consumption Among Women Who Are Pregnant or Who Might Become Pregnant—United States, 2002. Centers for Disease Control and Prevention. www.acbr.com/fas.

Charles, C. 1974. *Teachers' petit Piaget.* San Francisco: Fearon.

Charles, C. 2000. *The synergetic classroom.* Boston: Allyn & Bacon.

Charles, C. 2002. *Essential elements of effective discipline.* Boston: Allyn & Bacon.

Chavkin, N., and Gonzalez, J. 2000. Mexican immigrant youth and resiliency: Research and promising programs. ERIC Digests. ED447990. www.ericdigests.org.

Cheng, L. 1996. Enhancing communication: Toward optimal language learning for limited English proficient students. *Language, Speech and Hearing Services in Schools,* 28(2), 347–354.

Cheng, L. 1998. Enhancing the communication skills of newly-arrived Asian American students. ERIC Digests. www.ericdigests.org/1999-1/asian.html.

Claitor, D. 2003. Breaking Through: Interview of Ruby Payne. www.hopemag.com/issues/2003/septOct/breakingThrough.pdf.

Clark, E., Jutke, J., Minnes, P., and Ouellette-Kuntz. 2004. Secondary disabilities among adults with fetal alcohol spectrum disorder in British Columbia. *Journal of FAS International (2)*, 1–12.

Coker, D. 1988. Asian students in the classroom. *Education and Society, 1*(3), 19–20.

Coloroso, B. 1990. *Discipline: Creating a positive school climate.* Booklet; video; audio. Littleton, CO: Kids are worth it!

Coloroso, B. 2002. *Kids are worth it!: Giving your child the gift of inner discipline.* New York: Quill.

Coloroso, B. 2003. *The bully, the bullied, and the bystander: How parents and teachers can break the cycle of violence.* New York: HarperCollins.

Cook, P. 2004a. Behaviour, learning and teaching: Applied studies in FAS/FAE (Distance Education Curricula). Winnipeg, MB, Canada: Red River College.

Cook, P. 2004b. Sensory Integration Dysfunction: A Layperson's Guide. Booklet available from Paula Cook. pcook59@shaw.ca.

Cook, P. 2005. Rage: A Layperson's Guide to What to Do When Someone Begins to Rage. Booklet available from Paula Cook. pcook59@shaw.ca.

Cook, P., Kellie, R., Jones, K., and Goossen, L. 2000. *Tough kids and substance abuse.* Winnipeg, MB, Canada: Addictions Foundation of Manitoba.

Cornett, C. 1983. *What you should know about teaching and learning styles* (Fastback No. 191). Bloomington, IN: Phi Delta Kappa Foundation.

Cox, B., and Ramirez, M. 1981. Cognitive styles: Implications for multiethnic education. In J. Banks (Ed.), *Education in the 80s: Multiethnic Education* (pp. 61–71). Washington, DC: National Education Association.

Curwin, R. 1992. *Rediscovering hope: Our greatest teaching strategy.* Bloomington, IN: National Educational Service.

Curwin, R. 2003. *Making good choices: Developing responsibility, respect, and self-discipline in grades 4–9.* Thousand Oaks, CA: Corwin Press.

Curwin, R., and Mendler, A. 1988. *Discipline with dignity.* Alexandria, VA: Association for Supervision and Curriculum Development. Revised editions 1992, 1999, 2002.

Curwin, R., and Mendler, A. 1997. *As tough as necessary. Countering violence, aggression, and hostility in our schools.* Alexandria, VA: Association for Supervision and Curriculum Development.

Curwin, R., and Mendler, A. 2005. Practical Discipline Guidelines. www.disciplineassociates.com/dwd.htm.

Danielson, C. 1996. *Enhancing professional practice: A framework for teaching.* Washington, DC: Association for Supervision and Curriculum Development.

Davidson, H. 1993. *Just ask! A handbook for instructors of students being treated for mental disorders.* Calgary, AB, Canada: Detselig Enterprises Ltd.

DeAngelis, T. 2004. Children's mental health problems seen as 'epidemic'. *APA Monitor on Psychology: 35*(11), p. 38.

Diamond, M., and Hopson, J. 1998. *Magic trees of the mind: How to nurture your child's intelligence, creativity, and healthy emotions from birth through adolescence.* New York: Dutton.

Diller, D. 1999. Opening the dialogue: Using culture as a tool in teaching young African American children. *Reading Teacher, 52*(8), 820–858.

Dreikurs, R., and Cassel, P. 1995. *Discipline without tears.* New York: Penguin-NAL. Originally published in 1972.

Drye, J. 2000. Tort liability 101: When are teachers liable? Atlanta, GA: EducatorResources. www.Educator-Resources.com.

Dunn, R., Griggs, S., and Price, G. 1993. Learning styles of Mexican-American and Anglo-American elementary-school students. *Journal of Multicultural Counseling and Development,* 21(4): 237–247.

Echternach, C., and Cook, P. (2004). The Rage Cycle. Paper available from Paula Cook. pcook59@shaw.ca.

Education Trust, The. 2003. African American Achievement. Washington, DC. www.edtrust.org.

Faircloth, S., and Tippeconnic, J. 2000. Issues in the education of American Indian and Alaska Native students with disabilities. ERIC Digests. EDO-RC-00-3. www.ericdigests.org.

Faraone, S. 2003. *Straight talk about your child's mental health.* New York: The Guilford Press.

Feldman, E. 2004. Impact of mental illness on learning. Keynote Address at the 9th Midwest Conference on

Child and Adolescent Mental Health. Grand Forks, ND.

Feng, J. 1994. Asian-American children: What teachers should know. ERIC Digests. EDO-PS-94-4. www. ericdigests.org.

Foster, M. 1999. Teaching and learning in the contexts of African American English and culture. *Education and Urban Society. 31*(2), 177ff.

Gardner, H. 1983. *Frames of mind: The theory of multiple intelligences.* New York: Harper and Row.

Gardner, H. 1999. *Intelligence reframed: Multiple intelligences for the 21st century.* New York: Basic Books.

Gay. G. 2005. A Synthesis of Scholarship in Multicultural Education. North Central Regional Educational Laboratory. www.ncrel.org/sdrs/areas/issues/educatrs/leadrshp/le0gay.htm.

Ginott, H. 1971. *Teacher and child.* New York: Macmillan.

Ginott, H. 1972. I am angry! I am appalled! I am furious! *Today's Education, 61,* 23–24.

Ginott, H. 1973. Driving children sane. *Today's Education, 62,* 20–25.

Glasser, W. 1969. *Schools without failure.* New York: Harper & Row.

Glasser, W. 1986. *Control theory in the classroom.* New York: HarperCollins.

Glasser, W. 1992. The quality school curriculum. *Phi Delta Kappan, 73*(9), 690–694.

Glasser, W. 1998a. *Choice theory in the classroom.* New York: HarperCollins.

Glasser, W. 1998b. *The quality school: Managing students without coercion.* New York: HarperCollins.

Glasser, W. 1998c. *The quality school teacher.* New York: HarperCollins.

Glasser, W. 2001. *Every student can succeed.* Chatsworth, CA: William Glasser Incorporated.

Glavac, M. 2005. Summary of Major Concepts Covered by Harry K. Wong. The Busy Educator's Newsletter. www.glavac.com.

Goorian, B., and Brown, K. 2002. Trends and Issues: School Law. ERIC Clearinghouse on Educational Management. http://eric.uoregon.edu/trends_issues/law/index.html.

Gordon, T. 1970. *Parent Effectiveness Training: A tested new way to raise responsible children.* New York: New American Library.

Gordon, T. 1974, 1987. *T.E.T.: Teacher Effectiveness Training.* New York: David McKay.

Gordon, T. 1976. *P.E.T. in action.* New York: Bantam.

Gordon, T. 1977. *Leader Effectiveness Training, L.E.T.* New York: Wyden Books.

Gordon, T. 1989. *Discipline that works: Promoting self-discipline in children.* New York: Random House.

Gossen, D. 1993. *Restitution: Restructuring school discipline.* Chapel Hill, NC: New View Publications.

Gossen, D., 2002. What do you want? Student behavior. *yA! Magazine for Middle Level Educators, 3*(3).

Gossen, D. 2004. *It's all about we: Rethinking discipline using restitution.* Saskatoon, SK, Canada: Chelsom Consultants Ltd.

Gossen, D. 2005. Diane Gossen on Restitution. www.realrestitution.com.

Gossen, D., and Andersen, J. (1995). *Creating the conditions: Leadership for quality schools.* Chapel Hill, NC: New View Publications.

Grandin, T. 2005. Website on Temple Grandin. www.templegrandin.org.

Greene, R. 2001. *The explosive child.* New York: Harper Collins.

Griggs, S., and Dunn, R. 1996. Hispanic-American Students and Learning Style. http://ceep.crc.uiuc.edu/eecearchive/digests/1996/griggs96.html.

Hall, P., and Hall, N. 2003. *Educating oppositional and defiant children.* Alexandria, VA: Association for Supervision and Curriculum Development.

Hargan, L. 2003. Teaching Students of Poverty, NCL Brief. www.ctlonline.org/ESEA/newsletter.html.

Harmon, M. 1993. Reducing the risk of drug involvement among early adolescents: An evaluation of drug abuse resistance education (DARE). Schaffer Library of Drug Policy, (posted 2005). www.druglibrary.org/schaffer/index.htm.

Hill, P. 2005. Pharmacological Treatment of Rage. www.focusproject.org.uk/SITE/UPLOAD/DOCUMENT/Hill.

Huang, G. 1993. Beyond culture: Communicating with Asian American children and families. ERIC Digests. ED366673. www.ericdigests.org.

Institute of Medicine. 1996. Fetal Alcohol Syndrome: Diagnosis, Epidemiology, Prevention, and Treatment. www.come-over.to/FAS/IOMsummary.htm.

Interstate New Teacher Assessment and Support Consortium. 2003. Website: http://www.ccsso.org/intascst.html#preface

Irvine, J., and Fraser, J. 1998. Warm demanders. *Education Week on the WEB.* www.edweek.org/ew/1998/35irvine.h17.

Jones, F. 1987a. *Positive classroom discipline.* New York: McGraw-Hill.

Jones, F. 1987b. *Positive classroom instruction.* New York: McGraw-Hill.

Jones, F. 2001. *Fred Jones's tools for teaching.* Santa Cruz, CA: Fredric H. Jones & Associates.

Jones, J. 2002. *The video toolbox.* Santa Cruz, CA: Fredric H. Jones & Associates.

Kagan, L., Scott, S., and Kagan, S. 2003. *Win-Win discipline course workbook.* San Clemente, CA: Kagan Publishing.

Kagan, S. 2001. Teaching for character and community. *Educational Leadership, 59*(2), 50–55.

Kagan, S. 2002. What is Win-Win Discipline? *Kagan Online Magazine, 1*(15). www.KaganOnline.com.

Kagan, S., Kyle, P., and Scott, S. 2004. *Win-win discipline.* San Clemente, CA: Kagan Publishing.

Kellerman, T. 2003. The FAS Community Resource Center. www.comeover.to/FASCRC.

Kim, B. 1985. (Ed.). *Literacy and languages. The second yearbook of literacy and languages in Asia, International Reading Associations special interest group.* Seoul, South Korea: International Conference on Literacy and Languages (August 12–14, 1985).

Kohn, A. 1993. *Punished by rewards: The trouble with gold stars, incentive plans, A's, praise, and other bribes.* Boston: Houghton Mifflin.

Kohn, A. 1999. *The schools our children deserve: Moving beyond traditional classrooms and "tougher standards."* Boston: Houghton Mifflin.

Kohn, A. 2001. *Beyond discipline: From compliance to community.* Upper Saddle River, NJ: Merrill/Prentice Hall. 1996 edition published Alexandria, VA: Association for Supervision and Curriculum Development.

Kounin, J. 1971. *Discipline and group management in classrooms.* New York: Holt, Rinehart & Winston. Reissued in 1977.

Kranowitz, C. 1998. *The out-of-sync child.* New York: Skylight Press.

Kranowitz, C., Szkut, S., Balzer-Martin, L., Haber, E., and Sava, D. 2003. Answers to Questions Teachers Ask About Sensory Integration. Las Vegas, NV: Sensory Resources LLC.

Krovetz, M. 1999. *Fostering resiliency: Expecting all students to use their minds and hearts well.* Thousand Oaks, CA: Corwin Press.

Ladson-Billings, G. 2000. Fighting for our lives: Preparing teachers to teach African American students. *Journal of Teacher Education, 51*(3), 206–214.

Latinos in School: Some facts and findings. 2001. ERIC Digests. www.ericdigests.org.

Learning Disabilities Association of America. 2005. Accommodations, Techniques, and Aids for Teaching. www.ldanatl.org/aboutld/teachers/understanding/accommodations.asp.

Levine, M. 2003. *A mind at a time.* New York: Simon and Schuster Adult Publishing Group.

Levinson, H. 2000. *The discovery of cerebellar-vestibular syndromes and therapies: A solution to the riddle—dyslexia.* (2nd ed.). Lake Success, NY: Stonebridge Publishing, Ltd.

Lockwood, A., and Secada, W. 2000. Transforming education for Hispanic youth: Exemplary practices, programs, and schools. U.S. Department of Education. www.ncela.gwu.edu/pubs/resource/hispanicyouth/ch6.htm.

Lucas, T., Henze, R., and Donato, R. 1990. Promoting the success of Latino language minority students. An exploratory study of six high schools. *Harvard Educational Review, 60,* 315–340.

Marshall, M. (Monthly since August, 2001). Promoting Responsibility & Learning: The Monthly Newsletter. www.MarvinMarshall.com.

Marshall, M. 1998. *Fostering social responsibility.* Bloomington, IN: Phi Delta Kappa.

Marshall, M. 2001. *Discipline without stress punishments, or rewards: How teachers and parents promote responsibility & learning.* Los Alamitos, CA: Piper Press.

Marshall, M. 2005a. A Letter Worth Reading. www.marvinmarshall.com/aletterworthreading.html.

Marshall, M. 2005b. A Principal's Experience. www.marvinmarshall.com/principal.htm.

Marshall, M. 2005c. Classroom Meetings. www.disciplinewithoutstress.com/sample_chapters.html.

Marshall, M. 2005d. Collaboration for Quality Learning. www.disciplinewithoutstress.com/sample_chapters.html.

Marshall, M. 2005e. Promoting Positivity, Choice, and Reflection. www.MarvinMarshall.com/promoting_positivity.htm.

Marshall, M. 2005f. Reducing Perfectionism. www.disciplinewithoutstress.com/sample_chapters.html.

Marshall, M. 2005g. Samples of Hierarchies for Promoting Learning. www.marvinmarshall.com/hierarchy.htm.

Matsuda, M. 1989. Working with Asian Family members: Some communication strategies. *Topics in Language Disorders, 9*(3), 45–53.

McCollough, S. 2000. Teaching African American students. *Clearing House, 74*(1), 5–6.

McGregor, D. 1960. *The human side of enterprise.* New York: McGraw-Hill.

McKinley, J. 2003. Leveling the Playing Field and Raising African American Students' Achievement in Twenty-nine Urban Classrooms. New Horizons for Learning. www.newhorizons.org.

Mee, C. 1997. *2,000 voices: Young adolescents' perceptions and curriculum implications.* Columbus, OH: National Middle School Association.

Mendler, A. 2001. *Connecting with students.* Alexandria, VA: Association for Supervision and Curriculum Development.

Mendler, A., and Curwin, R. 1999. *Discipline with dignity for challenging youth.* Bloomington, IN: National Education Service.

Morrish, R. 1997. *Secrets of discipline: 12 keys for raising responsible children.* Fonthill, ON, Canada: Woodstream Publishing.

Morrish, R. 2000. *With all due respect: Keys for building effective school discipline.* Fonthill, ON, Canada: Woodstream Publishing.

Morrish, R. 2003. *FlipTips.* Fonthill, ON, Canada: Woodstream Publishing.

Morrish, R. 2005. What Is Real Discipline? www.realdiscipline.com.

National Alliance for the Mentally Ill (NAMI). 2004. About NAMI. www.nami.org/Template.cfm? Section=About_Nami.

National Center for Education Statistics. 2001a. Overview of Public Elementary and Secondary Schools and Districts: School Year 2001–02 http://nces.ed.gov/programs/quarterly/vol_5/5_2/q3_5.asp#top.

National Center for Education Statistics. 2001b. Public Alternative Schools and Programs for Students At Risk of Education Failure: 2000–01 Executive Summary. http://nces.ed.gov/surveys/frss/publications/2002004.

National Coalition of Advocates for Students. 1994. *Delivering on the promise: Positive practices for immigrant students.* Boston: Author.

National Council for Learning Disabilities. 2005. The ABCs of Learning Disabilities. www.ncld.org.

National Education Association. 1975. Code of Ethics of the Education Profession. www.nea.org/aboutnea/code.html.

National Institute of Mental Health. 1999. Mental Health: A Report of the Surgeon General. www.surgeongeneral.gov/library/mentalhealth.

National Institute of Mental Health. 2005. Health Information Quick Links. www.nimh.nih.gov.

National Institute on Drug Abuse. 2004. InfoFacts. www.drugabuse.gov.

Nelsen, J. 1996. *Positive discipline.* New York: Ballantine.

Nelsen, J., Lott, L., and Glenn, H. 1993, 2000. *Positive discipline in the classroom.* Rocklin, CA: Prima.

North Central Regional Educational Laboratory. 2005. Culturally Responsive African-American Teachers. info@ncrel.org.

Oregon School Boards Association 2004. Breaking barriers: Poverty—The elephant in the room. www.osba.org/hotpics/gap/poverty.htm.

Packer, L. 2005. Overview of Rage Attacks. www.tourettesyndrome.net/rage_overview.htm.

Papolos, D., and Papolos, J. 2002. *The bipolar child.* New York: Broadway Books.

Parents' Guide to Helping Kids with Learning Difficulties. 2005. www.schwablearning.org/index.asp.

Payne, R. 2001. *A framework for understanding poverty.* Highlands, TX: Aha! Process, Inc.

Payne, R. 2003. Quoted in Claitor, D. 2003. Breaking Through: Interview of Ruby Payne. www.hopemag.com/issues/2003/septOct/breakingThrough.pdf.

Pellegrino, K. 2005. The Effects of Poverty on Teaching and Learning. www.teachnology.com/tutorials/teaching/poverty.

Pewewardy, C., and Hammer, P. 2003. Culturally responsive teaching for American Indian students. ERIC Digests. ED482325. www.ericdigests.org.

Philips, S. 1983. *The invisible culture.* New York: Longman.

Piaget, J. 2001. *The psychology of intelligence.* London: Routledge & Kegan Paul.

Portland Public Schools. 2003. Supporting American Indian/Alaska Native Students in School. Title IX Indian Education Project Staff and Parent Board. http://comped.salkeiz.k12.or.us/indian-ed/ai-an.htm.

Qualities of effective programs for immigrant adolescents with limited schooling. 1998. ERIC Digest. ED423667. www.ericdigests.org.

Rammler, L. 2005. Interview with Linda H. Rammler. Ask the Expert. www.explosivekids.org/pdf/ rammler.pdf.

Reed, R. 1988. Education and achievement of young black males. In J. W. Gibbs (Ed.), *Young, black, and male in America: An endangered species.* Dover: Auburn Publishing Company.

Redl, F., and Wattenberg, W. 1951. *Mental hygiene in teaching.* New York: Harcourt, Brace & World. Revised and reissued in 1959.

Reducing Adolescent Risk: Toward An Integrated Approach. (D. Rowe, Ed.). 2003. Newbury Park, CA: Sage Press. www.sagepub.com/book.aspx?pid=9315.

Schwartz, F. 1981. Supporting or subverting learning: Peer group patterns in four tracked schools. *Anthropology and Education Quarterly, 12*(2), 99–120.

Schwartz, W. 2000. New trends in language education for Hispanic students. ERIC Digests. ED442913. www.ericdigests.org.

Schwartz, W. 2002. School practices for equitable discipline of African American students. ERIC Digests. ED455343. www.ericdigests.org.

Shaywitz, S., and Shaywitz, B. 2003. Drs. Sally and Bennett Shaywitz on Brain Research and Reading. www.schwablearning.org/Articles.asp?r=35.

Skinner, B. 1953. *Science and human behavior.* New York: Macmillan.

Skinner, B. 1954. The science of learning and the art of teaching. *Harvard Educational Review, 24,* 86–97.

Skinner, B. 1971. *Beyond freedom and dignity.* New York: Knopf.

Spence, G. 1995. *How to argue and win every time.* New York: St. Martin's Press.

St. Germaine, R. 1995. Drop-out rates among American Indian and Alaska Native Students: Beyond cultural discontinuity. ERIC Digests. Eric document reproduction service no ED 388 492.

Starr, L. 1999. Speaking of Classroom Management— An Interview with Harry K. Wong. *Education World.* www.education-world.com/a_curr/ curr161.shtml.

Storti, C. 1999. *Figuring foreigners out: A practical guide.* Yarmouth, ME: Intercultural Press.

Strategies for Teaching Minorities. 2004. www.as .wvu.edu/~equity/general.html.

Strategies for Teaching Science to African American Students. 2005. www.as.wvu.edu/~equity/african .html.

Streissguth, A., Barr, H., Kogan, J., and Bookstein, F. 1997. Primary and secondary disabilities in fetal alcohol syndrome. In A. Streissguth and J. Kanter (Eds.), *The challenge of fetal alcohol syndrome: Overcoming secondary disabilities* (23–39). Seattle: University of Washington Press.

Swisher, K. 1991. American Indian/Alaskan Native learning styles: Research and practice. ERIC Digest. ED335175. www.ericdigests.org.

Teplin, L. 2001. OJJDP Fact Sheet. Assessing Alcohol, Drug, and Mental Disorders in Juvenile Detainees. U.S. Department of Justice. Office of Juvenile Justice and Delinquency Prevention.

Tobler, N., and Stratton, H. 1997. Effectiveness of school-based drug prevention programs: A meta-analysis of the research. *Journal of Primary Prevention, 18*(1), 71–128.

Trueba, H., and Cheng, L. 1993. *Myth or reality: Adaptive strategies of Asian Americans in California.* Bristol, PA: Falmer Press.

University of Sheffield. 2005. Teaching students with mental health conditions. www.shef.ac.uk/disability/ teaching/mental/10_examples.html.

U.S. Department of Education. 1998. *Preventing bullying: A manual for schools and communities.* www.cde.ca.gov spbranch/ssp/bullymanual.htm.

Walsh, C. 1991. Literacy and school success: Considerations for programming and instruction. In C. Walsh and H. Prashker (Eds.), *Literacy development for bilingual students.* Boston: New England Multifunctional Resource Center for Language and Culture Education.

Wierzbicka, A. 1991. Japanese key words and core cultural values. *Language in Society, 20*(3), 333–385.

William Glasser Institute. 2005. Control Theory. www .wglasser.com/whatisct.htm.

Wong, H. 2001. Selection of Tips for Teachers. www.glavac.com/harrywong.htm.

Wong, H., and Wong, R. 2000a. The First Five Minutes Are Critical. Gazette Article. Teachers.net. http:// teachers.net/gazette/NOV00/wong.html.

Wong, H., and Wong, R. 2000b. The Problem Is Not Discipline. Gazette Article. Teachers.net. http:// teachers.net/ gazette/SEP00/wong.html.

Wong, H., and Wong, R. 2000c. Your First Day. Gazette Article. Teachers.net. http://teachers.net/gazette/ JUN00/covera.html.

Wong, H., and Wong, R. 2002. How to Start School Successfully. Gazette Article. Teachers.net. http:// teachers.net/gazette/AUG02/wong.html.

Wong, H., and Wong, R. 2004a. A Well-Oiled Learning Machine. Gazette Article. Teachers.net. http:// teachers.net/wong/MAR04.

Wong, H., and Wong, R. 2004b. *The first days of school: How to be an effective teacher.* Mountain View, CA: Harry K. Wong Publications.

Wong, H., and Wong, R. 2005. The First Ten Days of School. Gazette Article. Teachers.net. http://teachers.net/wong/JAN05.

Yong, F., and Ewing, N. 1992. A Comparative Study of the Learning-Style Preferences among Gifted African-American, Mexican-American and American Born Chinese Middle-Grade Students. *Roeper Review, 14*(3), 120–123.

Academic difficulties, in neurological-based behavior, 38
Acceptance, Albert on, 95
Acknowledgment
    Gordon on, 82
    Marshall on, 215
Active student involvement (Fred Jones), xxiv, 113–126
    backup systems, 123–124
    bell work, 117–118
    body language, 113–114, 116, 118–119
    classroom structure, 117
    concept cases, 127–128
    general rules, 117
    Grandma's rule, 121
    group concern, 122–124
    helpless handraising, 124
    incentives, 120–124
    massive time wasters, 114–115
    nonverbal communication, 115
    omission training, 123
    physical proximity, 119
    preferred activity time (PAT), 121–124
    providing help efficiently, 124–125
    Say, See, Do teaching, 115–116, 119–120
    setting limits, 118–119
    specific rules, 117
    summary suggestions, 127
    visual instruction plan (VIP), 120, 125
    work the crowd, 116
Advising, 83
Affection, Albert on, 95
Affective disorders, 36, 41
Affirmation, Albert on, 95
African American students
    improving classroom experiences for, 23–24, 30–31
    information about, 23–24
Agendas, for classroom meetings, 107, 109
Aggression
    Curwin and Mendler on handling, 176–177
    as disruptive behavior, 156, 157
Agreements
    Charles on, 270–271
    Glasser on, 76–77
    Jones on, 118

Alaska Native students. *See* American Indian/Alaska Native students
Albert, Linda (Cooperative Discipline), xxiii, 93–99
Alcohol, in fetal alcohol spectrum disorder (FASD), 36, 45–46
American Indian/Alaska Native students
    improving classroom experiences for, 26–28, 30–31
    information about, 26–28
Analyzing, 83
Anarchy, Marshall on, 211
Anger
    Curwin and Mendler on handling, 176–177
    hostile teachers (Canter and Canter), 66–67
    Kagan, Kyle, and Scott on handling, 159
    rage cycle, phases of, 46–49
Anxiety disorders, 36, 37
Appreciation
    Albert on, 95
    Ginott on, 61
    Nelsen and Lott on, 107, 108
Asian American/Pacific Islander students
    improving classroom experiences for, 26, 30–31
    information about, 24–26
Asperger syndrome, 44
Assertive Discipline (Canter and Canter), xxii, 55, 65–69
    assertive teachers, 66, 67
    corrective actions, 67–69
    discipline hierarchy in, 67–69
    hostile teachers, 66–67
    nonassertive teachers, 66, 67
    positive recognition, 67
    response styles, 66–67
    student rights in the classroom, 65
    teacher rights in the classroom, 65
At-risk students, Curwin and Mendler on, 172–173
Attention, Albert on, 95
Attention-deficit hyperactivity disorder (ADHD), 36, 37, 40, 45–46
Attention seeking
    Albert on, 94, 96
    Dreikurs on, 63
    Kagan, Kyle, and Scott on, 158

Authority, Morrish on, 232–233
Autism spectrum disorder (ASD), 36, 44–45
Avoidance
    Albert on, 97–98
    Charles on, 252–253

Basic student needs
    Charles on, 247
    Glasser on, 73–74
Behavior. *See also* Misbehavior
    as choice (Canter and Canter), 65–66
    as choice (Charles), 252
    as choice (Glasser), xxii
    as choice (Marshall), 210, 214, 218–219
    as choice (Morrish), 233–234
    difficulties, in neurological-based behavior, 38
    of economically disadvantaged students, 29–30
    general suggestions for working with students, 30–31
    misbehavior versus, 8
    structure and limits on student, 87–88, 118–119
    value systems and, 20–28
Behavior management, discipline versus, 9–10
Behavior shaping (Skinner), xxii, 55, 57–58
Belonging
    Albert on, 94
    Dreikurs on, 63
    Gossen on, 191–192
Bipolar disorder, 36, 41
Black students. *See* African American students
Body carriage, Jones on, 119
Body language, Jones on, 113–114, 116, 118–119
Borba, Michele (moral intelligence theory), xxv, 187, 195–205
Bored students
    Kagan, Kyle, and Scott on, 160
    misbehavior and, 254–255
Bossing
    Glasser on boss teaching, 75
    Marshall on, 211, 216
Brain injuries, 37

Brainstorming, in classroom meetings (Nelsen and Lott), 108
Breach of duty, 17
Breathing, Jones on, 118
Bullying
    Curwin and Mendler on, 178–179
    Marshall on, 211

Canter, Lee and Marlene (Assertive Discipline), xxii, 55, 65–69
Caucasian American students
    information about, 21–22
    values of, 21
Character traits, in fostering moral intelligence, 201–203
Charisma, Charles on, 248–249
Charles, C. M. (Synergistic Discipline), xxiv, 245–262
Charles, Gail, sample discipline plan of, 279–281
Childhood mental health conditions, 36–37
Choice Theory (Glasser), xxiii, 72, 73–78
    basic needs, 73–74
    behavior agreements, 76–77
    boss teaching, 75
    concept cases, 90–91
    connecting habits, 77
    lead teaching, 75–76
    quality curriculum, 74
    quality education, 74
    quality learning, 74
    quality schoolwork, 76
    quality teaching, 75
    seven deadly habits, 77
    SIR, 75
    standards of conduct, 76
    student needs, 73–74
    summary suggestions, 90
Chores, Jones on, 117
Classroom discipline, 1–19. See also Misbehavior
    through active student involvement (Jones), xxiv, 113–126
    through Assertive Discipline (Canter and Canter), xxii, 55, 65–69
    as basic competency of teachers, 7–10
    behavior management versus, 9–10
    through Choice Theory (Glasser), xxiii, 72, 73–78
    through Classrooms as Communities (Kohn), xxv, 72, 84–89
    comparing classrooms, 1–2
    through congruent communication (Ginott), xxii, 55, 60–62
    through Cooperative Discipline (Albert), xxiii, 93–99

    through democratic teaching (Dreikurs), xxii, 55, 63–65
    through Discipline with Dignity (Curwin and Mendler), xxiii, 168–183
    evolution of, 54–69
    through Group Dynamics (Redl and Wattenberg), xxi, 54, 55–56
    through Inner Discipline (Coloroso), xxiv, 99–104
    intervention aspect of, 261–262, 269–270
    through lesson and group management (Kounin), xxii, 58–60
    through maintaining hope (Curwin), xxiii, 179–180
    through moral intelligence theory (Borba), xxv, 187, 195–205
    personal system of, 11–16, 266–284
    through Positive Discipline (Nelsen and Lott), xxiv, 104–109
    through pragmatic classroom management (Wong and Wong), xxiv, 130–147
    problems with, 228
    through Raise Responsibility System (Marshall), xxv, 208–223
    through Real Discipline (Morrish), xxv, 227–242
    through self-restitution theory (Gossen), xxvi, 187–195
    through shaping desired behavior (Skinner), xxii, 55, 57–58
    through student self-control (Gordon), xxiii, 72, 79–84
    through Synergistic Discipline (Charles), xxiv, 245–262
    teacher–student relationships in, 237–238, 278–281
    timeline of contributions to field, xxi–xxvi
    through Win-Win Discipline (Kagan, Kyle, and Scott), xxvi, 151–165
    working with students, 10–11
Classroom meetings
    Kohn on, 85
    Marshall on, 217
    Nelsen and Lott on, 106–109
Classrooms as Communities (Kohn), xxv, 72, 84–89
    compliant behavior, 85–86
    concept cases, 90–91
    constructivist theory, 86
    learning communities, 84–85
    perspective taking, 85
    summary suggestions, 90

Coercion, student misbehavior based in, 257
Collaboration
    Gordon on, 80
    Marshall on, 215
Coloroso, Barbara (Inner Discipline), xxiv, 99–104
Communication skills. See also Congruent communication (Ginott)
    Charles on, 249, 257
    in classroom meetings (Nelsen and Lott), 107
    I-messages in, 61, 79–82, 107
    listening, 82, 216
    nonverbal communication, 113–116, 118–119
    you-messages in, 61, 80
Community alliances, Kagan, Kyle, and Scott on, 163
Competencies of teachers
    Danielson on, 7
    discipline as, 7–10
    INTASC recommendations, 2–6
    Praxis Series, 6–7
Compliance, Morrish on, 230–233, 240–241
Compliments, Nelsen and Lott on, 107, 108
Conduct disorder, 36, 37
Conflict resolution
    Albert on, 99
    Charles on, 249–250, 262
    Curwin and Mendler on, 176–177
    Gordon on, 83–84
    Gossen on, 195
    Marshall on, 217
Conformity, Marshall on, 211
Confrontation
    Albert on, 97–98
    Charles on, 262
    Curwin and Mendler on, 176–177
    as disruptive behavior, 156, 157
    Gordon on, 81–82
Congruent communication (Ginott), xxii, 55, 60–62
    appreciative praise, 61
    conferring dignity, 61
    defined, 60–61
    evaluative praise, 61
    genuine discipline, 62
    hidden asset, 61
    I-messages, 61
    inviting cooperation, 61
    laconic language, 61
    sane messages, 62
    self-discipline, 61, 62
    teachers at their best, 61
    teachers at their worst, 61

why questions, 61
you-messages, 61
Conscience, Borba on, 197
Consequences
    Albert on, 96, 98–99
    Curwin and Mendler on, 170,
        174–175
    Dreikurs on, 64
    Kagan, Kyle, and Scott on, 162
    Morrish on, 238–239
    sample discipline plan emphasiz-
        ing, 275–278
Contracts, Kagan, Kyle, and Scott on,
    162
Control seeking, Kagan, Kyle, and
    Scott on, 159
Conventional consequences, Curwin
    and Mendler on, 175
Cook, Paula, and neurological-based
    behavior, 34, 35
Cooperation
    Albert on. *See* Cooperative Disci-
        pline (Albert)
    cooperative work groups, Wong
        and Wong on, 146
    inviting by teacher (Ginott), 61
    Marshall on, 211
Cooperative Discipline (Albert), xxiii,
    93–99
    attention, 95
    attention-getting mechanisms
        (AGMs), 94, 96
    avoidance-of-failure behavior, 97
    belonging, 94
    circle of friends, 95
    class code of conduct, 96
    concept cases, 110–111
    confrontation avoidance,
        97–98
    consequences, 96, 98–99
    encouragement, 95
    Five A's of connecting, 95
    Four R's of consequences, 99
    genuine goal, 94
    graceful exits, 98
    mistaken goals, 94
    power, 94, 96–97
    revenge, 94, 97
    Six-D conflict resolution plan, 99
    summary suggestions, 110
    Three C Committee, 95
    Three C's, 94–95
    withdrawal, 94
Coopetition, 249
Criticizing, 83
Curriculum, quality (Glasser), 74
Curwin, Richard (Discipline with
    Dignity), xxiii, 168–183

Curwin, Richard (maintaining hope),
    xxiii, 179–180

Danielson, Charlotte, professional
    teaching competencies and, 7
Democratic teaching (Dreikurs), xxii,
    55, 63–65
    attention seeking, 63
    autocratic classrooms, 63
    belonging, 63
    democratic classroom, defined, 63
    encouragement, 64
    genuine goal of behavior, 63
    inadequacy, 63
    logical consequences, 64
    mistaken goals, 63
    permissive classrooms, 63
    power seeking, 63
    revenge seeking, 63
    self-control, 63
    social interest, 64
    true discipline, 64
Desires, misbehavior and thwarted, 251
Difficult-to-control students, Curwin
    and Mendler on, 172–173
Dignity
    conferring, by teacher (Ginott), 61
    Curwin and Mendler on. *See* Disci-
        pline with Dignity (Curwin and
        Mendler)
Discipline. *See* Classroom discipline;
    Misbehavior
Discipline plans
    Charles on, 258–261
    Morrish on, 234–237
    sample, 275–281
    Wong and Wong on, 134–135
Discipline with Dignity (Curwin and
    Mendler), xxiii, 168–183
    bullying and, 178–179
    concept cases, 184
    conflict and, 176–177
    consequences, 170, 174–175
    core values, 170–171
    dignity, defined, 168
    hate crimes and, 178–179
    motivating students, 180
    preventing escalation, 175–176
    rules, 170, 174–175
    sense of hope and, xxiii, 179–180
    with students who are aggressive,
        176–177
    with students who are behaviorally
        at risk, 172–173
    with students who are difficult to
        control, 173–176
    with students who are hostile,
        176–177

with students who are violent,
    176–177
    summary suggestions, 183
    teacher preparation and change for,
        171, 180–182
Disengagement, as disruptive behav-
    ior, 156, 157
Disruptive behaviors
    Curwin and Mendler on, 172–177
    Kagan, Kyle, and Scott on,
        154–161
    student positions and, 154–158,
        161–162
    types of, 156, 157
Dreikurs, Rudolf (democratic teach-
    ing), xxii, 55, 63–65
Due diligence, 17
Dyscalcula, 42
Dyslexia, 42, 43
Dyspraxia, 42

Economically disadvantaged students
    general suggestions for working
        with, 30–31
    improving classroom experiences
        of, 29–30
    information about, 28–30
Educational Testing Service (ETS),
    Praxis Series, 6–7
Effective teachers
    Jones on, 115–116
    Wong and Wong on, 132, 146
Efficient help, Jones on, 124–125
Egocentric personality, misbehavior
    and, 253
Empathy, Borba on, 196–197
Encouragement
    Albert on, 95
    Dreikurs on, 64
    Marshall on, 215
Energetic students, Kagan, Kyle, and
    Scott on, 159
Ethics of instruction, 18–19, 248
Ethnic and cultural backgrounds,
    20–28
    African American, 23–24, 30–31
    American Indian/Alaska Native,
        26–28, 30–31
    Asian American/Pacific Islander,
        24–26, 30–31
    Caucasian American, 21–22
    general suggestions for working
        with, 30–31
    Hispanic American, 22–23, 30–31
    recently arrived immigrants, 28,
        30–31
Expediency, misbehavior and, 251
Eye contact, Jones on, 119

Facial expression, Jones on, 119
Failure avoidance
    Albert on, 97
    Kagan, Kyle, and Scott on, 158–159
Fairness, Borba on, 200
Fetal alcohol syndrome disorder (FASD), 36, 45–46
Follow-up, Kagan, Kyle, and Scott on, 155, 160, 161–162

Generalized anxiety disorder (GAD), 37
Generic consequences, Curwin and Mendler on, 175
Gibbs, Nathan, 137–141
Ginott, Haim (congruent communication), xxii, 55, 60–62
Glasser, William (Choice Theory), xxiii, 72, 73–78
Gordon, Thomas (Self-Control), xxiii, 72, 79–84
Gossen, Diane (self-restitution theory), xxvi, 187–195
Grandma's rule (Jones), 121
Group behavior, misbehavior and, 253–254
Group Dynamics (Redl and Wattenberg), xxi, 54, 55–56
    appraising reality, 56
    group dynamics, defined, 55
    punishment, 56
    situational assistance, 56
    student roles, 55–56
    supporting student self-control, 56
    teacher roles, 56

Habits
    Charles on, 252, 255
    Glasser on, 77
Hate crimes, Curwin and Mendler on, 178–179
Helpless handraising (Jones), 124
Hispanic American students
    improving classroom experiences for, 22–23, 30–31
    information about, 22–23
Hope, Curwin on, xxiii, 179–180
Hostility. *See* Anger

I-messages
    of Ginott, 61
    of Gordon, 79–82
    of Nelsen and Lott, 107
Immigrant students, improving classroom experiences for, 28, 30–31
Incentives, Jones on, 120–124
Inner Discipline (Barbara Coloroso), xxiv, 99–104

concept cases, 110–111
defined, 100
ownership of the problem, 102
punishment, 100–101
reconciliation, 101
resolution, 101
restitution, 101
summary suggestions, 110
Three F's of punishment, 100–101
Three R's of reconciliatory justice, 101–102
Instructional environment
    Jones on, 117
    misbehavior and, 254–255
Instruction aspect of discipline, 268
Insubordination rule, Curwin and Mendler on, 175
Interstate New Teacher Assessment and Support Consortium (INTASC), 2–6
Intervention aspect of discipline, 261–262, 269–270

Jondahl, Sarah, first day of school and, 141–145
Jones, Fred (active student involvement), xxiv, 113–126

Kagan, Spencer (Win-Win Discipline), xxvi, 151–165
Kindness, Borba on, 199
Kohn, Alfie (Classrooms as Communities), xxv, 72, 84–89
Kounin, Jacob (lesson and group management), xxii, 58–60
Kyle, Patricia (Win-Win Discipline), xxvi, 151–165

Lack of stimulation, misbehavior and, 255
Language development
    in neurological-based behavior, 38
    of recently arrived immigrant students, 28
Latino students. *See* Hispanic American students
Learning disabilities (LD), 42–43
Lecturing, 83
Legal issues, 17–18
    breach of duty, 17
    due diligence, 17
    negligence, 17
    physical contact with students, 18
Lesson and group management (Kounin), xxii, 58–60
    group alerting, 59
    momentum, 59
    overlapping, 59

satiation, 59
smoothness, 59
withitness, 58
Life skills, Kagan, Kyle, and Scott on, 155, 162–163
Limit setting
    Gossen on, 192–194
    Jones on, 118–119
    Kohn on, 87–88
    Morrish on, 232
Listening skills
    active and passive (Gordon), 82
    Marshall on, 216
Logical consequences
    Curwin and Mendler on, 174
    Dreikurs on, 64
Lott, Lynn (Positive Discipline), xxiv, 104–109
Lucero, Ed, pragmatic classroom management and, 147

Make a Better Choice, 154
Marshall, Marvin (Raise Responsibility System), xxv, 208–223
Meaninglessness, misbehavior and, 255
Medications, for students with behavioral issues, 49–50
Meetings. *See* Classroom meetings
Mendler, Allen (Discipline with Dignity), xxiii, 168–183
Misbehavior, 7–9. *See also* Classroom discipline
    Albert on, 96–97
    behavior versus, 8
    Charles on, 250–257, 261–262, 271–272
    class peers and groups as cause of, 253–254
    Coloroso on, 101–102
    defined, 8
    Gordon on, 81
    individual students as cause of, 250–253
    instructional environment as cause of, 254–255
    interventions for, 261–262, 269–270
    Jones on, 114–118
    Marshall on, 218–220
    serious, 271–272
    strategies for handling, 7–8
    teachers or personnel as cause of, 255–257
    types of, 8–9, 96–97
    Wong and Wong on, 134–135
Mistaken goals
    Albert on, 94
    Dreikurs on, 63

Moral intelligence theory (Borba), xxv, 187, 195–205
  concept cases, 206
  essential virtues, 196–200
  five-step approach to teaching moral values, 201–203
  fostering moral intelligence, 201–203
  fostering prosocial behavior, 203
  four-step approach to discipline, 204–205
  moral core, 196–198
  moral intelligence, defined, 196
  reasons for building moral intelligence, 200–201
  summary suggestions, 205
Morrish, Ronald (Real Discipline), xxv, 227–242
Motivation
  Curwin and Mendler on, 180
  Marshall on, 213
  Morrish on, 239–240

Name calling, 83
National Education Association (NEA), standards for professionalism and, 16–17
National Institute of Mental Health (NIMH), 49
Native American students. See American Indian/Alaska Native students
NBB. See Neurological-based behavior (NBB)
Negligence, 17
Nelsen, Jane (Positive Discipline), xxiv, 104–109
Neurological-based behavior (NBB), 34–51
  brain injuries, 37
  defined, 36
  extent of, 36–37
  improving classroom experiences for students with, 50
  indicators of, 38–39
  medications for, 49–50
  people first language and, 34–35
  sensory integration dysfunction in, 39
  types of mental health diagnoses, 36–37, 40–49
Neurological differences, 36
New teachers, 2–10
  Danielson and competencies of, 7
  discipline as basic competency of, 7–10
  INTASC competency recommendations, 2–6

personal system of classroom discipline, 11–16, 266–284
  Praxis Series and, 6–7
  Wong and Wong on, 141–146
Nontraumatic brain injuries, 37
Nonverbal communication, Jones on, 113–116, 118–119

Obsessive compulsive disorder (OCD), 37
Oppositional defiant disorder (ODD), 36, 40–41
Orders, 82
Ownership of problem
  Coloroso on, 102
  Gordon on, 80, 81–82

Pacific Islander students. See Asian American/Pacific Islander students
Pantoja, Melissa, first day of school and, 144–145
Parent alliances, Kagan, Kyle, and Scott on, 163
Payne, Ruby, on teaching economically disadvantaged students, xxv, 29, 30
People first language, 34–35
Personal system of classroom discipline, 11–16, 266–284
  clarifying ideas about discipline in, 14–16
  defined, 11
  finalizing, steps in, 281–284
  philosophy of discipline and, 266–267
  practice of discipline and, 268–273
  principles for building, 11–14, 273–274
  sample discipline plans, 275–281
  theory of discipline and, 267–268
  thoughts of students preparing to be teachers, 274–275
Philosophy of discipline, personal, 266–267
Physical contact, with students, 18
Physical proximity, Jones on, 119
Picture It Right, 154, 160
Positive Discipline (Jane Nelsen and Lynn Lott), xxiv, 104–109
  barriers to relationships, 105
  builders of relationships, 105
  classroom meetings, 106–109
  concept cases, 110–111
  eight building blocks, 106–108
  I-statements, 107
  summary suggestions, 110
Positivity, Marshall on, 210, 214
Posttraumatic stress disorder, 36

Poverty. See Economically disadvantaged students
Power seeking
  Albert on, 94, 96–97
  Dreikurs on, 63
Practice of discipline, personal, 268–273
Pragmatic classroom management (Wong and Wong), xxiv, 130–147
  classrooms in, 132
  concept cases, 148–149
  discipline in, 133
  first day of class and, 132, 133, 141–145
  first week of teaching and, 133, 145–146
  pragmatic, defined, 130
  in primary grades, 137–141
  procedures in, 132, 136–141
  roles and responsibilities in, 132
  routines, 137–141
  school in, 131
  in secondary grades, 147
  summary suggestions, 148
  support buddy, 146
  support groups, 146
  teaching in, 131–132
  testing and evaluation in, 133
Praise, 83
  Ginott on, 61
  Morrish on, 239–240
Praxis Series, 6–7
Preaching, 83
Preferred activity time (PAT), Jones on, 121–124
Prevention
  as aspect of discipline, 268–269
  Gordon on, 80–81
  sample discipline plan emphasizing, 278–281
Problem solving
  Charles on, 249
  in classroom meetings (Nelsen and Lott), 108
  Marshall on challenges versus, 216
Procedures, Wong and Wong on, 132, 136–141
Professionalism, standards for, 16–17
Prosocial behavior, 203
Provocation, misbehavior and, 253, 256–257
Pryor, Alison K., on developing respect in classroom, 274
Punishment
  Canter and Canter on, 67–68
  Charles on, 257
  Coloroso on, 100–101
  discipline versus, 100–101

Punishment (*continued*)
  Dreikurs on, 64
  Redl and Wattenberg on, 56
  Skinner on, 57
  student misbehavior based in, 257

Questioning, 83
  Ginott on, 61
  Marshall on, 214

Rage, 46–49. *See also* Anger
Rage cycle, phases of, 46–49
Raise Responsibility System (Marshall), xxv, 208–223
  choice in, 210, 214
  concept cases, 224
  external motivation in, 213
  four classical virtues in, 217
  guided choices in, 218–219
  hierarchy of social development in, 210–213
  internal motivation in, 213
  positivity in, 210, 214
  raising responsibility, defined, 208–209
  reflection in, 210, 214
  reflective questions in, 214
  self-diagnostic referral in, 219–220
  summary suggestions, 223
  tactics for, 214–217
  Theory X and, 209
  Theory Y and, 209
Real Discipline (Morrish), xxv, 227–242
  concept cases, 242–243
  consequences in, 238–239
  mindset for, 229–230
  motivation in, 239–240
  planning for, 234–237
  Real Discipline, defined, 228–229
  rewards in, 239–240
  student failure to comply, 240–241
  summary suggestions, 242
  teacher–student relationships in, 237–238
  three-phase approach to, 230–234
Reality
  appraisal of (Redl and Wattenberg), 56
  in classroom meetings (Nelsen and Lott), 107
  in problem solving (Coloroso), 103–104
Reassuring, 83
Recognition
  Canter and Canter on, 67
  Marshall on, 215

Redl, Fritz (Group Dynamics), xxi, 54, 55–56
Reflection, Marshall on, 210, 214
Reinforcement Theory (Skinner), xxii, 55, 57–58
Respect
  Borba on, 198–199
  Pryor on, 274
Revenge seeking
  Albert on, 94, 97
  Dreikurs on, 63
Rewards
  Morrish on, 239–240
  reinforcement and (Skinner), 57
Role-playing, in classroom meetings (Nelsen and Lott), 108
Roles
  Redl and Wattenberg on, 55–56
  Wong and Wong on, 132
Room arrangement, Jones on, 117
Routines, Jones on, 117–118
Rules, classroom
  breaking, as disruptive behavior, 156, 157
  Canter and Canter on, 67
  Curwin and Mendler on, 170, 174–175
  Gossen on, 194
  Jones on, 117
  Kagan, Kyle, and Scott on, 154
  Marshall on, 215–216
  Morrish on, 231–232
  sample discipline plan emphasizing, 275–278
  Wong and Wong on, 132, 134–135

Say, See, Do teaching (Jones), 115–116, 119–120
Scott, Sally C. (Win-Win Discipline), xxvi, 151–165
Self-control
  Borba on, 198
  Dreikurs on, 63
  Gordon on. *See* Self-Control (Gordon)
  Redl and Wattenberg on, 56
Self-Control (Gordon), xxiii, 72, 79–84
  acknowledgment responses, 82
  active listening, 82
  collaborative rule setting, 80
  communication roadblocks, 82–84
  concept cases, 91
  confrontive I-messages, 82
  confrontive skills, 81–82
  coping mechanism, 80
  defined, 79
  door openers, 82

helping skills, 82–84
  I-messages, 79–82
  misbehavior, 80
  no-lose method of conflict resolution, 84
  noncontrolling methods, 79, 80
  participatory classroom management, 80–81
  passive listening, 82
  positive influence, 80
  preventive I-messages, 80
  shifting gears, 82
  summary suggestions, 90
  who owns the problem, 80, 81–82
  you-messages, 80
Self-diagnostic referral (Marshall), 219–220
Self-discipline (Ginott), 61, 62
Self-esteem, Morrish on, 240
Self-presentation, Vigil on, 274–275
Self-restitution theory (Gossen), xxvi, 187–195
  bottom line, 194
  collapsing the conflict, 195
  concept cases, 206
  "Does it really matter?," 191
  least coercive road, 190–195
  managers of restitution, 195
  "My job, your job," 192–193
  restitution, characteristics of, 188–189
  restitution triangle, 189–190
  rules, 194
  self-restitution in, 187–189, 194–195
  social contracts, 191–192
  summary suggestions, 205
  "Yes, if . . . ," 191
Sensory integration dysfunction (SID), 39
Sensory processing disorder, in neurological-based behavior, 39
Seroyer, Chelonnda, pragmatic classroom management and, 147
Skill clusters, Jones on, 117–125
Skinner, B. F. (behavior shaping), xxii, 55, 57–58
Slovenske, Jane, first week of school and, 145–146
Smith, Jeff, pragmatic classroom management and, 147
Social development hierarchy (Marshall), 210–213
  levels of, 211
  teaching to students, 212–213
  value of, 211–212
Space, Rachel, on relating to and connecting with students, 274

Students
  at-risk, and Discipline with Dignity (Curwin and Mendler), 172–173
  difficult-to-control, and Discipline with Dignity (Curwin and Mendler), 173–176
  discipline and working with, 10–11
  disruptive behaviors of (Kagan, Kyle, and Scott), 154–161
  needs of (Charles), 247, 250
  needs of (Glasser), 73–74
  physical contact with, 18
  positions in Win-Win Discipline, 154–158, 161–162
  raising responsibility of (Marshall), xxv, 208–223
  relating to and connecting with (Space), 274
  relationships with teachers, 237–238, 278–281
  rights in classroom (Canter and Canter), 65
  roles of (Redl and Wattenberg), 55–56
  self-control of (Redl and Wattenberg), 56
  social development hierarchy (Marshall) and, 212–213
Study Group Activity Guide, 125–126
Sund, Deborah, sample discipline plan of, 276–278
Support aspect of discipline, 269–270
Support groups, Wong and Wong on, 146
Synergistic Discipline (Charles), xxiv, 245–262
  basic student needs and, 247
  charisma in, 248–249
  class conditions for, 248
  communication in, 249
  concept cases, 263–264
  coopetition in, 249
  discipline plans in, 258–261
  ethics in, 248
  fundamental hypothesis of, 245
  interventions for student misbehavior, 261–262
  nature of, 246
  problem solving/conflict resolution in, 249–250
  student misbehavior and, 250–257, 261–262
  summary suggestions, 263
  Synergistic Teaching in, 246
  synergy, defined, 246–247

teacher misbehavior and, 258
trust in, 248
Synergy
  defined, 246–247
  developing, 273

Teachers. *See also* Classroom discipline; New teachers
  assertive, 66–67
  competencies of, 2–10
  Discipline with Dignity (Curwin and Mendler) program and, 171, 180–182
  effective, 115–116, 132, 146
  misbehavior of, 258
  relationships with students, 237–238, 278–281
  rights in classroom (Canter and Canter), 65
  roles of (Redl and Wattenberg), 56
  self-presentation of, 274–275
  student misbehavior based in, 255–257
  at their best (Ginott), 61
  at their worst (Ginott), 61
Tedium
  Kagan, Kyle, and Scott on, 160
  misbehavior and, 254–255
Temptation, misbehavior and, 251–252
Testing, Wong and Wong on, 133
Theory of discipline, personal, 267–268
Theory X, 209
Theory Y, 209
Threats, student misbehavior based in, 257
Tolerance, Borba on, 199–200
To You . . . To Me, 154
Traditional instruction
  improvements in, 89
  problems with, 88
Training
  omission (Jones), 123
  for Real Discipline (Morris), 230–233, 235–237
Transgression, misbehavior and, 251
Traumatic brain injuries, 37
Triggers, in rage cycle, 46–49
Trust
  Charles on, 248
  Marshall on, 217

Uninformed students, Kagan, Kyle, and Scott on, 160

Value systems, 20–28
  African American, 23–24

American Indian/Alaskan Native, 27
Asian American/Pacific Islander, 24–25
Caucasian American, 21
Curwin and Mendler on, 170–171
defined, 20
Hispanic American, 22
recently arrived immigrant, 28
Variety, Marshall on, 215
Video Toolbox, 125–126
Vigil, Manuel, on self-presentation, 274–275
Violence, Curwin and Mendler on handling, 176–177
Visual instruction plans (VIPs), 120, 125

Warnings, 83
Wattenberg, William (Group Dynamics), xxi, 54, 55–56
White students. *See* Caucasian American students
Why questions (Ginott), 61
Win-Win Discipline (Kagan, Kyle, and Scott), xxvi, 151–165
  ABCD disruptions, 154, 156, 157, 158–161
  class rules, 154
  concept cases, 166
  follow-ups and goals, 155, 160, 161–162
  goal of, 152–153
  moment-of-disruption structures, 154–155, 160–161
  parent and community alliances, 163
  premises of, 153
  promoting life skills through, 155, 162–163
  student positions, 154–158, 161–162
  summary suggestions, 165
  Three Pillars, 153, 156, 161, 163–164
Withdrawing
  Albert on, 94
  Gordon on, 83–84
  Kagan, Kyle, and Scott on, 156, 157
Wong, Harry and Rosemary (pragmatic classroom management), xxiv, 130–147

You-messages
  of Ginott, 61
  of Gordon, 80